IN
FRAGMENTS

OTHER BOOKS BY JOHN DOMINIC CROSSAN

In Parables: The Challenge of the Historical Jesus

Raid on the Articulate: Comic Eschatology in Jesus and Borges

The Dark Interval: Towards a Theology of Story

Finding Is the First Act: Trove Folktales and Jesus' Treasure Parable

Cliffs of Fall: Paradox and Polyvalence in the Parables of Jesus

A Fragile Craft: The Work of Amos Niven Wilder

IN
FRAGMENTS
The Aphorisms of Jesus

"Gather up the fragments left over, that nothing may be lost"
John 6:12

JOHN DOMINIC CROSSAN

1817

HARPER & ROW, PUBLISHERS, SAN FRANCISCO

Cambridge, Hagerstown, New York, Philadelphia
London, Mexico City, São Paulo, Sydney

for
Margaret
in
memory

IN FRAGMENTS. THE APHORISMS OF JESUS. Copyright © 1983 by
John Dominic Crossan. All rights reserved. Printed in the United States
of America. No part of this book may be used or reproduced in any
manner whatsoever without written permission except in the case of brief
quotations embodied in critical articles and reviews. For information
address Harper & Row, Publishers, Inc., 10 East 53rd Street, New York,
NY 10022. Published simultaneously in Canada by Fitzhenry & White-
side, Limited, Toronto.

FIRST EDITION

Designer: Jim Mennick

Library of Congress Cataloging in Publication Data

Crossan, John Dominic.
  IN FRAGMENTS.

  Bibliography: p.
  Includes index.
    1. Jesus Christ—Words.   2. Aphorisms and apothegms.
  I. Title.
  BT306.C76   1983   232.9'54   83-47719
  ISBN 0-06-061608-3

83 84 85 86 87 10 9 8 7 6 5 4 3 2 1

Contents

Introduction

The title of this book is deliberately evocative of my book *In Parables* of ten years ago. I subtitled that work *The Challenge of the Historical Jesus*. My major focus of interest is still the historical Jesus. But continuing studies on the parabolic tradition have made it very clear that divergent versions of Jesus' parables are not destructive changes nor even deflective alterations of the original parabolic structure; rather, they are much more the inevitable interpretations and ineluctable responses to the parabolic challenge itself. The problem of the historical Jesus thereby translates itself and transforms itself into the problem of the hermeneutical Jesus. Instead of the multiplicity of textual interpretations cutting the tradition off from the parabler himself, its very plurality links it most fully to the creative matrix from which it came. Polyvalence is not the parable's failure or betrayal, but rather its victory and success.

My next step was to attempt an investigation of the aphoristic tradition similar to that already effected for the parabolic tradition. Two major differences were soon evident. The parabolic tradition—that is, the transmission and/or creation of separable narrative metaphors or short stories—is restricted, for all practical purposes, to Matthew, Mark, Luke, and the *Gospel of Thomas* from Nag Hammadi (CG II,2). For example, the *Apocryphon of James*, also from Nag Hammadi, has Jesus assert: "For after the [end] you have compelled me to stay with you another eighteen days for the sake of the parables. It was enough for some ⟨to listen⟩ to the teaching and understand 'The Shepherds' and 'The Seed' and 'The Building' and 'The Lamps of the Virgins' and 'The Wage of the Workmen' and 'The Didrachmae' and 'The Woman.' " (CG I,8:1–11.) Titles and themes start to replace plots and narratives. Seven titles is not a lot for eighteen days, and less if that should be read as eighteen months. Put simply, the parabolic genre did not exactly grasp the tradition's imagination. The opposite is true of the aphoristic genre. In transmission and creation, in exegesis and mimesis, the aphorisms of Jesus extend like hermeneutical tentacles throughout both intracanonical and extracanonical sources and throughout both first and second centuries. And this establishes a second distinction between parables and aphorisms, that is, between the narrative and discourse sayings of Jesus in the tradition. Parables are much fewer in number and far easier to locate and identify. Aphorisms are far more numerous and often extremely difficult to isolate from each other and their surroundings. Those two distinctions establish, respectively, the importance and the difficulty of the task.

When I started work on this book, I thought I would be able to discuss all the aphorisms of Jesus just as all the parables were discussed, in detail or in passing, by In Parables. I even thought that the line between transmission and creation, between the problem of the historical and the hermeneutical Jesus, could be studied for the aphoristic as for the parabolic tradition: in a single book. The sheer quantity of material, as well as the minute details of the differentiation within even a single aphorism, soon dispelled those grandiose plans. I decided that, for this book, it would be more than enough to make a proper beginning. I have as consolation the thought that while very many books have been written on the parabolic or narrative tradition of Jesus' sayings, none has ever been written on the non-narrative or aphoristic tradition alone. Works, for example, on the "sayings" (logoi) of Jesus usually consider such diverse genres as aphorisms and parables, dialogues and debates.

There are, therefore, two limitations on the present work. First, the corpus is limited to those aphorisms found in Mark and Q, all their independent versions elsewhere and anywhere, as well as their dependent versions in Matthew and Luke. This proposes a data base of 133 aphorisms. I presume, of course, that independent and dependent versions are found within both intracanonical and extracanonical sources. I also presume that a dependent version may be every bit as hermeneutically interesting as an independent one. The limitation of the data base was an imperative of time and space, not a presumption of value and interest. As such it points necessarily towards more complete studies in the future. Second, the question of originality is not raised even within that corpus. My present concern is with how the aphoristic tradition works and what the aphoristic tradition does with its materials. Afterwards there will be time (and maybe only afterwards should there be time) to discuss the products rather than the processes of the aphoristic tradition and to attempt a final isolation of what is from Jesus, what is from exegesis, and what from mimesis.

My method was, first, to establish a transmissional analysis for each of those 133 sayings. This was done with very great concern for their present context, especially for their location in the compositional design of Mark and Q. Second, during those analyses a basic generative model for the aphoristic tradition began to form itself and this was adapted and developed as the work progressed (see Figure 9.1). Third, the major elements of that model became the chapter headings for the book. Fourth, a selection was made among the analyses to fill out those chapters, which meant that most of the analyses were never used in the book itself (see Appendix 1). Fifth, the advantage of this method was that the selection could choose those particular aphorisms that (1) best exemplified the process in question, (2) best exemplified the diverse sources and problems involved, and (3) best exemplified the theological problems at issue in the tradition.

The following are my general presumptions concerning sources. By presumptions I do not mean positions that are beyond controversy, but working hypotheses whose operational validity is tested and checked by their usage. I consider that Q is a discourse gospel whose sequential structure and even redactional strata can be plausibly demonstrated, and whose content was adopted, along with Mark, by both Matthew and Luke. But because of recent criticism of this Two Source theory, I did not simply presuppose the existence of the gospel Q, but I worked out its aphorisms against the background of a total review of the document itself (see Appendix 2). I consider that John's present text indicates Synoptic influence, but that there is equal evidence of independent traditions within it. That forced me to consider almost every case for itself; but in all the aphorisms studied for this book, the Johannine versions were independent of their Synoptic parallels. I consider that the *Gospel of Thomas* (CG II,2) is completely independent of the intracanonical gospels because (1) its order is totally different from theirs and yet it has no compositional sequence demanding such radical reorderings, and (2) it lacks precisely those redactional (as distinct from traditional) elements whose presence would definitively prove its dependence on those gospels whose redactional elements we know. I consider that those three paradigmatic possibilities—that is, dependent traditions, as with Matthew and Luke on Q and Mark; both independent and dependent traditions, as with John on the Synoptics; and completely independent traditions, as with *Thomas* on the intracanonical gospels—must always be considered for both apocrypha and patristica until such times and such places as the intracanonical texts became normative, definitive, and exclusive.

I wish to thank Professors Donald Morton and James Williams of Syracuse University for introducing me to the work of Professor Gerhard Neumann. I am especially grateful to Professor Morton for the use of his translations of the essays by Neumann, Mautner, and Asemissen from Neumann's anthology on the aphoristic genre (1976b). I have cited, with permission and gratitude, from those translations in my own first chapter. I am also very grateful to DePaul University for a quarter's sabbatical in the midst of the book's research.

Prologue

Y exploraremos también el espacio vacío que dejaste en tu poema,
el espacio vacío que dejaste en cada palabra
y hasta en tu propia tumba
para alzar el futuro.

And we will explore besides the empty space that you left in your poem,
the empty space that you left in each word
and even in your own tomb
to build the future.

ROBERTO JUARROZ, *Vertical Poetry*,
trans. W. S. Merwin
(Santa Cruz, CA: Kayak Books, 1977), pp. 44–45

1
Aphoristic Genre

I hear noises which others don't hear and which disturb for me the music of the spheres, which others don't hear either.

Many share my views with me. But I don't share them with them.

KARL KRAUS (Zohn: 30)

A. APHORISM AND GENRE

The prose miniature has many names: adage, aphorism, apothegm, epigram, fragment, *gnome*, proverb, maxim, sentence (*sententia*), or saying. In Holman's A *Handbook to Literature*, the following definitions appear. *Adage* is "a proverb or wise saying made familiar by long use" (7). *Aphorism* is "a concise statement of a principle or precept given in pointed words" (36). *Apothegm* is "a sharply pointed and often startling maxim, more particularly centered and practical than an aphorism, although like it in other respects" (39). *Epigram* is "any pithy, pointed, concise saying" (196). *Proverb* is "a sentence or phrase which briefly and strikingly expresses some recognized truth or shrewd observation about practical life and which has been preserved by oral tradition, though it may be preserved and transmitted in written literature as well" (421). *Sentence* is "a rhetorical term formerly in use in the sense of apothegm or maxim (Lat. *sententia*), usually applied to quoted 'wise sayings'" (486). Each of those definitions is quite satisfactory in itself. But if you bring them all together comparatively you must wonder what differences, if any, exist between the terms and things defined. Specifically, what is the essential difference between proverb and aphorism? More specifically, what is an aphorism within the spectrum of the prose miniature? "What exactly is the aphorism, by what marks shall we know it when we find it, of what substance is it composed, and what is the form of its composition? What are the advantages and what the drawbacks and limitations of this way of expression?" (Smith, 1928:3).

1. THE DANCE OF ART AND THOUGHT

Franz H. Mautner's 1933 study of "The Aphorism as a Literary Genre" complained that "whatever the contour of the shortest prose can contain within itself, be it seed, fruit, or refuse of scholarly, literary, or poetic activity, or of solitary reflection, must expect the name 'aphorisms.' . . . To put it simply, but not more simply than it is: every otherwise undefinable short prose piece is considered an aphorism" (1933:31). Later he repeats this complaint that "every formless, isolated, sudden idea that is brought forth, every unsystematic discussion, every quotation, every catchy extract from a book, every literary sketch has, without further ado, a right to be called 'aphorism' " (1933:35). But within the French tradition of La Rochefoucauld(1613–1680), Pascal(1623–1662), La Bruyère(1645–1696), Chamfort (1740–1794), and Joubert (1754–1824), or the German one of Lichtenberg (1742–1799), Goethe (1749–1832), Novalis (1772–1801), Friedrich Schlegel (1772–1829), and Nietzsche (1844–1900), there is a much more specific use and understanding of aphorism as a literary genre, and "no other genre is so sensitive to the upsetting of its inner balance as this one, whose essence almost is its vacillating participation in the fields of art and thinking" (1933: 37).

This generic dance of art and thought is well described by Mautner: "Be it more or less conscious, a personal, *subjective*, and programmatic isolation, following from the solitary situation of thought, is an essential feature of the aphorism. In this way it offers in each case a freshly *original* and often bold worldview. (This, too, is a difference with respect to the proverb and the true 'sentence'.) The inspiration of the moment and/or the individuality of the thinker has newly resolved an old problem or offered an old solution in a new form, due either to the unusual viewpoint from which the 'perspective' was achieved, or to the unusual power of metaphor or expression (recall Kraus) by which it becomes conscious and vivid, or to the frequently used means of comparison by which it enters into a new system of relations" (1933:51–52). Art and thought, artistic isolation, and conceptual originality must integrate perfectly to set the aphoristic genre at its purest. But if Mautner distinguishes *aphorism* from *proverb* primarily in terms of thought, he distinguishes it from *treatise* primarily in terms of art: "A sentence in the form of an aphorism is an aphorism in the strict sense of a poetic genre . . . only if it subjects itself from the beginning to the generic character of the aphorism, that of isolation . . . the pithy *unity* and ability to stand without proof separate the aphorism from the treatise and from the essay" (1933:52). Such "programmatic isolation" is intensified rather than modified when aphorisms are gathered together in "the context of a totality of isolations" (1933:52).

2. THE CINDERELLA OF LITERARY SCHOLARSHIP

In 1949 Hermann Ulrich Asemissen called aphorism "the Cinderella of literary scholarship" and began his discussion with the same complaint as Mautner's: "The application of the word from Hippocrates until today embraces everything in prose which does not yield itself to a systematic context and to the customary literary classification" (159,160).

Asemissen's own contribution is itself proposed in primarily aphoristic style. He reiterates Mautner's art *and* thought as autonomy *and* insight. Autonomy: "The good aphorism needs no premise, no conclusion, and no commentary. It is sufficient in itself. All aphorisms found to be effective show that. And the counter example shows it too. If one deprives them of their autonomy, one deprives them of their effectiveness" (162). Insight: "It never gives the insight simply as something already comprehended. It would then be open to question. Rather it conveys insight as process, as the seizure of insight. But it doesn't let that process show" (163). Autonomy *and* insight: "Aphorisms say something which is not self-evident. But they say it so that it is apparently self-explanatory" (163). Out of this combination grows the powerful heuristic drive of the aphorism. "The aphorism in its representative form is the monument of its own process of thought. Whoever grasps its meaning is compelled to rethink and reflect, and goes through, in focusing the train of thought, the reasons and the reasons behind the reasons which lead to the illuminating end result" (164). And the heart of this heuristic provocation is: "the contradiction. Every effective aphorism is characterized by contradiction. To oppose is its passion. . . . The more perplexing the contradiction, the greater the tension, the greater the resulting attraction. Therefore the aphorism contradicts precisely all those things that appear unshakeable in their authority and that enjoy unquestioned general recognition" (165). But here, as always, art and thought, autonomy and insight, form and content, go together: "Thus even its form is a spirited contradiction of the powerful tradition of systematic deductive thinking. And thus in its content it especially likes to contradict authoritative opinions, habits, customs, conventions, and traditions of all kinds" (165).

At this point the distinction between proverb and aphorism starts to become clear. In terms of content the aphorism's passion for contradiction leads inevitably (even if not always) to paradox "as its ideal form of action," since "the paradoxical self-contradiction is the most astonishing of all contradictions and as such is the best suited to the purpose of the aphorism" (166). Paradox is also, however, the aphorism's greatest danger: "It imperils the insight which is the goal of the aphorism by threatening (permanently) to become absurd . . . but the special danger accords it a special charm. In the self-consciousness of its strength, it plays with the danger" (166,167). Asemissen also notes that the aphorism "likes to make use of ready-made formulations, proverbial expressions for example, which it modifies in a surprising way for its purposes or brings into a paradoxical relationship" (171). Such a complicated relationship between aphoristic frame and proverbial core will have to be considered again later.

In terms of form, however, Asemissen's analysis is less persuasive. His earlier statement, "it is alarming that the effective aphorisms turn out to be a very small minority" (161), is necessitated by his claim that the aphorism's "structure of tension and equilibrium inevitably occasion a two-part formal structure, which it can vary only incidentally by additions and ornamentations. The only possibility of formal development remaining open to the aphorism is to subdivide its members and to repeat the basic structure in its parts" (169–170). This necessitates a clear preference for the "maxims" of the French moralists and the "fragments" of the German romantics, but it also demands an intolerable act of constant discrimination as one reads through the works of both traditions. It seems better and wiser to distinguish, if one must at all, between a "closed form" as in the maxims of a La Rochefoucauld and an "open form" as in the fragments of a Novalis or a Valéry, but to admit that both forms appear side by side in the works of most aphorists (so Mautner, 1966:410).

In the final analysis, however, Asemissen admits that such taxonomic difficulties are not just due to scholarly incapacity but to the nature of the aphorism, which is "itself responsible for the fact that its theory has not yet been written. It is not only that the theoretician would have to be artist, philosopher, philologist, psychologist, and sociologist—he could nevertheless fulfill his task only imperfectly. For just as the aphorism resists every system, so also it resists systematic observation" (176).

3. THE FORM OF SCATTERED OCCASIONS

In 1959 Joseph Peter Stern published a magnificent study of Georg Christoph Lichtenberg (1742–1799). Like Francis Bacon (1561–1626) before him, Lichtenberg stood astride the distinction between science and literature and, also like Bacon, found in aphorism a precarious bridge across that widening chasm. In his *De Augmentis*, Bacon used the expression "the Doctrine concerning Scattered Occasions" to introduce his own commentary on thirty-four "Aphorisms or Proverbs of Solomon" (5.35–37). Stern's work on Lichtenberg bows then to Bacon with its subtitle, "A Doctrine of Scattered Occasions."

Stern has both an historical and theoretical thesis to defend. He proposes the former thesis as follows: "The connection between the Hippocratic aphorism and the modern genre of literature which bears this name is usually considered to be 'merely verbal,' meaning that it is merely fortuitous. In order to find out whether this is really so, we must briefly consider some aspects of its history. For this purpose it may be convenient to distinguish three stages in the genre: the scientific, the hypothetical, and the literary types of the aphorism. The assertion to be proved is that the first of these is a rudimentary form of the last" (Stern: 104). And Lichtenberg is himself the historical medium of this process: "Lichtenberg's work effects the transition between the two types of aphorism; or, to put it biographically, the transition from the scientific aphorism to the aphorism as a genre in literature traces Lichtenberg's own journey from science to literature" (Stern: 110). Or, again: "Our main argument—that the scientific aphorism is a rudimentary form of the aphorism as a genre in literature—is reflected and consolidated in a particular finding: that both the raw material of Lichtenberg's aphorisms (their 'images') and his manner of assembling that material was determined, predominantly but not exclusively, by his work as a practicing and philosophizing scientist" (112). This historical thesis is argued most persuasively by Stern's analysis of Lichtenberg. It is also corroborated by a moment's consideration of Hippocrates himself. It is true that most of his medical definitions and diagnoses seem far from the aphorisms of either French moralists or German romantics. "In disorders of the bowels and vomitings, occurring spontaneously, if the matters purged be such as ought to be purged, they do good, and are well borne; but, if not, the contrary" (Adams: 292), will not be found in most aphoristic anthologies. But, on the other hand, "Wherever a doctor cannot do good, he must be kept from doing harm" is included in the best contemporary anthology (Auden and Kronenberger: 213). Or, consider the justly famous aphorism that opened his collection of medical sayings: "Life is short, and the Art long" (Adams: 292). But this is short, as are all aphorisms. Which, then, are they—life or art?

Stern's second thesis, contained primarily in his section on "A Literary Definition of the Aphorism" (189–226), is much more difficult to summarize. He proposes two major aspects of the aphoristic genre. First, "the condition of the aphorism's presence in the realm of art . . . is an integration of matter and form which issues in a poetical reversal of the functions of both" (Stern: 200). Stern illustrates this by an extremely close and subtle reading of some of Lichtenberg's aphorisms. But for my present purpose I shall simply recall those two Hippocratic aphorisms just cited. I already indicated how form and content reverse themselves in "Life is short, and the Art long." The form of the saying, the form-as-short, becomes the content of the aphorism. So also with the first Hippocratic example above. A first or fast reading might take as *content* this: "Wherever a doctor cannot do good, *he must not do harm.*" But then the specific form pulls us back for a second reading: "*he must be kept from doing harm.*" And this formal element becomes a new content as we begin to wonder why this is so, why is there such a drive *to do* that it will do harm rather than do nothing? Hence, from this first aspect, Stern defines an aphorism as "a self-contained, pithy sentence whose organization involves a partial reversal of the traditional matter-and-form dichotomy and a second look at a part of itself" (200). The second aspect of aphorism proposed by Stern is just as subtle: "the aphorism is the most *self-conscious* of all literary genres" (214). This does not, of course, mean that the aphorist need be any more or less self-conscious than any other artist. But it means that the aphorism's ineluctable isolation renders any failure glaringly evident.

I conclude with a long quotation that sums up Stern's understanding of the genre (216–217):

> The aphorism, we have found, is a strange and suprisingly complex configuration of words. Its charm hides in an antithesis, perfectly integrated, issuing from a double look at a word or an idea. It conceals its autobiographical source yet displays its process of generation. It is self-conscious, yet never exhibits its author's self-consciousness unmodified. It is something of an experiment in words and ideas, yet it commits

aphorist and reader alike to an irretrievable occasion in experience. It
uses ideas and sentiments culled from all manner of experience, or again
the findings of science, philosophy, literary theory, and any number of
other inquiries, yet it defies all the systems to which they belong and all
coherence wider than itself. It strikes us as both remarkably philosophical
and remarkably literary. To one side of it loom empty puns, to the other
fragmentary reflections. It and its definition involve us in a great many
second thoughts about distinctions which common sense thought firmly
established. And it gives one insight while suggesting many—indeed we
find it difficult to tell how many, since it is always a little more than their
occasion and a little less than their cause. In brief, it is the most paradoxical of genres. Defining a paradox as that formulation of a partial or
ostensible contradiction which originates from a particular experience
and in its effects elicits an abundant range of insights, we conclude that
the aphorism is *the literary emblem of paradox.*

This summation concludes, as did that of Asemissen earlier, by
involving a particularly close relationship between aphorism and
paradox. For Asemissen, the aphorism "discovered as its ideal form
of action: the paradox" (166) and for Stern "the aphorism is *the
literary emblem of paradox.*"

4. THE DIALECTIC OF MIMESIS AND UTOPIA

In the preceding sections I cited studies by Mautner (1933, 1966),
Asemissen (1949), and Stern (1959). Those three articles and a revision of Stern's analysis were included in an anthology of theoretical
discussions on the aphorism assembled by Gerhard Neumann in
1976. He himself contributed an "Introduction" to the volume
(Neumann, 1976a:1–18), and in the same year he published an
immense volume on the German aphorists, Lichtenberg, Novalis,
Friedrich Schlegel, and Goethe (Neumann: 1976b).

Neumann begins by insisting that we "treat the problem of defining such a genre dialectically: by being aware of the individuality of
each author in all its distinctiveness and then appealing to a flexibly
handled overarching concept, a process which opens rather than
closes the scope of the genre" (1976a:1). His own "overarching con-

cept" is the *between* status of the aphorism, but not a between that seeks serene mediation, rather one that accentuates the overt interstitial conflict of such a position. For example: *between* the particular and general, concrete and abstract, sense and thought, experience and system: "it insists precisely on this *representation of the conflict* between the particular, the observed, the noticed, the sensuously apprehended, on the one hand, and its elevation into the general, the maxim-like, the reflected, that which is something abstracted by the intellect, on the other hand" (1976a:5; see also 1976b:828–830).

Neumann then uses this "overarching concept" on "the structure of the aphorism as a form of epistemological conflict" (1976a:6) to trace the shifts of the genre from Hippocrates to the moderns. But he is especially interested in Lichtenberg, Novalis, Friedrich Schlegel, and Goethe because "here the problematic relationship of the particular and the general achieves 'transcendental' significance. It becomes the center of the question on the 'condition of the possibility' for human understanding" (1976a:8).

Then, having grounded the epistemological problem ontologically, transcendental aphoristics turns to politics. But not to the prudent tactics of Baconian advancement. Rather, for example, to those of a Lec: "In a war of ideas it is people who get killed." Thus, for Neumann, "the writing of political aphorisms approaches eminent significance because above all it makes concrete a connection that, more or less concealed, has always been in effect in the form of the aphorism: the connection between Mimesis and Utopia, between representation and model of reality" (1976a:12). But, once again, the aphoristic "connection" is a very special type of interstitial phenomenon: "It is the 'being-under-way' of Mimesis towards Utopia. Consequently, the aphorism in general, but the political aphorism in particular, proves to be the literary form in which the relationship of 'the representation of reality' and 'the projection of the not (yet) real' is expressed most crassly, but also most candidly, as conflict. Of all the forms of utopian schemes, it behaves (in Karl Mannheim's sense) least 'ideologically' because it reflects—unceasingly and in all self-critical acuteness—the conflicting relationship of reality and conception and challenges the reader continuously to this reflection" (1976a:13).

B. APHORISM AND PROVERB

Imagine that one has read widely among the great aphorists. Imagine, at least or as well, that one has read through the "more than 3,000 selections from more than 400 authors" in *The Viking Book of Aphorisms* (Auden and Kronenberger). Imagine, finally, that one has studied the best theoretical discussions on the genre such as, for example, the two works of Neumann (1976a,1976b). As one progresses, and despite or because of the seductive brilliance of analyses such as those of Stern or Neumann, a problem becomes steadily more evident and insistent. On the one hand, aphorism is defined in a way that is correct for aphorism but equally correct for proverb. On the other hand, aphorism is defined in a way clearly incorrect for proverb, but unfortunately also incorrect for most aphorisms. For example: On the one hand, Neumann's *between* features can be as true of proverbs as of aphorisms; on the other, self-criticism and paradox are seldom found in proverbs, but neither are they found in all or even most aphorisms. For another example· Take the not-so-simple English proverb *a stitch in time saves nine*. It is hard to imagine much more formal interlocking in six words: (1) three strophes in unstressed/stressed rhythm: *a/stich, in/time, saves/nine*; (2) the stressed syllable is always *-i*: *stitch, time, nine*; (3) the three strophes are bound by the *st* in *stitch*, which is reversed in the *ts* of *time saves*; (4) the first and second strophes are bound together by the initial *-ti* -of *stitch* and *time*; (5) the second and third strophes have a double connection, bound both by the resonance of *in* and *nine* and their terminal four-letter words both with *-i-e*: *time* and *nine*; and (6) the first and third strophes are linked together by their initial *a*: *a* and *saves*. Many of the aspects of aphorism cited in the previous section would be just as true of this proverb: *between* general and particular etc., reversal of form and content with that terminal *nine* drawing attention to the form quite self-consciously. The *nine* comes from form, not content; the only alternative is *five*, but then you lose the assonance between *in* and *nine*.

The dilemma is now clear: the best theories of aphorism define it either in ways that include most proverbs or else exclude most aphorisms.

1. HEURISTIC AND EPIDICTIC MODALITIES

The problem is intensified by a consideration of Stephenson's criticism of the Baconian aphoristic tradition.

Brian Vickers has shown that "to Bacon's contemporaries the aphorism was a thing to be reckoned with and respected, and its major connotation seems to have been not so much pithiness but intellectual authority" (61). Nevertheless, although Bacon was working within a Renaissance tradition of the aphorism, Vickers admits that "as regards the detailed rationale of their suitability as a guide to life, Bacon is more articulate than any other source known to me, in his insistence on the particularity of the process" (71). What exactly is this "suitability" of the aphorism for Bacon?

Francis Bacon (1561–1626), Baron Verulam, Viscount St. Albans, Lord Chancellor of England (1618–1621), has explained and also defended his own aphoristic style in several places throughout his voluminous writings. The classic location is Book II of his *Advancement of Learning* because there the aphorism is praised for three reasons, corresponding respectively to its Sender, Message, and Recipient—that is, to the three major facets of any communication (Bacon: 3.405):

> Another diversity of Method, whereof the consequence is great, is the delivery of knowledge in Aphorisms, or in Methods; wherein we may observe that it has been too much taken into custom, out of a few Axioms or observations upon any subject to make a solemn and formal art; filling it with some discourses, and illustrating it with examples, and digesting it into a sensible Method; but the writing in Aphorisms hath many excellent virtues, whereto the writing in Method doth not approach.

For first, it trieth the writer, whether he be superficial or solid: for Aphorisms, except they should be ridiculous, cannot be made but of the pith and heart of sciences; for discourse of illustration is cut off; recitals of examples are cut off; discourse of connexion and order is cut off; descriptions of practice are cut off; so there remaineth nothing to fill the Aphorisms but some good quantity of observation: and therefore no man can suffice, nor in reason will attempt, to write Aphorisms, but he that is sound and grounded. But in Methods . . . the arrangement and connexion and joining of the parts has so much effect, as a man shall make a great shew of an art, which if it were disjointed would come to little. Secondly, Methods are more fit to win consent or belief, but less fit to point to action; for they carry a kind of demonstration in orb or circle, one part illuminating another, and therefore satisfy; but particulars, being dispersed, do best agree with dispersed directions. And lastly, Aphorisms, representing a knowledge broken, do invite men to enquire farther; whereas Methods, carrying the shew of a total, do secure men, as if they were at furthest.

Aphorism is thus opposed to treatise, essay, or the more systematic forms of discourse. With it, the Sender (author, speaker, writer) is severely tested; the Message (content) tends to action; and the Recipient (hearer, reader) is challenged to hermeneutics. In the other places where Bacon praises the aphoristic genre, he does so either in terms of Message alone or Recipient alone. For example, on Message, he says in Book I of the *Advancement of Learning*: "But as young men, when they knit and shape perfectly, do seldom grow to a further stature; so knowledge, while it is in aphorisms and observations, it is in growth, but when it once is comprehended in exact methods, it may perchance be further polished and illustrate(d), and accommodated for use and practice, but it increaseth no more in bulk and substance" (Bacon: 3.292). Or again, in Book VIII of *De Augmentis*: "For knowledge drawn freshly and in our view out of particulars knows best the way back to particulars again; and it contributes much more to practice, when the discourse or discussion attends on the example, than when the example attends upon the discourse" (5.56). But it is specially the effect of aphorism on the Recipient that is most important for Bacon. In *Filum Laby-*

rinthi this is again stated in polemical contrast to systematic treatises
(3.498):

> He thought also, that knowledge is uttered to men, in a form as if
> every thing were finished; for it is reduced into arts and methods, which
> in their divisions do seem to include all that may be. And how weakly
> soever the parts are filled, yet they carry the shew and reason of a total;
> and thereby the writings of some received authors go for the very art:
> whereas antiquity used to deliver the knowledge which the mind of man
> had gathered, in observations, aphorisms, or short and dispersed sen-
> tences, or small tractates of some parts that they had diligently meditated
> and laboured; which did invite men, both to ponder that which was
> invented, and to add and supply further. But now sciences are delivered
> to be believed and accepted, and not to be examined and further discov-
> ered; and the succession is between master and disciple, and not between
> inventor and continuer or advancer: and therefore sciences stand at a
> stay, and have done for many ages, and that which is positive is fixed,
> and that which is question is kept question, so as the columns of no
> further proceeding are pitched. And therefore he saw plainly, men had
> cut themselves off from further invention; and that it is no marvel that
> that is not obtained, which hath not been attempted, but rather shut out
> and debarred.

The same polemic appears in the *Novum Organum* (4.85):

> For they set them forth with such ambition and parade, and bring
> them into the view of the world so fashioned and masked, as if they were
> complete in all parts and finished. For if you look at the method of them
> and the divisions, they seem to embrace and comprise everything which
> can belong to the subject. And although these divisions are ill filled out
> and are but as empty cases, still to the common mind they present the
> form and plan of a perfect science. But the first and most ancient seekers
> after truth were wont, with better faith and better fortune too, to throw
> the knowledge which they gathered from the contemplation of things,
> and which they meant to store up for use, into aphorisms; that is, into
> short and scattered sentences not linked together by an artificial method;
> and did not pretend or profess to embrace the entire art. But as the
> matter now is, it is nothing strange if men do not seek to advance in
> things delivered to them as long since perfect and complete.

The same point is made, but in a less polemical format, in his preface to *Maxims of the Law* (7.321):

> This delivering of knowledge in distinct and disjoined aphorisms doth leave the wit of man more free to turn and toss, and to make use of that which is so delivered to more several purposes and applications. For we see all the ancient wisdom and science was wont to be delivered in that form; as may be seen by the parables of Solomon, and by the aphorisms of Hippocrates, and the moral verses of Theognis and Phocylides: but chiefly the precedent of the civil law, which hath taken the same course with their rules, did confirm me in my opinion.

The Baconian aphorism is, then, in the different metaphors of James Stephens, a case of "paths illuminated by starlight" (87), or "a method for handing on the lamp, as he calls it; it works to deliver knowledge by stimulating the thirst for it" (106), or, finally, "a building block in the structure of the next man's intellectual heritage" (106).

R. H. Stephenson has severely criticized the Baconian or heuristic model of the aphorism, which he finds to be "pervasive throughout the literature" (4). His argument can be traced over four steps. First, he interprets the heuristic modality as restricted to the case where *new and original* knowledge is communicated: "What was to be passed on, although perhaps common knowledge to the members of the previous generation of scholars, was new, specialized knowledge to those receiving it" (12). Second, he objects that such a restriction puts all the emphasis on content while it ignores considerations of form, and, above all, it ignores the fact that many aphorisms contain commonplaces and not new or original conceptions. Third, then, he proposes the epidictic rather than the heuristic modality as being much more appropriate to such polished commonplaces. The Greek theoreticians divided oratory into *political*, *legal*, and *epidictic* situations. The first two situations were "real contests in which two opponents sought to gain the adherence on debated topics of an audience that would decide on the issue of a trial or on a course of action to be followed," but the third one was "more reminiscent of a procession than of a struggle" so that it was "practised by those who, in a society, defend the traditional and accepted values, those which are the object of education, not the new and revolutionary values which stir up controversy and polemics. . . . Being in no fear of contradiction, the speaker readily converts into universal values, if not eternal truths, that which has acquired a certain standing through social unanimity" (Perelman and Olbrechts-Tyteca: 47,51). Fourth, both the heuristic model, which emphasizes content, and the epidictic model, which emphasizes form, need to be subsumed within a theory of *aesthetic discourse*: "There is the conceptual structure, in which other linguistic features are subordinated to the conceptual relations, and there is the poetic structure in which conceptual relations are coordinated with all other. These two modes of language co-exist in 'aesthetic discourse' [Schiller] in a relation of reciprocal subordination, now one, now the other being predominant, depending on the needs and interests of the reader" (Stephenson: 16).

I do not find this criticism of the Baconian theory at all convincing. First, there is actually no compelling reason to restrict that model to new and original content. What is new is the *formed content* and it is, first and above all, the *external isolation of formed content* rather than just the *internal integration of formed content* that constitutes the heuristic power and hermeneutical challenge of the aphorism. Second, within the British tradition itself, the presence of *commonplaces* within aphoristic content is openly acknowledged. In 1887 Lord Morley noted that, "the truism, however, and the commonplace may be stated in a form so fresh, pungent, and free from triviality, as to have all the force of new discovery" (61). So also Logan Pearsall Smith (1928:13) said that,

> To polish commonplaces and give them a new lustre; to express in a
> few words the obvious principles of conduct, and to give to clear thoughts
> an even clearer expression; to illuminate dimmer impressions and bring
> their faint rays to a focus; to delve beneath the surface of consciousness to

new veins of precious ore, to name and discover and bring to light latent and unnamed experience; and finally to embody the central truths of life in the breadth and terseness of memorable phrases—all these are the opportunities of the aphorist.

But Stephenson's article, and even the title of his 1944 University of London dissertation, *Goethe's Transmutation of Commonplaces*, raise most forcibly the problem of aphorism and proverb. If one cannot distinguish them in terms of new versus old knowledge or original versus commonplace insight, and if both can be polished truisms, what difference is left between them?

2. COLLECTIVE AND INDIVIDUAL AUTHORITY

It is at this point that James G. Williams's recent book, *Those Who Ponder Proverbs: Aphoristic Thinking and Biblical Literature*, is extremely important.

(1) Pondering Proverbs. I shall discuss two points from this study in relation to the present problem of proverb and aphorism.

(a) The Book's Problem. The book's title might seem to suggest that proverb and aphorism are but different names for the same thing. The following problem is posed, however, at the very start and its formulation is quite significant: "Is there a generic relationship between the traditional proverb transmitted in an ancient, conservative society and the aphorism of the modern writer whose thinking is informed by the relativity of knowledge and the tenuousness of language?" (14). By that formulation of the problem Williams combines (i) the generic relationship of proverb and aphorism and (ii) the historic relationship of ancient conservatism and modern relativism as if these were parallel or at least similar questions, as if *ancient proverbial conservatism* and *modern aphoristic relativism* were a simple dialectic rather than a double one. We are, however, dealing with a double one; that is, the proverb/aphorism dialectic is found *both* among the ancients *and* the moderns. For example, Diogenes Laertius' *Lives of Eminent Philosophers*, in discussing

Pyrrho of Elis (c. 360–270 B.C.), attributes the following statement to the Sceptics: "Every saying has its corresponding opposite" (Hicks: 2.488–489). The Greek version has *panti logō logos antikeitai* which is an elegantly executed chiasm with a(*anti*), b(*log*), b'(*log*), a'(*anti*). And this self-consciousness with regard to form is matched with an equal self-consciousness in terms of content. "The Sceptics . . . laid down nothing definitely, not even the laying down of nothing" (2.487). Thus that quoted saying refers not only to all the sayings but especially to itself: "Even this statement has its corresponding antithesis, so that after destroying others it turns round and destroys itself, like a purge which drives the substance out and then in its turn is itself eliminated and destroyed" (2.489–491). I do not, of course, suggest that all ancients were Sceptics but, then, neither are all moderns Moderns. Hence it is necessary to keep quite separate the problem of proverb/aphorism and of ancient/modern and not to consider them the same dichotomy.

(b) The Book's Solution. Williams's solution begins with the following negative summation (80):

> Our viewpoint is that it is not helpful to distinguish proverb and aphorism too sharply in formal terms. The real difference between them is not so much formal as it is a matter of purpose and function. What was the intended use, and does the saying in question pretend to speak for a populace or tradition, or for an individual? The attribution of specific authorship to aphorism, and of popular origins and appeal to proverb are useful but not decisive characteristics.

This acknowledges much of the difficulty seen with earlier assessments. The *form* of a proverb can be every bit as elegantly structured as that of an aphorism. Indeed, as *aphorisms* phase into *fragments*, elegant internal cohesion often cedes place to deliberately broken, unfinished, and open internal constructions. And neither is *content* always a secure criterion of distinction. It is certainly true that aphorisms may contain vertiginously paradoxical content or extremely self-critical or self-conscious material, but not all need contain such challenges. Williams's proposed distinction is this (80):

What is decisive in this writer's view, is the difference in principle between a *collective* voice and an *individual* voice. Both proverb and aphorism may employ metaphor. Proverb may be more associated with "homespun" language, but it can be quite clever and sophisticated. Both are non-narrative forms that reveal and conceal a tension between the general (truth, principle, concept) and the particular (case, experience of subject), each seems to provide and evoke insight, and both may be paradoxical, although aphorism in modern western history is more associated with paradox and irony. What really distinguishes the two, if and when the distinction is valid, is their function, a function that does not always show itself in formal literary signs. The proverb expresses the voice of the human subject as ancient, collective wisdom, whereas aphorism (certainly the modern literary aphorism) brings the subjectivity of the individual more to the fore. But both accord a significant role to the human origin of the word spoken, whatever the ultimate grounding of authority of the utterance.

(2) Gnomic Discourse. I consider, therefore, that we have a single genre which I term *prose miniature, gnomic discourse,* or, simply, the *saying.* I use that last expression as always exclusive of the *story* or the *parable,* that is, as a non-narrative formulation. I divide this genre as in Figure 1.1.

Figure 1.1

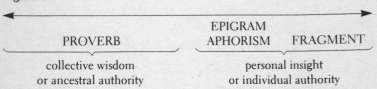

I think that the dynamic power of the genre lies precisely in its continuum status so that the line above should be formed into a circle: A fragment *could* eventually become a proverb and a proverb *could* be transformed into a fragment. What is fundamental to the genre is the isolated status of its units. No matter how banal the proverb may be, and no matter how totally it may seem to espouse the common mind and the collective authority, that internal integration of form and matter and that external isolation from continu-

ing discourse render it eternally unstable. One can easily imagine
the process of linguistic self-consciousness:

(a)   saying
(b)   saying versus saying
(c)   saying (saying versus saying)
(d)   saying [saying (saying versus saying)]

(a) One could begin with: "Like snow in summer or rain in harvest,
so honor is not fitting for a fool" (Prov. 26:1).

(b) One might even move to a point where one becomes conscious
of the opposing advice of proverbial wisdom: "Answer not a fool
according to his folly, lest you be like him yourself. Answer a fool
according to his folly, lest he be wise in his own eyes" (Prov. 26:4–
5). In most cases opposing proverbs are less obvious in their contradiction; but in this "celebrated case" (Collins, 1980:5) the sage simply juxtaposes two quite obviously contradictory proverbs on the
same problem.

(c) A next stage would be to formulate a saying on the contradictory
possibilities of sayings. For example, Santayana's dictum "Almost
every wise saying has an opposite one, no less wise, to balance it"
(Smith, 1928:53). Does Santayana include this saying itself among
such wise sayings? Does he exclude it by his "almost every"? Or
does he even consider it a wise saying at all?

(d) In this stage of self-consciousness, as distinct from the preceding
instance, one is quite certain that the saying comprehends its own
paradoxicality. Recall, for example, the saying from the Sceptics
cited above, or Clifton Fadiman's comment: "An aphorism (this
one of course excepted) can contain only as much wisdom as overstatement will permit" (5).

  In moving through those four points along a trajectory of increasing self-consciousness, one has moved as well from the collective
wisdom of the common mind to the more intensely personal vision
of individual challenge.

(3) Epigram and Fragment. For my present purpose I shall not make any programmatic distinction between *aphorism* and *epigram*. In itself I can do no better than cite the distinction suggested by Auden and Kronenberger (vii): "An epigram need only be true of a single case, for example, *Coleridge opened his mouth and a moth flew out*. . . . An aphorism, on the other hand, must convince every reader that it is either universally true or true of every member of the class to which it refers. . . . Again, an epigram must be amusing and brief, but an aphorism, though it should not be boring and must be succinct in style, need not make the reader laugh and can extend itself to several sentences." On the continuum suggested in Figure 1.1, I located both epigram (single case) and aphorism (general case) in the middle. But, once again, one must concede the constant pull of the continuum. It is possible, for example, that an epigram could become not only proverbial on its single case but even be extended, metonymically or metaphorically, to become a general proverbial expression: He has a bad case of Coleridge's mouth. But, for my present purpose in this book, I make no distinction between aphorism and epigram. I take very seriously, however, the warning of F. K. Bradley that, "Our live experiences, fixed in aphorisms, stiffen into cold epigram" (no. 25). Some of Jesus' aphorisms have stiffened not only into cold epigram, but even cold and anti-Semitic proverb.

Neither, for my present purpose, shall I make any distinction between *aphorism* and *fragment*. No matter how "closed" the form/matter integration of the aphorism may make it appear, and no matter how untouchable its isolated status may make it appear, despite or precisely because of those facets, it is always a heuristic matrix and a hermeneutical challenge. The form/matter integration of the *fragment* does no more than make such openness more overtly evident. Indeed, what the *fragment* does is push to an extreme possibilities always latent in the *aphorism*. Leonard Forster comments on *Das Atheneum*, the "little review" started in 1798 by the brothers August Wilhelm and Friedrich Schlegel, Friedrich von Hardenberg (Novalis), and Johann Ludwig Tieck, as follows (99):

In their review they operated with high-level intellectual shock tactics. The most obvious of these was the employment of the 'Fragment', a concentrated aphorism in prose designed to make people think. Friedrich Schlegel said that a 'Fragment' must be self-contained and rounded-off like a curled-up hedgehog. The apt simile brings out an important feature of the new literary form: it was meant to be prickly. It stood in direct contrast to the normal medium of intellectual communication—the learned or literary treatise, often in the form of a series of fictitious letters, proceeding discursively and developing an ordered argument.

In the *fragment*, the provocative overstatement that is characteristic of the *aphorism* moves in the direction of the *manifesto*: "Provocation is one of the functions of the literary manifesto, which aims at arousing interest and attention, not at stating sober truths" (Forster: 105). As the content of the *fragment* moved towards *manifesto* provocation, so also did its form remain in conjuction with that intention. "One of its functions was no doubt to outrage the orthodox, but it was also a gadget with which the early Romantics struck sparks out of each other's high-tension minds, in conversation and in letters as well as in print. This 'formless form' corresponds to an idea of wit remote from that of the eighteenth century and for which Friedrich Schlegel finds electrical metaphors" (Magill: 85).

The term *fragment* extends, then, the hermeneutical challenge of the *aphorism*. It dares the hearer or reader to envisage the whole of which this is but a part, to imagine the total vision of which this is but a fractured insight. "For surely one of the reasons why the, fragments are fragmentary, ruins and not complete edifices, is that Schlegel wants us to intuit what might have been but never was, wants us to take the fragment and make of it a whole, take the ruin and reconstruct the edifice" (Firchow: 18).

In this book I have used the term *fragment* and *aphorism* interchangeably in the title. I consider that the words used by Hans Eichner in describing Friedrich Schlegel's fragments are true of the miniaturist, aphorist, or fragmentalist in any place or time. We are confronted with "a collection of aphorisms, each of which was formulated so as to create an impression of independence from the rest and which were deliberately not arranged in a systematic order, but depended, in fact, on each other for mutual support and clarification" (48).

(4) Proverb and Aphorism. The distinction between *aphorism* and *proverb* is, however, of importance throughout this book. As stated before, I understand it as described by Williams (80). But since I consider the generic continuum of the prose miniature with its dialectic of collective and individual voices to be of great importance, I need to look at aphorism and proverb more closely.

There are two situations that need special attention. The first is primarily concerned with form. What of the case of those speakers or writers whose work is composed of newly or even brilliantly polished commonplaces? I consider such persons to be aphorists, because their very success is dangerous to the secret and anonymous processes of common mind and collective wisdom. It may be far safer never to see how dependent content is on form, how dependent proverbial truth is on artistic form, and how dependent that common mind and collective wisdom is on individual thought and personal contribution. I believe that those who tamper only with form are the most dangerous and necessary people around.

The second case is primarily concerned with content. Williams shows throughout his book how "Kohelet breaks away from the authority of the ancient collective voice" (27) of Israel's wisdom tradition. He gives two examples of how Kohelet uses proverbial and collective sayings in a quite unproverbial and individual manner (59). The first example is his use of Prov. 6:10 in Koh. 4:5–6. Proverbs 6:10 says that "a little folding of the hands to rest" is bad. Koh. 4:5 agrees: "The fool folds his hands, and eats his own flesh." But then he contradicts it in 4:6: "Better is a handful of quietness than two hands full of toil and a striving after wind." And that juxtaposition is a much more serious one than the case seen earlier in Prov. 26:4–5. The second example is Koh. 7:1. The first half of the verse reads at least like a proverbial piece of collective wisdom: "A good name is better than precious ointment." But the second

half of the verse says: "And the day of death, than the day of birth."
As Williams says, that second half "is as jarring as a zen koan" and
"whatever be the interpretation of these two lines, the rather conservative and traditional affirmation contained in the first proverb cannot have the same sense after having been joined to 7:1b. In fact,
the seeming literary illogic of the joining of these two texts may
have been Kohelet's method of indicating the absurdity of life: a
good name amounts to little or nothing if the name's bearer must
face the fickleness of fortune and a brief life span fading into death"
(Williams: 59–60).

I draw one very important conclusion from this for the present
book. One may quote proverbs in an anti-proverbial manner. One
may quote proverbs in such a way that one's personal vision is
challenging the common mind and collective wisdom of ancestral
tradition. In such a case it is better to talk of a *proverbial* or collective vision and order being countered by an *aphoristic* and personal
counter-vision and counter-order (but see Williams: 35–63).

The continuum of the prose miniature is therefore even more
important than its differentiation into proverb and aphorism. Both
are short and pithy formulations. And both resolutely refuse to append any reason, argument, or explanation. But proverb gives no
reason since none is necessary; it is the summation of the wisdom of
the past. Aphorism, on the other hand, gives no reason because
none is possible; it is the formulation of the wisdom of the future.
Proverb is the last word, aphorism the first word. And the aphorist
is quite content if one gets mixed up and cannot tell aphorism from
proverb. But whether in form alone or content alone or in form and
content together, the aphorism appears as a voice from Eden, a
dictum of dawn.

C. APHORISM AND AUTHORITY

The aphorist may or may not attack the *content* of community
wisdom. It is already dangerous enough to use the gnomic *form* of

its assertions for one's own propositions. Aphorism is thus an authoritative form, no matter what may be its content. Who is this who dares to speak from Eden?

"If any of you should be bitten with an unhappy passion for the composition of aphorisms, let me warn such an one that the power of observing life is rare, the power of drawing new lessons from it is rarer still, and the power of condensing the lesson in a pointed sentence is rarest of all. Beware of cultivating this delicate art" (Morley: 87–88). The warning of Lord Morley resounds again and again throughout the theoretical literature on the aphorism. Auden and Kronenberger agree that "aphorisms are essentially an aristocratic genre of writing. The aphorist does not argue or explain, he asserts; and implicit in his assertion is a conviction that he is wiser or more intelligent than his readers" (vii–viii). This authority begins with the very form of the aphorism, with the very fact that the aphorist adopts a form that the common mind or ancestral traditions uses for its own accumulated wisdom. But it is earned thereafter in formed content. It is not important whether the aphorist uses the "I" format, as Karl Kraus (1874–1936) does in the two aphorisms used as epigraphs for this chapter. With or without an overt "I," the individuality of the aphorist as authoritative visionary is always present. Logan Pearsall Smith (15) goes so far as to say that,

> finally—and this is their supreme perfection—aphorisms should bear, like coins, the personal image, delicate and delicately cut, of the lord of thought from whose mint they issue. The thought, in the other words, must be stamped with the hall-mark of the mind that thinks it. The individual quality of his temper, his imagination, the timbre of his voice, must mark his sayings as his own; we must feel that they are his, that he, and only he, could have said them.

This may well be true of some aphorisms and some aphorists, but surely not of all. Every aphorism, however, does bear the mark of individuality over against collectivity, even if not *always* of this individuality over against that one.

Clifton Fadiman has suggested that "a certain indescribable air of

authority" inherent in aphoristic speech makes it rather unfashiona-
ble at the moment. He cites the lines of Ogden Nash,

> The maxim, the apothegm, yea, even the aphorism,
>   die like echoes in the distance,
> Overwhelmed by such provocative topics as clothes,
>   beauticians, taxes and the scarcity of competent
>   domestic assistants,

to show that we prefer safer subjects, that is, safer contents and also
safer forms. "But an original mind entering a room bearing in his
hand the precious candle of an original statement may well set the
house afire" (15–16).

There is, finally, the question of aphoristic truth. Both aphorists
and commentators agree that aphorism is often deliberately exaggerated and overstated. "An aphorism," according to Karl Kraus,
"never coincides with the truth: it is either a half-truth or one-and-
a-half-truths" (Zohn: 67). In an interesting discussion, Patricia Topliss called "*hyperbole* . . . the master figure of the *Pensées*. It epito-
mizes the aggressiveness of Pascal's approach, his 'shock tactics,' his
determination to force acceptance of Christianity upon a stunned and
bewildered reader" (288). Then she concluded with this comparison:
"It is curious that La Rochefoucauld, obliged as an inventor of
maxims to generalize, is nevertheless much more careful of the truth
than Pascal, much less prone to prefer the bold to the accurate" (292).
Such provocation is, of course, part of the aphorism's heuristic power:
"it conveys a portion of a truth with such point as to set us thinking
on what remains" (Morley: 61).

Overstatement and exaggeration, hyperbole and paradox, are
often mentioned as facets of aphoristic truth. But understatement,
the even more delicate art of letting everything hang on a single
word, is also typical of the aphorism. Clifton Fadiman gives two
magnificent examples (12–13):

> The aphorist is a miser of words. If he could have spoken more tersely,
> he has failed. Sometimes an aphorism's whole life vibrates in a single
> word. President Lowell of Harvard, conferring the degree of Doctor of

Science upon the great entomologist William Morton Wheeler, composed a gem whose radiance depends upon a shy adverb: *Profound student of the social life of insects, who has shown that they also can maintain complex communities without the use of reason.* Ambrose Bierce, one of the most scarifying aphorists who ever lived, used a single simple verb to equally good effect: *Mythology: The body of a primitive people's beliefs concerning its origin, early history, heroes, deities and so forth, as distinguished from the true accounts which it invents later.*

Sometimes an aphorism may even lose its life in translation. " 'An aphorism need not be true, but it should overtake truth,' he [Karl Kraus] once wrote. 'It must get beyond it *in einem Satz.*' The last part of the aphorism defies translation; the German phrase means both 'in one sentence' and 'with one leap,' and Kraus was fond of playing with—and even physically illustrating—this linguistic fortuitousness" (Zohn: 23; see Williams: 108 note 40).

D. APHORISM AND JESUS

What exactly does all this—and particularly the proverb/aphorism continuum—have to do with the Jesus tradition? For the moment only a general answer will be offered, and this is done as discussion of Charles E. Carlston's thoughtful article, "Proverbs, Maxims, and the Historical Jesus."

1. PROBLEM

Carlston notes that "the whole point of proverbial wisdom is the communication of the generally accepted, the universal, the tried and true, not the striking or innovative. Almost by definition, therefore, a proverb does not represent the unique experience or outlook of the one who first coins it" (1980:88). He then goes on to propose three major conclusions concerning the use of such proverbial wisdom in the Jesus tradition.

(1) Amount. "My very rough and inexact count gives 102 sayings in the Synoptics which could be considered wisdom-sayings . . . Mk 32; Q 38; M 16: L 16" (91 and note 24). He concludes: " . . . the fact that wisdom-sayings are ascribed to Jesus in such considerable

numbers is significant, perhaps more significant than many commentators are willing to grant" (90).

(2) Subject. This concerns those subjects *not* touched in the Jesus tradition. "Our historical judgments about how Jesus might be related to the wisdom-tradition must take cognizance of the fact that education, personal character and habits, friendship, women and family relationships, ethnic matters, politics, and prudence are all missing from the proverbial material in the surviving Jesus-tradition" (98–99).

(3) Content. Finally, the materials of many proverbs in the Jesus-tradition are essentially the same as ones known before or contemporary with Jesus (99–102). This must be mentioned, he maintains, just as much as the fact that "Jesus' teaching differs in its use of hyperbole, its paradoxical formulations, its extremism, its demand for bold action, and perhaps above all in its eschatological conditioning" (102).

My primary concern in this book is not with the products of the historical Jesus, but with the process and procedures of the Jesus tradition. However, Carlston's article touches as much on this latter as that former question. In terms of *originality*, the problem is this: Did Jesus regularly quote proverbs and speak proverbially, and if he did, why was the tradition interested in remembering and recording them? In terms of *stratigraphy*, the problem is this: Did proverbial materials generally enter the tradition at the original, transmissional, or redactional levels, or did it enter more or less evenly at all levels? That second or stratigraphic problem is crucial for an understanding of the tradition's processes.

2. Case

The following detailed case study of a single aphorism will help to clarify the problem.

Aphorism 78: *On Hindering Others*

(1) There are three independent versions: (a) Q/Matt. 23:13 = Luke 11:52; (b) *Gos. Thom.* 39a; and (c) *Gos. Thom.* 102. (See Table 1.1.)

Table 1.1

Matthew 23:13	Luke 11:52
But woe to you, scribes and Pharisees, hypocrites! because you shut the kingdom of heaven against men; for you neither enter yourselves, nor allow those who would enter to go in.	Woe to you lawyers! for you have taken away the key of knowledge; you did not enter yourselves, and you hindered those who were entering.

(2) The Q Context. This aphorism forms part of the concluding diatribe of Q's third section concerning *Jesus and Opponents* (see Appendix 2).

(3) The Q Text. This is better preserved in Luke than in Matthew (Polag, 1979:56–57), but the Q/Luke term "key" (*kleida*) is still visible in the Matthean verb "shut" (*kleiete*).

(4) Oxyrhynchus Papyri. Aphorism 78 appears not only in the Coptic *Gospel of Thomas* from Nag Hammadi, but also in some Greek papyrus fragments of it found about fifty years earlier at Oxyrhynchus:

(a)   Oxy P 654 = *Gos. Thom.* Prologue, 1,2,3,4,5,6.

(b)   Oxy P 1 = *Gos. Thom.* 26,27,28,29,30 + 77b,31,32,33b.

(c)   Oxy P 655 = *Gos. Thom.* 36,37,38,39.

(a) Discovery of the Fragments. "On the edge of the Libyan desert, 120 miles south of Cairo, a series of low mounds, covered with Roman and early Arab pottery, marks the spot where stood the capital of the Oxyrhynchite nome" (Grenfell and Hunt, 1897:5). Although "a flourishing city in Roman times, and one of the chief centers of early Christianity in Egypt . . . it declined rapidly after the Arab conquest, and its modern representative, Behnesa, is a mere hamlet" (1897:5). Excavating there on behalf of the Egypt Exploration Fund in the winter of 1896–1897, Bernard P. Grenfell

Table 1.1 (cont.)

Gospel of Thomas 39a	Gospel of Thomas 102
The Pharisees and the scribes	Woe to the Pharisees,
have taken the keys of Knowledge and hidden them. They themselves have not entered, nor have they allowed to enter those who wish to.	for they are like a dog sleeping in the manger of oxen, for neither does he eat nor does he let the oxen eat.

and Arthur S. Hunt, both from the University of Oxford, discovered "in the rubbish-heaps of the town . . . large quantities of papyri, chiefly Greek, ranging in date from the first to the eighth century, and embracing every variety of subject" (1897:5). Among those papyri, and given immediate pride of place, was Oxy P 1.

"After an interval of six years . . . we returned in February 1903 to Oxyrhynchus, with a view to an exhaustive examination of what has been on the whole the richest site in Egypt for papyri" (1904b:9). Among that season's discoveries were Oxy P 654 and 655, but this latter was not recognized as part of the same original text as Oxy P 1 and 654.

(b) Date of the Fragments. After their discovery and editing of Oxy P 1, Grenfell and Hunt concluded: "(1) that we have here part of a collection of sayings, not extracts from a narrative gospel; (2) that they were not heretical; (3) that they were independent of the Four Gospels in their present shape; (4) that they were earlier than 140 A.D., and might go back to the first century" (1898:2). They decided on that date as follows: "Since the papyrus itself was written not much later than the beginning of the third century, this collection of sayings must go back at least to the end of the second century. But the internal evidence points to an earlier date. The primitive cast and setting of the sayings, the absence of any consistent tendency in favour of any particular sect, the wide divergences in the familiar sayings from the text of the Gospels, the striking character of those which are new, combine to separate the fragment from the 'apocryphal' literature of the middle and latter half of the second century, and to refer it back to the period when the Canonical Gospels had not yet reached their pre-eminent position" (1897:16). That is to say, the date of the text's *composition*, as distinct from the date of the text's *transcription*, was "earlier than 140 A.D., and might go back to the first century" (1898:2).

The discovery of Oxy P 654 did not alter that proposed date for the collection's creation. Although Oxy P 1 was a fragment from a valuable codex and Oxy P 654 was from an unimportant roll (1904a:10,1904b:20), Oxy P 1 belonged to earlier decades of the third century than did Oxy P 654. But, of course, since the original editors already recognized "that the present text [Oxy P 654] represents the beginning of a collection which later on included the original 'Logia' [Oxy P 1]" (1904a:1–2,1904b:10), they still "proposed A.D. 140 as the latest date to which the composition of the Sayings could be referred" (1904a:14,1904b:25).

(c) Relationship of the Fragments. We now know that Oxy P 1, 654,655 represent parts of Greek versions of the *Gospel of Thomas* whose Coptic translation was discovered at Nag Hammadi in 1945. "It is now certain that the three Oxyrhynchus fragments (1,654,655) . . . represent three different copies of the Greek text made at different times and give evidence of a fairly frequent copying of it in the third century" (Fitzmyer, 1974:362). Thus, although this has been disputed (Garitte: 1960ab; Guillaumont: 1960), the Coptic *Gospel of Thomas* should be considered as a translation of a Greek original, fragmentary versions of which had been discovered about fifty years earlier.

Detailed comparisons between the Greek and Coptic texts make it evident, however, that the latter is not just a straight translation of the former but is, minimally, a deliberate redaction of it, "an adapted translation" (Fitzmyer, 1974:416), or, maximally, both are "very different recensions of the *GTh*" (Marcovich: 64). On this point the combination of *Gos. Thom*. 30 + 77b in Oxy P 1 is very significant since that conjunction is a special indication "that the Coptic version is not a direct translation of the Greek, for we have here a bipartite saying, whereas the Coptic has preserved the two parts separately" (Fitzmyer, 1974:398). It is of course a separate question whether it was the Coptic translation that redactionally separated an originally unified Greek saying (Hofius: 187; Kuhn: 1960:317–318), or whether it was the Greek recension in Oxy P 1 that did so while the different and more original Greek recension translated into Coptic did not (Marcovich: 69). That former interpretation seems preferable, and in that case the Coptic would be a much more gnosticizing version of the Greek (Jeremias, 1964:106–111).

(5) *Gos. Thom*. 39a and Oxy P 655. Oxy P 655 is "eight fragments of a papyrus in roll form . . . the largest . . . measuring 8.2 × 8.3 cm. and comprising parts of the middles of two narrow columns" (Grenfell and Hunt, 1904b:37; see also 1904a:22). After the Nag Hammadi discoveries it is clear that this "fragment of a lost gospel" is actually a third Oxyrhynchus portion of the Greek *Gospel of Thomas* and that the original of this very badly mutilated papyrus "contained a continuous parallel to G. Thom. 24–39" (Kraft: 262), although now only sayings 24b and 36–39 are persuasively decipherable.

Of the twelve lines in this saying's Greek version, the first two are totally missing and the others contain only from two to five letters at the start of each line. Nevertheless, when the Greek text is restored in the light of the Coptic translation, it agrees substantially with its content (Hofius: 191; Kraft: 255; Fitzmyer, 1974:413–414). I give it in Fitzmyer's restoration and translation, but indicating the lacunae involved: ["Jesus says, 'The Pharisees and the scribes have] re[ceived the keys] of [knowledge and have] hid[den them; neither have they] enter[ed nor permitted those who would] enter. [But you] bec[ome wi]se a[s the serpents and g]uileless [as the dov]es" (see also Hennecke and Schneemelcher: 1.112–113).

(6) *Gos. Thom*. 102. Strictly speaking this is not, of course, a

definite variation of *Gos. Thom.* 39a. But Quispel has said that "these words have the sensuousness of good tradition" (1957:204). And Wilson described it as "a similar saying against the Pharisees" to *Gos Thom.* 39a. He even goes on to say that "the fact that it is a proverbial saying need create no difficulty: the originality lies not in the saying, but in its application, in the rapier-like thrust of the attack. There would seem to be grounds for including this among those apocrypha with some claim to authority" (1960a:76–77).

My present concern is not with *Gos. Thom.* 102 as a possibly original saying of Jesus. My more limited question is whether *Gos. Thom.* 102 represents an earlier stage of the aphorism's transmission than does either Q/Matt. 23:13 = Luke 11:52 or *Gos. Thom.* 39a. That is, was the *proverbial* form earlier or later than the other one? I repeat that what is at stake here is an understanding of how, where, and when proverbial expressions enter the Jesus tradition.

3. Solution

The "dog in the manger" is apparently a Greek proverb going back to "very ancient times" (Moravcsik: 85). (1) It is included among the Greek proverbs attributed to Aesop: "a dog lying in the manger who does not eat himself but hinders the donkey from doing so" (Perry, 1952:276). (2) It is also among the Latin fables as follows: "A dog without conscience lay in a manger full of hay. When the cattle came to eat of the hay he would not let them, but showed his teeth in ugly mood. The oxen protested: 'It is not right for you to begrudge us the satisfaction of indulging our natural appetite when you yourself have no such appetite. It is not your nature to eat hay, and yet you prevent us from eating it' " (Perry, 1952:696; 1965:597). (3) Lucian of Samosata (c. A.D. 125–180) gives the following version in "Timon, or The Misanthrope": "Not that they were able to enjoy you themselves, but that they were shutting out everyone else from a share in the enjoyment, like the dog in the manger that neither ate the barley (*tōn kithōn*) herself nor permitted the hungry horse to eat it" (Harmon: 2.342–343). (4) Again, in "The Ignorant Book-Collector," he says: "But you never lent a book to anyone; you act like the dog in the manger, who neither eats the grain (*tōn kithōn*) herself nor lets the horse eat it, who can" (Harmon: 3.210–211). One notes, of course, the inevitable oral variations on the dog (male or female), the fodder (hay or grain), and the hindered animals (donkey, cattle, horse).

Theoretically, then, the proverb could have infiltrated Aphorism 78 at a later stage of its transmission (so Stroker, 1970:111–113). But there is one very serious objection to seeing *Gos. Thom.* 102 as a simple proverbalization of *Gos. Thom.* 39a. This is the fact that *Gos. Thom.* 102 is a Woe, but 39a is not. One can hardly claim that 102 simply proverbalized the content of 39a, since that does not explain the Woe format of 102. The following stages are therefore indicated: (1) *Gos. Thom.* 102 with Woe/Proverb; (2) a stage with Woe/Non Proverb, which is the common source for (3) Q/ Matt. 23:13 = Luke 11:52 with Woe/Non Proverb, and (4) *Gos. Thom.* 39a with Non Woe/Non Proverb.

In the present case, at least, the proverbial content entered the aphorism's transmission at an earlier rather than a later stage. Bultmann, in discussing "secular meshalim which have been made into dominical sayings in the tradition" (102), noted that "it is even more precarious to try to indicate which of the logia Jesus could have taken from secular wisdom and made his own. In itself it is obviously by no means impossible that he should have taken the widespread figure of the doctor who tends the sick and not the healthy (Mk. 2:17), and used it to defend his own way of going to work" (104–105). He therefore concludes that "it is necessary to see that the tradition has taken many logia from popular wisdom and piety into itself, and to reckon with the fact that it has done so now and then because Jesus has made use of or coined such a saying" (105).

Accordingly, in this book my working hypothesis will be as follows. (1) The decision as to when proverbial expression entered the Jesus tradition must be worked out in each individual case with no absolute rule such as *always original* or *always early* or *always late* to solve situations automatically. (2) If a proverbial expression is recalled and remembered in the tradition, it may well be that its continuance is due to contextual or circumstantial data that render it memorable and not just to the proverbial content itself. (Millions of Americans said "Nuts," but only McAuliffe's is remembered.) (3) Such usage is not so much *proverbial* in the sense given by Carlston —"the communication of the generally accepted, the universal, the tried and true, not the striking or innovative" (1980:88)—as it is *aphoristic* in the sense proposed by Williams, speaking of Kohelet and Jesus (81):

> What they pose against the timeless types of traditional order is an intuition or vision of a counter-order—a reality or dimension of reality that is over against the traditional or commonly accepted view of the world. For Kohelet this is the dimension of immediate experience where one may ironically receive and enjoy his "portion" in the very process of work, eating, and intimate human relations. For Jesus the counter-order is a transcendent state of things which is announced as God's arriving rule.

Throughout this book, then, I shall speak of aphorisms and of aphoristic tradition even or especially when proverbial contents or expressions are concerned. As Asemissen said, "Longwindedness goes against the aphorism's nature. To say as much as possible with as little as possible is its watchword. For this reason it likes to make use of ready-made formulations, proverbial expressions for example, which it modifies in a surprising way for its purposes or brings into a paradoxical relationship" (171).

2
Aphoristic Core

When people can no longer hear a man thinking, he must speak. As soon as he reaches a point where he can again presuppose thoughts of the same nature as his, he must stop speaking. Most books contain nothing between two interesting points but the most ordinary common sense: a heavily drawn line where a dotted one would have sufficed.

GEORG CHRISTOPH LICHTENBERG (Mautner, 1959:25)

The wisest of the Ancients consider'd what is not too Explicit as the fittest for Instruction, because it rouzes the faculties to act. I name Moses, Solomon, Esop, Homer, Plato.

WILLIAM BLAKE (Keynes: 793)

On the whole, he who draws his thoughts (as Coleridge says) from a cistern and not from a spring, will generally be more sparing of them than to give ten ideas in a page instead of ten pages to an idea.

JOHN STUART MILL (Mill: 209)

A. ORAL SENSIBILITY

It is easy enough to distinguish the pure forms of orality and scribality. It is the intermediate cases that are difficult.

If a people have never invented writing and have never acquired it from others, they remain inevitably and exclusively oral. Oral sensibility is the triumph of sense over sequence, of structure over syntax. With the acquisition of writing, however, a new and different sensibility becomes possible. Scribal sensibility can conceive of *ipsissima verba* in ways utterly beyond the capacity and even the conceivability of oral imagination. Scribal sensibility is the victory of exact sequence and precise syntax. This in no way denigrates the magnificent power of oral memory but it insists that, apart from short formulaic sets, it is a memorization primarily of structure.

Imagine the following question. What did President Franklin Roosevelt say:

(a)   The only thing we have to fear is fear itself.
(b)   The only thing you have to fear is fear itself.
(c)   The only thing there is to fear is fear itself.
(d)   We have nothing to fear but fear itself.
(e)   You have nothing to fear but fear itself.
(f)   There is nothing to fear but fear itself.

In oral sensibility that is a meaningless question, since all those sentences are the same. And in oral sensibility, even if one asked the speaker what had been said, the repetition would be not so much verbatim repetition as repetition *ad sensum* and *ad structuram*. But for a scribal sensibility such questions are meaningful and important. If I were quoting Roosevelt, for example, I would probably try to check the *ipsissima verba* from a written version of the speech, and find (a) to be correct. That is scribal sensibility. Oral sensibility and *ipsissima verba* are, however, contradictions in terms. Or, put otherwise, even if orality speaks of *ipsissima verba* it means *ipsissima structura*. One can see this quite clearly in the four different openings of the story of "Marko and Nina" collected by Milman Parry (Lord: 236) and given in Table 2.1.

Intermediate situations are more difficult. What of a people at an historical moment when they are shifting from oral to scribal sensibility? And what especially of a writer for whom oral sensibility is still very much alive? I do not believe in any intrinsic superiority

Table 2.1

Parry 6	Parry 804	Parry 805	Parry 846
Marko	Marko arises early in his stone tower	Marko arises early in his tower in Prilip	Marko arises early in his stone tower.
is drinking wine with his mother, his wife, and his sister.	and drinks raki. With him are his mother, his wife, and his sister Andelija.	and drinks raki. With him are his mother, his wife, and his sister Andelija.	With him are his mother and his wife.

between orality and scribality in either direction (but see Ong). It is clear, however, that peoples or individuals caught in the transition from orality to scribality may well compare the advantages of the former with the disadvantages of the latter and decide that the movement is only loss (see Kelber, 1983). My present concern is not with such hierarchical suggestions, but simply with the mechanics of a *writer* for whom *orality* is still quite dominant. When such a one is actually copying from a written source in which a saying is given complete syntactical formulation, it is always possible that the verbal structure will be taken and the verbal syntax will be reformulated. This should not be explained as "oral tradition" in the sense that an oral *version* of the saying wins out over the written one. If that actually happened, we were not dealing with an oral version but with a scribal version transmitted orally. An *oral* version is a structure, a *scribal* version is a sequence. It is because of that ambiguity that I avoid the term "oral tradition," since it often confuses oral transmission within oral sensibility (basic structure) and oral transmission within scribal sensibility (exact saying).

I would like to go over this point in some detail, since the tradition of Jesus' aphorisms represents a transition from oral beginnings to scribal conclusions. When one speaks or writes, one does so with a sequentially formulated and syntactically invested verbal structure. One can only say it or write it one way at a time. Imagine, for example, that what Jesus said on a dawning Galilean morning was "ask and you will receive." His own oral sensibility and the oral memory of any hearer will retain that as a verbal *structure* that contains within itself immediate possibilities of:

(1) *contraction* (especially of two stichs, if present, to one);
(2) *expansion* (especially of one to two stichs);
(3) *conversion* (from positive to negative, or vice versa);
(4) *substitution* (of one synonymous term for another);
(5) *transposition* (of first for second part, or vice versa).

For example, Jesus' own or any subsequent formulations may (1) move freely among the basic verbs on either side as long as one from each side is present; (2) shift from positive to negative, to positive and negative, or negative and positive formulations; (3) use imperative ("ask") or conditional ("if you ask") or relatival ("whoever asks") formats; or (4) even reverse the sequence of the two sides: "he receives who has asked." Etc., etc., etc.

Because of this situation of initial orality, I consider that the basic unit of transmission is never the *ipsissima verba* of an aphoristic saying but, at best and at most, the *ipsissima structura* of an aphoristic core.

B. PERFORMANCE AND HERMENEUTIC

That first distinction between *orality* and *scribality* is crucial. If, for example, Jesus had uttered oral aphorisms and then drilled some disciples in oral mnemonics so that they could repeat them verbatim, and even if none of them could read or write, they would have been operating within scribal sensibility. This would not have been intrinsically impossible, since writing was long known in their tradition. Had Jesus so done, of course, the results we have would indicate his instruction to have been the worst in the long history of pedagogical technique.

A second distinction follows directly. This is between performance and hermeneutic or between performancial variations and hermeneutical variations.

I use the term *performance* for the necessarily diverse ways in which the transmission will formulate the aphoristic core into syntactically complete sayings. Thus all the versions of the *Ask and Receive* core suggested above would represent performancial variations. And Matthew and Luke looking at a specific aphoristic saying in Mark or in Q might well display oral sensibility and formulate it differently, not only because of theological or grammatical or stylistic reasons, but simply because of residual orality, residual reluctance to be bound finally and irrevocably to one ultimate formulation.

I want to distinguish these *performancial variations* from what I term *hermeneutical variations*. Suppose that paradigmatic *Ask and Receive* core is formulated as:

(a) Ask and you will receive immediately
(b) Ask and you will receive eventually.

Or, suppose it is formulated as:

(c) Ask and you will receive always
(d) Ask and you will receive sometimes.

I term those hermeneutical variations because they give an interpretation as well as a performance. But notice that we cannot say they interpret it away from or against some absolute original meaning. All four formulations seem possible interpretations *within* and not *against* the basic core. This is an extremely delicate and important point. There may, of course, be situations where we are willing to say that a hermeneutical variation *changes*, for better or for worse, for richer or for poorer, some more original meaning. But especially when one is dealing with aphoristic phenomena, there will be many cases where we can record divergent hermeneutical variations without being able to say that they are *changes against* rather than *interpretations within* the aphoristic core itself. It is also obvious that many interesting things will take place not on the extreme ends of the distinction but towards the middle, where it may not be clear at all whether we arc dealing with performancial or hermeneutical variation.

One final point. On May 13, 1940, England's new Prime Minister, Winston Churchill, said in the Commons, "I have nothing to offer but blood, toil, tears, and sweat." One often hears that phrase recalled as "blood, sweat, and tears." The original formulation is, however, sequentially perfect: (1) *blOOd, tOil/tEArs, swEAt*; (2) the medial *Toil/Tears*; (3) the connections of *blooD, Toil*, and of *tearS, Sweat*; and (4) the final *sweaT* to recall the medial *Ts*. It is, in fact, quite unforgettable. It is orally unforgettable not only as a structure but as a prose sequence. What, then, of "blood, sweat, and tears"? Is that formulation an example of oral memory and performancial variation? Not exactly. An oral mind is not the same as a tin ear.

C. PERFORMANCIAL VARIATIONS

At the moment I am considering those performancial variations that are to be included *within* the aphoristic core itself. Cases where, for example, Matthew or Luke performancially vary their received Mark or Q text as exercises in residual orality are not the present concern. But independent versions of an aphorism often contain variations about which it is either impossible or unprofitable to speculate on greater or lesser originality. In the light of oral sensibility, I find it better to locate certain variations within the core itself. The main ones are (1) *contraction*, (2) *expansion*, (3) *substitution*, (4) *transposition*, and (5) *conversion*. The meaning of these terms will be clear from the following examples.

Aphorism 111: *First and Last*

(1) There are three independent versions: (a) Mark 10:31 = Matt. 19:30; (b) Q/Matt. 20:16 = Luke 13:30; and (c) *Gos. Thom.* 4b. (See Table 2.2.)

(2) Mark 10:31. Externally, "the material from Mark viii 27 to x 25 is constructed in an overall pattern of three. The three passion

Table 2.2

Mark 10:31	Matthew 19:30	Matthew 20:16	
But many that are first will be last, and the last first.	But many that are first will be last, and the last first.	So the last will be first, and the first last.	

predictions establish a framework for a lengthy amount of material and provide a dramatic progression to the . . . lengthiest and most dramatic form of the saying in x 33–34" (Robbins, 1981a:102). This gives three major units in (i) 8:27–9:29, (ii) 9:30–10:31, and (iii) 10:32–45.

Internally, that second unit is composed as in Figure 2.1.

Figure 2.1

9:30 – 32	prophecy and incomprehension
9:33 – 37/38 – 50	disciples/John (aphoristic monologue)
10:1 – 9	outsider (journey)
10:10 – 12	disciples
10:13 – 16	disciples
10:17 – 22	outsider (journey)
10:23 – 27/28 – 31	disciples/Peter (aphoristic dialogue)

(a) After the opening prophecy in 9:30–32, there are two sections in 9:33–10:12 and 10:13–31 that are paralleled internally and also joined together externally. *Internally* (b) each section begins with a *children* episode in 9:33–37 and 10:13–16, and

(c) continues with outsiders encountered on the journey who enter into dialogue with Jesus in 10:1–9 and 10:17–22 before Jesus turns to the disciples in 10:10–12 and 10:23–31. *Externally*

(d) the beginning of the first section and the conclusion of the last section are linked together by (i) a dialogue with the disciples in

Table 2.2 (cont.)

Luke 13:30	Gospel of Thomas 4b
And behold, some are last who will be first, and some are first who will be last.	For many who are first will become last, and they will become one and the same.

9:33–37 and 10:23–27 giving way to one with a named disciple, John in 9:38–39 and Peter in 10:28–31; (ii) an aphoristic monologue combining the sayings in 9:40–50, but an aphoristic dialogue combining those in 10:23–31; and (iii) the incomplete opening aphorism looking to the concluding complete one:

first/last//—/servant   (9:35)
first/last//last/first   (10:31)

This means that Mark redacted 10:31 into its present position as the climactic conclusion to all of 9:30–10:31. It should be noted, also, that the two–stich Aphorism 14 in 9:35 is in positive/negative// (positive)/negative format while 10:31 is in chiastic positive/negative/ /negative/positive construction.

(3) Matt. 19:30. This is verbatim the same as in Mark 10:31 and in the same context.

(4) Q/Matt. 20:16 = Luke 13:30. The aphorism appears in quite different contexts in Matthew and Luke, but in each case as the climactic conclusion to a unit. In Matt. 20:16 it terminates the parable of the Workers in the Vineyard in 20:1–15, which had contained in it mention of "last/first" (8), "first" (10), and "last" (12,14). Despite this word-linkage, however, the association is less than perfect. The format of the parable is not that the last to be hired are the first to be paid and the first to be hired are the last to be paid. The point is that first and last are equated and, while the pay is just and fair, it is against both their expectations: one expected less, the other more.

In Q/Luke 13:23–30 it concludes a six-unit *aphoristic cluster* whose first five units are word-linked together (see Appendix 2). Although there is no word-linkage between those five and this sixth saying, its position as aphoristic conclusion stems most likely from Q rather than from Luke, as does indeed the entire composition of Q/Luke 13:22–30 (but see Hoffmann: 1967). As Jacobson (1978: 227) has noted: "Near what seems to be the end of Q, we encounter material where it is clear that Israel has finally been abandoned and her position taken by Gentiles (Lk 13:34f par; Lk 13:28–29 par; Lk 14:15–24 par)." The context says that the *Jews*, who were first, will not enter the Kingdom of God, that is, will become last, in 13:25–27 and 13:28. And conversely, the *Gentiles*, who were last, will enter and become first, in 13:29. And this is summed up in 13:30.

But the aphorism in Q is in negative/positive//positive/negative construction. This is not dictated by the context (Jews/Gentiles), which rather dictates the reverse or Markan chiasm. Thus the differences in sequence between Mark and Q are most likely simple performancial variations.

(5) *Gos. Thom.* 4b. This saying is found both in the Coptic text of Thomas and also among its Greek fragments found at Oxyrhynchus. It is contained in Oxy P 654. "This consists of forty-two incomplete lines on the verso of a survey-list of various pieces of land, thus affording another example of the not uncommon practice of using the back of ephemeral documents for literary texts" (Grenfell and Hunt, 1904a:1,1904b:9). The fragment measures 24.4 × 7.8 cm., but only the first half of lines 1–31 are extant, and thereafter even the opening of each line steadily diminishes from two letters absent in line 33 to only two letters present in line 42 (1904a:3, and its Plate I; 1904b:11, and its *Frontispiece*). The Greek text, as restored by Marcovich (60; see Hofius: 32), rather than Fitzmyer (1974:379), can be translated and compared with the translated Coptic, as in Table 2.3. Marcovich (60; see Schrage, 1964a:258) concludes that the Coptic translator or copyist has omitted "and the

Table 2.3

Oxyrhynchus Papyrus 654	*Gospel of Thomas* 4b
For many who are f[irst shall become last ⟨and⟩] the last first, and they shall [become one]	For many who are first will become last, and they will become one and the same.

last first" by simple oversight. This means that the two-stich aphorism was originally in *Thomas*, and in the Markan sequence and
opening rather than in the Q formulation. It also means that the
original chiastic two-stich aphorism was expanded by the addition of
a third stich: "and they will become one and the same" (Lambdin:
118) or, possibly better, "and they shall become a single one" (Guillaumont, 1959:5; Wilson, 1973:511).

Klijn (271) has noted that "three different words are used to render the word 'single one' " in *Thomas*: (1) *wa* (11,22,106); (2) *wa
wōt* (4,22,23); (3) *monachos* (16,49,75). The meaning is the same,
and that last (Greek) expression "cannot have its usual meaning
'monk' in this early text" (Till: 452 note 2). The meaning of this
very important Thomistic theme has been summarized by Klijn
(272) as follows: "(a) The word 'single one' is equivalent to the elect
and saved ones. (b) Originally man was a 'single one,' but he
became 'two.' In order to be saved he has to become a 'single one'
again. This means that he has to return to his original state. (c) The
original 'single one' has become 'two' by becoming male and
female. This means that originally man was not male and female.
As a result we may say that the Gospel of Thomas speaks about
salvation as a return to the original state and that it rejects the
division of man into male and female." When *Gos. Thom.* 4 is
compared with *Gos. Thom.* 22, one can conclude that "becoming
as a child, and entering the kingdom, and achieving a state of asex-
uality are very nearly interchangeable terms" (Kee, 1963:313; see
also Ménard, 1975:83).

Table 2.4

Mark 9:40	Luke 9:50b	Matthew 12:30	
For he that is not against us is for us.	for he that is not against you is for you.	He who is not with me is against me, and he who does not gather with me scatters.	

(6) Conclusion. The differences between the aphorism in Mark, Q, and the first half of *Gos. Thom.* 4b are all performancial variations on the same chiastic two-stich saying. The variation is what I term *transposition* because the stichs (*first/last* or *last/first*) can be transposed with either coming first. Notice, by the way, how hard it is to recall which way one has just cited the saying even for oneself. But the second half of *Thomas's* version is not performancial but hermeneutical variation.

Aphorism 71: *For and Against*

(1) There are, I would judge, three independent versions: (a) Mark 9:40 = Luke 9:50b; (b) Q/Matt. 12:30 = Luke 11:23; and (c) Oxy P 1224. (See Table 2.4.)

(2) Mark 9:40. The saying in Mark is word-linked (see Table 5.6 below) to the preceding 9:38–39 by a simple Markan "for" (*gar*). It rebukes another "misunderstanding" on the part of the disciples and proposes a more open and accepting attitude to outsiders. This *inclusive* formulation where "not against" means "for" fits well into this whole section in Mark.

(3) Luke 9:50b. This is verbatim Mark 9:40 but with "you" for "us." Thus Luke 9:50b with "you" and 11:23 with "me" combine to equate the Markan version with its "us."

(4) Q/Matt. 12:30 = Luke 11:23. Q's Beelzebul controversy continues with Aphorisms 69–70 and concludes with Aphorism 71 (see Appendix 2). That is, it was preceded in Q's Aphorism 69 by an acknowledgment from Jesus of the validity of other Jewish exorcisms

Table 2.4 (cont.)

Luke 11:23	Oxy P 1224
He who is not with me is against me, and he who does not gather with me scatters.	For he who is not [against you] is for you. [He who today] is far-off—tomorrow will be [near to you]

as well as his own: "And if I cast out demons by Beelzebul, by whom do your sons cast them out? Therefore they shall be your judges" (Luke 11:19 = Matt. 12:27). "It is certainly true that the juxtaposition of Lk 11:19 and 20 par jeopardizes the eschatological uniqueness of Jesus. But . . . where Jesus is understood as a messenger of Wisdom, such ideas as this are possible. . . . Jesus contends that his exorcisms, like those of the other Jewish exorcists, are manifestations of the Kingdom of God. . . . Neutrality has ceased to be possible. . . . But since neutrality is impossible, the situation can actually be formulated in seemingly opposite ways: he who is not with me is against me (Lk 11:23 par); he who is not against us is for us (Mk 9:40)" (Jacobson, 1978:165–166).

Thus Mark 9:40 and Q/Matt. 12:30a = Luke 11:23a are but performancially diverse ways of stating, *with specific allusion to exorcisms*, that neutrality is impossible: *All* exorcists are on the side of Jesus. But what of the saying's second stich in Matt. 12:30b = Luke 11:23b? This more metaphorical restatement of the same principle is probably to be read in the context of Q/Matt. 9:37–38 = Luke 10:2 (Jacobson: 166). It is also probable that Q doubled the aphorism to make this connection.

(5) Oxy P 1224. This represents two fragments from the tops of leaves of a papyrus book dating from the early fourth or even late third century. Of the first fragment "so little is preserved that no reconstruction is practicable" although "the words *amēn hy[min legō]* show that the Saviour is speaking"(Grenfell and Hunt, 1914:2). It is the second and larger fragment (6.3 × 13.1 cm.) whose recto contains the present saying (Hennecke and Schneemelcher: 1.114; see Grenfell and Hunt, 1914:6,9–10). The verso has the following unit: "And the scribes and [Pharisees] and priests, when they sa[w] him, were angry [that with sin]ners in the midst he [reclined] at table. But Jesus heard [it and said:] The he[althy need not the physician]" (Hennecke and Schneemelcher: 1.114; see Grenfell and Hunt, 1914:5,8–9). That unit indicates, however, that this "unknown gospel," if it was actually such, was more narratival than aphoristic.

The present saying appears within an *aphoristic cluster* in Oxy P

1224 containing: (a) a preceding saying, "and pray for your enemies" (see Aphorism 35); (b) Aphorism 71, word-linked to its predecessor by "for you(r)," *hyper . . . hymōn*; (c) an otherwise unknown saying: and (d) a fourth saying, linked to the third by "and in" but thereafter so mutilated as to be presently undecipherable save that it mentions "of the adversary" and so presumably continues the cluster's theme of relations with enemies (Grenfell and Hunt, 1914:6,9–10).

Jeremias considers that third saying as an authentic saying of Jesus (1964:96–97). Be that as it may, it should not be considered as part of Aphorism 71, but simply as part of an *aphoristic cluster* concerning contacts with "enemies." It is not the same as the Q *expansion* in Matt. 12:30b = Luke 11:23b, which is parallel to Q/Matt. 12:30a = Luke 11:23a. But the two sayings in the middle of Oxy P 1224 (Fr. 2 recto. Col.i) concern opposite rather than parallel situations: (a) not against/for, and (b) far off/near.

I consider Oxy P 1224 to be an independent version of Aphorism 71. It has a participial opening as does Q's version, "he who" (*ho ōn*), rather than a relatival opening, as in Mark, "he that" (*hos*). But it has the Markan format of *not against/for* rather than Q's *not for/against*.

(6) Conclusion. The saying appears as an *aphoristic addition* to a story concerning exorcism in both Mark 9:38–39 (as 9:40) and Q/Matt. 12:22–28 = Luke 11:14–15,17–20 (as Q/Matt. 12:30 = Luke 11:23) but within an *aphoristic cluster* concerning one's opponents in Oxy P 1224.

In all cases, in Greek, the construction is chiastic: *is/us//us/is*. This formal unity underlines the fact that the inclusive (not against, for) and the exclusive (not for, against) versions are simple performancial variations stressing in both cases the impossibility of *neutrality*. Luke must have seen this and so finds no problem in giving both versions of the aphorism. But Matthew, in omitting Mark completely, *may* have read it in an exclusive sense. But in itself the variation between Mark and Oxy P 1224, on the one hand, and Q, on the other, is primarily performancial rather than hermeneutical.

It is *neutrality* that the saying categorically denies in either variation, and it does so by *substitution* of "for" and "against" for one
another within the same chiastic framework. There is also an example of *expansion* in Q/Matt. 12:30b = Luke 11:23b, but this is
probably from Q and not from the aphoristic core itself.

Aphorism 38: *The Golden Rule*

(1) There are three independent versions of this saying: (a) Q/
Matt. 7:12 = Luke 6:31; (b) *Gos. Thom.* 6b; and (c) *Did.* 1:2b. (See
Table 2.5.)

(2) Forms. The version from Q is given positively, but that from
Thomas and the *Didache* is formulated negatively.

The negative form, "and what you hate, do not do to anyone,"
appears in the book of Tobit, at 4:15, a book "composed, possibly in
Aramaic, in the last quarter of the third century B.C. . . . from
orthodox circles in Egypt" (Charles: 1.174). But both negative and
positive forms appear in the *Letter of Aristeas* 207: "As you wish that
no evil should befall you, but to be a partaker of all good things, so
you should act on that same principle." This Alexandrian apology
"was issued in its present form at the commencement of the Christian era . . . —but the large part of it—possibly the whole except the
law section, §§ 128-71—was in existence before and belongs to the
period 130-70 B.C." (Charles: 2.87). Thus, although the negative
form is more common in Jewish literature, for example as Hillel's
one-sentence summation of the Law (see Strack-Billerbeck: 1.459–
460), Bultmann has warned that, "It is a piece of self-deception to

Table 2.5

Matthew 7:12	Luke 6:31	
So whatever you wish that men would do to you; do so to them for this is the law and the prophets.	And as you wish that men would do to you, do so to them.	

suppose that the positive form of the rule is characteristic for Jesus, in distinction from the attested negative form among the Rabbis. The positive form is purely accidental, for whether it be given positive or negative formulation the saying, as an individual utterance, gives moral expression to a naif egoism" (103). Manson's judgment, although considerably milder, is equally sweeping: "The question whether the positive form states a higher moral ideal than the negative is one of little moment" (52). Hence positive and/or negative versions are simple performancial variations within the aphoristic core rather than hermeneutical improvements in morality or ethics. Dihle has traced the "Golden Rule" back to the fifth century Sophists (85–95), but denies any difference between its negative and positive forms (8–11). He also gives a list of early Christian citations where it appears negatively (seventeen times), positively (seven times), and positively/negatively (three times). It is even in negative construction in the western readings of Acts 5:20,29 (Metzger: 430–432). Although, therefore, the negative/positive differentiation *could* be interpreted as a minimal/maximal morality, such an interpretation is neither logically nor theologically necessary. And, in any case, no reading should feed the chauvinism it forbids.

(3) The Q Context. The Q context of Aphorisms 35–38 is still evident in Luke, although redactionally relocated by Matthew (see Appendix 2). For Q, Aphorism 38 served (a) to conclude the encapsulation of that terrible Aphorism 36 (see Luke 6:29), which was already somewhat modified at least from violent to nonviolent self-despoiling by its alignment with Aphorism 37 (see Luke 6:30), and

Table 2.5 (cont.)

Gospel of Thomas 6b	Didache 1:2b
do not do what you hate	And whatsoever thou wouldst not have done to thyself; do not thou to another.

(b) to stand as a summary of the *aphoristic cluster* in 6:27–31 before turning to Q's composition of the *aphoristic commentary* in 6:32–35 (see Appendix 2) "Apparently, Matthew has delayed his use of the saying to sum up the considerable number of Q sayings in 6:22–7:11. In short, he alters Luke's order for editorial reasons" (Taylor, 1959:251; Lührmann, 1972:419). The Matthean relocation also begets the redactional addition, "For this is the law and the prophets," placed here before Matthew turns to his concluding warnings in 7:13–27.

(4) The Q Text. Once the Matthean concluding addition is removed, the two texts are extremely close, with only a minor difference in the opening words. Polag proposes the Q reading: "Whatever you wish that men would do to you, do so to them" (1979: 36–37). But, whatever the precise opening expression, it is quite clear that *The Golden Rule* is here formulated in *positive* fashion and with plural "you."

(5) *Gos. Thom.* 6b. This somewhat truncated version of the rule's negative formulation has the following context. "His disciples questioned Him and said to Him, 'Do you want us to fast? How shall we pray? Shall we give alms? What diet shall we observe?' Jesus said, 'Do not tell lies, and do not do what you hate, for all things are plain in the sight of Heaven. For nothing hidden will not become manifest, and nothing covered will remain without being uncovered.' "

The text is found not only in the Coptic translation of *Thomas*, but also among the Oxyrhynchus Papyri fragments of the Greek *Thomas* in Oxy P 654. The badly mutilated Greek text has been restored from the Coptic version as follows: [*ha mis*]*eite me poieit*[*e*] or "[what] you [ha]te do not do" (Hofius: 41; see also Fitzmyer, 1974:385; Marcovich: 65). The Coptic version is a close translation of that sequence: "that which you hate, do not do" (with Wilson, 1973:511; rather than Guillaumont, 1959:5; or Lambdin: 118). Thus the sequence here is as in Tob. 4:15, *ho miseis, mēdeni poiēsēs*, although the former is plural "you" while this latter is singular "you." Those differences are dictated primarily by context. It is, of course, quite unlikely that *Thomas* is in any way quoting directly from Tobit (Ménard, 1975:87). But his negative version says: What you hate (done to you) do not do (to others).

(6) *1 Clem.* 13:2. This is "a letter sent by the church of Rome to the church of Corinth in consequence of trouble in the latter community which had led to the deposition of certain Presbyters" and "it must be dated between 75 and 110 A.D.; but within these limits there is a general agreement among critics to regard as most probable the last decade of the first century" (Lake: 1.3,5).

In *1 Clem.* 13:2 there is a series of seven sayings introduced by the phrase "remembering the words of the Lord Jesus which he spoke when he was teaching gentleness and longsuffering. For he spoke thus" (Lake: 1.30–31). Koester has argued, I think correctly, that this cluster is independent of the intracanonical gospels (1957a: 12–16,259). But he has also suggested that the saying, "as ye do, so shall it be done unto you," which appears third in the aphoristic cluster of *1 Clem.* 13:2 (Lake: 1.30–31), is an example of *The Golden Rule* given in positive formulation. I cannot agree with this, since that aphoristic cluster seems more concerned with human action and *divine* reaction than with human reaction: "As ye do (to others), so shall it be done unto you (by God)."

(7) *Did.* 1:2b. The situation with *Did.* 1:2b is much more difficult. "The Teaching of the Twelve Apostles" (*Didachē tōn Dōdeka Apostolōn*) has a very complicated textual history (see Lake: 1.305–307). It opens with the moral catechism called the "Two Ways" in *Did.* 1–6. But this unit also exists "in a self-contained Latin version, usually cited as *Doctrina Apostolorum*," which "*omits the Christianizing passage = Did.* 1.3b–2.1 and otherwise shows only the most external signs of Christianization" so that originally it "was almost certainly a Jewish didactic work, used in the Hellenistic synagogue before the *Didache* was compiled. The 'Two Ways' document's continuing existence within the Christian community, independent of the *Didache*, is also shown by its use in the letter of Barnabas (18.1–20.2) and in later works" (Layton, 1968:379). Hence, although "the chronology of this complex document is very obscure"

the "original 'Two Ways' may be early first century or even earlier" (Lake: 1.307).

This means that the negative citation of *The Golden Rule* in *Did.* 1.2b has nothing whatsoever to do with Q/Matt. 7:12a = Luke 6:31 (Glover: 13), but represents the more general Jewish (negative) tradition which dominates also in the later Christian tradition, despite Q (Koester, 1957a:169).

(8) Conclusion. The positive/negative versions are neither morally superior/inferior nor maximal/minimal variations but simple performancial variations. The negative version (because of the negativity of the Ten Commandments?) predominated in the Jewish and also the Christian tradition, despite Q/Matt. 7:12a = Luke 6:31. This tradition had, after all, its own quite different positive formulation, from Lev. 19:18 and Mark 12:31.

I use the term *conversion* for variations between negative and/or positive formulations of an aphorism, and this would be an example of such performancial variation. But the expansion in Matt. 7:12, "for this is the law and the prophets," is hermeneutical variation, and is similar to that attributed to Hillel the Elder (c. 20 B.C.–A.D. 20), "What is hateful to you, do not do to anyone else; that is the whole Law, all else is commentary. Go and learn."

D. HERMENEUTICAL VARIATIONS

In discussing performancial variations of *substitution*, *transposition*, and *conversion* above, but within the aphoristic core, we have also seen hermeneutical variations outside it, for example, *Gos. Thom.* 4b or Matt. 7:12. In this section I consider a hermeneutical variation that could be mistaken for *contraction* and *transposition* within a performancially varied aphoristic core. It *could* be but it *should* not be.

Aphorism 1: *Kingdom and Repentance*

(1) There is only one independent version: Mark 1:15 = Matt. 4:17b. (See Table 2.6.)

Table 2.6

Matthew 4:17b	Mark 1:15
Repent, for the Kindom of heaven is at hand.	The time is fulfilled, and the Kingdom of God is at hand; repent, and believe in the gospel

(2) Luke 4:15. Luke has totally avoided the Markan formulation by summarizing with the phrase, "And he taught in their synagogues, being glorified by all."

(3) Matt. 4:17b. Matthew retains half of it, but drastically changes its meaning and its impact. (a) It is no longer uniquely Jesus' message, since earlier the Baptist (3:2, verbatim) and later the disciples (10:7, nothing about repentance) preached the same announcement. (b) The double parallels of Mark (twin perfects, twin imperatives) are reduced to a single one, so that one can no longer interpret one side of the parallelism by the other. (c) He reverses the Markan order to imperative-perfect and inserts "for" (because) between them so that "what is announced in Matt. 4:17 is not the present arrival but the imminent coming of the Kingdom" (Kelber, 1974:10). For Matthew, the call is to repent in preparation for the coming Kingdom.

(4) Mark 1:15. Bultmann called 1:15 "a quite secondary formulation . . . which might very well derive from Mark himself" (118). Pryke describes Mark here as "summarising the content of Jesus' preaching in a celebrated bridge passage" (74) and places all of 1:14–15 among his "redactional text of Mark" (151–152). But it is especially Kelber who has shown how thoroughly Mark's own theological concerns have dominated both the form and the content of 1:15, especially by the "advanced position" (9) of the parallel verbs *fulfilled* and *is at hand*, which are in perfect tense and inaugural position in the Greek text (*Fulfilled the time! Arrived the Kingdom!*). Since "no other New Testament theologian saw fit to put on the lips

of Jesus the bold assertion" (Kelber, 1974:9), one understands why Matthew and Luke handle Mark's text so carefully.

The one who speaks in Mark 1:15 is *not* the historical Jesus but the Markan Jesus. He announces that the Kingdom *has* arrived, but it has arrived in a most unexpected mode of mysterious humility and hidden divinity. Therefore its advent demands *repentance*—that is, a radical change in one's way of thinking and being, and also *faith*. Later, when it arrives "in power," one will not need to believe but to see (Mark 9:1; 13:26; 14:62).

(5) Conclusion. Mark 1:15 is a thoroughly Markan formulation. Because of this Luke avoided it completely. Matt. 4:17b effected a *contraction* and *transposition* on Mark 1:15, but this is by no means a performancial variation within the aphoristic core. It is a deliberate hermeneutical variation upon a source text.

Table 2.7

Matthew 24:43–44	Luke 12:39–40	
But know this, that if the householder had known in what part of the night the thief was coming, he would have watched and would not have let his house be broken into.	But know this, that if the householder had known at what hour the thief was coming, he	
	would not have left his house to be broken into.	
Therefore you also must be ready;	You also must be ready;	
for the Son of man is coming at an hour you do not expect.	for the Son of man is coming at an unexpected hour.	

E. PERFORMANCIAL OR HERMENEUTICAL VARIATION?

In the preceding two sections it was relatively easy to differentiate between performancial and hermeneutical variations. My final example concerns a saying where it is very difficult to say which we are dealing with, but where that decision is also of some importance.

Aphorism 99: *Knowing the Danger*

(1) There are three independent versions: (a) Q/Matt. 24:43 = Luke 12:39; (b) *Gos. Thom.* 21c; and (c) *Gos. Thom.* 103. There are also independent but residual mentions of the theme in: (d) 1 Thess. 5:2; (e) 2 Pet. 3:10; (f) Rev. 3:2–3; and (g) Rev. 16:15. (See Table 2.7.)

Table 2.7 (cont.)

Gospel of Thomas 21b	*Gospel of Thomas* 103
Therefore I say to you, if the owner of a house knows that the thief is coming, he will begin his vigil before he comes and will not let him dig through into his house of his domain to carry away his goods. You, then, be on your guard against the world. Arm yourselves with great strength lest the robbers find a way to come to you, for the difficulty which you expect will (surely) materialize.	Fortunate is the man who knows where the brigands will enter, so that he may get up, muster his domain, and arm himself before they invade.

(2) The Q Context. The general context is Q's fourth and final section on *Jesus and Apocalypse* (see Appendix 2). The more immediate context is in Q/Matt. 24:43–51 = Luke 12:35–48. Here the close combination of metaphorical but non-narrative aphorisms and metaphorical, narrative parables makes it sometimes uncertain which is which. The complex is a graphic illustration of the point where aphorism and parable meet. I am considering *Knowing the Danger* as an aphorism primarily because of *Gos. Thom.* 103, but it is really on the precise borderline between the developed aphorism and the very short parable.

The proximate Q complex involves the six units given in Table 2.8. Those six units will be considered briefly before concentrating on Unit 2, which is Aphorism 99.

(a) *Q?/Luke* 12:35–38. There is no Matthean equivalent for this unit. It seems very probable, however, that it was here in Q, but that Matthew omitted it in favor of his own Matt. 25:1–13 (Manson: 115; Polag, 1979:62–63). This is supported by the formal parallelism between Units 1 and 4. In both cases a *beatitude* is inserted into the middle of a *parable*. Although both these forms are characteristic of Q (Jacobson, 1982:373,377), that combination makes it very difficult to distinguish aphorisms and parables in this whole integrated complex (see Bultmann: 118–119). In the present case the inserted beatitude reduces the parable to narrative "debris" (Crossan, 1973:99), while it is the beatitude which takes over precedence. The *parable* proper is still visible in Luke 12:35–36, 38a, but the *beatitude* receives emphatic chiastic expansion in 12:37,38b:

Table 2.8

	Genre	Content	Matthew	Luke
1	Parable	*The Waiting Servants*		12:35–38
2	Aphorism 99	*Knowing the Danger*	24:43	12:39
3	Aphorism 100	*The Unknown Time*	24:44	12:40
4	Parable	*Steward and Servants*	24:45–51	12:(41)42–46
5	Parable	*Servants and Beatings*		12:47–48a
6	Aphorism 101	*Much and More*		12:48b

(a) "blessed . . . those . . . "
(b) "comes . . . finds . . . " (Greek order)
(c) "truly, I say to you (that) . . . "
(b') "comes . . . finds . . . "
(a') "blessed . . . those . . . "

Despite Bultmann's idea (118) that Luke 12:35 "could well have been originally independent," I prefer to see all of Luke 12: 35,36,38a as a parabolic situation involving servants waiting for their master's late-night return from a wedding feast. This parable appears now in (i) Mark 13:33–36; (ii) Q/Luke 12:35,36,38a; (iii) *Did.* 16:1, in more aphoristic than parabolic form; and (iv) Matt. 24:42 even more briefly (from Mark 13:35). The *Did.* 16:1 instance is very interesting because that text (a) has *lamp/loins* as negative rather than positive and in reversed order from Q; (b) is probably an independent variant not derived from our gospels (Koester, 1957a:175–177); and (c) is "the only example of the Didachist using material peculiar to Luke" so that the unit was probably in Q (Glover: 21–22; as against Butler: 1960). This will be seen again under Aphorism 100.

(b) Q/Matt. 24:43 = Luke 12:39. Aphorism 99 appears as a beatitude in *Gos. Thom.* 103, opening with the Greek loan-word *makarios* (see also Rev. 16:15 below). Since Q has a beatitude inserted into units 1 and 4, it is possible, *but not much more*, that Q knew Aphorism 99 also in beatitude format.

(c) Q/Matt. 24:44 = Luke 12:40. This is a separate and independent aphorism that has attached itself to both the parables of *The Waiting Servants* and *Knowing the Danger* in the tradition (see Appendix 2).

(d) Q/Matt. 24:45–51 = Luke 12:42–46. Here again an inserted beatitude in Q/Matt. 24:46–47 = Luke 12:43–44 breaks up the parable in Q/Matt. 24:45,48–51 = Luke 12:42,45–46. This parabolic situation is not that of a doorkeeper awaiting a master returning late at night from a feast, as in unit 1, but rather a steward awaiting a

master returning unexpectedly from a journey. But, in both Units 1
and 4, the inserted beatitude introduces a positive aspect into what
is otherwise a rather negative and threatening image, and they may
well have been inserted by Q precisely to effect that change. The two
beatitudes (Q/Luke 12:37 and Q/Matt. 24:46–47 = Luke 12:43–44)
compare as follows, in their Greek word-order:

"blessed are those servants . . .	"blessed is that servant
whom	whom
when he comes (*elthōn*)	when he comes (*elthōn*)
the master finds . . .	his master finds . . .
truly I say to you that	truly I say to you that
(*hoti*) . . . "	(*hoti*) . . . "

(e) Q?/Luke 12:47–48a. The section in Q/Luke 12:35–40 *could* be
considered as applying to all and not just to the disciples. The question of Peter in Q?/Luke 12:41 distinguishes, however, between "for
us" and "for all." The next parable considers a servant who is set
over other servants, and thus the complex turns internally "for us"
rather than "for all." This internal process is considered in Q?/Luke
12:47–48a. The major question is whether Luke 12:41,47–48 is
from Q, but omitted by Matthew, or from Luke himself (see Polag,
1979:86–87)?

I consider, but rather tentatively, that Luke 12:41,47–48 is from
Q. My reason is that there is a similar parabolic distinction of outsiders ("citizens") and insiders ("servants") and then among insiders
themselves in the double-parable of Luke 19:11–27. Matt. 25:14–30
also avoided this Q parable, and chose instead an alternative version
of it that lacked any conflation between *The Pounds* and *The Throne
Claimant*. But both in Q/Luke 12:41–48 and in Q/Luke 19:11–27
there is a double distinction: first, between outsiders and insiders,
and, second, between successful and unsuccessful insiders.

(f) Q?/Luke 12:48b. Bultmann suggested that 12:48b "May perhaps
have been originally independent and given rise to the parable-like
amplification in vv. 47,48a. In any case vv. 47,48a are secondary

formulations, concerning the Christian teacher and layman" (119, see 84). I consider that Q has adapted what may have been a prover-bial saying (*much demands much*) into a much sterner one (*much demands more*) in the twin halves of Q/Luke 12:48b.

All that initial discussion of Q/Matt. 24:43–51 = Luke 12:35–48 intended only the isolation of Q/Matt. 24:43 = Luke 12:39 as a separate aphorism.

(3) Aphorism 99 in Q/Matt. 24:43 = Luke 12:39. There are two minor differences.

(a) Matt. 24:43 has "watch," Luke 12:39 has "hour." It is the latter word that is used for the Son of Man's advent in the following Aphorism 100 (Q/Matt. 24:44 = Luke 12:40), and it also appears along with "day" in Q/Matt. 24:50 = Luke 12:46. I would consider Luke an assimilation, an inevitable one once the image is applied to the Son of Man's "hour."

(b) "The original Lukan text seems to have lacked *egrēgorēsen an kai* ['he would have watched and']" but it became assimilated "to the longer reading found in the parallel passage (Mt 24.43), whereas there is no good reason that would account for the deletion of the words had they been present originally" (Metzger: 161–162). Granted that, what was in Q? Once again, I prefer Matthew's to Luke's version as being closer to Q, since both Thomas texts also mention the owner's precautionary measures (see Sieber: 256).

(4) *Gos. Thom.* 21c. In form *Gos. Thom.* 21 combines an *apho-ristic dialogue* (21a) with an *aphoristic cluster* (21bcde). The present unit is the second one of four in that cluster (21c). Its content combines a third-person metaphor with a second-person appli-cation, as is also effected by the combination of Aphorisms 99 and 100 in Q.

The *metaphor* is clear enough and similar to that in Q/Matt. 24:43 = Luke 12:39. The awkward phrase, "his house of his do-main" (Lambdin: 120) or "his house of his kingdom" (Guillaumont, 1959:14–15; Wilson, 1973:513) is probably a Coptic mistranslation for an original "the house of his domain/kingdom" (Quecke; Ménard,

1975:112). Why the double *house* and *domain/kingdom* should be present at all will be discussed under *Gos. Thom.* 103 below.

The *application* is more difficult since its translation is not too certain (Bartsch, 1959–1960:260). It is clear, however, that it warns about the world rather than the parousia. And therein lies the difficulty: The *image* actually works better for the unexpected and momentary irruption of the end than for the expected and permanent onslaught of the world. Hence the concluding sentence's translation could be: "for the difficulty which you expect will (surely) materialize" (Lambdin: 120) or "because they will find the advantage which you expect" (Guillaumont, 1959:16–17) or "since the advantage for which you look they will find" (Ménard, 1975:60).

But, however that concluding phrase be interpreted and translated, the use of the Greek loan-word in the plural for "robbers" or "brigands" in the application differs from the use of the Coptic word in the singular for "thief" in the image. And this will be of importance in the next section.

(5) *Gos. Thom.* 103. There are five major differences between this version and the preceding one. (a) The form of 21c was metaphor succeeded by application, that of 103 is beatitude, beginning with the Greek loan-word *makarios*. (b) In 21c the protagonist is a *householder*, but in 103 he is simply a *man*, and there is no mention at all of a house. (c) In 21c the metaphor mentions a singular *thief*, but the application mentions plural *brigands* or *robbers*. In 103 there is only mention of brigands or robbers, using the same Greek loan-word as earlier in 21c. (d) In 21c it is a question of knowing the *time* of attack, but in 103 it is the *place* of attack that is in question. There is, however, a textual problem here. The Coptic reads literally: "Blessed is the man who knows in what part the robbers are coming" (Wilson, 1973:521). The problem is whether "part," using the Greek loan-word *meros*, is to be taken as "part (of the property)," that is, "where" (so Lambdin: 129), or "part (of the night)," that is, "when" (so Guillaumont, 1959:52–53). I am accepting the Lambdin interpretation because there are enough *other* differences between *Thomas* and Q on this saying to render intru-

sions from Q into *Thomas* on this point at least doubtful. (e) This is also an important point but it depends on an even greater textual problem, one of restoration rather than interpretation. In 21c the phrase "his house of his domain" (*tefmᵉntero*) appears, as was seen earlier. In 103 the protagonist sets out to "muster his *mᵉnᵉt* [. . .]." That is, the object of that action is uncertain because of a bad tear in the manuscript's outside top corner. Most translators attempt no reconstruction after "his." They simply leave a gap. But Lambdin proposes reading "muster his domain," presuming *mᵉnter* (domain, kingdom) as the missing word. If that reconstruction is correct, it is an important connection between 21c and 103, and it would indicate that 103 has infiltrated the application not only by the plural "robbers" or "brigands," but also by the term "domain" or "kingdom." I find this reconstruction very appealing, *but* there is a major problem in that the manuscript's photographic copy evidences a fourth letter after that opening triad (*mnt*), a fourth letter that is mostly lost in the lacuna but which could not be *e* or *r*. Accordingly, although I accept Lambdin's "muster his *domain*," I do so with some doubts.

But even apart from that reconstruction, it is now clear that there are important content differences between *Gos. Thom.* 21c and 103. (a) That latter text concerns *a man knowing the place where brigands will invade his property*. Place, not time, is what is important. The former text concerns *a householder knowing that a thief is going to attack his house*. One could presume here that time (when) rather than place (where) is the significant point. But I would emphasize that time is not explicitly mentioned within the metaphor itself and that place would seem even more indicated in the application ("find a way to come to you"). (b) That application in 21c links even more closely with the distant image in 103 than with the proximate and preceding one in 21c itself. One sees, in other words, a slight movement from explicit place in 103 to implicit time in 21c's metaphor, but with 21c's application still capable of moving in either direction.

(6) "Girded Loins" in *Gos. Thom.* 21c, 103. In itself the meta-

phor of *girded loins* is a standard metaphor for readiness to move or act (see Eph. 6:14; 1 Pet. 1:13). It is associated with the parable of *The Waiting Servants* in Q/Luke 12:35 and *Did.* 16:1a. But the second metaphor of *lit lamps* is a more specific one and demands a more specific context, such as that of the master returning late at night from a feast. Thus, although I consider *Did.* 16:1 to be independent of the Q version of the parable, I also consider it an abbreviated version of that parable. It should be noted that the combination of second-person admonition and third-person parable in (a) Mark 13:33–37 and (b) Q/Luke 12:35–38 has been smoothed into consistent two-person address in (c) *Did.* 16:1a.

The aphorism in *Gos. Thom.* 21c and the application of the aphorism in *Gos. Thom.* 103 also contain the phrase about *girded loins*. The Coptic expressions translated by Lambdin as "arm yourselves" (21c) and "arm himself" (103) read, literally, "gird up his loins" (Guillaumont, 1959:16–17, 52–53; Wilson, 1973:513,521; Ménard, 1975:60,73). I do not think, however, that this creates any special connection between the parable of *The Waiting Servants* and the aphorism on *Knowing the Danger*. It is simply the common presence of a standard image of readiness.

(7) Other Texts. Four other texts in the New Testament touch on this aphorism: (a) "For you yourselves know well that the day of the Lord will come like a thief in the night" (1 Thess. 5:2); (b) "But the day of the Lord will come like a thief" (2 Pet. 3:10); (c) "If you will not awake (*gregorēsēs*), I will come like a thief, and you will not know at what hour I will come upon you" (Rev. 3:3); (d) "Lo, I am coming like a thief! Blessed is he who is awake, keeping his garments that he may not go naked and be seen exposed!" (Rev. 16:15).

First, all four texts agree on the phrase "as a thief." Second, they use different verbs for "come": *erchomai* in (a) and (d) but *hēkō* in (b) and (d). Third, in Revelation it is Jesus the Lord who likens himself to the thief, but in the other two texts it is the writers themselves that describe the "day of the Lord" as a thief. Fourth, the text in Rev. 16:15 is probably the most interesting of the four. It breaks unexpectedly into its present context; it is a beatitude; and it mentions the theme of "watching" or "being awake" (*gregorōn*), as in Q/Matt. 24:43. I consider, however, that Aphorism 99 is quite separate and independent originally from Aphorism 100, despite its present combination in Q/Matt. 24:43–44 = Luke 12:39–40 and Rev. 3:3; 16:15. What has happened here is that Aphorism 100 was connected to (i) Aphorism 99 in Q/Matt. 24:43–44 = Luke 12:39–40 and Rev. 3:3; to (ii) the parable of *The Waiting Servants* in Mark 13:(32)33–37 and *Did.* 16:1; to (iii) the parable of the *Steward and Servants* (by Q) in Q/Matt. 24:50 = Luke 12:46; and to (iv) the parable of *The Bridesmaids* (by Matthew?) in Matt. 25:1–13. That is, Aphorism 100: *The Unknown Time* was easily attached, both early and late, to metaphorical aphorisms or parables concerning *watching*, *waiting*, and *being ready*.

(8) Conclusion. All that detailed analysis has been given here to raise one basic question. Do the variations within this aphorism's versions (and especially those between *Gos. Thom.* 103 and *Gos. Thom.* 21c's *application*, on the one hand, and all other versions on the other) represent simple performancial or deliberate hermeneutical variations? Does the shift from (a) a man knowing *where* the brigands are to invade his territory to (b) a householder knowing *when* the thief will invade his house represent a performancial or a hermeneutical shift?

I propose that the basic shift is much more hermeneutical than performancial. (i) The aphorism's trajectory started with a beatitude concerning a man's knowledge of the *place where* his property (domain, kingdom) was to be invaded by brigands. Hence *Gos. Thom.* 103, the *application* but not the text of *Gos. Thom.* 21c, and the form of Rev 16:15. (ii) The text of *Gos. Thom.* 21c has moved to the metaphor of *time when*, but it is quite muted as yet: "knows that the thief is coming." This is probably still a simple performancial variation on *Gos. Thom.* 103. In 21c it is applied to the gnostic's situation before the world (as thief), and that means that the inbreaking is still seen in a negative light. (iii) But in all the other texts this is very different. The thief is now quite positive: He is "the day of the Lord" in 1 Thess. 5:2 and 2 Pet. 3:10; he is the "I" of Jesus in Rev. 3:3 and 16:15; and he is the Son of Man in the combination of Aphorisms 99 and 100 in Q/Matt. 24:43–44 = Luke 12:39–40. And so also does the *time when* motif receive far greater emphasis: "in what part (watch) of the night" in Q/Matt. 24:43. I consider all of this change to be deliberate hermeneutical variation as the returning Lord becomes the thief in the night. This aphorism's trajectory, then, is a graphic if very complicated illustration of the delicate interface between performancial and hermeneutical variations.

3
Aphoristic Saying

In the literary prism
Nothing more enlightens, nothing hooks
Ampler meaning than the aphorism,
Scoring better than a shelf of books.
Half a truth is ideal,
Three-quarters would be unreal.

Roy C. Bates (Zohn: 28)

A. CORE AND SAYING

In oral sensibility one speaks or writes an aphoristic *saying*, but one remembers and recalls an aphoristic *core*. The only exceptions are those superbly special cases where the crafted sequence is so precisely memorable that one cannot recall the structure without also recalling the sequence and the syntax. Hence all of what was seen in the last chapter is still operative in this one. But here I intend to concentrate on two special aspects of the aphoristic *core/saying* dynamic, namely, the openings and the stichs.

B. OPENINGS

I am here concerned with three types of aphoristic opening, between which there is frequent variation both within oral tradition and even genetic scribal transmission. These openings are the relatival, conditional, and participial formats.

1. Performancially Varied Openings

Before turning to the Jesus tradition, I cite two examples from elsewhere in the New Testament to indicate how easily one moves from one opening to another.

(1) 1 Cor. 11:27,29. "Whoever, therefore, eats the bread or drinks the cup of the Lord in an unworthy manner will be guilty of profaning the body and blood of the Lord. . . . For anyone who eats and drinks without discerning the body eats and drinks judgment upon himself." The first verse in 11:27 is in *relatival* opening: "whoever . . . eats" (*hos an esthiē*) but the second one in 11:29 is in *participial* format in Greek: "any one who eats" (*ho . . . esthiōn*). Sometimes such divergent Greek openings do not even show up in English translation.

(2) 1 John 1:6–2:11. In 1:6,7,8,9,10; 2:1b there are six sayings with *conditional* openings: "if (*ean*)." Then there is a group of five sayings in 2:4,6,9,10,11 with a *participial* format in Greek: "he who (*ho . . .*)." But in among those five there is also a single *relatival* opening in 2:5 with "whoever (*hos d'an*)."

This can now be seen for an aphorism within the Jesus tradition itself.

Aphorism 6: *Let Him Hear*

(1) There are *probably* six independent versions: (a) Mark 4:9 = Matt. 13:9 = Luke 8:8b; Mark 4:23 = Matt. 13:43b; (b) Matt. 11:15; (c) Luke 14:35b; (d) Rev. 2:7,11,17,29; 3:6,13,22; 13:9; (e) *Gos. Thom.* 8,21,24,63,65,96; (f) *Soph. Jes. Chr.* CG III, 97:21–23; 98: 22–23; 105:10–12; BG 8502, 107:18–108:1. (See Table 3.1.)

Table 3.1

Mark 4:9	Mark 4:23	Matthew 11:15; 13:9, 43b	Luke 8:8b; 14:35b	Revelation 2:7, 11, 17, 29; 3:6 13, 22
He who (*hos*) has ears to hear, let him hear	If any man (*ei tis*) has ears to hear, let him hear	He who (*ho*) has ears, let him hear	He who (*ho*) has ears to hear, let him hear	He who (*ho*) has an ear, let him hear

(2) Mark 4:9,23. When Mark is judged a collector and editor rather than a composer and author, it is possible to find a coherent pre-Markan unity behind Mark 4 (Kuhn: 99–146). But the more problematic that presupposition becomes, the more likely it is that Mark 4 was composed by Mark himself from originally separate and isolated materials, save of course, for 4:3–8 and 14–20 (Lambrecht, 1974a:303, but add "not" in the first line). One theme that holds his new unity together is that of "hearing" in 4:3,9,12,15, 16,18,20,23,24,33. It is within this overarching theme that his two citations of the present aphorism (4:9,23) are to be considered.

Despite Jeremias (1963:14 note 11), "there are no conclusive arguments for ascribing the three *kai elegen* ["and he said"] of *Mk.*, IV (vv. 9,26,30) to a pre-Markan source" (Lambrecht, 1974a:298). Thus "the Sower would have existed before Mark without the logion of v. 9" (299). But by adding it there Mark framed the Sower parable with his "hearing" theme in command (4:3) and in aphorism (4:9).

Mark's second use of the aphorism is placed with equal care. Lambrecht (303) proposed a chiastic structure for 4:1–34 as follows: A(Introduction, 1–2), B(Seed, 3–20), C(a:Lamp, 21–22; b:Hear, 23–24a; a':Measure, 24b–25), B'(Seed, 26–32), A'(Conclusion, 33–34). Dewey (1980:150) has a quite similar proposal: A(Introduction, 1–2a), B(Parable Material, 2b–20), C(Sayings Material, 21–25),

Table 3.1 (cont.)

Revelation 13:9	Gospel of Thomas 8, 21	Gospel of Thomas 24, 63 65, 96	Sophia of Jesus Christ
If any one (*ei tis*) has an ear,	Whoever has ears to hear,	Whoever has ears,	Whoever has an ear to hear,
let him hear	let him hear	let him hear	let him hear

B'(Parable Material, 26–32), A'(Conclusion, 33–34). Thus 4:21–25 is the structure's center.

Although I recognize full well the classic prejudice against too great Markan creativity even in a unity such as 4:21–25 (Best, 1974:30–32), I agree with Lambrecht that "the assembling, composing, and structuring of IV, 21–25 by Mark are as good as proved" (287). It is Mark himself who first combined 4:21,22,23,24,25, and he did so in a formally parallel manner: "All indications with regard to the content as well as to the style suggest that it is Mark who composed and structured this unity" (Lambrecht, 1974a:290). That is, the five aphorisms in 4:21–25 were originally separate (Schneider:195) but formed by Mark into an *aphoristic cluster*. And in Markan context, "hearing" (4:23,24a) is the center of 4:21–25 and so of 4:1–34.

(3) Matthew. The three uses of this phrase in Matt. 11:15; 13:9, 43 are verbatim the same. He avoids the double "hear" of Mark and opens with a *participial* construction. His 13:9 is a rephrasing of Mark 4:9, and 13:43 is presumably a relocation of Mark 4:23. But 11:15 is not directly from Mark, and Matthew has made all his own citations uniform with this performancial variation of the aphorism.

(4) Luke. Luke 8:8b, from Mark 4:9, and Luke 14:35b, from elsewhere, are also rendered uniformally, but with a different uniformity from that of Matthew.

(5) Thomas. The six uses in Thomas have the double "hear" in *Gos. Thom.* 8,21 (as in Mark and Luke), but the single "hear" in 24,63,65,96 (as in Matthew). It is used mostly to conclude parables (8,21,63,65,96), but once to introduce an aphorism (24). Since Coptic has no participle, the opening is the equivalent of the Greek *relatival* format.

(6) Revelation. The first seven uses in 2:7,11,17,29; 3:6,13,22 are *relatival* and uniformally conclude each of the letters: "He who has an ear, let him hear what the Spirit says to the churches." The eighth usage is *conditional* in opening, but this seems to have happened under the influence of the succeeding verse. "*If any one* has an ear, let him hear: *If any one* is to be taken captive, to captivity he

goes; *if any one* slays with a sword, with the sword must he be slain"
(13:9–10). The form omits the double "hear" of Mark and Luke and
is closer to the Matthean formulation. The "ear" is singular, but
this is phonetically quite effective through the resonance of *ous* (ear)
and *akousato* (let him hear).

(7) *The Sophia of Jesus Christ*. The third of the Nag Hammadi
codices contains a tractate, *Eugnostos the Blessed*, which is immediately followed by another one, *The Sophia of Jesus Christ*. The
former is "a religio-philosophical epistle written by a teacher to his
disciples," while the latter is "a revelation discourse given by the
risen Christ to his followers. Despite their different forms, these
tractates are two versions of the same original document. The former is without apparent Christian influence, while the latter is
highly Christianized" (Parrott, in Robinson, 1977:206). In the process of turning the non-Christian source into the Christian *Sophia
of Jesus Christ*, the present aphorism was inserted four times (see
Robinson and Koester: 90). It appears in uniform citation in CG III,
97:21–23; 98:22–23; 105:10–12; BG 8502, 107:18–108:1 (Robinson,
1977:211,212,217,221). But now "ear" is always in the singular, as
in Revelation.

(8) Oxy P 1081. "This interesting fragment of heretical literature
consists of a leaf from a papyrus book, copied probably in the earlier
decades of the fourth century" (Hunt: 16). It contains a dialogue
between disciples and Jesus on the recto side: "The disciples [ask
him,] Lord, how then can we find faith? The Saviour saith unto
them . . . " (19). The fragment may have come from a writing "in
the form of a Gospel . . . and probably its revelations were placed,
as often in the later apocryphal gospels, in the period after the resurrection" (17).

Puech has now identified Oxy P 1081 as a fragment of the Greek
text of *The Sophia of Jesus Christ* (Hennecke and Schneemelcher:
1.245). It corresponds to CG III, 97:16–99:13 (Robinson, 1977:
211–213). But what is of present interest is that here Aphorism 6
appears not as in the Coptic text with the singular "ear," but with
the more usual plural "ears."

Hunt had restored the Greek text of the first citation on the fragment's verso, lines 6–8, as *ho echōn ō[t]a t[a onta] peran tōn [a]ko-[ō]n akouetō*, and translated with, "He who hath hearing beyond his ears, let him hear" (18–19). The second citation lacks that gloss and reads more simply, *ho echōn ōt[a akou]ein akouetō*, "He who hath ears to hear, let him hear" (18–19), on the verso, lines 35–36.

Puech claimed that Oxy P 1081 has "proved that the Sophia Jesu Christi was originally composed in Greek, and not in Coptic" (Hennecke and Schneemelcher: 1.245). If that is accepted, its version of Aphorism 6 may have originally been the same as those of Luke. And in that case the versions in the Coptic *Sophia of Jesus Christ* would be translational and performancial variations.

(9) Scribal glosses. Besides these usages in Mark (2), Luke (2), Matthew (3), *Sophia* (4), *Thomas* (6), and Revelation (8), there is also a scribal tendency to add it on "especially to parables" (Robinson and Koester: 90) in certain manuscripts.

(a) Mark 7:16. Both Mark 4:9 and 23 have the double "to *hear*, let him *hear*," but while 4:9 has the *relatival* format (*hos*), 4:23 uses the *conditional* (*ei tis*). The latter also appears in Mark 7:16, but "this verse, though present in the majority of witnesses, is absent from important Alexandrian witnesses . . . [and] . . . appears to be a scribal gloss" (Metzger, 1971:94–95). It should be considered, however, as a very well-chosen gloss both in form (4:23 = 7:16) and location (compare 4:10 with 7:17).

(b) Matt. 25:29–30; Luke 8:15; 12:21; 13:9; 21:4. In certain manuscripts the aphorism is found at these places as well. It is given in Lukan format and is introduced by: "having said these things, he cried out. . . ." The case of Luke 12:21 will serve as instance for this whole series.

The parable of the Rich Fool appears in Luke 12:16–21 and "at the close of the verse several of the later manuscripts have added (perhaps from 8:8 or Mt 11:15) the stereotyped expression" (Metzger, 1971:161) of the aphorism in its standard Lukan format. The aphorism is also appended, however to *Thomas*'s version of this parable in *Gos. Thom.* 63. Thus Wilson asks: "Have we here an influence of apocryphal tradition on manuscripts of the ninth or tenth century? Or was the addition original to Luke? Or was it in the tradition behind Luke? It must be noted that Thomas gives it in the Matthean form, whereas the manuscripts referred to have the form used in Luke, so that pure coincidence cannot be ruled out" (1960a:135; see also 1960b:238). Birdsall has shown how such a pure coincidence might have occurred by noting that the phrase, "having said these things he cried out, He who has ears to hear, let him hear," is added after Matt. 25:29 or 30; Luke 8:15; 12:21; 13:9; 21:4 in some manuscripts, but that "the general nature of the un-cials [in question] is not such as to arouse great confidence: most of them have traces of ancient texts, but hidden beneath the encroach-ing flood of the Byzantine recension" (334). The reason for the addition "suggests the needs of the Lectionaries" (334) and "this investigation brings us to a late point, not an early, in the history of the New Testament text" (335).

(10) Conclusion. Aphorism 6 was used primarily as an example of the performancially oral and even genetically scribal shift in openings between the *relatival* (Mark 4:9), *conditional* (Mark 4:23; Rev. 13:9), and *participial* (Matt. 11:15; 13:9,43; Luke 8:8b; 14:35b; Rev. 2:7,11,17,29; 3:6,13,22) formats. But it is also a classic exam-ple of oral sensibility, of the triumph of structure over syntax. There are three separable elements of variation: (a) the opening (*relatival*, *participial*, *conditional*); (b) the *ear* (singular or plural); and (c) the *hear* (single or double). And thereafter it is almost pure performan-cial variation.

2. Translationally Varied Openings

Besides *performancial* and *hermeneutical* variations there is a third type and, like them, it cuts across the distinction of oral and scribal transmission. This problem of *translational* variations connects with the preceding discussion as follows.

Aphorism 6 appears in Mark 4:9 as *relatival*(R), but in Matthew and Luke as *participial*(P). Since Matt 11:15 and Luke 14:35b are not from Mark, how is this *participial* agreement to be explained?

Best (1976) has proposed the existence of: (1) a connected oral and presumably Aramaic source containing a sequence of sayings on discipleship; (2) which now appears through *"translation variants"* as *relatival*(R) in Mark, having *hos (e)an* usually with the subjunctive but sometimes with the indicative, but as *participial*(P) in Q; and (3) which has the great majority using a parallel or double-stich rather than a single-stich construction.

In discussing this important suggestion I will be *adapting* Best's list to my own purposes. I distinguish, as he does not, between two sets of examples. The first set involves aphorisms that appear in Mark and then in either Matthew alone or Luke alone. These are given in Table 3.2, using the following abbreviations: R = *relatival*, P = *participial*, and C = *conditional* opening. The second set involves aphorisms that appear in Mark and then in both Matthew and Luke—that is, in Q. These are given in Table 3.3.

What, then, of Best's proposal in the light of Tables 3.2 and 3.3? (1) It seems clear that the *relatival*(R) form dominates in Mark, and that, despite frequent irregularities—possibly from Markan influence—the *participial*(P) form dominates in Q, and in fact every-

Table 3.2

Aphorism	MARK		
	Matthew	Mark	Luke
	12:50(R)	3:35(R)	8:21(P)
6	13:9(P)	4:9(R)	8:8b(P)
14	23:11(P)	9:35(C)	9:48c(P)
	20:26(R)	10:43(R)	
	20:27(R)	10:44(R)	
19		10:15(R)	18:17(R)

where else except Mark. The occasional *conditional*(C) form can be
left aside for the moment. (2) I find *simple* performancial variation
inadequate to explain all this. One would have to claim that a
certain preference was also at work: that Mark preferred to articulate
the structure of certain aphoristic cores relativally and Q preferred to
do so participially. In itself there is no problem with such a situation. The speaker or writer has simply accepted a standard construct
on how certain cores are to be formulated. It need not be done
always and inevitably; it can be done generally or mostly. (3) Preferred performance or individual style may be quite sufficient to
explain the phenomena noted by Best, but it is *possible* that we are
dealing here with translational variation and that (pre?)Mark or
(pre?)Q has translated divergently from Aramaic sayings. I prefer to
think, however, that we are dealing with preferred performancial
variations with these openings. (4) I find no necessity to postulate a
consistent and thematically unified Aramaic source behind those
sayings.

The importance of Best's article is that it draws acute attention to
the delicate borderline between *preferred performances* and *translation variants*. If an author consistently and stylistically formulates
aphoristic cores in a certain set opening, it may be very difficult to
distinguish such results from the use of a set and sequential source.

Table 3.2 (cont.)

Matthew	Luke	Other
	11:28(P)	
11:15(P)	14:35b(P)	Rev. 2:7 etc.(P)
	22:26a(P) 22:26b,27(P)	(John 13:16)
18:3(C)		John 3:3(C) John 3:5(C)

Table 3.3

	MARK		
Aphorism	Matthew	Mark	Luke
61	18:5(R)	9:37a(R) 9:37b(R)	9:48a(R) 9:48b(R)
71		9:40(R)	9:50(R)
89		8:38(R)	9:26(R)
90	(12:31a) (12:31b)	(3:28) 3:29(R)	
118	19:9(R)	10:11(R) 10:12(C)	
129	16:25a(R) 16:25b(R)	8:35a(R) 8:35b(R)	9:24a(R) 9:24b(R)
132	13:12a(R) 13:12b(R)	4:25a(R) 4:25b(R)	8:18a(R) 8:18b(R)

C. STICHS

It is obvious that an aphorism may be long enough to be broken into *parts* or *sections*. This is not my present concern. By *stichs* I refer especially to those parts or sections that could stand quite adequately alone. Jeremias cited "the judgment of E. Norden that, after the putting of the verb in first place, parallelism of clauses was the most certain Semitism to be found in the New Testament" (1971:14). Stichs are to be understood especially within this phenomenon of Semitic parallelism in all its varieties.

C. F. Burney, continuing the work and terminology of an earlier Oxford scholar, Bishop Lowth (1778), proposed four different types

Table 3.3 (cont.)

| Q | | Other |
Matthew	Luke	
10:40a(P) 10:40b(P)	10:16ab(P) 10:16c(P)	John 13:20a(P) John 13:20b(P) John 5:23(P) John 12:44(P) John 12:45(P)
12:30a(P) 12:30b(P)	11:23a(P) 11:23b(P)	Oxy P 1224, 2d:i/b Oxy P 1224, 2r:i/c
10:32(R) 10:33(R)	12:8(R) 12:9(P)	
12:32a(R) 12:32b(R)	12:10a(R) 12:10b(P)	
5:32a(P) 5:32b(R)	16:18a(P) 16:18b(P)	
10:39a(P) 10:39b(P)	17:33a(R) 17:33b(R)	John 12:25a(P) John 12:25b(P)
25:29a(P) 25:29b(P)	19:26a(P) 19:26b(P)	

of parallelism within the sayings of Jesus: (1) *synonymous parallelism*, where the second stich *repeats* the first one, for example, Mark 10:38 (Burney: 63); (2) *antithetic parallelism*, where the second *contrasts* the first, for example, Matt. 7:17 (Burney: 72); (3) *synthetic parallelism*, where the second simply *continues* the first, for example, Matt. 23:5b (Burney: 89); and (4) *step-parallelism*, where the second *climaxes* the first, for example, Mark 9:37 (Burney: 91).

That fourfold typology is both useful and dangerous. It makes it seem that sheer *repetition* is at the heart of the phenomenon and that variations on repetition are its modalities. And it forces all the vast repertoire of examples into one of four slots. Kugel (1) reacted against this classical understanding of biblical parallelism and

proposed instead that "A is so, and *what's more*, B" is the way such
couplets should be read. He notes that (7), "the ways of parallelism
are numerous and varied, and the intensity of the semantic parallelism established between clauses might be said to range from 'zero
perceivable correspondence' to 'near-zero perceivable differentiation' (i.e., just short of word-for-word repetition)." He concludes,
therefore, that " 'what's more,' in whatever sense or strength, is
always part of the meaning" (45). I consider, however, that neither
repetition nor *climax* is the genius of this form. Its power lies in
interaction, in the way the twin phrases vibrate with one another,
creating by their polarities a field of force within which the mind
vibrates in response. This throws, of course, a certain emphasis on
the second phrase since its arrival establishes the interaction; but
that is a result of linear necessity and not of the second's intrinsic
"more." It is vibration, dialectic, interaction, and especially all the
multiple possibilities of such interaction that is the form's most powerful challenge.

When I use parallelism here my basic emphasis is always on
interaction and not just *repetition*. And my first example is deliberately chosen because it manages, in its development, to exemplify a
wide range of *interaction*, that is, of the classical "types" of *repetition*.

Aphorism 4: *Man and Sabbath*

(1) There is only one independent version to be considered:
Mark 2:27–28 = Matt. 12:8 = Luke 6:5. (See Table 3.4.)

Table 3.4

Matthew 12:8	Mark 2:27–28	Luke 6:5
For the Son of man is lord of the sabbath.	The sabbath was made for man, not man for the sabbath; so the Son of man is lord even of the sabbath.	The Son of man is lord of the sabbath.

(2) Mark 2:1–3:6. Dewey proposed the following chiastic structure for Mark 2:1–3:6: A(2:1–12); B(2:13–17); C(2:18–22); B'(2:23–28); A'(3:1–6). Although she argues that "on literary and theological grounds it would seem that the present structure is due to Mark" (1973:399), she is willing to accept Kuhn's thesis of an earlier, pre-Markan "collection of four units: the healing of the paralytic, the eating with the tax-collectors (without vss. 13–14), the question about fasting, and the plucking of grain on the sabbath without its OT reference" (401). A major reason for her acceptance of this proposed pre-Markan *structure* is that, "the one fact not accounted for by the assumption of a Markan construction from previously independent units of tradition is the occurrence of the title of Son of Man in stories A and B'" (400). This does less than justice to Mark's creativity. Mourlon Beernaert (141) had, at about the same time, but without mentioning Kuhn, proposed this chiastic structure: A(2:1–9); B(2:10–12); C(2:13–17); D(2:18–22); C'(2:23–26); B'(2:27–28); A'(3:1–6). In this chiasm the two Son of Man sayings are in appropriate balance as B/B'. This would mean that only *units* came to Mark, their chiastic combination came from Mark. This structural creativity must be kept as background in the discussion of his 2:27–28.

(3) Mark 2:23–28. It is clear that a separation exists between 2:23–26 and 2:27–28 as indicated by the Markan redactional phrase (Pryke: 76,118,154): "And he said to them" (*kai elegen autois*). But it is debated whether the original dialectical story was 2:23–26, to which 2:27–28 was *appended* (Lohse: see Neirynck, 1975:228–235), or the original unit was 2:23–24, 27–28 into which 2:25–26 was *inserted* (Beare; Kuhn: 76; Hultgren, 1972; see Neirynck, 1975: 235–237). Because of the redactional nature of the connective in 2:27, Mark would presumably have to be the one who appended or inserted the later unit. Although the former opinion (that Mark appended 2:27–28 to 2:23–26) seems the more likely, the debate itself is enough to warrant considering 2:27–28 here among the aphoristic sayings rather than bracketing it with the dialectical stories.

(4) Luke 6:5 and Matt. 12:8. Both Luke and Matthew found

Mark's text quite unacceptable, and making it acceptable took four minor agreements against him (Neirynck, 1974:76). Negatively, they both omitted (a) all of the 2:27, (b) the "so" (*hōste*), and (c) the "even" (*kai*) of 2:28. Positively, they (d) changed the word order in Greek from (literally): "So lord is the Son of Man even of the sabbath" to "Lord is of the sabbath the Son of Man." There is a clear logic behind the four changes and it is this logic that makes it possible to imagine Luke and Matthew separately and independently making exactly the same four "corrections." They remove aspects of Mark's text that greatly diminish the apodictic value of a shorter version, such as: "The Son of Man is Lord of the sabbath" appended directly to the preceding Mark 2:23–26. In Mark's version (a) 2:27 places man, in general, over the sabbath; (b) the "so" gives this to Jesus almost as a subordinate consequence, as being simply one man among many; (c) the "even" makes this power seem just barely achieved rather than going almost without saying; and (d) the Greek word order in Mark, apart from problems of syntax (Pryke: 117–118), throws the emphasis climactically on the sabbath rather than on the Son of Man.

(5) Mark 2:27–28. But all these problems, seen and solved by Luke and Matthew centuries ago, come back to haunt the exegete considering Mark 2:27–28 itself.

Was 2:27–28 originally two separate aphorisms joined into their present unity either by the pre-Markan tradition or the Markan redaction? (Gils; see Neirynck, 1975:242–246). On the *level of the Markan redactional composition*, the balanced presence of the Son of Man sayings in 2:10–12 and 2:27–28 certainly refers *now* to Jesus as the titular Son of Man (Perrin, 1968a:360–361) and not just to "man" in general or even the Christian community in particular (Hay). But 2:10 is to be considered a Markan insertion (Donahue: 241), and *at least* 2:27 must also be considered as a Markan addition. Still the question remains, even granted all that, whether Mark received 2:23–26 and 2:28 from the tradition and inserted 2:27 to create the present unity? That would mean that, whether he joined 2:27 to 2:23–26,28 or joined 2:27 to 2:28 to 2:23–26, Mark is the one who forged the present aphorism in 2:27–28. The major objection to this compositional possibility is that, *on the level of Markan compositional theology*, the combination of 2:27 with 2:28 seems as unfortunate today as it did to Luke and Matthew in the first century. It is understandable that an author, involved and preoccupied with the primary creativity of compositional structure, could have accepted 2:27–28 from the tradition as a unit, accepted 2:27, that is, because he wanted 2:28. And it is equally understandable that careful readers, such as Luke and Matthew and, indeed, later copyists as well (Neirynck, 1978:233), employing on Mark the secondary creativity of editorial scrutiny, would have decided that his 2:27–28 required some radical surgery. The conclusion would be, therefore, that Mark found separately and combined together two units, 2:23–26 and 2:27–28.

(6) Pre-Markan 2:27–28. The objection is that Mark, whose titular use of the Son of Man is so obviously important (Perrin, 1971), would never have drastically weakened 2:28 by adding 2:27 to it. But this same objection must be maintained for the pre-Markan tradition, even if on a milder level. Succinctly: once Son of Man is titular (for Jesus or even for another transcendental authority), the combination of 2:27 and 2:28 is scarcely comprehensible. At this point there seems only one solution. Mark 2:27–28 was a unit at a period or in a context when the Son of Man was not titular but atitular. The combination ("man"/"son of man") was accepted by Mark even when the atitular had become titular ("man"/"Son of Man"), but it was not tolerable for Luke and Matthew. Two arguments can be suggested for this conclusion.

(a) The first argument is internal. Pryke is not exactly clear what is source(S) and what is redaction(R) in Mark 2:27–28. Concerning constructions with "so" (*hōste*) he says that, "of the thirteen examples used by the evangelist, eleven are followed by the accusative + infinitive construction, and the other two by the indicative (2:28S, 10:8S). Seven of the thirteen are found with redactional material, while six are source. The two examples of *hōste* with the in-

dicative are from the source verses and not from the redactional"
(115–116). But later he locates 2:28 among "Conversion of S to R:
2:28" and describes it as follows: "2:28 comes under peculiarities of
syntax which Zerwick labels 'Sperrungen' " [blockages], in the case
of this text between the noun 'lord' and its accompanying genitive—
'of the sabbath' (117). And, finally, in his reconstruction of the
"redactional text of Mark," he gives all of 2:28 as redactional (154).
Thus 2:28 has gone from S to S/R to R. It seems, however, that the
"so" (*hōste*) and indicative construction renders 2:28 as source(S)
and that, *at the most*, redaction(R) is to be seen in the separation of
"lord" and "of the sabbath." But since 2:28 is traditional (source)
precisely in and by its connective (*hōste* and indicative), it must
originally have been connected to and consequent upon something
else. There was hardly ever a separate aphorism beginning with: "so
(*hōste*). . . ." Since, then, 2:27 came also to Mark from source (see
Pryke: 133,note 3), it seems quite likely that all of 2:27–28, combined and connected by "so" (*hōste*), came to Mark from the tradition.

(b) The second argument is external, but possibly even more important. It concerns the possibility of an atitular reading for "son of
man." The suggestion is certainly not new: "The theory of the misunderstanding of *bar nasha* used generically found here its best
illustration. It is still a widespread opinion that mistranslation for
'man' is a valid explanation of the origin of *ho huios tou anthrōpou*
in sayings with reference to the earthly ministry of Jesus, and some
authors who are opposed to that theory are willing to make an exception for Mark II,28" (Neirynck, 1975:237–238; see also Black,
1978:10). But the question must now be reconsidered in the light of
the recent debate between Vermes and Fitzmyer.

There are four possible contemporary meanings for the term "son
of man" outside the New Testament. (i) *Titular Meaning:* this usage denoted a transcendental figure with apocalyptic and/or mes-
sianic functions. (ii) *Atitular Meaning:* this usage could be either (a)
generic (man, mankind, humans), or (b) indefinite (anyone, some-

one—or the corresponding negatives), or (iii) circumlocutional and reflexive ("I").

Concerning (i), the *titular* usage, Vermes and Fitzmyer coincide on one very important point: "I agree that the titular use of *bar 'ĕnāš* is unknown in any extrabiblical Aramaic texts prior to or contemporary with the New Testament (Fitzmyer, 1979a:65; see Vermes, 1967:327–328, 1973:188, 1978a:130–132 = 1978b:26–27; and Fitzmyer, 1968:428, 1973–1974:397, 1975:93, 1979b:153, 1980:21).

Concerning (ii), the atitular usage, they also coincide on (a) and (b). That is, there is no debate concerning the *generic* or *indefinite* meanings: "of the three classes of meaning that V. detects for *br nš(')* in Jewish Aramaic texts, there is no quarrel with his first two, 'a human being' or 'man,' and the indefinite 'someone.' " (Fitzmyer, 1968:427; see Vermes, 1967:316–319, 1978a:124 = 1978b:20; and Fitzmyer, 1973–1974:397, 1975:92–93, 1979b:147–148, 1980: 20).

Thus the main debate concerns (iic), the circumlocutional, paraphrastic, or reflexive use of "son of man" to denote obliquely and indirectly the speaker ("I"). But even here the actual point of debate is quite narrow. On the one hand, Fitzmyer notes that while the generic and indefinite usages of "son of man" are "now clearly attested in Qumran Aramaic . . . there is no instance of its use . . . as a surrogate for 'I' " (1973–1974:397; see 1975:93), and, outside Qumran: "It is never found prior to the Late Phase [of Aramaic, i.e., A.D. 200–700 (or later)] in the paraphrastic usage, i.e., as a substitute for a personal pronoun (e.g., 'I,' 'me')." On the other hand, that last quotation continues: " . . . even though a number of NT parallels in the Synoptic Gospels would seem to indicate its use in the time of Jesus" (1980:20), and, earlier, "though I, like many others, suspect that the circumlocution 'Son of Man' for 'I' in Matt. 16:13 reflects current Palestinian Aramaic usage, neither Vermes nor anyone else has yet uncovered any *contemporary* evidence for that usage" (1979a:59). Actually, therefore, Vermes and Fitzmyer agree on the circumlocutional usage of "son of man" as a speaker's self reference ("I") at the time of Jesus and the Synoptic Gospels.

But *while Vermes claims that he has (indirect) proof of it, Fitzmyer correctly rejoins that he has no (direct) proof of it.* Note, for example, the *indirect* nature of the arguments in Vermes (1973:190–191; 1978a:127–130 = 1978b:23–25).

At this point the whole long debate (1967–1980) seems in danger of disappearing from view. But it should not be allowed to disappear too swiftly, because there is an important difference in emphasis that can be placed on all this data. If "son of man" has a *generic* ("man") and/or *indefinite* ("someone") sense, then *the former must and the latter could include the speaker* circumlocutionally ("I"). Hence "son of man" will very often contain the speaker in his assertion (see Jeremias, 1971:261). But it must be stressed (and here precisely is where Fitzmyer really differs from Vermes) that a speaker using "son of man" would not intend to separate himself apart or above others, but would rather intend (at most) to include himself among or with others. In this sense, "son of man" is not only atitular, it is almost antititular.

E. C. Maloney (267–275), in a doctoral dissertation under Fitzmyer, has shown that this atitular (generic or indefinite) usage shows up in poetic parallelism (man/son of man or men/sons of men) not only in biblical Hebrew, but also in Qumran Hebrew and Qumran Aramaic. In the Hebrew Bible there is (a) "God is not man, that he should lie, or a son of man, that he should repent" in Num. 23:19; (b) "When he commits iniquity, I will chasten him with the rod of men, with the stripes of the sons of men" in 2 Sam. 7:14; (c) "O Lord, what is man that thou dost regard him, or the son of man that thou dost think of him" in Ps. 144:3. In Qumran Hebrew there is (d) "And I, I know that righteousness does not belong to mankind nor perfection of way to a son of man" in 1QH 4:30; (e) "knowledge is hidden from mankind and the counsel of prudence from sons of men" in 1QS 11:6. And in Qumran Aramaic there is (f) "[and al]l men (are) gazing upon it (an injustice) and the sons of men will examine it" in 11QtgJb 28:2–3. Hence the atitular (generic or indefinite) usage not only appears before and contemporary with Jesus, but it does so in poetic parallelism as man/son of man or men/sons of men.

(7) Conclusion. Bultmann (84) had already noted that Mark 2:27 "could have existed as a saying in its own right, as in fact a Rabbinic saying was also handed down: 'The Sabbath was given to you, not you to the Sabbath.'" As such an independent aphorism, Mark 2:27 is an example of chiastic (*sabbath/man//man/sabbath*) antithetical parallelism. This first stage of *antithetical parallelism* was changed into a second stage by the pre-Markan addition of 2:28. But in this second stage, 2:27–28 was *synonymous parallelism* in that *man/son of man* usage is here atitular and generic. Mark's own compositional usage, however, proximately within 2:1–3:6 and remotely within the gospel as a whole, reads 2:27–28 as climactic parallelism (man/Son of Man). That is to say, Son of Man is now titular and specific. Finally, in a fourth stage, both Matthew and Luke independently recognize that 2:27–28 is very, very bad climactic—in fact, anticlimactic—parallelism, and so they deleted 2:27 completely.

1. SINGLE AND DOUBLE STICHS

This is the distinction Bultmann made between the "single-stranded" and "double-stranded mashal" (81). What is of importance here for transmissional processes is the ease with which the tradition moves from single to double or from double to single formulation within the trajectory of the same aphorism. All of this is greatly facilitated by the background of Semitic parallelism.

Cases where single-stich aphorisms have been doubled in transmission will not be considered here. This involves the much wider problem of *aphoristic expansion*, which would require a whole chapter to itself. I am considering here the contraction from two stichs to one, but also the difficulty of deciding at times which way the development actually moved. Was it from single to double stichs, or vice versa?

Aphorism 43: *Disciple and Servant*

(1) There are two independent versions to be considered: (a) Q/ Matt. 10:24–25a = Luke 6:40, and (b) John 13:16; 15:20 (see Table 3.5.)

Table 3.5

Matthew 10:24–25a	Luke 6:40	
A disciple is not above his teacher nor a servant above his master; it is enough for the disciple to be like his teacher, and the servant like his master.	A disciple is not above his teacher, but everyone when he is fully taught will be like his teacher.	

(2) The Q Text. The Q context (see Appendix 2) makes it clear how Q understood this text: *the disciple of a blind teacher can hope at best for blindness.* But did the Q text contain only Luke 6:40, or all of Matt. 10:24–25a? I would propose that Q had the full Matthean text and that Luke shortened it here to avoid the redundancy of the parallelism, disciple/teacher and servant/master (so Bultmann: 93,99).

I disagree, therefore, with Jacobson's comment that "Lk 6:40 fits only poorly into this polemical scheme, and has no discernible connection with 6:39" (1978:63). Q has, poorly or not, fitted 6:39,40, and 41–42 into a criticism of blind teachers of blind students in this polemical half of Jesus' great Inaugural Sermon.

(3) John. John 13:16 is a double-stich parallelism whose first stich uses the latter of the twin comparisons in Q/Matt. 10:24–25a (*servant/master*) just as Luke 6:40 had used the former one (*disciple/teacher*). The second stich in John 13:16 has "he who is sent" (*apostolos*) and "he who sent" (*tou pempsantos*). However, the two terms, "Teacher and Lord" (or Master), appear together in John 13:13, and 13:16 is the only use of *apostolos* in John (Brown, 1966–

Table 3.5 (cont.)

John 13:16	John 15:20
Truly, truly, I say to you	
a servant is not greater than his master;	a servant is not greater than his master
nor is he who is sent greater than he who sent him	

1970:2.570), so that John's double-stich version may well be a per-formancial or even redactional version of Matthew's. I do not propose here any direct connection between Matthew and John, but simply variations on a basic double-stich parallelism (see Dodd, 1963:335–338).

In John 15:20 there "is a literal citation of xiii 16," but as a single-stich version and now promising suffering rather than enjoining humility (Brown, 1966–1970:2.687).

These positive uses of this saying in John should not distract from the pejorative connotation given to the saying in its Q context. And this connotation is underlined by the appended comment, which *might* possibly derive from Q itself, that the subordinate can at best be "like" (*hōs*) the superior.

(4) Conclusion. In this case an original double-stich aphorism in synonymous parallelism (*disciple/teacher//servant/master*) appears in Q/Matt. 10:24. The same form is in John 13:16, but with performancially or even hermeneutically varied content. Because of the theological importance of "sending" in John, the parallelism in 13:16 might even be considered *synthetic* or *climactic*. Here and always

it is necessary to recall the warning of Kugel (58) that "all parallelism is really 'synthetic': it consists of A, a pause, and A's continuation B (or B + C)." The aphorism is reduced to a single-stich saying in Luke 6:40 (disciple/teacher) and John 15:20a (servant/master). But Matt. 10:24–25a, or possibly even Q itself, turned the double-stich into a quadruple-stich aphorism, and now it is in overall antithetical parallelism (*not alone*/*be like*) with the negative preceding the positive stich (see Jeremias, 1971:15 note 3). All of this indicates, once again, how easily aphorisms expand and contract along the lines of stich and parallelism.

2. ANTITHETICAL PARALLELISM

"As far as the sayings of Jesus in particular are concerned, C. F. Burney . . . came to the conclusion that of the different kinds of Semitic parallelism (synonymous, antithetic, synthetic, and climactic), antithetic parallelism 'characterizes our Lord's teaching in all the gospel sources.' Indeed, he goes so far as to say that we are nearer to the *ipsissima verba* of Jesus in cases of marked antithetic parallelism 'than in any sentence otherwise expressed.' " (Jeremias, 1971:14). I bracket for here all considerations of *ipsissima verba*, or even of the obviously more correct phrase *ipsissima structura*. But antithetical parallelism *is* so pervasive among the Jesus sayings that this particular double-stich phenomenon deserves special consideration.

Table 3.6

Matthew 16:25	Mark 8:35	Luke 9:24
For whoever would save his life will lose it, and whoever loses his life for my sake . will find it.	For whoever would save his life will lose it; and whoever loses his life for my sake and the gospel's will save it.	For whoever would save his life will lose it; and whoever loses his life for my sake, he will save it.

Jeremias has made two important points concerning antithetical parallelism in the double-stich Jesus sayings. (1) "Whereas in cases of antithetic parallelism in the Old Testament the second member serves, on the whole, to illuminate and to deepen the first by an opposed statement . . . in the sayings of Jesus exactly the opposite is the case: there the stress is almost always on the second half" (1971: 18). (2) The parallelism is achieved by "numerous technical devices . . . the use of nouns, adjectives or verbs as opposites (usually pairs of opposites), by negation (usually of the second member), by the contrast of question and statement, by inversion, by polarization, by complementary expressions (including periphrases for totalities), and very often by the combination of an opposition with a negation" (1971:16). Those assertions are quite copiously documented by Jeremias (1971:14–20).

My chosen example is one of inverted or chiastic antithetical parallelism, Aphorism 129 (see Burney: 73,74,77,81,85,141; Jeremias, 1971:15 note 1, 16 note 3).

Aphorism 129: *Saving One's Life*

(1) There are three independent versions to be considered. (a) Mark 8:35 = Matt. 16:25 = Luke 9:24; (b) Q/Matt. 10:39 = Luke 17:33; and (c) John 12:25. (See Table 3.6.)

(2) Form. The opening of this aphorism is another example of that performancial preference in which Mark has a *relatival* and Q

Table 3.6 (cont.)

Matthew 10:39	Luke 17:33	John 12:25
He who finds his life will lose it, and he who loses his life for my sake	Whoever seeks to gain his life will lose it, but whoever loses his life	He who loves his life loses it, and he who hates his life in this world
will find it.	will preserve it.	will keep it for eternal life.

(as in Matt. 10:39 rather than Luke 17:33) a *participial* format. The version in John 12:25 is also participial in construction.

In itself the aphorism is (a) a double-stich structure whose twin parts contain (b) both positive and negative poles. These are (c) arranged chiastically so that (d) the positives frame the negatives: positive/negative//negative/positive. It is thus inverted antithetical parallelism.

(3) Mark 8:35. In terms of form the Markan verbs are *save/lose// loses/save*. Thus one verb serves both positives and another verb both negatives.

In terms of content Mark has linked 8:35 with his aphoristic cluster in 8:34–9:1 by means of "for" (against Pryke: 128,131–132) and "would" (Turner: 355–356). But the much more important point is the phrase "for my sake and the gospel's," which qualifies the third of his four verbs. This will now be studied in some detail.

Any discussion of the double qualification in 8:35 must keep in mind the structural parallelism redactionally created by Mark between:

"For my sake and the gospel's"   (8:35)
"Of   me   and   my words" (8:38)

(a) *"and the gospel's."* It is usually accepted that at least the second qualification is a redactional addition (Marxsen: 120,125,128) as is the parallel expansion "and my words" in 8:38 (Pryke: 53 note 1, see also 132). But the first qualification is much more problematic.

(b) *"for my sake."* The dualism of the qualification was obviously a problem both for the synoptics and the later Markan textual tradition (Metzger, 1971:99). But is this first half of the specification pre-Markan and traditional (so Best, 1970:330) or Markan and redactional?

The decision concerning "for my sake" (*heneken emou*) will have to consider its use throughout Mark and Q as well. The context of these uses is always that of disciples suffering *for the sake of*. . . .

There are three cases in Mark. (i) In Mark 8:35 both Matt. 16:25

and Luke 9:24 accept his "for my sake." (ii) In Mark 10:29 each of them changes it: Matt. 19:29 has "for my name's sake" and Luke 18:29 (see 18:25) has "for the sake of the kingdom of God." (iii) In Mark 13:9, Matt. 10:18 retains the phrase, but Luke 21:12 changes it (see 21:17) to "for my name's sake."

There are two *possible* cases in Q. (iv) Matt. 5:11 has "Blessed are you when men revile you and persecute you . . . on my account (*heneken emou*)"; but Luke 6:22 has "Blessed are you when men hate you . . . on account of (*heneka*) the Son of man." *Gos. Thom.* 68 has simply "Blessed are you when you are hated and persecuted." Was "on my account" (*heneken emou*) in Q? If it was, Luke would have had to make the change to his version, but "one cannot find any specifically Lukan Son of Man Christology in his Gospel" (Colpe, 1972:459; see also Vielhauer, 1957:57; Tödt: 123). Thus *heneken emou* in Matt. 5:11 is most likely redactional and not traditional, from Matthew and not from Q. The final case is (v) the Q version of the present *Saving One's Soul* aphorism. Once again Matt. 10:39 has *heneken emou*, but Luke 17:33 does not. On the analogy of the preceding instance, it seems better to presume the phrase's absence from Q.

This means that the expression "for my sake" (*heneken emou*) has entered the synoptic tradition only from and through Mark (against Satake: 8–11). Hence Mark (a) added the second qualification, "and my words," to the "me" of 8:38, and (b) created the double qualification of "for my sake and the gospel's" in 8:35.

(4) Matt. 16:25. Matthew follows Mark verbatim for the first stich, but makes some changes in the second one. He drops "and the gospel's" presumably as redundant. Similarly, when Mark 10:29 has the same dualism, Matt. 19:29 reduces it to a single "for my name's sake." He also changes the fourth verb, "save," to "find," thereby bringing Mark into closer agreement with the Q version's concluding "find," but destroying the Markan dualism in the process. There is thus an intrusion from Q into Mark in Matt. 16:25.

(5) Luke 9:24. Luke also stays close to Mark's first stich, but makes changes in the second one. He agrees with Matt. 16:25 in

switching "loses" from indicative to subjunctive, and in omitting "and the gospel's" (see also Luke 18:29 against Mark 10:29). Finally he adds "he" (*houtos*) to the fourth and final verb.

(6) The Q Context. This aphorism *may* have been located in Q as now in Luke 17:33. Matt. 10:39 would then have relocated it (see Manson: 145; Polag, 1979:78–79). One could even argue that it continues the theme of Lot's flight as in Gen. 19:17 ("flee for your *life*"). However, it really is not that contextually appropriate. In Q/Luke 17:31 the flight theme is a way of expressing Sodom-like catastrophe rather than a blueprint for escape (as in Mark 13:15–16). In 17:33 flight is reprehensible and forbidden. I therefore consider that Luke relocated Q/Matt. 10:39 = Luke 17:33 here just as Matthew did elsewhere. Its Q location is now lost (see Appendix 2). It would also follow that, if it was Luke who placed 17:33 in its present position, it was hardly Luke who also added on 17:32 to 17:31. Luke 17:33 really contravenes 17:31–32.

(7) Luke 17:33. Luke has handled the Q text in 17:33 (= Matt 10:39) in an unusual manner. He adapted Q *formally* to Mark 8:35 = Luke 9:24 by accepting the relatival rather than the participial opening for each stich. But he also differentiated it *verbally* (the positive verbs) from Mark 8:35 = Luke 9:24 to avoid complete repetition. However, in doing this he has as his four verbs, *gain/lose// loses/preserve*, which destroys the chiastic structure still evident in the Matt. 10:39 version of Q. Thus 17:33 is Lukan redaction rather than a variant translation from the Aramaic (against Black: 188). It should be noted that the verb "gain" (*peripoieomai*) appears only here and in Acts 20:28; 1 Tim. 3:13; the verb "preserve" (*zōogoneō*) appears only here and in Acts 7:19 and 1 Tim. 6:13 (see also Metzger, 1971:167).

(8) Matt. 10:39. The Q form is much better preserved in Matt. 10:39 than in Luke 17:33, whence it has almost entirely vanished. Besides the participial openings of "he who" (*ho heurōn, ho apolesas*), there is also the chiastic structure of the verbs: *finds/lose//loses/ find*. This means that Mark and Q agree on this structure and also

that the negative verb ("lose") has remained stable even though the positive verb appears as "save" in Mark and "find" in Q. Matthew's major deviation for Q is his insertion of "for my sake" from Mark 8:35 = Matt. 16:25 into Matt. 10:39 (see Bultmann: 93).

(9) John 12:25. There are three points concerning this text. (a) John has the participial format as in Q rather than the relatival one as in Mark, and "there is no real proof for treating the Johannine form of the saying as an adaptation of a Synoptic pattern" (Brown: 1.474). (b) The fourfold verbal structure is now *loves/loses//hates keep* so that the chiastic structure is gone completely and only a single use of "'loses" links John's verbs to those of Q and Mark. Since John uses "love" (*phileō*) almost twice as often as the Synoptics (Brown: 1.497), and has the verbs "love" and "hate" in general parallelism in 15:19, it seems most likely that these are John's rephrasing of his source rather than a direct reflection of its wording. His final verb "keep" appears also in John 12:47 and 17:12, and that second place has the same general antithetical parallelism between "keep" (*phylassō*) and "lose" (*apollymi*) as in 12.25: "I have guarded (*ephylaxa*) them, and none of them is lost (*apōleto*)." Hence the verbs *love/hate* and *keep* are typical Johannine rephrasings. (c) So also do the twin qualifications for the final verbs in John "represent the familiar Johannine contrast between the life of this world and eternal life" (Brown: 1.474,505–508). Since these qualifications are redactional, this text represents another version of the Q and pre-Markan unqualified aphorism.

(10) Conclusion. In terms of form the chiastic rhythm of positive/negative//negative/positive held for all versions and the chiastic verbalization held for Mark (*save/lose//lose/save*) and Q (*find/lose// lose/find*) but not for John (*love/lose//hate/keep*). In terms of content, the relatival (Mark) and participial (Q, John) openings are more likely preferred performancial variations than they are "two different ways of rendering the Aramaic original in Greek" (Brown: 1.473). In the verbal changes it is the positive verbs that tend to diverge, while the negative ones hold firm for Mark and Q and even once for

John ("lose":*apollymi*). The Q positive verbs ("find") and the Markan positive verbs ("save") "cannot be *traced* to translation of Aramaic" (Black: 189 note 1). But Brown has noted that the "Greek verb [*apollymi*] . . . is always the same but seems to be used in its different meanings of 'lose' and 'destroy' " (1.473). Hence it is the twin meanings of the negative verb *apollymi* in Greek which has pulled the positive verb either as in Mark (*save/destroy//destroy/save*) or in Q (*find/lose//lose/find*). But all three sets of verbs (Mark, Q, John) are probably no more than performancial variations with much the same meaning. The qualifications, however, are a different matter. The specifications added to the second stich in Mark and John are hermeneutical variations that serve to interpret the paradoxicality of the saying (see Dodd, 1963:338–343).

In all of this, the chiastic antithetical parallelism exerts a powerful control over the aphorism's development.

Table 3.7

Mark 11:24	Matthew 21:22	Matthew 7:7–8	
Therefore I tell you, whatever you ask in prayer, believe that you have received it, and it will be yours.	And whatever you ask in prayer, you will receive, if you have faith.	Ask, and it will be given you; seek, and you will find; knock, and it will be opened to you. For every one who asks receives, and he who seeks finds, and to him who knocks it will be opened.	

3. TRIPLE STICHS

Because of the phenomenon of parallelism, it is easier to find dou-ble- or even quadruple-stich sayings than triple-stich sayings. But the following is a fascinating triple-stich example.

Aphorism 67: *Ask, Seek, Knock*

(1) There are *at least* four independent versions: (a) Mark 11:24 = Matt. 21:22; (b) Q/Matt. 7:7–8 = Luke 11:9–10; (c) *Gos. Thom.* 94 (see also 92 and 2); and (d) John 15:7b. I say *at least* because Q, probably, and *Thomas*, possibly, may have independent versions behind their multiple texts of this saying. (See Table 3.7.)

(2) Mark 11:24. I propose that the following phrases in 11:24 are part of Mark's redactional word-linkage for 11:22–25: (a) "in prayer" (*proseuchesthe*), which is a "synonymous expression" with "ask" (*aiteisthe*; see Neirynck: 1972:104); (b) "believe" (*pisteuete*); and (c)

Table 3.7 (cont.)

Luke 11:9–10	*Gospel of Thomas* 94	John 15:7b
And I tell you, Ask,		Ask whatever you will
and		and
it will be given you; seek, and you will find; knock, and it will be opened to you. For every one who asks receives, and he who seeks finds, and to him who knocks it will be opened.	He who seeks will find, and [he who knocks] will be let in.	it shall be done for you.

"it will be yours." That leaves as pre-Markan only, "Therefore I tell (say to) you, whatever you ask in prayer . . . received. . . ." I propose that in the process of his redaction Mark changed the aphorism's given apodosis from "you will *receive*" into the present "believe that you have *received*, and it will be yours." Then the pre-Markan version would be close to this: "Therefore, I tell (say to) you, whatever you ask in prayer, you will receive."

(3) Matt. 21:22. Matt. 21:21–22 has redacted the two sayings in Mark 11:22–24 quite heavily, and he has no equivalent here to Mark 11:25 (but see Matt. 6:14–15). His redaction consisted primarily in removing all of Mark's carefully created word-linkage, that is, he omitted Mark's doubling of (a) "I say to you," (b) "believe(s)," and (c) "it will be." In 21:22, however, while he still retains mention of "prayer" and "faith" added by Mark to his 11:24, he has changed the ending away from Mark's redaction and back towards Mark's given apodosis: "you will receive" (*lēmpsesthe*). This change is not, of course, purely coincidental since the verb "receive" is still visible in Mark's "received" (*elabete*), and even more directly in the Q version at Matt. 7:8 ("receives," *lambanei*).

(4) The Q Context. The context of Aphorism 67 in Q is the enthusiastic and even rhapsodic ending of Q's second section on *Jesus and Disciples* (see Appendix 2), and this situation is important in understanding its *double* assertion in Q.

(a) Its present Q context is in the complex that begins with the *Revelation to Babes* prayer (not aphorism) in Q/Matt. 11:25–26 = Luke 10:21 (see Appendix 2). In its overall Q context this ecstatic prayer must be taken as "a reinterpretation of the recalcitrance of Israel. It is now said that it was God's will that Israel did not believe" (Jacobson, 1978:141). But this differs completely from the general Deuteronomistic theology seen repeatedly as Q's background: "The Deuteronomistic tradition is not only unmentioned here, it is contradicted. There is no place in the Deuteronomistic tradition for a thanksgiving concerning Israel's unbelief, even if it is willed by God. We may also note that the expectation found elsewhere in Q that

Israel should repent presupposed Israel's knowledge of God; now this knowledge is denied" (Jacobson, 1978:141; see pp. oo below).

Three important conclusions derive from this change in the interpretation of the Q community's failure to convert Israel. First, the change moves, within the wisdom tradition, from one to another description of Wisdom's rejection by the world. In one explanation, for example in Aphorism 53 (Suggs, 1970:44; Jacobson, 1978:132), Wisdom comes, calls, fails, and, in retribution, departs, and abandons the refusers to their fate. In the other, "Wisdom is inaccessible except to God (see Job 28). The first solution dominates most of Q; the second occurs in Lk 10:21–22 par." (Jacobson: 143). Second, this change means that Q/Matt. 11:25–26 = Luke 10:21, and much of the following material in Q/Aphorisms 62–68 (see Appendix 2) is "later addition" (Jacobson, 1978:142,144 and "it seems to represent a basic shift in the theology of the community which stands behind Q" (221). Third, this reinterpretation may be correlated with historical change within that community itself: "Recent research on Q has recognized the most distinctively Wisdom sayings of Q to belong to a later layer in the tradition, as the Q tradition moved out of its Palestinian milieu into the wider Hellenistic Jewish Christian environment where the final redaction took place" (Robinson, 1975:8).

(b) Bultmann already suggested that Q/Matt. 7:7–11 = Luke 11:9–13 "had several stages of development, or has been enlarged by the addition of originally independent sayings" (87). It is in fact an *aphoristic cluster* constituted from a double assertion of the *Ask, Seek, Knock* saying (Aphorism 67) leading into the *Good Gifts* saying (Aphorism 68). But what exactly is its contextual purpose within
• Q?

Q enshrined the two *prayers* of Q/Matt. 11:25–26 = Luke 10:21 and Q/Matt. 6:9–13 = Luke 11:2–4 within a series of Aphorisms 62–68 (see Appendix 2). Aphorisms 67–68 are both a commentary on the Lord's Prayer and an appropriate conclusion for this *later* Q Wisdom theology (Jacobson, 1978:217–222). But those aphorisms enshrine the Lord's Prayer in somewhat of a *corrective* commentary. In other words, I propose (i) that the Lord's Prayer was earlier but secret Q tradition; (ii) that it was known to Q in the Jewish-Christian seven-petition form that was accepted in Matt. 6:9–13 but changed to the Gentile-Christian five-petition format by Luke 11:2–4 (see Jeremias, 1967a:89); and (iii) that it was acceptable to the later Q theology *only* as commented on by Aphorisms 67–68. What exactly do these add to its content? First of all, the double assertion of Aphorism 67 creates an atmosphere of "remarkable confidence . . . there are no conditions mentioned here as there are, e.g., in 1 John 3:22" (Jacobson, 1978:217), and that latter text deliberately corrects this sort of conditionless gnosticizing confidence. Second, having greatly increased the positive side of the petitions in the Lord's Prayer in Aphorism 67, the single negative aspect is corrected in Aphorism 68. The final word: "And lead us not into temptation. But deliver us from evil" (Q/Matt. 6:13), which is also problematic in James 1:17, is corrected by Aphorism 68: the heavenly Father gives *only good gifts*. Note also the word-linkage between "evil" in Q/Matt. 7:11 = Luke 11:13 (*ponēroi*) and Q/Matt. 6:13 (*ponērou*). It is against this background of rhapsodic confidence and enthusiastic certainty that one must understand the Q text of Aphorism 67.

Table 3.8

Oxyrhynchus Papyrus 654	*Gospel of Thomas* 2
Let him who see[ks] not cease [seeking until] he finds and when he finds, [he will be astounded, and] having been [astoun]ded,	Let him who seeks continue seeking until he finds. When he finds, he will become troubled. When he becomes troubled, he will be astonished, and he will rule over the All.
he will reign an[d having reigned], he will re[st].	

(5) Q/Matt. 7:7–8 = Luke 11:9–10. The Q complex is composed of (a) a triple-stich saying repeated twice in 7:7 = 11:9 and 7:8 = 11:10; (b) with the protasis/apodosis of the former triptych in *imperative/future* format but that of the latter in *participle/present* format; (c) with all three stichs of the former having second person emphasis ("given you . . . you will find . . . opened to you"), but all three of the latter having third-person emphasis; and (d) with the only content change being the first stich's "given" in the first triptych appearing as "receives" in the second triptych.

The major question this raises is whether Q has simply doubled a given triptych or combined together two given versions of the same triptych. But the answer to this will have to be postponed until after a consideration of *Thomas* and John.

(6) *Thomas.* There are three different texts to be seen in *Gos. Thom.* 2,92,94, and the first of these is also present in Oxy P 654. (See Table 3.8.)

(7) *Gos. Thom.* 2.

(a) The restoration of the Greek text in Oxy P 654, of which only the first half of each line is extant, is relatively secure due to its citation by Clement of Alexandria (Fitzmyer, 1974:372–373; Hofi-

Table 3.8 (cont.)

Gospel of Thomas 92	*Gospel of Thomas* 94
Seek and you will find. Yet what you asked Me about in former times and which I did not tell you then, now I do desire to tell, but you do not inquire after it.	He who seeks will find and [he who knocks] will be let in.

us: 27; Marcovich: 56). In form it is a quadruple-stich saying climactically word-linked from one stich to the next: seeks/finds//
finds/astounded//astounded/reign//reigned/rest (see Hennecke and Schneemelcher: 1.164).

(b) On the other hand, the version in *Gos. Thom.* 2 breaks both the form and content of that Greek version: seeks/finds//finds/troubled//
troubled/astonished// — / reign. The result is that the Coptic version climaxes with "rule" while the Greek text climaxes with "rest" (see Bammel, 1969). It is fairly certain that the Greek version is more original, but it is difficult to explain the Coptic deviation since "rest" is one of *Thomas*'s major themes (Vielhauer, 1964:297). The best explanation is probably some form of misreading of his Greek original by the Coptic translator (see Marcovich: 57; or Ménard, 1975:79).

(c) For my present purpose it suffices to note from Oxy P 654, (i) that only the *seek/find* stich is used; (ii) that it is accompanied not with two other parallel stichs as in Q, but with three climactically linked stichs; and (iii) that the *seek/find* stich is in participial and thus third-person format: "him who seeks" (*ho zētōn*).

(8) *Gos. Thom.* 92. As in the preceding instance, only the *seek/find* stich is present; but now it is accompanied by another saying whose meaning is not exactly clear. More significant for my own purpose is the fact that the stich's version here is in imperative/
future format and thus in the second person.

(9) *Gos. Thom.* 94. There is a lacuna in this text because the left bottom corner of the manuscript page is missing. But the restoration is probably as certain as such things can be. The restored "[he who knocks]" presumes the Coptic [*pettohm e*]*hūn* (literally, "knocks inward," see Crum: 458b), and this is still residually visible in the final tip of the -*h*- and the complete -*ūn*. And "will be let in" is, literally, "they will open to him," which is normal circumlocution for Coptic's absent passive voice (see Guillaumont, 1959:49; Wilson, 1973:520).

(10) Q *and Thomas.*

(a) With regard to *content*, the three stichs of Q (*asks, seeks, knocks*) appear either as one stich in *Gos. Thom.* 2,92 (*seeks*), or as two stichs in *Gos. Thom.* 94 (*seeks, knocks*).

(b) With regard to *form*, both the Q constructions are present in Thomas:

  (i)   Imperative/Future and Second Person:
        Matt. 7:7 = Luke 11:9 = *Gos. Thom.* 92
  (ii) Participial Opening and Third Person:
        Matt. 7:8 = Luke 11:10 = Oxy P 654 (*Gos. Thom.* 2)

The form in *Gos. Thom.* 94 is closer to (b) but, lacking here any Greek original, it is impossible to tell whether the Coptic is translating a Greek participial or relatival version.

I conclude, therefore, that Q did not redactionally double the triad in Matt. 7:7–8 = Luke 11:9–10, but that he knew two performancially distinct versions of the triptych and that he gave us both. The twin versions were also known to Thomas, but there the three stichs have already become two (94) or even one (2,92) and, as the aphoristic core decreases, so does the gnostic contextual commentary increase from *Gos. Thom.* 94 to 92 to 2. And having been abbreviated from *ask/seek/knock* (Q) to *seek*, and then redeveloped into *seeks/finds/astounded/reign/rest* (Oxy P 654), this sequence could become the structural and theological basis for the *Dialogue of the Savior* (Robinson, 1977:229–238), where "discussion of the sayings proceeds in an order indicated by the second saying of the *Gospel of Thomas*, which speaks of an *ordo salutis* of *seeking, finding, marvelling, ruling, resting*" (Pagels and Koster: 68). On the gnostic trajectory, then, the triad of *ask/seek/knock* (as in Q) is contracted first to *seek/knock* (*Gos. Thom.* 94), then to *seek* alone (*Gos. Thom.* 92), and then expanded to *seek/find/astounded/reign/rest* (*Gos. Thom.* 2; Oxy P 654), and finally this becomes *rest* (CG III, 120:5–10; 121:5–10), *seek* (126:5–10; 129:15–20; 131:20–25; 137:15–25), *find* (129:15–20), *wonder* (136:1–5), *rule* (138:5–20), and *rest* (141:1–15).

(11) John. In John, however, the *seek/knock* part of the Q triad

disappears and it is the *ask* theme which appears repeatedly throughout the Last Supper discourse in 14:13–14; 15:7,16; 16:23–24,26 (Brown, 1966–1970:2.634). I propose the following sequential steps for the theme's development within John.

(a) 15:7. "If you abide in me, and my words abide in you, *ask* whatever you will, *and it shall be done for you.*" This combines (i) the Johannine theme of indwelling with (ii) the *ask* theme using the imperative (*aitēsasthe*), and (iii) it cites explicitly no recipient for the prayer nor granter of its request (*genēsetai hymin*).

(b) 16:23–24,26. "In that day you will ask nothing of me. Truly, truly, I say to you, if you ask anything of the Father, he will give it to you in my name. Hitherto you have asked nothing in my name; *ask, and you will receive,* that your joy may be full. . . . In that day you will ask in my name; and I do not say to you that I shall pray the Father for you. . . ." Once again, (i) there is a version of the ask theme using the imperative (*aiteite*) and the future (*lēmpsesthe*), but (ii) it is now the Father who receives and answers the prayer (iii) in the name of Jesus.

(c) 15:16. "that *whatever you ask* the Father in my name, *he may give it to you.*" Although firmly imbedded in specific Johannine themes, the imperative form of the saying was still clearly visible in 15:7 and 16:23–24 (26). But here there is a relatival opening much closer to that of Mark 11:24. That latter's "whatever you ask" (*panta hosa aiteisthe*) is similar to the "whatever you ask" (*ho ti an aitēsēte*) of 15:16. But, once again, it is the Father who receives and answers in the name of Jesus.

(d) 14:13–14. "*Whatever you ask* in my name, *I will do it*, that the Father may be glorified in the Son; *if you ask* me anything in my name, *I will do it.*" At this final stage (i) the form is again relatival (*ho ti an aitēsēte*) in 14:13, exactly as in 15:16, but it shifts to the conditional format (*ean ti aitēsēte*) in 14:14; and (ii) the receiver and granter of the prayer is now Jesus himself (on the "me" of 14:14, see

Metzger, 1971:244), but (iii) with the Father's glory also mentioned.

(e) 1 John 3:21–22; 5:14–15. These versions, with the relatival opening in the former (*ho ean aitōmen*) and both relatival (*ho ean aitōmetha*) and conditional ones (*ean ti aitōmetha*) in the latter, never mention Jesus but refer only to God. Notice, for example, how the "name of *his Son* Jesus Christ" is specified in 3:23. Their cautionary emphasis on ethics ("commandments . . . please him . . . his will") indicates, however, that they are not earlier and more primitive versions of the *ask* theme, but rather the final stage in its development, with the author reacting to specific problems within the Johannine community (see Brown, 1979:128–130).

In all of this it seems most probable that John is making "independent use of traditional material" (Dodd, 1963:352) rather than working directly from the synoptics.

(12) *Conclusion*. The earliest recoverable core is a three-stich aphorism (*ask/seek/knock*) whose elements are also known from outside this tradition (Bultmann: 87,107; Sieber: 81). This inaugural triad appears in two performancially distinct versions in Q, with the *imperative* in Matt. 7:7 = Luke 11:9 and with the *participle* in Matt. 7:8 = Luke 11:10. The triad then splits along an *ask* and a *seek/knock* trajectory. The *ask* line appears within Mark 11:24 (*relatival*) and John where it proceeds from 15:7 (*imperative*) to 16:23–24,26 (*imperative*) to 15:16 (*relatival*) to 14:13–14 (*relatival, conditional*) and on into reaction with 1 John 3:21–22; 5:14–15 (*relatival, conditional*). The *seek/knock* trajectory appears as such in Gos. Thom. 94 (*relatival*), but the *knock* theme is then dropped and only the *seek* theme continues to develop; first into Gos. Thom. 92 (imperative) with rather unclear contextual commentary; then into Gos. Thom. 2, but as in Oxy P 654 (*seek/find/wonder/rule/rest*); and finally into the theological structure of the *Dialogue of the Savior* (CG III,5), which "may indeed prove to be a *topos* in other gnostic literature as well" (Pagels and Koester: 74). Thus while I would

agree that "Q, insofar as it is known through Matthew and Luke, cannot have been the source for the other sayings on 'seeking and finding' " (Koester, 1980b:243), I consider that the earliest recoverable version of this triadic saying is that of Q in its *imperative* and *relatival* variations. Even more important, however, is Koester's suggestion that the gnostic trajectory may well represent the saying's more original reference and meaning; that is, "the theme of 'seeking and finding' is not yet formulated as an ecclesiastical admonition for prayer, but reflects the older sapiential theme of seeking after wisdom, revelation, and salvation" (1980b:244). The triadic saying's original drive was not towards general assurance concerning one's prayerful requests, but towards a very specific assurance along the lines of that other Q/Aphorism 95: *Seek the Kingdom* in Q/Matt. 6:31–33 = Luke 12:29–31. This, therefore, continues the connections between the complex of later Q wisdom theology in the prayer of Q/Matt. 11:25–26 = Luke 10:21 and Q/Aphorisms 62–68 (see Koester, 1980b:238–250).

The triple-stich version is not, therefore, an expansion of a single- or double-stich text. But the more original triple saying (*ask, seek, knock*), as in Q, has become contracted into shorter forms with *ask* alone (Mark, John), or *seek* alone (*Gos. Thom.* 2,92), or even a *seek/knock* diptych (*Gos. Thom.* 94).

4. QUADRUPLE STICHS

My final example is a quadruple-stich formulation. But in this case, and in distinction from the preceding one, I consider that the more original version was a single-stich format that became quadrupled in the transmission.

Aphorism 61: *Receiving the Sender*

(1) There are *at least* four independent versions: (a) Mark 9:37 = Matt. 18:5 = Luke 9:48; (b) Q/Matt. 10:40 = Luke 10:16; (c) John 5:23; 12:44–45; 13:20; and (d) Ign. *Eph.* 6:1. I say *at least* because it is most likely that John has independent variants behind 12:44 and 13:20. Because of the number of texts involved I use only Mark

9:37 for the Markan tradition (= Matt. 18:5 = Luke 9:48), and, since Ign. *Eph.* 6:1 is so divergent, I omit it from parallel columns and give it by itself below. (See Table 3.9.)

(2) Relatival and Participial Opening. This is another example of that divergence of opening format noted before in sayings from Mark (*relatival*) and Q or John (*participial*). The *relatival* opening appears in Mark 9:37 (twice), Matt. 18:5 (once), and Luke 9:48 (twice). But the *participial* style is in Q/Matt. 10:40 (twice), Luke 10:16 (thrice), and John 5:23 (once), John 12:44–45 (twice), and John 13:20 (twice).

(3) Internal Structure. There are four separate aspects to the internal structure: protagonists, verbs, stichs, and constructions.

(a) Protagonists. We are dealing with three protagonists by whatever name expressed: *disciples/Jesus/God*. These three protagonists are organized into two sets: (i) *disciples/Jesus*, and (ii) *Jesus/God*.

(b) Verbs. What is important here is whether the verb is positive or negative. They can be distinguished as follows: (i) *positive verbs*: receive, hear, see, believe; (ii) *negative verbs*: reject, not honor.

(c) Stichs. When the two sets of protagonists are combined with the two sets of verbs, one has a possible quadruple-stich formulation:

a: Positive (Disciples/Jesus)
a': Negative (Disciples/Jesus)
b: Positive (Jesus/God)
b': Negative (Jesus/God)

These possibilities appear as the following textual actualities, with single, double, and triple stichs.

a: Matt. 18:5 (from Mark 9:37); Ign. *Eph.* 6:1
b: John 12:44,45
b': John 5:23
ab: Mark 9:37 = Luke 9:48; Matt. 10:40; John 13:20
aa'b': Luke 10:16

Table 3.9

Mark 9:37	Matthew 10:40	Luke 10:16	John 5:23	
Whoever receives one such child in my name receives me;	He who receives you receives me,	He who hears you hears me, and he who rejects you rejects me,		
and whoever receives me, receives not me but him who sent me.	and he who receives me receives him who sent me.			
		and he who rejects me rejects him who sent me	he who does not honor the Son does not honor the Father who sent him	

In our present texts there is no example of *aa'bb'* but, as I shall suggest below, Q must have had the full fourfold version (see under Luke 10:16).

(d) Constructions. There are two types of construction to be considered: those with *ab* or *a'b'* structure and those with *a* or *b* or *b'* structure alone.

(i) In all cases of *ab* or *a'b'* formulation, for example: *you/me// me/sender*, the hinge of the two stichs is formed by having the same ordered expression terminate the first and initiate the second stich. The Greek order is *object-verb* in both expressions of Mark 9:37; Luke 9:48ab; Matt. 10:40; Luke 10:16bc; John 13:20 (for example, *eme dechetai//eme dechētai* in Mark 9:37). Further, in all such

Table 3.9 (cont.)

John 12:44	John 12:45	John 13:20
		Truly, truly, I say to you, he who receives any one whom I send receives me;
he who believes in me, believes not in me but in him who sent me.	And he who sees me sees him who sent me	and he who receives me receives him who sent me.

cases, but with the exception of Mark 9:37, the two stichs are constructed around that central hinge in an intricate chiastic arrangement, as in Figure 3.1.

There is, in other words, an internal chiastic structure within each stich (left brackets) and also an external chiastic connection (right brackets) between both stichs.

(ii) In all cases of *a* or *b*, *a'* or *b'* (that is, *you/me* or *me/sender*) the internal chiastic structure of verb/object//object/verb holds for *a* in Matt. 18:5 and *a'* in Luke 10:16a; but it is absent for *b* in John 12:44,45 and *b'* in John 5:23b, whose structure is instead verb/object//verb/object.

(4) The Markan Context. First, there is the wider context of 8:27–10:45 which, like 4:1–8:26 (see Petersen), has a core structure

Figure 3.1

Structure	Luke 9:48ab	Matthew 10:40	Luke 10:16bc	John 13:20
verb	*dexētai*	*dechomenos*	*athetōn*	*lambanōn*
object	*paidion*	*hymas*	*hymas*	*tina*
object	*eme*	*eme*	*eme*	*eme*
verb	*dechetai*	*dechetai*	*athetai*	*lambanei*
object	*eme*	*eme*	*eme*	*eme*
verb	*dexētai*	*dechomenos*	*athetōn*	*lambanōn*
verb	*dechetai*	*dechetai*	*athetai*	*lambanei*
object	*ton* . . .	*ton* . . .	*ton* . . .	*ton* . . .

that is repetitive and internally and externally tradic (see Perrin and Duling: 248; Robbins, 1981a:102–105):

(a) Passion-Resurrection
     Prophecy   8:27–30   9:30–32   10:32–34
(b) Apostolic
     Misunderstanding   8:31–33   9:33–34   10:35–41
(c) Corrective Teaching   8:34–9:1   9:35–50   10:42–45

Second, within the middle section of the triad there is evidence of another large compositional unity wherein two sections concerning the *child* frame one concerning *divorce*: A(9:36–39 within 9:33–50), B(10:1–12), A'(10:13–16). The thematic importance of this juxtaposition has been well explained by Kelber: "The marriage relationship is singled out as the one exception to the eschatological experience of separation and divorce. By the same token neither wife nor husband are included among the goods to be renounced" (10:29). And so, "while the ties to the past are severed, the link to the future is strengthened" (1974:91; note that the "children" to be abandoned in Mark 10:29 are *tekna* not *paidia*). The twin framing units concerning children (*paidia*) are carefully paralleled by a chiastic balance of positive ("whoever receives . . . child") and negative ("whoever does not receive . . . child") aphorisms. This is detailed in Table 3.10.

(5) Mark 9:37. The fact that Mark alone has any mention of *child(ren)* in this *Receiving the Sender* aphorism can best be understood against that parallelism: Mark himself introduced the *child (ren)* from Mark 10:13–16 into 9:36–37 by (a) creating 9:36 from 10:16 and (b) adding "one such child in my name" to the pre-Markan 9:37 (see Pryke: 165) from 10:14b–15. By so doing he effected not only a verbal and thematic parallelism but he also gave his own understanding of the pre-Markan sayings behind 9:37 and 10:14b–15 (Fleddermann: 61–64).

The pre-Markan version of 9:37 must have designated the disciples either directly or indirectly (*disciples/me//me/sender*), but Mark changes this quite emphatically. This interest is not on those who must receive the disciples, as in Q and John, *but on those whom the disciples must receive*. By combining 9:33–35 with his created and modified 9:36–37, Mark insists that the disciples must be the servants of all (9:35), even or especially of the least and the lowest of all (9:37). In such acts of abject humility one receives God.

(6) Matt. 18:5. Matthew accepts only the first of Mark's two stichs, and this is part of his restyling of Mark's word-linked composition in 9:33–50. Matthew (a) removed Mark 9:38–40 completely, (b) relocated Mark 9:41 to Matt. 10:42, and thereby (c) brought Mark 9:37 = Matt. 18:5 ("one such child") and Mark 9:42 = Matt. 18:6 ("one of these little ones") into immediate sequence. In such a conjunction, and especially with a different Q version for Mark 9:37 at Matt. 10:40, Matthew reduced Mark 9:37's double-stich aphorism to its first stich. But he also changed the Markan word order so that the chiastic sequence of verb/object//object/verb from the Q first stich reappears even here.

(7) Luke 9:48ab. A similar phenomenon occurs in Luke. On the one hand, he accepts Mark's double-stich format, with minor alterations such as dropping Mark's "receives not me but." On the other, he has the full inner and outer chiastic construction seen in Q and John 13:20 (Figure 3.1). One must presume a very powerful

Table 3.10

			Mark 9:36–39	
A	Action by Jesus on child		9:36, "taking him in his arms" (*enagkalisamenos auto*)	
B	Aphorism by Jesus about child(ren)		9:37, "whoever receives . . . child" (*hos an . . . paidiōn dexētai*)	
C	a'	Action by outsiders	9:38a	
	b'	Reproach by disciples	9:38b	
	b'	Counter-reproach to disciples by Jesus	9:39a, "do not forbid" (*mē kōlyete*)	
	a'	Aphorism by Jesus on action by outsiders	9:39b	
B'	Aphorism by Jesus about child			
A'	Action by Jesus on children			

pull from this structure still operative on Matt. 18:5 and Luke 9:48ab, despite following Mark 9:37.

(8) The Q context. In Q this saying followed immediately upon Q/Matt. 11:21–24 = Luke 10:13–15 (Taylor, 1953:29; 1959:254–55; Polag, 1979:46–47). It therefore closed Q's "mission" discourse by reverting to the opening theme: "I send (*apostellō*) you" in Q/Luke 10:3 and "who sent (*aposteilanta*) me" in Q/Luke 10:16. (See the *Jesus and Disciples* section in Appendix 2.)

(9) Luke 10:16. This text is composed of (a) a positive single-stich

Table 3.10 (cont.)

Mark 10:13–16
10:13a
10:13b
10:14a, "do not hinder" (mē kōlyete)
10:14b
10:15, "whoever does not receive . . . child" (hos an mē dexētai . . . paidion)
10:16, "took them in his arms" (enagkalisamenos auta)

saying and (b) a negative double-stich saying. It has thus three out of the four parts of a balanced positive/negative quadruple-stich version. Manson (78) has suggested that the "original form of the saying was fuller" than any of the existing versions and was, in fact, such a balanced quadruple-stich aphorism. He also noted "that the Aramaic verb qabbēl means both 'to receive' and 'to hear' in the sense of 'obey'" (see Mark 6:11), so that Luke 10:16a (hear) is but a translational variation of Mark 9:37 (receive). Most likely, then, Q was a balanced positive/negative format with two stichs in each side, and this agrees with similar positive/negative parallelisms in Q/ Matt. 7:24–27 = Luke 6:47–49 and in Q/Matt. 10:7–8,14 = Luke 10:8–11 (Aphorism 59). The emphasis on *hearing* is also characteristic of Q, as in Q/Luke 6:27 (Aphorism 35) or Q/Matt. 7:24–27 = Luke 6:47–49, once again. I consider, therefore, that Luke himself shortened the redundancy by omitting the second stich of the positive. But the intricate chiastic pattern is still visible in 10:16a and 10:16b despite that omission.

(10) Matt. 10:40. "About Mt. 10:40 one may have doubts whether it should be labelled Q or M" (Manson: 78, see also 183). On the one hand, its position is explicable as a Q relocation and both its participial opening and intricate chiastic structure is that of Q. On the other hand, those last two items are also true of John 13:20. It is probably best to consider it the Q text relocated and reduced to the two-stich positive format but rewritten in terms of Mark 9:37 = Matt. 18:5.

(11) John. The texts in John may be outlined as in Table 3.11. In all double-stich instances the second stich (me/ —) rather than the first one (— /me) is present in John (see Borgen, 1979–1980:24–25). Four of the texts include the phrase that elsewhere concludes the aphorism in almost formulaic fashion: "him who sent me" (*ton aposteilanta me* in Mark and Q; *ton pempsanta me* in John). I shall concentrate on this first foursome since the other four are more like fragmentary variations of those fuller ones.

(12) John 12:44–45. John 12:44 is the *only case anywhere* that has a parallel to Mark 9:37 with its qualification "receives not me

Table 3.11

including "who sent me"			
single stich		double stich	
positive	negative	positive	negative
12:44 12:45	5:23	13:20	

but" (*ouk eme dechetai alla*). Yet despite this striking parallel, John 12:44 differs from Mark 9:37 in having a participial opening and also in its verb/object//verb/object structure, which is certainly not the chiastic construction of Q in John 13:20 but is not that of Mark 9:37 (*object/verb//object/verb*) either.

The presence of John 12:45 after 12:44 creates a unique situation of two second-stich versions of this saying. But it should also be noted that the qualification "not me but" is absent from 12:45.

When one recalls the Johannine appropriateness of the verb "believes" (especially as *pisteuō eis*) in 12:44 and "sees" (*theōreō*) in 12:45 (Brown, 1966–1970:1.501–503,512–513), it seems most likely that (a) John 12:45 is a redactional doubling of 12:44 (note this same verbal conjunction in 6:40) and that (b) the verbs in John are not so much simple performancial variations as deliberate Johannine redactions.

(13) John 13:20. If John 12:44 was close to Mark's version, this is much closer to Q's. It has the Q participial opening and the Q chiastic structure. But "receives" is *lambanō* here as against *akouō* in Q or *dechomai* in Mark, and "sends" is *pempō* here as against *apostellō* for Q and Mark; and, more importantly, the saying is in the third person ("any one whom") rather than the second ("you"). Those first two elements should be considered as simple translational or performancial variations; but the third feature is more significant, since "a change from the specific to the general . . . would be contrary to the main tendency of the Farewell Discourse, in which we repeatedly find sayings which in the earlier part of the gospel had

Table 3.11 (cont.)

excluding "who sent me"			
single stitch		double stitch	
positive	negative	positive	negative
8:19	15:23		
14:7			
14:9			

a general or indefinite form now applied specifically to the disciples" (Dodd, 1963:344). In other words this element is not redactionally Johannine, so that "any one whom" must be considered as traditional and pre-Johannine. On the other hand, this is the *only* text that brings the verb "to send" from the second (Jesus/God) into the first (disciples/Jesus) stich. This is, of course, logically implicit in the double-stich parallelism. And it is already rendered explicit in Q by his framing connection between the start and finish of the "mission" discourse: "I send you" in Q/Matt. 10:16 = Luke 10:3 and "who sent me" in Q/Matt. 10:40 = Luke 10:16. But here it is rendered explicit within a version of the aphorism itself. Thus within the phrase "any one whom/I send" there are both earlier and pre-Johannine as well as later and Johannine elements. What has happened in John 13:20 repeats what had occurred just before in 13:16, "Truly, truly, I say to you, a servant is not greater than his master; nor is he who is sent (*apostolos*) greater than he who sent (*pempsantos*) him." In this Johannine rephrasing of a traditional double-stich aphorism (servant/master//apostle/sender), the emphasis is now totally on Jesus-as-sender and there is no mention of God-as-sender at all (see Aphorism 43 in Appendix 1).

(14) John 5:23. This is a single-stich and *b'*-construction version of the saying (*me/sender*). It has the participial opening and the verb/object//verb/object format. This means that it is the negative balance of John 12:44 (without "not me but") rather than of John 13:20. It is possible, but not at all certain, that John knows a parallel to the full Q version of double stich positive and double stich negative. This arises from the fragmentary mention in 12:48 within the commentary of 12:46–50 on 12:44,45. The common "he who rejects" (*ho atheton*) of Q/Luke 10:16 and of John 12:48 might indicate this (Borgen, 1979–1980:28). But the verse is too fragmentary to be sure about it, and 12:48 might be just another redactional negation of 12:44 or 13:20 just as in 5:23 or 15:23.

(15) John 8:19; 14:7,9; 15:23. These four sayings lack any mention of "him who sent me" and this separates them from all other versions whether in Mark, Q, or John. Otherwise they are formally diverse. On the one hand 8:19 and 14:7 have *conditional*, while

14:9 and 15:23 have *participial* openings. But, on the other, 8:19 and 15:23 have object/verb//object/verb sequence, 14:9 has verb/object//verb/object sequence, and only 14:7 has some chiastic construction with verb/object//object/verb.

(16) Ign. *Eph.* 6:1. On his way "to Rome to be killed by the beasts in the amphitheatre," Ignatius, bishop of Antioch, stopped at Smyrna whence "he wrote letters to Ephesus, Magnesia, Tralles, and Rome, and later on, when he reached Troas he wrote to the Philadelphians, Smyrnaeans, and Polycarp the bishop of Smyrna." Concerning his death "there is a general tendency to think that Ignatius was really a martyr in Rome in the time of Trajan (98–117 A.D.)" (Lake: 1.166).

"Ignatius is exceedingly anxious in each community to strengthen respect for the bishop and presbyters" (Lake: 1.167), and this shows up clearly in the following injunction in *Eph.* 6:1 (Lake 1.178–181): "For everyone whom the master of the house (*ho oikodespotēs*) sends to do his business (*eis idian oikonomian*) ought we to receive as him who sent him (*hos auton ton pempsanta*). Therefore it is clear that we must regard the bishop as the Lord himself (*hōs auton kyrion*)."

Koester has argued convincingly that Ignatius of Antioch, like Clement of Rome, makes no use of any canonical gospel (1957a: 60–61,259). The version of Aphorism 61 in *Eph.* 6:1 is thus independent of the canonical gospels (1957a:40–42,259). It uses *pempei* for "sends," as in John 13:20, rather than *aposteilanta* as in Mark 9:37 = Luke 9:48 and Q/Matt. 10:40 = Luke 10:16. But it uses *dechesthai* for "receives" as in Mark 9:37 = Matt. 18:5 (= Matt. 10:40, despite Q) = Luke 9:48 rather than *lambanei* as in John 13:20. And, of course, it introduces the householder/household theme which also appears in several synoptic parables (Koester, 1957a:42). This latter image fits well with Ignatius' application of the aphorism specifically to the monarchical bishop.

It should also be noted, however, that this independent version is, in form, a single stich, with *a* construction, in reversed order (*sends/receive*), and, in content, it has Jesus-as-sender rather than God-as-sender. That is, just as in John 13:16, 20a, the protagonists are disciples/Jesus but translated, within Ignatian concerns, into bishop/Lord. Ignatius has, like John, moved the emphasis to Jesus-as-sender, to "Jesus Christ our Lord" (*Eph.* 7:2). But, in so doing, he has moved quite far from all the other *forms* of this saying known to us within the tradition.

(17) Scribal Emendation. The love of parallelism is also evident in scribal additions made to the gospel manuscripts. There are two very interesting examples.

(a) On Luke 10:16. I proposed earlier that Q's quadruple *aa'bb'* construction was shortened into Luke's *aa'b'* structure. Certain manuscripts have "corrected" this, but either into *aa'b* construction (Codex D), or else into full quadruple structure but now as *aa'b'b* (Θ Φ it syr^{sc}). (See Table 3.12.)

(b) On John 12:44. In the Sinai Palimpsest, the Old Syriac manuscript from St. Catherine's, that single stich *b* construction of John 12:44 becomes a *b'b* construction: "But Jesus cried out and said, he who is not like unto me is not like unto him that sent me. And he who believeth in me, believeth not in me, but in him that sent me" (Lewis: 249 and Appendix 4,x).

All of those should be considered as secondary emendations (Jeremias, 1964:16,36), that is, of "secondary analogous formulation, patterned on the one to which it is joined" (Stroker: 436–437).

(18) Conclusion. There are two clearly distinguished lines of de-

Table 3.12

(a)	He who hears you, hears me,	
(a')	and he who rejects you, rejects me,	
(b)	and he who hears me, hears him who sent me.	

velopment. (a) There is the pre-Markan double-stich positive saying in *ab* structure (*disciples/me//me/sender*) with the qualification, "not me but," and which also appears but in single-stich positive with *b* construction in John 12:44 (*me/sender*). In this line (i) the intrusion of the *child* in Mark 9:37 (from 10:15) = Matt. 18:5 = Luke 9:48ab and (ii) the creation of John 12:45 are redactional. (b) There is also the carefully balanced and intricately chiastic structure of a double-stich positive (*hears: you/me//me/sender*) and a double-stich negative (*rejects: you/me//me/sender*). This quadruple *aa'bb'* structure appears with three stichs intact for form and content in Q/Luke 10:16 (*aa'b'*), but with only the two positive stichs (*ab*) formally intact in John 13:20, while the disformed negative (*b'*) appears in John 5:23 (and 15:23). In other words both the pre-Markan and the Q forms reappear in John, but with some important differences. And in all of this special care must be given to formal considerations.

I propose three consecutive stages in the growth of the saying, and this leaves aside performancial variations and redactional creations. (a) First, there is the single-stich positive or *b* construction, but with negating qualification (*me, not me but/sender*). This is still visible in John 12:44 and is not chiastic. (b) Second, this is expanded into a double-stich positive (*ab: disciples/me//me/sender*), against a more missionary background. This is visible in Mark 9:37 (with *child* redactionally replacing disciples) and in John 13:20 (with disciples still traditionally general and impersonal: "any one whom").

Table 3.12 (cont.)

(a)	He who hears you, hears me,
(a')	and he who rejects you, rejects me,
(b')	and he who rejects me, rejects him who sent me,
(b)	and he who hears me, hears him who sent me.

Mark is not chiastic but retains the negating qualification ("not me but"), while John 13:20 lacks the qualification but has a chiastic construction. (c) Third, there is a stage that can be seen working in different directions. In a positive and intra-Christian development, there is a tendency to emphasize not so much God-as-sender as Jesus-as-sender. This is implicit, of course, in the aphorism's second stage, but it becomes externally explicit in the connection of Q/Matt. 10:16 = Luke 10:3 with Q/Matt. 10:40 = Luke 10:16 and internally explicit in John 13:20, more so in 13:16, and especially in Ign. *Eph.* 6:1. In a negative and extra-Christian development, against a background of missionary disappointment, and presumably *done separately in the Q and John traditions*, both the single-stich positive or *b* stage and the double-stich or *ab* stage develop negative counterparts, as *b'* or *a'b'*. Thus the single-stich positive of John 12:44,45 develops the single-stich negative of John 5:23 (verb/object//verb/object). And the double-stich positive, which remains at the second stage in John 13:20 (*ab*), now appears as the third stage in the double-stich negative of Q/Luke 10:16 (*a'b'*). But while Q continues and copies the intricate chiastic design of the double-stich positive and thus keeps the quadruple-stich construction together, John 5:23 (and see also John 15:23) has the negative or *b'* structure saying quite separate even if structurally parallel to the positive second-stich at John 12:44. One might see the negative and positive (in that order) coming together, but much changed and much later, in 1 John 2:23, "No one who denies the Son has the Father. He who confesses the Son has the Father also." Thus while second and third stages appear in Mark and Q respectively, all stages appear in John: (a) 12:44, and rephrased and abbreviated in 12:45; 8:19; 14:7,9; (b) 13:20; (c) 5:23, and so on into (d) 15:23, and even (e) 1 John 2:23. But it is especially that negating qualification, "not me but," present in Mark 9:37c and John 12:44, which both breaks the symmetry of the double-stich format and indicates that a single-stich format was most likely original.

In terms of the present chapter, then, the quadruple-stich formulation is not an original version whose dismembered parts are scattered as triple, double, and single stichs across the gospels. The original version was the single-stich or *b* formulation, but with negating ("not me but") qualification. Thereafter increasing parallelism took over the aphorism's destiny.

In terms of this book as a whole, there is one final point to be noted. Aphorism 61 appears as an isolated *aphoristic saying* in concluding frame to the *aphoristic discourse* in Q/Matt. 10:40 = Luke 10:16. It also appears within a redactionally created *aphoristic* story in Mark 9:36–37. But, as Borgen (1979–1980) has shown so clearly, John 12:44–50 has developed the *aphoristic saying* into a full *aphoristic commentary*. (a) John first cites one traditional version of the saying in 12:44. (b) Then he repeats it, but omitting the negating qualification ("not be but") in 12:45. This elimination brings the saying into closer unity with John's other version in 13:20, which also lacks the negating qualification (see also 5:23; 8:19; 14:7,9; 15: 23). Finally, (c) there is the appended *commentary* in 12:46–50. "The expository character of *vv.* 46–50 is seen from the fact that fragments from the Logion are paraphrased in a way that corresponds to Paul's paraphrase of tradition-fragments in I Cor. 11.27ff. and 10.16–17.21" (Borgen, 1979–1980:27).

All this tremendous activity, from gospel text to scribal emendation, and from aphoristic saying into aphoristic story and aphoristic discourse, begins from a single formulation: *He who receives me, receives not me but him who sent me.*

4

Aphoristic Compound

A fragment, like a miniature work of art, has to be entirely isolated from
the surrounding world and be complete in itself like a porcupine.

FRIEDRICH SCHLEGEL (Firchow: 189)

As Schlegel said, porcupines and aphorisms share a prickly isolation from the world around them. But as Schlegel did not say,
porcupines get on very well in pairs. And so also do aphorisms.

Bertil Gärtner used the term "compound texts" (40) for such
combinations of *two* sayings. What is of importance in such *aphoristic compounds* is that (1) the sheer juxtaposition often creates hermeneutical dynamics between the two aphorisms, and (2) verbal
and thematic osmosis often occurs from one aphorism into the
other. This is the phenomenon that concerns me in the present
chapter.

Gärtner exemplifies this process from *Gos. Thom.* 33, where "two
sayings have been coupled together, the latter interpreting the former" (41), as Figure 4.1. In that case two aphorisms, only one of
which is in Mark and both of which are quite separate in Q, appear
in close conjunction in *Thomas.*

Figure 4.1

Gos. Thom. {	33a = Aphorism 85: *Open Proclamation.* (Q/Matt. 10:27 = Luke 12:3)
	33b = Aphorism 74: *Lamp and Bushel.* (Mark 4:21 = Luke 8:16; and Q/Matt. 5:15 = Luke 11:33)

The difference between *aphoristic compound* and *aphoristic cluster* is basically quantitative. I use the former expression for combinations of only two aphorisms, and the latter for all combinations of more than two. The distinction is worth noting, however, since verbal, thematic, and hermeneutical interaction is much more intensive in the case of the *aphoristic compound*, and because of this it deserves special consideration.

The sequence of the examples given in this chapter evinces increasing complexity and importance within the aphoristic compound itself. The first example is quite deliberately chosen to link with the close of the last chapter, since it could be seen either as a quadruple-stich aphoristic saying or else as an aphoristic compound.

Aphorism 3: *Patches and Wineskins*

(1) There are three independent versions to be considered: (a) Mark 2:21–22 = Matt. 9:16–17; (b) Luke 5:36–38; and (c) Gos. Thom. 47b. (See Table 4.1.)

(2) Mark 2:19–22. The three aphorisms in 2:19–20,21,22 all involve *impossible combinations:* wedding and fasting, unshrunk with shrunk cloth, new wine in old wineskins. Despite their formal diversity, therefore, they do have a certain thematic unity and, indeed, one could claim that the "imagery of the parables continues the nuptial theme: it plays on the two essentials of a Jewish wedding, decent clothes and good supply of wine" (Muddiman: 279). However, the separation of 2:19–20 in Gos. Thom. 104 and of 2:21–22 in Gos. Thom. 47b, which agrees with the formal distinction of *dialogue* and *aphorism*, renders it quite possible that it was Mark himself who first united them in 2:19–22 (Kuhn: 89).

(3) Mark 2:21–22. The relationship of Mark 2:21 and 2:22 represents a more difficult problem since they appear together, *but in reversed order*, in Mark and Thomas, as in Table 4.2. Bultmann has said that "it is possible at least to ask the question whether Mk. 2:22 is an analogous formulation to 2:21" (86), following a "tendency of the tradition . . . when to a saying already in circulation a new

Table 4.1

Matthew 9:16–17	Mark 2:21–22	
And no one *puts* a piece of unshrunk cloth	No one sews a piece of unshrunk cloth	
on an old garment,	on an old garment; if he does,	
for the patch tears away from the garment,	the patch tears away from it, the new from the old,	
and a worse tear is made.	and a worse tear is made.	
Neither is new wine put into old wineskins; if it is, the skins burst, and the wine is *spilled* and the skins are destroyed; but new wine is *put* into fresh wineskins, and so both are preserved.	And no one puts new wine into old wineskins; if he does, the wine will burst the skins, and the wine is lost, and so are the skins; but new wine is for fresh skins.	

formulation (analogous formulation) is fitted and occasioned by it" (85). But in this case the answer should probably be in the negative since the point of the twin aphorisms is not *new vs. old* in both cases (against Bultmann: 98). The point of 2:21 is *unshrunk vs. shrunk* and while, presumably, the former would usually be newer than the latter, this is at most a secondary point: unshrunk (new or old) does not work with shrunk (new or old). Indeed, the combination of the categories of *unshrunk/shrunk* from the *cloth* metaphor with the categories of *new/old* from the *wine* metaphor has resulted in the infiltration (Mark), confusion (Thomas), and eventual domination

Table 4.1 (cont.)

Luke 5:36–37	Gospel of Thomas 47b(3–2)
No one tears a piece from a new garment and *puts* it upon an old garment; if he does, he will tear the new, and the piece from the new will not match the old.	
	An old patch is not sewn onto a new garment, because a tear would result.
And no one puts new wine into old wineskins; if he does, the new wine will burst the skins and it will be *spilled* and the skins will be destroyed. But new wine must be *put* into fresh wineskins.	And new wine is not put into old wineskins, lest they burst;
	nor is old wine put into a new wineskin lest it spoil it.

(Luke) of the latter over the former categories. Since this process shows up in all the versions available, it seems best to consider the two sayings as a *double aphorism* and so combined from the earliest recoverable stage of its transmission. In confirmation it should be

Table 4.2

	Matthew	Mark	Luke	Thomas
Patch and Garment	9:16	2:21	5:36	47b(3)
Wine and Wineskin	9:17	2:22	5:37–38	47b(2)
Drinking Old Wine			5:39	47b(1)

noted that the *Drinking Old Wine* aphorism is always appended *outside* and never inside the unity of the *Patches and Wineskins* aphorism: it is added *before* it in Thomas and *after* it in Luke, but never *inside* it.

(4) Luke 5:36–39. There is one final preliminary problem before turning directly to the double aphorism in *Patches and Wineskins*.

(a) There are five minor agreements (positive) of Matthew and Luke against Mark in this unit (Neirynck, 1974:73). Two are visible only in Greek: (i) *de* in Matt. 9:16 and Luke 5:36, but not in Mark 2:21; (ii) *ge* in Matt. 9:17 and Luke 5:37, but not in Mark 2:22. The other three are italicized in Table 4.1 above: (iii) "puts,"; (iv) "spilled,"; (v) "put." Alone, or even together, these five changes are such that they could be accepted as independent alterations although they already make one wonder if Matthew and Luke know here another version of Mark's unit. But three other points (b, c, and d, below) are even more important.

(b) Luke 5:36 begins with a special opening: "He told them a parable also."

(c) The rest of Luke 5:36 is quite different from Mark 2:21 and yet this does not seem to be clearly a Lukan redactional change (Hahn: 362).

(d) The combination of the *Drinking Old Wine* aphorism with that on *Patches and Wineskins* (in reversed order) in both Luke and *Thomas* can scarcely be coincidental. When these four points are taken together it must be considered as (i) *very probable* that Luke 5:36–39 has another version of Aphorism 3 besides Mark 2:21–22 (Schramm: 107–109), and that Luke's aphoristic trilogy (5:36,37–38,39) appears in an earlier version in *Gos. Thom.* 47b (against Schürmann; Dehandschutter); (ii) *slightly possible* that Matthew also knew this non-Markan source but decided to omit the *Drinking Old Wine* saying (see Schramm: 105); (iii) *barely imaginable* that this non-Markan source is Q itself. Only (i) can be accepted with any degree of certainty.

(5) Luke 5:36–38. The confusion of the *unshrunk/shrunk* categories from Aphorism 3a (*Patch and Garment*) with the *new/old* categories from Aphorism 3b (*Wine and Wineskins*) comes to consummation in Luke 5:36, which ruthlessly solves the confusion by rephrasing the aphorism completely. All mention of *unshrunk/ shrunk* is gone and the saying now states: no one tears up a new garment to get a patch for an old one because that results in a new garment ruined and an old one patched and mismatched. Quite true, of course, but also rather obvious. In this case Luke's non-Markan source is of little assistance in reconstructing the original.

(6) Matt. 9:16–17. Matt. 9:16 remains quite close to Mark but cuts back the categorical confusion somewhat by eliminating Mark's phrase "the new from the old." He also adds his own positive comment in 9:17b.

(7) Mark 2:21–22. There are two main features to be noted. The infiltration of categories from Aphorism 3b into 3a shows up in the sequence: "unshrunk/old" (2:21a) and "new/old" (2:21b). But there is also the concluding comment in 2:22b, which gives aphorism 3b the sequence: new wine/old wineskins//new wine/*new wineskins*. This second element is of special importance when Mark 2:21–22 is compared with *Thomas*.

(8) *Gos. Thom.* 47b (2–3). From the combination of Mark and *Thomas* there arises the strong possibility that this double aphorism was originally a double-diptych or quadruple-stich aphorism with each diptych in reversed parallelism (abb'a'). This must be considered not only for *Gos. Thom.* 47b(2) on wine (Turner and Montefiore: 65; and see especially Nagel), but for both *Gos. Thom.* 47b(2 and 3) on wine and on cloth (Quispel, 1957:194–195). Thus the double diptych involved (a) a combination of two metaphors: cloth-patching and wine-storing; (b) with a different set of categories for each; (c) in chiastic arrangement: unshrunk/shrunk//shrunk/unshrunk and new/old//old/new. Two processes worked upon this original structure: (d) an internal process whereby the new/old categories eventually prevailed over the unshrunk/shrunk, and (e) an external process that found it appropriate to retain the new/old

aspect but not the old/new side of each diptych. Finally, (f) the internal process has changed *Thomas* even more than Mark (where "unshrunk" is still present), but the external process, with its concern for Jesus as the new, has changed Mark and Luke much more than *Thomas* (where "old/new" is twice present). The only vestiges of this old/new still visible in Mark or Luke is its residue within that concluding and unnecessary comment about "new wine/new wineskins." But here, of course, old/new has become new/new.

The logic of this complete process can be outlined as in Table 4.3. Stage I is, of course, a hypothetical reconstruction to explain; Stage II, which can be seen in Mark (unshrunk/old and new/old// new/new); Stage III, which can be seen, with the metaphors reversed, in *Thomas* (new/old//old/new and old/new); and Stage IV (new/old and new/old), which can be seen in Luke.

The three stichs of the quadruple-stich (double-diptych) aphorism, which appear in *Thomas*, all append a reason for their assertions; that is, they note the disastrous consequences attached to contravening them. So also do the two parts of the four-part structure remaining in Mark and Luke. The reconstruction of the missing reason *may* be possible if it is residually present in Mark (that is, in so far as the two parts of the *Patch and Garment* aphorism have been combined into one there, as the *old wine/ new wineskins* was residually present in Mark's "new wine/new wineskins"). Thus (a)

Table 4.3

Metaphor	Categories	Stage I
Cloth-patching	Unshrunk	Unshrunk
	Shrunk	Shrunk
		Shrunk
		Unshrunk
Wine-storing	New	New
	Old	Old
		Old
		New

unshrunk/shrunk: patch will tear away; (b) shrunk/unshrunk: garment will get (worse) tear; (c) new/old: wineskins will burst; and (d) old/new: wine will spoil.

(9) Conclusion. The earliest recoverable saying is a double diptych whose twin metaphors (cloth, wine) use a set of categories in reversed parallelism: unshrunk/shrunk//shrunk/unshrunk and new/old//old/new. The point of the double aphorism is not the victory of the new over the old, but the impossibility of bringing together certain objects. The stress is on combinational impossibility, not on novel superiority. It is necessary to underline this combinational impossibility and not simply claim that "the theme is not old versus new but the danger of loss through thoughtless and inappropriate action" (Kee, 1970:20).

It is theoretically possible that there were originally two separate aphorisms, one on *Patch and Garment* and another on *Wine and Wineskin* brought together into *aphoristic compound*. But, lacking any textual evidence for this, I conclude that there was originally a quadruple-stich aphorism that presently appears as two stichs in Mark 2:21–22 and Luke 5:36–37, as three stichs in *Gos. Thom.* 47b. It was thus the opposite case to Aphorism 61. I have included Aphorism 3 here, however, both as a transition from the preceding chapter and more especially to illustrate the infiltration of one section into another which takes place both in double- or quadruple-stich aphorisms and also in aphoristic compounds.

Table 4.3 (cont.)

Stage II	Stage III	Stage IV
Unshrunk	New	New
Old	Old	Old
Old	Old	
New	New	
New	New	New
Old	Old	Old
Old	Old	
New	New	

Aphorism 97: *Treasure in Heaven*

Aphorism 98: *Heart and Treasure*

(1) There are two independent versions to be considered for Aphorism 97: (a) Q/Matt. 6:19–20 = Luke 12:33; (2) *Gos. Thom.* 76b; but only one for Aphorism 98: Q/Matt. 6:21 = Luke 12:34. (See Table 4.4.)

(2) Aphoristic Compound. I begin with Aphorisms 97–98 because they are a very simple case and involve no very important implications one way or another. The problem is whether there is a multiple-stich aphorism present in Q but abbreviated in *Thomas*, or, an *aphoristic compound* in Q which has not been created as such in *Thomas*.

Bultmann had already noted this problem and on a programmatic level. He says that there is "a distinct tendency in the tradition to combine different but similar sayings" (82), that is, in my terms, to create *aphoristic compounds* and *clusters* (see also Gärtner: 35–43). He considers that "it is possible" that Q/Matt. 6:21 = Luke 12:34

Table 4.4

Matthew 6:19–20	Luke 12:33	
Do not lay up for yourselves treasures on earth, where moth and rust consume and where thieves break in and steal, but lay up for yourselves treasures in heaven, where neither moth nor rust consumes and where thieves do not break in and steal.	Sell your possessions, and give alms; provide yourself with purses that do not grow old, with a treasure in the heavens that does not fail where no thief approaches and no moth destroys.	
Matthew 6:21	Luke 12:34	
For where your treasure is, there will your heart be also.	For where your treasure is, there will your heart be also.	

"could have been originally an independent maxim" (84). He also warns, however, that "in a whole series of these instances we are admittedly dealing simply with probabilities, or even bare possibilities. But it is a necessity of right method that we should be concerned with such possibilities, because the sure instances make the tendency of the tradition clear, and we still have to reckon with the tendency even when the sources do not permit of an unambiguous judgment. But it would be wrong even here to talk about a law that had no exceptions, for I should be far from denying that occasionally a saying has been abridged" (84).

Although it is probably more important to underline the ambiguity and fluidity between aphoristic sayings and compounds in these instances than to demand a certain decision in each case, I think that *Gos. Thom.* 76b, which has no mention of *Heart and Treasure*, tips the balance, but delicately, towards considering Q/ Matt. 6:19–21 = Luke 12:33–34 an aphoristic compound wordlinked together.

(3) Contexts. In Q's fourth and final section, *Jesus and Apocalypse*, with its inception at Aphorism 84 in Q/Matt. 10:26 = Luke

Table 4.4 (cont.)

Gospel of Thomas 76b
You too, seek his unfailing and enduring treasure where no moth comes near to devour and no worm destroys.

12:2 (see Appendix 2), there is a constant interaction of sapiential and eschatological motifs so that the former are taken up into an apocalyptic atmosphere. Notice, for example, the phrase, "therefore I say to you" in Q/Matt. 6:25 = Luke 12:22 (Polag, 1979:60–61), which links Aphorisms 89–92 with Aphorisms 93–96. This general *apocalyptic parenesis* would also indicate that Luke 12:33a is his own interpretation of the saying rather than the Q introduction.

The context in Gos. Thom. 76 makes the saying into an *aphoristic addition* appended interpretatively to the parable of *The Pearl Merchant*.

(4) Matt. 6:19–20. Matthew's text is a perfectly balanced doublestich negative/positive saying. This might recommend its originality (see Polag, 1979:60–61), but it might just as well recommend Matthew's own sense of poetic parallelism. The term *brōsis*, usually translated "rust" could also be taken as "worm," as in the RSV note (Sieber: 57).

(5) Luke 12:33 and Gos. Thom. 76b. Both Luke and *Thomas* are totally positive and lack Matthew's antithetical parallelism. Yet Luke has a parallelism of his own:

> (a)   purses—not grow old
> (b)   treasure—not fail
> (b′) no thief
> (a′) no moth

This version makes most sense of "moth," since if purses are eaten through by moths, their contents can easily be lost. *Thomas*, on the other hand, reads like the remnants of that parallelism:

> (a)   — unfailing
> (b) treasure — enduring
> (c) no moth
> (d) no worm

Although the precise word for "purses" (*ballantia*) may well reflect Lukan terminology (Sieber: 57), I prefer to consider Luke as the Q version, a tradition reflected more brokenly by *Thomas*. The fact that Luke's *thief/moth* and *Thomas*'s *moth/worm* appear in Matthew as *moth/worm/thieves* may indicate an independent variant there, rather than simple redactional restyling.

(6) Q/Matt. 6:21 = Luke 12:34. This Aphorism 98 has been word-linked chiastically into aphoristic compound with Aphorism 97: *treasure/where//where/treasure*. There is thus a closer linkage with the singular "treasure" of Q/Luke 12:33 than the plural "treasures" of Matt. 6:20 (note singular also in *Gos. Thom.* 76b).

(7) Conclusion. This first aphoristic compound is a very simple case of verbal and formal juxtaposition, but there is no infiltration of one aphorism into the other.

Aphorism 113: *Hating One's Family*
Aphorism 114: *Carrying One's Cross*

(1) There are two independent versions to be considered for Aphorism 113: (a) Q/Matt. 10:37 = Luke 14:26; and (b) *Gos. Thom.* 101, 55a; but three for Aphorism 114: (a) Mark 8:34b = Matt. 16:24 = Luke 9:23; (b) Q/Matt. 10:38 = Luke 14:27; (c) *Gos. Thom.* 55b. (See Table 4.5.)

(2) The Q Context. The Q parable of *The Great Supper* in Q/Matt. 22:2–10 = Luke 14:16–24 was already absorbed by Luke himself within the symposiac unity of Luke 14:1–24 (Meeus), but 14:25–35 is a quite separate unit. It is *possible, but not much more*, that Aphorisms 113,114,115 followed after Q/Luke 14:16–24 in Q (Taylor, 1953:30; Polag, 1979:70–71).

(3) Aphorism 113 in Q. In *form*, Aphorism 113 appears as a double-stich saying in Matt. 10:37 but a single-stich version in Luke 14:26. Because of *Gos. Thom.* 55 I think that the double-stich format was in Q (against Polag, 1979:70–71). In *content*, there are differences in the Matthean and Lukan versions concerning *verbs*, *members*, and *results*.

(a) The *verbs* are "loves more than me" in Matthew, but "does not hate" in Luke, and the latter represents Q (Bultmann: 160; Polag, 1979:70–71).

Table 4.5

Matthew 16:24	Mark 8:34b	Luke 9:23	Matthew 10:37–38
			He who
			loves father or mother more than me is not worthy of me; and he who loves son or daughter
			more than me is not worthy of me;
If any man would come after me, let him deny himself and take up his cross and follow me.	If any man would come after me, let him deny himself and take up his cross and follow me.	If any man would come after me, let him deny himself and take up his cross daily and follow me.	and he who does not take his cross and follow me is not worthy of me.

(b) The *members* have two pairs, "father/mother" and "son/daugh-
ter," in Matthew, but three pairs in Luke: "father/mother, wife/
children, brother/sisters." The first pair, "father/mother" was in Q.
The middle pair, "wife/children" is Luke's own addition, just as he
himself added "wife" to the family members of Aphorism 21 in
Matt. 19:29 = Mark 10:29–30 = Luke 18:29–30. The final pair
would have been "brothers/sisters" in Q, as still in Luke, and also in
Gos. Thom. 55. Matt. 10:37 changed Q to "son/daughter" as a
word-linkage to *his* preceding Aphorism 103 in Matt. 10:34–36 =
Luke 12:51–53.

(c) The *results* are "not worthy of me" in Matthew but "cannot be
my disciple" in Luke. Again in the light of *Gos. Thom.* 55 and 101,

Table 4.5 (cont.)

Luke 14:26–27	*Gospel of Thomas* 55	*Gospel of Thomas* 101
If any one comes to me	Whoever	Whoever
and does not	does not	does not
hate his own	hate his	hate his
father and mother	father and his mother	father and his mother as I do
	cannot become a disciple to Me. And whoever	cannot become a disciple to Me. And whoever
and wife and children and brothers and sisters, yes, and even his own life, he cannot be my disciple. Whoever	does not hate his brothers and sisters and take up his cross in My way will not be worthy of Me.	does [not] love his father and his mother as I do cannot become a [disciple] to Me. For my mother [gave me falsehood],
does not bear his own cross and come after me, cannot be my disciple.		but [My] true [Mother] gave me life.

I consider that Q originally had "cannot be my disciple."

Finally, Luke himself has made two small changes in Q, under the influence of the text and context of the Markan *Carrying One's Cross* saying. The Markan sequence is:

> Aphorism 114 (*Carrying One's Cross*): Mark 8:34b = Matt. 16:24 = Luke 9:23
>
> Aphorism 129 (*Saving One's Life*): Mark 8:35 = Matt. 16:25 = Luke 9:24

The conditional opening, "if anyone comes to me" (*ei tis . . . er-chetai*) in Luke's Aphorism 113 derives from the phrase "if any man would come after me" (*ei tis . . . erchesthai*) of Mark/Luke's Aphorism 114. Similarly, the intrusive phrase, "yes, and even his own life" in Luke's Aphorism 113 derives from Mark/Luke's Aphorism 129. Hence the original Q opening of Aphorism 113 was most likely participial, and had no mention of "one's life."

(4) Aphorism 114 in Q. The opening was relatival in Q/Matt. 10:38 (*hos*) = Luke 14:27 (*hostis*), despite Aphorism 113's participial opening in Q/Matt. 10:37 (*ho*), but was conditional in Luke 14:26 (*ei tis*). The *result* is "not worthy of me" in Matthew, but "cannot be my disciple" in Luke. Thus Aphorisms 113–114 are consistent, with "not worthy of me" thrice in Matthew, but "cannot be my disciple" twice in Luke. I consider that "is not worthy of me" was the original Q expression in Aphorism 114, but that there has been infiltration within the Q *aphoristic compound* as follows:

	Matthew	Luke
Q/Aphorism 113: "cannot be my disciple"	10:37 ↑	14:26 ↓
Q/Aphorism 114: "is not worthy of me"	10:38 ↑	14:27 ↓

This, once again, depends on considerations from *Gos. Thom.* 55 and 101.

(5) Aphorism 114 in Markan Context.

(a) 8:27–10:45. This wider context was already discussed above.

(b) 8:27–9:13. Recent redactional studies on Mark have argued for a chiastic structure in 2:1–3:6 (Mourlon Beernaert; Dewey, 1973, 1980). That former author has also proposed such an arrangement for 8:27–9:13 (Lafontaine and Mourlon Beernaert) as follows: A(8:27–28), B(8:29–30), C(8:31–33), D(8:34–9:1), C' (9:2–6), B' (9:7–10), A' (9:11–13). That chiasm depends more on content and concept than on form and word, so that one may well not be persuaded by it, as the authors themselves admit (545).

(c) 8:34–9:1. Those preceding authors are much more persuasive on the chiastic structure of this unit since they invoke verbal and structural criteria here (see Clark). I accept Aphorism 114 within their construction.

(6) Aphorism 114 in Mark 8:34b. The opening in 8:34a with its

"double group of persons" (Neirynck, 1972:109) is redactionally Markan (Pryke: 51,163) and this is the introduction for the entire Markan complex of 8:34b–9:1.

The aphorism is in *conditional* form, "if any man" (*ei tis*) and contains one element that could be Markan addition, "let him deny himself." This use of a "synonymous expression" (Neirynck, 1973: 103) would have intended to explain and emphasize the central image of cross-carrying. Its presence, however, actually weakens the image since it gives the hearer a degree of initiative and control over the process. Yet "the strangely incomprehensible and repulsive logion of Jesus" (Fletcher: 162–163) bespeaks a situation where something terrible is forced upon another.

Leaving aside this possible Markan addition, the aphorism is chiastically arranged in Greek: a(me), b(follow), c(take up cross), b' (follow), a' (me).

(7) Matt. 16:24. This is verbatim as in Mark, save that "come" replaces Mark's first "follow," which thereby spoils the chiasm but not the meaning.

(8) Luke 9:23. Luke also replaces Mark's first "follow," but, more importantly, he qualifies "take up his cross" with "daily." Like Mark's addition of "deny himself," this seems to increase the seriousness of the aphorism's demand and yet it actually has the opposite effect. The terrible once-and-for-all quality of cross-carrying has been diminished to become an image for daily abnegation (see Griffiths: 362–363).

(9) *Gos. Thom.* 55. The original *aphoristic compound* in Q involved a double-stich saying on *family* and a single-stich saying on *cross*. It would have looked like this:

> He who does not hate his father and mother
>   cannot be my disciple,
> and he who does not hate his brother and sister
>   cannot be my disciple.
> Whoever does not take up his cross and come
>   after me is not worthy of me.

Those twin aphorisms had already changed one another as Matthew and Luke rewrote Q, but an even greater mutual change occurs in

Gos. Thom. 55. Matt. 10:37–38 had retained three stichs, but Luke 14:26 had reduced the former double-stich saying to one. *Gos. Thom.* 55 also reduces the three stichs to two, but he does so by incorporating the *cross* saying within the second stich of the *family* saying:

> Whoever does not hate his father and mother
>   cannot become a disciple to Me,
> And whoever does not hate his brothers and sisters
>   [*cannot become a disciple to Me,*]
> And [*whoever does not*] take up his cross in My way
>   will not be worthy of Me.

Those lines in parentheses and italicized have dropped from *Thomas's* version in a different mode of amalgamation from either Matthew's or Luke's.

(10) *Gos. Thom.* 101. In all cases where *Thomas* has two or more versions of a synoptic aphorism, one is usually much more gnostic than the other. So also here. *Gos. Thom.* 101 "is a doublet of Saying 55. That part of its text which is parallel to the Lukan account of hating is almost identical with Saying 55. Its additional material seems clearly to be a more developed gnostic interpretation of the saying: hate this world, love the spiritual" (Sieber: 121). For my present purpose, it is less important to discuss this gnosticizing tradition of the triple-stich aphoristic compound than to note that, now, the *cross* saying has completely disappeared inside the *family* one, save for the common Coptic term behind "in My way" (55) and "as I do" (101). But *Gos. Thom.* 101 still retained the triple-stich format of the *aphoristic compound*. He even retained the double-stich parallelism of Aphorism 113, but the second stich is now in antithetical (*hate/love*) parallelism rather than in the original synonymous parallelism (*hate/hate*). *Gos. Thom.* 101 is a gnosticized redaction of *Gos. Thom.* 55.

(11) Conclusion. The double-stich Aphorism 113 (family) and the single-stich Aphorism 114 (cross) were formed into an aphoristic compound and came down as such to both Q and Thomas. There-

after there is steady unification. (a) In Luke's version of Q the *family* intrudes into the *cross:* "disciple" from the former replaces "worthy" in the latter. In Matthew's version the exact opposite takes place. Here the *cross* intrudes into the *family:* "worthy" from the former replaces "disciple" from the latter. (b) In *Gos. Thom.* 55 this process is intensified. The cross is now included within the second stich of the *family* aphorism. But it is still quite visible. (c) But in *Gos. Thom.* 101, the *cross* has almost totally disappeared within the *family* aphorism. It is but residually visible in the Coptic of "in my way" and "as I do" (55b = 101). Instead, *Gos. Thom.* 101, after retaining the first stich of the *family* aphorism, creates two new stichs as its gnosticizing commentary.

Aphorism 109: *Patriarchs and Kingdom*
Aphorism 110: *Gentiles and Kingdom*

(1) There are two independent versions to be considered for Aphorism 109: (a) Q/Matt. 8:11b–12 = Luke 13:28; and (b) 2 Esd. 1:30b,39–40; and the same two for Aphorism 110: (a) Q/Matt. 8:11a = Luke 13:29; and (b) 2 Esd. 1:38 (see Hennecke and Schneemelcher: 2.692–693). The sequence of motifs is so divergent that Table 4.6 does not attempt any exact line by line comparison.

(2) The Q Theology. Jacobson has proposed a basic understanding of Q based on (a) the Deuteronomistic and (b) Wisdom traditions but (c) united in a way unique to Q.

(a) In the Deuteronomistic tradition Israel's history is a persistent *rejection* of prophets sent by God to call her to repentance. The present call by John, Jesus, and the Q community is the final such call and the final such rejection. Thereafter there remains for Israel only *judgment,* and it is in this context that the example of the Gentiles is used as a last desperate effort to shame her into obedience.

(b) In the sapiential tradition Wisdom comes from on high to seek a dwelling place among men who will obey her. "In Sirach, the search has a happy ending; Wisdom 'pitched her tent in Jacob'

Table 4.6

Luke 13:28–29	Matthew 8:11–12	
There you will weep and gnash your teeth, when you see Abraham and Isaac and Jacob and all the prophets in the Kingdom of God and you yourselves thrust out. And men will come from east and west, and from north and south, and sit at table in the kingdom of God.	I tell you, many will come from east and west and sit at table with Abraham, Isaac, and Jacob in the kingdom of heaven, while the sons of the kingdom will be thrown into the outer darkness; there men will weep and gnash their teeth.	

(24:8) and found 'a resting place in the beloved city' (24:11). But the fragment embedded in 1 Enoch 42 repeats sadly that Wisdom was forced to return to heaven because she should find no dwelling-place among men" (Suggs, 1970:44). Q, like Prov. 1:20–33 before, follows that latter track, and Wisdom finding no resting place in Israel, returns whence she came and thereafter will *judge* Israel for that *rejection*.

(c) Those two traditions were already combined "by the Hasidic movement which, in the first half of the second century B.C.E., united several groups to form a common front against Hellenization and the deteriorating religious conditions, especially in the priest-hood and the urban population" (Jacobson, 1982:385). But within this general combining of traditions, it was the particular aspect of *Wisdom as sender of prophets* that represented the Q contribution: "Q is peculiar in having combined Wisdom motifs with the Deuteronomistic tradition" (Jacobson, 1978:234) since "the notion of Wisdom as sender of prophets as part of the Deuteronomistic tradition is not attested in pre-Christian tradition or elsewhere in early Christian traditions, even though the Deuteronomistic tradi-

Table 4.6 (cont.)

2 Esdras 1:30b, 38–40
But now, what shall I do to you? I will cast you forth from my presence! . . . And now, O Father, behold in glory and see thy people who come from the rising of the sun! To them will I give the dominion with Abraham, Isaac and Jacob, Elias and Enoch, Zachariah and Hosea, Amos, Joel, Micah, Obadiah, Zephaniah, Nahum, Jonah, Mattathias, Habakkuk and the twelve angels with flowers.

tion was adapted by Christians very early" (Jacobson, 1982:387). Thus Jacobson concludes that "particularly important to note are two passages (Luke 11:49–51 par; 13:34–35 par) which seem to give programmatic expression to the tendencies we have seen to be at work in much of the Q material" (1982:383). And it is precisely those two passages—that is, Aphorism 83: *Wisdom's Envoys* (Q/ Matt 23:34–36 = Luke 11:49–51) and Aphorism 112: *Jerusalem Indicted* (Q/Matt. 23:37–39 = Luke 13:34–35)—as well as the present Aphorisms 109–110, that raise the question of the relationship between Q and 2 Esd. 1–2.

(3) Q and 2 Esd. 1–2. "In the texts of the Latin Bible, the Fourth Book of Esra has two additional chapters at the beginning and at the end; these are missing in the Oriental translations. Chapters 1 and 2 are a Christian Apocalypse which is introduced in the MSS. before or after 4 Esra, and are known to some extent as the Fifth Book of Esra. Chapters 15 and 16 form an appendix" (Duensing in Hennecke and Schneemelcher: 2.689). That means that the Jewish apocalypse of 4 Ezra (Charles: 2.542–2.624; Collins, 1979: 33–34) is presently contained among the apocrypha as 2 Esd. 3–14. But "perhaps as early as the second century, a Christian editor prefaced

the Greek apocalypse with two chapters, which radically alter its tone. The basic shift is evident in the repeated assertion that God has forsaken Israel and given his name to other nations. . . . Mother Zion must take leave of her children permanently. . . . In her place is Mother church, who awaits her sons in the resurrection" (Nickelsburg, 1981:294). This Christian introduction in 2 Esd. 1–2 (= 5 Esra) "falls into two parts. The first turns against the Jewish people, the second is concerned with the Christians who must take their place. It is possible that in the first section material from a Jewish text has been used and has been worked over by a Christian hand (see 1.11; 1:24; 1.30 and especially 1.35–40)" (Hennecke and Schneemelcher: 2.689).

Stanton has proposed that "5 Ezra provides further evidence of the use of Matthew's Gospel by second-century writers" (67), that "the author of 5 Ezra has been deeply influenced by Matthew's Gospel" (70), and that "5 Ezra is probably directly dependent on no other part of the New Testament" (79). This is theoretically possible, but Stanton is very far from having proved his point. To prove *direct literary relationship* he would have to find *redactionally* Matthean verses or phrases in 2 Esd. 1–2. He speaks, for example, of Matthew having added 21:41b and 43 to Mark's parable of *The Wicked Husbandmen*, so that such verses are therefore redactionally Matthean (Stanton: 78). If he had found such verses in 2 Esd. 1–2, he would have had a strong point. But those Matthean verses are cited simply as a "link of continuity" between past and present, and this then is equated with 2 Esd. 2:10–12 where "the 'kingdom of Jerusalem,' 'mother of Jerusalem,' . . . passes from one people to the other" (Stanton: 78). I am not convinced, therefore, that direct literary dependence of 2 Esd. 1–2 on Matthew has been proved or even rendered strongly probable.

Jacobson has already linked Q and 2 Esd. 1–2 together (1978: 233):

> The Deuteronomistic tradition which plays so important a role in Q crops up elsewhere in early Christianity. A more advanced form of this tradition is found in Ignatius, *Mag.* 8:2 (cf. Acts 7:51f; GosThom 5)

where all the prophets are claimed as Christians or as spokesmen for Christ. Israel's resistance to the prophets is thus the struggle between Christianity and Judaism projected into the past. A more primitive form of the Deuteronomistic tradition—more akin to Q—presents the OT prophets not speaking of Christ but calling Israel to repentance. This more primitive form is found in 5 Ezra 1–2 (= Esdras 1–2); 1 Thess 2:15f (cf. Rom 11:3), and Barn 5:11.

The linkage is most likely to be explained by their common use of Christianized Deuteronomic traditions rather than by any direct borrowing by 2 Esd. 1–2 from Q, Matthew, or Luke. Myers (1974: 131) has noted that 2 Esd. 1–2 was "also keenly aware of contemporary thought and/or literature. A. Hilgenfeld has drawn up a list of what he refers to as citations from the New Testament though it is impossible to determine whether there was direct contact or whether II Esdras and New Testament writers drew upon floating sources."

It is, therefore, common Christianized Deuteronomic traditions that account for the quite specific contacts between Q and 2 Esd. 1–2 given in Table 4.7. Verbal and thematic parallels are specially evident between the Q/Aphorisms 83, 109–110, 112 and 2 Esd. 1:30 –40. It is quite clear that "the problems . . . of 5 Ezra [2 Esdr. 1–2) in relation to Q . . . require further investigation" (Jacobson, 1978: 214).

But, pending more detailed investigation, I do not think 2 Esd. 1:30–40 can be convincingly explained as simple dependence on Matthew or even on Matthew and Luke (see Stanton, 1977). I think, instead, that (a) the Christianized Deuteronomistic tradition is found independently in Q and 2 Esd. 1–2; that (b) it appears in Q as Aphorisms 83, 109–110, 112; that (c) in Q this was combined with the sapiential tradition and hence, in Aphorism 83, Wisdom speaks from the start of that tradition, just as in Aphorism 112 she speaks from its conclusion: She it was who sent those prophets to their death and it will be she who pronounces judgment on their murderers; that (d) there are allusions to Wisdom as Street Preacher (Prov. 1:20–33) and as Banquet Hostess (Prov 9:1–6) behind the sequence

Table 4.7

	Common Motifs	2 Esdras	Aphorism 83	
			Matthew	Luke
1	*Hen and Brood*	1:30a		
2	*Cast from Presence*	1:30b		
3	*Prophets Slain*	1:32a	23:34	11:49
4	*Blood Required*	1:32b	23:35a	11:50
5	*House is Desolate*	1:33a		
6	*Gentiles Coming*	1:38		
7	*Patriarchs and Prophets*	1:39–40		

of Q/Aphorisms 107–110; and that (e) Luke has preserved Q's sapiential allusions to a much greater extent than has Matthew: (i) compare Q/Aphorism 83 in Luke 11:49–51 ("Wisdom of God said, 'I will send' ") as against Matt. 23:34–36 ("I send") or (ii) Q/Aphorism 108 in Luke 13:26–27 ("We ate and drank in your presence, and you taught in our streets") as against Matt. 7:22–23 ("did we not prophesy in your name . . . ") but (iii) in Q/Aphorism 110 both Matt. 8:11a and Luke 13:29 retain Q's "sit at table," which recalls Wisdom's Banquet in Prov. 9:1–6.

(4) Aphorisms 109–110. As I mentioned above, there is a quite different sequence of motifs within Aphorisms 109–110 as given in Matt. 8:11–12, Luke 13:28–29, and 2 Esd. 1:30b,38–40. This sequence of motifs is given comparatively in Table 4.8.

(a) Luke and Matthew. The four motifs in Aphorisms 109–110 appear in Q/Luke as *1234*, but in Matthew as *4231*. That common *23* sequence indicates the basic Q sequence and I propose that it is Luke's *1234* that represents the original Q sequence and that Matthew's *4231* is his own redactional reversal of the first and last motifs. Why did Matthew do this? It is very clear that Matthew likes the expression "there men will weep and gnash their teeth," since he adds it on *at the end* of units in 13:42,50; 22:13; 24:51; 25:30. And in 22:13 and 25:30 it is preceded by "cast him into the outer darkness." Hence I conclude that Matt. 8:11–12 has changed the sequence in Aphorisms 109–110 in order not to begin with but to

Table 4.7 (cont.)

Aphorisms 109–110		Aphorism 112	
Matthew	Luke	Matthew	Luke
		23:37b	13:34b
8:12	13:28b		
		23:37a	13:34a
		23:38	13:35
8:11a	13:29		
8:11b	13:28a		

conclude with "there men will weep and gnash their teeth" (motif 1), and, in the process, he added in his own "thrown into the outer darkness." The Q sequence is Luke 13:28–29.

(b) Q and 2 Esd. 1:30b, 38–40. The motif sequence from Aphorisms 109–110 in 2 Esdras is *342*, since motif 1 is absent. This has the sequence *34* in common with Luke's *1234*, but the sequence *42* in common with Matthew's *4231*. I conclude, once again, that Q and 2 Esdras represent independent combinations of motifs from Christianized Deuteronomic traditions concerning rejected Israel's replacement by Gentile believers.

(5) Conclusion. Those motifs which were assembled in one manner by 2 Esdras into *You Cast Out* (1:30b) and *Gentiles, Patriarchs, Prophets* (1:38–40) were also assembled by Q, but into two different configurations—Aphorism 109 and 110—as in Luke 13:28 and 29. The Q *aphoristic compound* was facilitated by the word-linkage of "in the Kingdom of God." I would consider Q had "all

Table 4.8

Aphorisms	Motifs	Luke	Matthew	2 Esdras
Aphorism 109	(1) *Weep and Gnash*	13:28a	8:12b	
	(2) *Patriarchs and Prophets*	13:28b	8:11b	1:39–40
	(3) *You Cast Out*	13:28c	8:12a	1:30b
Aphorism 110	(4) *Gentiles and Kingdom*	13:29	8:11a	1:38

the prophets" as in Luke 13:28 against Matt. 8:11, since this is a very important point for Q: see Q/Aphorism 112 (Jacobson, 1978: 233–234; 1982:383). On the other hand, Matthew's "many" may well be originally Q, as a word-linkage with the opening Aphorism 106. Luke would have omitted it because it seemed a contradiction with the "few" of Q/Matt. 7:13–14 = Luke 13:23–24. But for Q the point of the aphoristic cluster is that there will be *few from Israel* but *many from the Gentiles* in the Kingdom of God.

In terms of the present chapter, then, the Q *aphoristic compound* in Luke 13:28–29 was rewritten by Matt. 8:11–12 into an integrated *aphoristic saying*. He did it so well that he has convinced many later

Table 4.9

Mark 14:21	Mark 9:42	Matthew 18:6–7	
. . . but woe to that man by whom the Son of man is betrayed! It would have been better for that man if he had not been born.			
	Whoever causes one of these little ones who believe in me to sin, it would be better for him if a great millstone were hung round his neck and he were thrown into the sea.	But whoever causes one of these little ones who believe in me to sin, it would be better for him to have a great millstone fastened round his neck and to be drowned in the depth of the sea. Woe to the world for temptations to sin. For it is necessary that temptations come, but woe to the man by whom the temptation comes!	

commentators that his is the original Q text (see Meyer, 1967:16 note 1; Polag, 1979:68–69).

Aphorism 119: *Woe for Scandal*
Aphorism 16: *Millstone for Scandal*

(1) There are three independent versions to be considered for Aphorism 119: (a) Mark 14:21 = Matt. 26:24 = Luke 22:22; (b) Q/Matt. 18:7 = Luke 17:1; and (c) 1 *Clem.* 46:8a; and two for Aphorism 16: (a) Mark 9:42 = Matt. 18:6 = Luke 17:2; (b) 1 *Clem.* 46:8b. (See Table 4.9.)

(2) Texts and Sources. There are two separate problems here. First, are we dealing with one or two aphorisms? With two separate

Table 4.9 (cont.)

Luke 17:1–2	1 *Clement* 46:8
Temptations to sin are sure to come; but woe to him by whom they come!	Woe unto that man:
	it were good for him if he had not been born than that he should offend one of my elect;
It would be better for him if a millstone were hung round his neck and he were cast into the sea,	it were better for him that a millstone be hung on him, and he be cast into the sea,
than that he should cause one of these little ones to sin.	than that he should turn aside one of my elect.

ones, as in Mark 9:42 and 14:21, or with one multiple saying, as in Matt. 18:6–7; Luke 17:1–2; and 1 *Clem*. 46:8? Second, how many independent sources are involved? Are there three: one in Mark 9:42/14:21, with this reappearing within Matt. 18:6–7 = Luke 17:1–2; another in Q, but also conflated within Matt. 18:6–7 = Luke 17:1–2 (Taylor, 1959:258; Polag, 1979:98–99); and a third one in 1 *Clem*. 46:8 (Lake: 1.88–89), which is not dependent on the intracanonical gospels (Koester, 1957a:16–19,23,259)? My working hypothesis, as suggested above, is that there are (a) two independent sayings and (b) three independent sources involved in this *aphoristic compound*.

(3) Forms. Sayings using the format: "better/for . . ./than . . . " are found both in the Old and New Testaments, for example, Prov. 15:16,17; 19:22; 27:10. In *form*, the New Testament examples are (a) introduced by terms such as *sympherei, kalon, kreitton, lysitelei*; (b) applied by a generalized dative personal pronoun; and (c) connected internally by *ē* or *kai mē*. In *content*, each "contains an exaggerated protasis and, when present, an admonitory apodosis which often is eschatological in nature" (Snyder: 120; see all of 117–120). It should also be noted that the complete form of "better/for . . ./than . . . " can be found side by side with an incomplete form such as "better/for . . . ":

    complete form: 1 Cor. 7:9;   Mark 9:42
    incomplete form: 1 Cor. 7:1,26; Mark 9:43,45,47

One cannot conclude, therefore, that the incomplete format represents a broken or disrupted saying. All of this is of importance for Aphorisms 119 and 16.

(4) Mark. As noted earlier, there are two separate sayings to be considered here: (a) Mark 14:21 = Matt. 26:24 = Luke 22:22 and (b) Mark 9:42 = Matt. 18:6 = Luke 17:2.

(a) Mark 14:21. The synoptic texts are given in Table 4.10.

I consider Mark 14:21 to be a Markan creation: (i) continuing his many mentions of Judas from 3:19 to 14:10,11,18,42,44; (ii) play-

Table 4.10

Matthew 26:24	Mark 14:21	Luke 22:22
The Son of man goes as it is written of him, but woe to that man by whom the Son of Man is betrayed! It would have been better for that man if he had not been born	For the Son of man goes as it is written of him, but woe to that man by whom the Son of man is betrayed! It would have been better for that man if he had not been born.	For the Son of man goes as it has been determined; but woe to that man by whom he is betrayed!

ing on "Son of Man" and "Man" here as earlier in 9:31 (Neirynck, 1972:183); (iii) specifying the more general core-saying known also in Q/Matt. 18:7 = Luke 17:1 and 1 *Clem.* 46:8a; and (iv) picking up its opening motif of *divine necessity* through "it is written." In form it is an incomplete "better/for . . ./than" saying but, as noted before, that does not necessarily indicate a broken or disjointed saying. This is especially true in the light of expressions such as, "It would have been better for them if they had not been born" in 1 Enoch 38:2 (Knibb, 1978:2.125), or "Woe to those who hear these words and disobey; it were better for them not to have been born" (*Herm. Vis.* IV.2:6). Mark 14:21 is followed completely by Matt. 26:24, incompletely by Luke 22:22, but not at all in John 13:18–20.

(b) Mark 9:42. There are two phrases in Mark 9:42 that deserve special attention.

(i) *"one of these little ones."* This phrase *(hena tōn mikrōn toutōn)* appears in the New Testament as follows:

(Mark 9:41) = Matt. 10:42
Mark 9:42 = Matt. 18:6 = Luke 17:2
                    Matt. 18:10
                    Matt. 18:14

That is, every single one of them derives either directly or indirectly from Mark. Direct derivation is clear in the case of Mark 9:42. And it is Matthew himself who added it to Mark 9:41 in relocating it to

Matt. 10:42. So also, it is Matthew himself who took it from Matt. 18:6 and repeated it twice in 18:10,14 as frames for the parable of *The Lost Sheep* in 18:12–14a (compare their absence in Luke 15:3–7). It is therefore Mark who introduced it into the synoptic tradition, but it is Matthew who expanded its usage (so Neirynck, 1966: 72). But why did Mark introduce it precisely here?

I have already suggested that Mark himself inserted the *child(ren)* from his 10:13–16 into the saying in 9:37 ("one such child," *hen tōn toutōn paidiōn*). And the word-linkage between this 9:37 and 9:42 was also already noted. But there seems to be more than mere compositional word-linkage at work between 9:37 and 9:42. In 9:37 the living disciples are told *positively and literally* to humble themselves before "one of these children," and in 9:42 they are told *negatively and metaphorically* not to damage "one of these little ones who believe [in me]." Thus 9:42 deliberately expands 9:37 from a literal to a metaphorical meaning and also balances a solemn positive with an even more solemn negative injunction concerning the relationship between disciples and believer. Pre-Mark probably read only: *hena tōn pisteuontōn [eis eme]*.

(ii) *"it would be better for him."* This is the same expression in 9:42 as in 14:21 (*kalon autǭ ei . . .*) and once again it is an incomplete version of the "better/for . . ./than . . . " construction. For 9:42, Matt. 18:6 (*sympherei autǭ hina*) and Luke 17:2 (*lysitelei autǭ ei*) have performancially varied openings. Note, however, the complete "better/for . . ./than . . . " constructions that follow Mark 9:42 in 9:43,45,47–48.

(5) Mark and Q. If Matt. 18:6–7 and Luke 17:1–2 are "conflations of material from Q and Mark" (Taylor, 1959:258, see also 1953:30), what exactly is from Mark and what from Q in this combination? Specifically, did the Q text contain any mention of the *millstone/sea* motif, or was this only in Mark?

Bultmann thinks that Q had the motif: "Matthew, who follows the Markan context, has first reproduced Mark's text in v.6 and then brings the surplus text of Q into v.7, while Luke uses only the Q text" (144; see also Manson: 138).

Neirynck, however, considers that Q did not have the *millstone/sea* saying but only the *woe* saying, since (a) "Luke 17,2 shows no specific similarity with Matthew 18,6, and negative agreements against Mark ('it is better' and 'to be thrown') only confirm that Mark 9,42 has been handled in two independent ways," and (b) "it is difficult to see in 17,1–2 a primitive connection because v.2b gives these verses a clearly edited character; the words 'than that he should cause to sin' limp lamely at the end and have been pushed out of their proper place by v.1c" (1966:70). Hence "Matthew and Luke both linked, each in his own way, the saying of Mark 9.42 with the apocalyptic saying from Q about the inevitability of scandal" (70).

I agree with Neirynck's analysis and consider, therefore, that the conflation is as follows:

(i) Q (*necessity/woe*):   Matt. 18:7b = Luke 17:1
(ii) Mark (*millstone/sea*): Mark 9:42 = Matt. 18:6 = Luke 17:2

That is, Matthew brings the Q text into the Markan context and so places Mark before Q, but Luke brings the Mark text into the Q context (see Appendix 2) and so places Q before Mark. This independent but common combination was facilitated, of course, by the common theme of *scandal* (i.e. temptation; tempting to sin; or causing to sin).

(6) Q/Matt. 18:7b = Luke 17:1.

(a) The redacted text in Mark 14:21 had three points: *necessity, woe, better unborn*. But the Q text in Matt. 18:7b = Luke 17:1 has only two elements: *necessity* and *woe*. Thus the *better unborn* motif was already omitted by the time the saying was included in Q. The woe, of course, can stand by itself quite well.

(b) There is a second *woe* saying in Matt. 18:7a with no Lukan parallel. This is not Q but a Matthean redactional connective between Mark in Matt. 18:6 and Q in Matt. 18:7b.

(c) Q/Matt. 18:7b had "woe to the man who" rather than Luke 17:1's "woe to him" (see Polag, 1979:74–75). Matt. 18:7b *might*

have had, and Q *then might also* have had, "woe to *that* man who"
(but see Metzger, 1971:44).

(7) 1 *Clem.* 46:8. The letter that opens with, "The Church of
God which sojourns in Rome to the Church of God which sojourns
in Corinth" has been traditionally attributed "to Clement, who was,
according to the early episcopal lists, the third or fourth bishop of
Rome during the last decades of the first century" (Lake: 1.3). "It is
safest to say that it must be dated between 75 and 110 A.D.; but
within these limits there is a general agreement among critics to
regard as most probable the last decade of the first century" (1.5).

Koester has argued most persuasively that this letter neither
knows nor uses the canonical gospels, so that the two formal citations of "the words of the Lord Jesus" in 1 *Clem.* 13:2 and 46:7–8
represent the redactional handling of extracanonical tradition, that
is, of sayings of Jesus transmitted independently of our intracanonical versions (1957a:4–23; 1957b:223–225; see also Mees, 1971).
Aphorisms 119,16 appear consecutively, therefore, in this independent 1 *Clem.* 46:8.

Two features of 1 *Clem.* 46:8 need consideration.

(a) The opening is very abrupt: "Remember the words of the Lord
Jesus; for he said, 'Woe unto that man'" (Lake: 1.89). This phrase
stands out in rather stark isolation as compared with the phrase's use
in either Mark 14:21 or Q/Matt. 18.7b. In other words, I am not
convinced that 1 *Clem.* 46:8a is a more primitive version of this
saying. There are three elements, albeit heavily redacted, in Mark
14:21 (*necessity, woe, better unborn*), but only the first two in Q/
Matt. 18:7b = Luke 17:1 (*necessity, woe*) and the last two in 1
Clem. 46:8a (*woe, better unborn*). I consider that the original of
Aphorism 119 included all three elements:

  (i) *Necessity:*   Mark (redacted!), and Q
  (ii) *Woe:*   Mark (redacted!), Q, and 1 *Clement*
  (iii) *Better Unborn:* Mark, and 1 *Clement*

It is the absence of (i) that makes the opening of 1 *Clem.* 46:8a so
abrupt, but it is also clear why it might have been omitted there.

(b) The two aphorisms are in *formal* alignment:

it were good (*kalon*) for him . . .	it were better (*kreitton*) for him . . .
. . . (unborn)	. . . (millstone)
than that (*ē*)	than that (*ē*)
he should offend (*skandalisai*)	he should turn aside *(dia-strepsai)*
one of my elect.	one of my elect.

I consider, therefore, that in bringing the two sayings into an aphoristic compound the motif of *offending one of my elect* has moved
from Aphorism 16 into 119. In terms of *content*, "one of my elect"
appears instead of the Markan "one of these little ones who believe
in me," and this was no doubt the pre-Markan text as well (see
Koester, 1957a:17 note 1; Mees, 1972:240–241). And that final
"turn aside" is probably a redactional replacement for the original
"offend," since Clement continues in 46:9 with, "your schism has
turned aside (*diestrepsen*) many" (see Koester, 1957a:17 note 1).

(8) Conclusion. There were originally two separate sayings that
were inevitably destined to be drawn together since they had the
same general *content*, against scandalizing (= tempting, causing to
sin, offending) and the same general *form*, complete or incomplete
versions of the "better/for . . ./than . . . " construction.

Aphorism 119 had three elements: *necessity, woe, better unborn*.
All three are repeated in Mark's creatively redacted 14:21, but only
the first two are in Q/Matt. 18:7 = Luke 17:1 and the last two in *1
Clem*. 46:8a. Aphorism 16 had two elements: *scandalize believer/
elect, better millstone*. These appear as *scandalize little ones who
believe, better millstone* in Mark 9:42 but, in reversed order, as
better millstone, scandalize elect in 1 Clem. 46:8b. Those two versions of Aphorism 16 represent, respectively, an incomplete and
complete instance of the "better /for . . ./than . . . " construction,
but I think it better to consider those as simple performancial variations.

Aphorisms 119 and 16 remained as separate sayings in Mark 14:
21 and 9:42. Only Aphorism 119 was in Q, but Matthew and Luke,

independently *but differently*, placed in *aphoristic compound* this Aphorism 119 from Q and 16 from Mark. They remained in both cases, however, quite distinguishable: Q is Matt. 18:7b = Luke 17:1 and Mark 9:42 is Matt. 18:6 = Luke 17:2.

Quite independently of all this, but under the same form/content attraction, *1 Clem.* 46:8 brought Aphorisms 119 and 16 together. In this version of the *aphoristic compound*, Aphorism 119 has lost its opening unit (*necessity*), but it has also received the element concerning *scandalize elect* from Aphorism 16. Thus the twin sayings are brought together in better parallelism than in the Q/Mark conflations created independently by Matthew and Luke. I do not consider it likely that Aphorisms 119 and 16 had already become an *aphoristic compound* in Q and thence into *1 Clem.* 46:8, or had already united in some common source for Q and *1 Clem.* 46:8. This is, of course, theoretically possible, but it does not seem warranted by the evidence.

The coincidences involved in the case of Aphorisms 119 and 16, from two separate sayings in Mark with only the former in Q, through independent but different formulations as an *aphoristic compound* by Matthew and Luke, and with another independent *aphoristic compound* in *1 Clement*, can conclude this chapter by underlining the powerful pull from one saying towards another materially and/or formally like it and thereafter the powerful osmotic influence of the one upon the other within an *aphoristic compound*.

5

Aphoristic Cluster

An aphorism need not be true, but it should surpass the truth. It must go beyond it with one leap.

You cannot dictate an aphorism into a typewriter. It would take too long.

One who can write aphorisms should not waste his time writing essays. Aphorisms call for the longest breath.

It is often difficult to write an aphorism if one knows how to do it. It is much easier if one does not.

KARL KRAUS (Ungar: 221)

A. TYPES OF CLUSTER

I use the term *aphoristic cluster* for the juxtaposition of three or more sayings into a small complex. In itself, therefore, an *aphoristic compound* is a minimal *cluster*. But I have treated it separately because mutual influence and interference is much more pronounced in the case of the *compound* than the larger *cluster*.

There are four different types of clustering to be considered and these types can, of course, be combined together. One can form *aphoristic clusters* by (1) *word*, (2) *form*, (3) *theme*, or (4) *structure*. These processes can initially be exemplified by a general discussion of the *Gospel of Thomas* and Q.

Robinson has shown that both these documents belong to the same genre and that "the trajectory of this genre of 'sayings of the sages' is traced from Jewish wisdom literature through gnosticism, where the esoteric nature of such collections can lead to the supplementary designation of them as 'secret sayings'" (Robinson and Koester: 71). Within that generic framework, Koester has suggested the following relationship: "Thomas does not use Q, but he does represent the eastern branch of the gattung [or genre] *logoi*, the western branch being represented by the synoptic *logoi* of Q, which was used in western Syria by Matthew and later by Luke" (Robinson and Koester: 136).

(1) Verbal Clusters. In this most minimal association, word-linkage alone connects the units. The classic example is the *Gospel of Thomas*. I am not presently concerned with how originally independent sayings are united *within* a given "numbered" saying, for example, the three units combined in *Gos. Thom.* 21. Rather is it a question of word linkage *between* "numbered" sayings. And my suspicion is that such word-linkage only occurred when and as the sayings, parables, etc., were first united into a written collection.

"The 'Sayings' follow one another without any thematic sequence; and thematically associated ones are separated within the collection. But quite often two consecutive 'Sayings' seem linked together by a word, which can be contextually quite secondary, but which appears in both" (Garitte, 1957:63). Examples of word-linkage, often more visible in Coptic, across two "numbered" sayings would be: 2–3 (rule/Kingdom); 7–8 (man); 22–23 (one); 25–26 (eye); 27–28 (world); 47–48 (two); 50–51 (repose); 55–56 (worthy/superior: see 111); 60–61 (Repose/rest); 61a–61b (*čloč* = bed/couch; "Salome said" starts a separate unit in 61b and should probably be numbered separately: see Stroker: 451); 64–65 (he sent his servant); 68–69a (persecuted); 74–75 (many); 83–84 (images); 92 + 94 (seek and find; is 93 part of 92?); 96–97 (woman); 99 + 101 (mother and father; is 100 part of 99?); 105–106 (son/sons); 106–107 (one); 108–109 (hidden); 110–111 (finds and world); 113–114 (Kingdom). All of these cases involve only two units of "Jesus said" differentiation. The only other examples of word-linkage involve four units: 58(life)–59(alive)–60(alive)–61(live); and 96–97–98–99 (Kingdom of the/My Father). It is already clear from this collection that word-linkage can be used as a simple scribal connection for *written* juxtaposition.

(2) Formal Clusters. In these cases sayings that are formally similar are juxtaposed. This also happens (but much less frequently) in the *Gospel of Thomas*. Beatitudes are placed sequentially in *Gos.*

Thom. 18–19 and 68–69a,b. Three parables with a very similar Coptic opening, "there was . . . a man," are so linked in 63–64–65; and three more parables with the opening, "The Kingdom of the Father is like" are linked together in 96–97–98. Similar formal clusters will be seen below in Q.

(3) Thematic Clusters. Verbal and formal clusters in *Thomas* do not have any close thematic connection save, of course, for the general theme of asceticism and gnosticism. But, as I shall propose in more detail below, the verbal and formal clusters in Q and Mark usually have thematic continuity as well. That is, their compositional juxtaposition and not just our exegetical imagination provides thematic integration. For Mark and Q, then, it is always a case of verbal/thematic or formal/thematic clusters.

I would also propose that, while the primary compositional unity of the *Gospel of Thomas* is purely verbal, that of Q is carefully thematic. Thus the mode of the smaller *aphoristic cluster* in *Thomas* or Q is also the mode of overall compositional unity for the two writings.

I agree completely with the position of Jacobson "that Q is a coherent document" (1978:17), and that "the relative compositional sophistication of Q becomes apparent when one compares it to the primitive structure of the Gospel of Thomas, which is a collection of largely unrelated sayings, each introduced with the stereotyped, 'Jesus said.' " (5). Thus Q was "apparently not just a random collection of sayings, but a carefully redacted composition produced some time after the middle of the 1st century A.D." (Koester, 1980a:112). Jacobson also proposes that "there is some development visible in the material, a development from John's opening warning to Israel to the view, expressed only at the end of Q, that Israel is being replaced by Gentiles"—that is, "if there was a plan to Q, it can be seen not in a narrative about Jesus but in an account of God's final controversy with Israel, beginning with John and ending with Gentiles streaming into the Kingdom" (231).

But not only is there a thematic unity to the smaller clusters in Q and to the overall compositional structure, there is also a thematic unity within the *four* major sections of Q. In 1937, Manson divided Q as follows (39–72,82,114):

(a) "John the Baptist and Jesus" (Q/Luke 3:7–7:35)
(b) "Jesus and His Disciples" (Q/Luke 9:57–11:13)
(c) "Jesus and His Opponents" (Q/Luke 11:14–12:34)
(d) "The Future" (Q/Luke 12:35–17:37)

Manson gave titles to his four sections and I have indicated the beginning and end of each section by using Q/Luke, although, of course, there is much more than Q present within each section. Forty years later, and on quite different analytical principles, Jacobson (1978: 24,127,156) also divided Q into four sections, but without using any titles: (a) Q/Luke 3:1–7:35; (b) Q/Luke 9:57–11:13; (c) Q/Luke 11:14–51; (d) Q/Luke 12:2–19:27. The two major differences are the question of where (b) ends and (c) begins, and of whether Luke 19:11–27 was present in Q.

My own proposal gives exactly the same four thematically unified sections as does Jacobson, but it underlines this by giving titles to those four units (see Appendix 2) and it maintains that Q concluded by moving directly from the double parable of *Pounds/Claimant* in Q/Luke 19:11–27 to the promise of Q/Luke 22:28–30.

In Q, therefore, thematic unity appears in the smaller clusters, in the four major sections, and in the overall compositional structure of the written document.

(4) Structural Clusters. In these clusters the unification is effected by an *external* construction that frames the originally independent aphorisms so that they appear as an integrated complex. I suppose one could consider the repetitive "Jesus said" of *Thomas* as an overall or large-scale structural clustering process. Similar structurally unified macroclusters can be seen in the ninth tractate (*Aboth* or "Fathers") of the fourth division (*Nezikin* or "Damages") of the *Mishnah* (Danby: 446–461). This tractate, which is also "called 'Pirkē Aboth,' or 'Sayings of the Fathers,' is a collection of maxims, mostly ethical and religious, uttered by Jewish teachers within a period extending from the third century B.C. to the third century

A.D." (Charles: 2.686). In this tractate the overall unification is effected by the repeated formulaic opening: (a) *Rabban* or *Rabbi* or R. plus the name, or else, *He*, followed by (b) *said* or *used to say*. At this point, such macrostructuring by means of minimal formulaic introductions is indicative of generic standing, as Robinson has shown so well (Robinson and Koester: 71–113).

My present concern is not, however, with such generic macrostructures, but rather with much smaller structural clusters, and here the best examples are in Mark (see C below).

B. WORD AND THEME

My first three examples are of *verbal clusters*. But, unlike such verbal clusters in *Thomas*, these also evidence a thematic unification.

1. VERBAL CLUSTER IN MARK 11:22–25

The cluster is composed of four aphorisms: (1) Aphorism 22: *Faith in God*; (2) Aphorism 23: *Moving a Mountain*; (3) Aphorism 67: *Ask, Seek, Knock*; and (4) Aphorism 65: *Reconciliation and Prayer*. The independent versions for these aphorisms are given in Table 5.1.

Mark 11:26 was "inserted by copyists in imitation of Mt 6.15" (Metzger, 1971:110), but Mark 11:22–25 were verbally linked together by Mark himself, as in Table 5.2.

I presume that it was Mark who first assembled this cluster and his primary change was to add to its theme of *prayer* the more basic theme of *faith* or *belief*. (a) His most important step was to create and prefix Aphorism 22 to the complex, thereby highlighting immediately the theme of faith. Notice, for example, how Matt. 21:21 inserts Mark's Aphorism 22 *within* the start of Aphorism 23 rather than independently preceding it. (b) He has also inserted the theme of faith ("believes that") into Aphorism 67, although it is not mentioned in any other versions of that saying. And his insertion in the form of "not doubt . . . but believes" is a "double statement:

Table 5.1

APHORISM	MARK			Q	
	Matthew	Mark	Luke	Matthew	Luke
22	21:21a	11:22			
23	21:21b	11:23			
67	21:22	11:24		7:7–8	11:9–10
65	6:14–15	11:25			11:4a

Table 5.2

(1) Aphorism 22	11:22			faith	
(2) Aphorism 23	11:23	I say to you		believes that	it will be
(3) Aphorism 67	11:24	I tell you	prayer	believe that	it will be
(4) Aphorism 65	11:25		praying		

negative-positive" (*mē-alla*) a characteristically Markan construction (Neirynck, 1972:89–94). (c) The given phrase, "I tell you" (*legō hymin*, without *hoti*) from 11:24 was added to 11:23, but rephrased in more Markan fashion as *amēn legō hymin*, now with *hoti* (see Pryke: 73–74). Finally (d) the given theme of "praying" (*proseuchomenoi*) in 11:25 was repeated into 11:24 as "in prayer" (*proseuchesthe*). In summary, then, the complex in 11:22–25 now underlines the Markan theme of "faith," which was inaugurally emphasized and programmatically announced in Mark's redactional 1:14–15 (see Kelber, 1974:13).

2. VERBAL CLUSTER IN Q/LUKE 6:43–45

The cluster is composed of five aphorisms: (1) Aphorism 45: *Tree and Fruit*; (2) Aphorism 46: *By Its Fruit*; (3) Aphorism 47: *Grapes*

Table 5.1 (cont.)

MATTHEW	JOHN	THOMAS	OTHER
18:19		48 106	Didasc. XV 1 Cor. 13:2 Ign. Eph. 5:2
	14:13–14 15:7 15:16 16:23–24 16:26	2 92 94	
5:23–24 6:12			Did. 14:2 Did. 8:2

and Thorns; (4) Aphorism 48: From One's Treasure; and (5) Aphorism 49: Heart and Mouth. The independent versions for these aphorisms are given in Table 5.3.

I consider that Luke presents the original Q sequence in 6:43–45 (Taylor, 1953:29; 1959:249; Polag, 1979:36–37). Matthew makes double use of the Q cluster, splitting it between 7:16–20 and 12:33–35, and redacting each usage extensively. But in Q the cluster was verbally linked as in Table 5.4.

The fact that Aphorisms 47–48–49 appear together in Gos. Thom. 45—that is, within the same "numbered" unit, the same "Jesus said"—indicates that Q did not create that threefold cluster. And the presence of Aphorism 45 in Gos. Thom. 43b may well

Table 5.3

APHORISM	Q			THOMAS	OTHER
	Matthew	Matthew	Luke		
45	7:17–18	12:33a	6:43	43b	
46	7:16a = 20	12:33b	6:44a		Ign. Eph. 14:2.
47	7:16b		6:44b	45a	
48		12:34b–35	6:45a	45bc	
49		12:34c	6:45b	45d	

Table 5.4

Aphorism 45	Q/Luke 6:43	for	tree/fruit		good(*kalon*)/bad(*sapron*)
Aphorism 46	Q/Luke 6:44a	for	tree/fruit		
Aphorism 47	Q/Luke 6:44b	for			
Aphorism 48	Q/Luke 6:45a			heart	good(*agathos*)/evil(*ponēros*
Aphorism 49	Q/Luke 6:45b	for		heart	

indicate that the entire fourfold cluster was already unified even
before Q used it.

3. VERBAL CLUSTER IN MARK 9:33–50

The cluster is composed of eight aphorisms: (1) Aphorism 14: *Leader as Servant*; (2) Aphorism 61: *Receiving the Sender*; (3) Aphorism 71: *For and Against*; (4) Aphorism 15: *Cup of Water*; (5) Aphorism 16: *Millstone for Scandal*; (6) Aphorism 17: *Against Temptation*; (7) Aphorism 18: *Salted with Fire*; and (8) Aphorism 115: *Salting the*

Table 5.5

APHORISM	MARK			Q	
	Matthew	Mark	Luke	Matthew	Luke
14	23:11 20:25–28	9:35 10:42–45	9:48c		
61	18:5	9:37	9:48ab	10:40	10:16
—		9:38–39	9:49–50a		
71		9:40	9:50b	12:30	11:23
15	10:42	9:41			
16	18:6	9:42	17:2		
17	18:8–9 5:29–30	9:43–48			
18		9:49			
115		9:50a		5:13	14:34–35a

Salt. The first two *aphoristic sayings* have been developed into *aphoristic stories* by Mark in 9:33–35 and 36–37. This is immediately followed by a *dialectical story* in 9:38–39 which I do not include in the aphoristic corpus but will consider here as part of the verbal cluster of 9:33–50. The independent versions of the units are given in Table 5.5.

The cluster is present only in Mark, and neither Matthew nor Luke accept it for more than three or four units. It is linked together verbally as indicated in Table 5.6.

It is clear that Mark himself considered the ninefold complex in 9:33–50 as a unit because of the redactional frames in 9:33 and 50b that he composed to hold it together. This raises two important questions for verbal clusters.

(1) Oral and Scribal Clusters. Does 9:33–50 indicate pre-Markan and even oral combination or could Mark himself use such a linkage as a redactional process? Taylor (1966:409) says of Mark 9:33–50: "Not to speak of the variety of the sayings, the structure of the

Table 5.5 (cont.)

LUKE	JOHN	OTHER
22:25–27	(13:4–17)	
	5:23 12:44–45 13:20	Ign. *Eph.* 6:1
		Oxy P 1224
		1 *Clem.* 46:8b

Table 5.6

Aphorism 14	Mark 9:33–35			
Aphorism 61	Mark 9:36–37 Mark 9:38–39			
Aphorism 71	Mark 9:40			
Aphorism 15	Mark 9:41			causes ... to
Aphorism 16	Mark 9:42			sin ... better causes ... to
Aphorism 17	Mark 9:43–48		fire	sin ... better
Aphorism 18	Mark 9:49	salted	fire	
Aphorism 115	Mark 9:50a Mark 9:50b	salt salt		

whole is artificial and must be set down to the work of a pre-Markan compiler who sought to assist catechumens in committing the sayings to memory." But Neirynck has warned against accepting this judgment too readily. "If the independent witness of Matthew and Luke collapses, it becomes difficult to prove that in Mark 9,33–50 we have a collection of sayings prior to Mark" since "we do not have the comparative matter which we need to detach the ordering of key words from the editing by the evangelist" (1966:67,68). I would conclude that it was Mark himself who first combined the nine units in 9:33–50, framing them as he did so with the compositional clamp of his own 9:33 and 9:50b and intensely redacting the entire complex in the process (see Fleddermann). Word-linkage, in other words, is a compositional device of Markan writing style, and also, indeed, of Matthew in 10:40–42 which is "a model of an editorial *linking up through the use of key words*" (Neirynck, 1966:72).

(2) Verbal and Thematic Clusters. It is clear, as already noted, that Matthew and Luke are not so impressed by the thematic unity of Mark 9:33–50 that they feel constrained to accept it as a whole.

Table 5.6 (cont.)

	for		discussed
one of these children	for	in (epi) my name in (en) your name in (epi) my name	
	for		
	for	in (en) the name	
one of these little ones			
			at peace

Does it actually have a thematic unity, or is it a mere verbal cluster somewhat in the style of *Thomas?*

This problem focuses on the relationship between Aphorism 17 and the rest of the cluster. With that aphorism the cluster seems to break in two: Before it, in 9:33–42, Jesus was discussing disciples and community; with and after 9:43, however, the emphasis seems to turn inward and personal. But is 9:43–48 to be taken hyperbolically and individually, or metaphorically and communally? In this discussion the *individual* usage in Matt. 5:29–30 must be ignored since the context there is clearly redactional. Koester (1978) has proposed that in Mark 9:43–48 "there is no attempt to relate it hyperbolically to the moral behavior of the individual. Rather, it is applied to the concept of the health of the community. . . . The image of the body as a communal metaphor is so widespread that one must assume that the saying of Mark 9:43–47 was originally designed to serve as a rule for the community: members of the Christian church who give offense should be excluded" (152; see also Hommel). In combining Mark 9:43–48 with the preceding units in 9:33–42, Mark is warning the community not only that it should expel certain members but that this applies even to the disciples themselves. Thus 9:43–48 is not a hyperbolic instruction for individuals but a metaphorical rephrasing of 9:42 for the community. This is indicated also by the structural parallelism between 9:42 and 9:43,45,47. If the leaders, the disciples, lead believers astray, they must be cut off from the community even though they are its hands, its feet, and its eyes. Thus the cluster in Mark 9:33–50 is both verbally and thematically unified, at least for Mark himself.

C. STRUCTURE AND THEME

A *structural cluster* is one in which an external framing device holds the independent aphorisms in present unity. My two examples are from Mark.

Table 5.7

APHORISM	MARK			Q		
	Matthew	Mark	Luke	Matthew	Luke	
74		4:21	8:16	5:15	11:33	
84		4:22	8:17	10:26		
6	13:9 13:43b	4:9 4:23	8:8b			
41		4:24		7:1–2	6:37–38	
132	13:12	4:25	8:18b	25:29	19:26	

1. STRUCTURAL CLUSTER IN MARK 4:21–25

The cluster is composed of five aphorisms: (1) Aphorism 74: *Lamp and Bushel*; (2) Aphorism 84: *Hidden Made Manifest*, (3) Aphorism 6: *Let Him Hear*; (4) Aphorism 41: *Measure and Measured*; (5) Aphorism 132: *Have and Receive*. The independent versions for these aphorisms are given in Table 5.7.

I have already discussed the overall Markan construction of Mark 4. The smaller cluster of five aphorisms in 4:21–25 is externally linked as in Table 5.8.

That construction indicates that Mark does not see this primarily as a cluster of five sayings, but as a parallelism of two newly composed units: (A) 4:21–23 and (A') 4:24–25. The theme of "hearing" is a verbal linkage between the two units, but the dominant linkage is structural rather than verbal. Indeed, Mark's new composition in 4:21–25 probably means that he is giving us five parables in 4:1–34:

Table 5.7 (cont.)

MATTHEW	LUKE	THOMAS	OTHER
		33b	
		5b 6b	
11:15	14:35b	8 21 24 63 65 96	Rev. 2:7, 11, 17, 29; 3:6, 13, 22; 13:9 *Soph. Jes. Chr.* CG III, 97:21–23; 98:22–23; 105:10–12; BG 8502, 107:18– 108:1
			1 Clem. 13:2
		41	

Table 5.8

(A)	"And he said to them" in 4:21a
	(a) Aphorism 74 (three strophes) in 4:21b
	(b) "for" connection
	(c) Aphorism 84 (four strophes) in 4:22
	(d) "Hear" *(akouetō)* in Aphorism 6 in 4:23
(A')	"And he said to them" in 4:24a
	(d') "Hear" *(akouete)* as Markan insertion in 4:24b
	(a') Aphorism 41 (three strophes) in 4:24c
	(b') "for" connection
	(c') Aphorism 132 (four strophes) in 4:25

(a) *Sower,* 4:1–9; (b) *Lamp,* 4:21–23; (c) *Measure,* 4:24–25; (d) *Seed Growing Secretly,* 4:26–29; and (e) *Mustard Seed,* 4:30–32 (see Lambrecht, 1974:303). There is, then, in Mark 4:21–25 both a structural and thematic cluster (see also Kelber, 1974:37–39).

2. STRUCTURAL CLUSTER IN MARK 8:34b–9:1

The cluster is composed of six aphorisms: (1) Aphorism 114: *Carrying One's Cross*; (2) Aphorism 129: *Saving One's Life*; (3) Aphorism 11: *What Profit?*; (4) Aphorism 12: *Life's Price?*; (5) Aphorism 89:

Table 5.9

APHORISM	MARK			Q	
	Matthew	Mark	Luke	Matthew	Luke
114	16:24	8:34b	9:23	10:38	14:27
129	16:25	8:35	9:24	10:39	17:33
11	16:26a	8:36	9:25		
12	16:26b	8:37			
89	16:27	8:38	9:26	10:32–33	12:8–9
13	16:28	9:1	9:27		

Before the Angels; and (6) Aphorism 13: *Some Standing Here*. The independent versions of the aphorisms are given in Table 5.9.

Although there are minor verbal links within Mark 8:34b–9:1, the major clustering principle here is structural. It is indicated in Table 5.10.

The cluster is structured as a miniature chiasm. And one notes especially that centrally poised "double question," a device common in Mark (Neirynck, 1972:125–126). It is therefore Mark himself who first united the cluster in 8:38–9:1. The preceding internal evidence is confirmed by external arguments. Three of the six sayings (Aphorisms 114,129,89) have Q parallels, but they are not combined together outside Mark. It is especially important to realize that even the combination of 8:34 and 8:35 is *not* present in Q, despite Matt. 10:38–39 (and Kuhn: 184 note 73), since they appear quite separately in Q/Luke 14:27 and Q/Luke 17:33. The thematic unity of 8:34b–9:1 needs no special comment (see Haenchen, 1963:96).

D. FORM AND THEME

In *formal clusters* the aphorisms are placed together because of their similarity in internal form. This was noted above for the form of

Table 5.9 (cont.)

JOHN	THOMAS	OTHER
	55b 101a	
12:25		
		Rev. 3:5 2 Tim. 2:12b

Table 5.10

	Aphorism	Mark	
a	114	8:34	and said (*eipen*) to them . . .any man (*tis*)
b	129	8:35	for whoever (*hos gar ean* and subj.) . . . for my sake and the gospe
c	11	8:36	for what . . . a man . . .his life?
c'	12	8:37	for what . . . a man . . .his life?
b'	89	8:38	for whoever (*hos gar ean* and subj.) . . . of me and my words
a'	13	9:1	and said (*elegen*) to them . . . some (*tines*)

Beatitude in *Gos. Thom.* 18–19 (two) and 68–69ab (three). My first example here is also *Beatitude*.

1. FORMAL CLUSTER OF BEATITUDES

Jesus' *Inaugural Sermon* in Q is still clearly visible in Luke 6:20–49 and to a lesser extent, because greatly expanded, in Matt. 5–7 (Taylor, 1953:29; 1959:249; Polag, 1979:32–39; Jacobson, 1978:46–66). It opens in Matt. 5:3–12 with nine beatitudes in a formal and synonymous cluster, while in Luke 6:20–26 there is a formal but antithetical cluster whose parallelism involves four beatitudes(B) in 6:20 –23 and four woes(W) in 6:24–26. Those openings are compared in Table 5.11.

How, in the light of these similarities and differences, did Q itself begin Jesus' *Inaugural Sermon?* That is, did Matthew add beatitudes and exclude woes, or did Luke add woes and exclude some

Table 5.11

Matthew	Beatitudes	Luke	Beatitudes	
B1Mt(5:3)	Poor	B1Lk(6:20b)	Poor	
B2Mt(5:4)	Mourning	B3Lk(6:21b)	Weeping	
B3Mt(5:5)	Meek			
B4Mt(5:6)	Hungry	B2Lk(6:21a)	Hungry	
B5Mt(5:7)	Merciful			
B6Mt(5:8)	Pure			
B7Mt(5:9)	Peacemakers			
B8Mt(5:10)	Persecuted			
B9Mt(5:11–12)	Persecuted/Reviled	B4Lk(6:22–23)	Persecuted/Reviled	

beatitudes? Bultmann's terse judgment that "I do not think these woes are a Lukan formulation, even if they seem not to have appeared at this point in Q" (111), is not exactly helpful. It is surely necessary to choose *one* of these options. Thus the first volume of Dupont's monumental study on the beatitudes concludes, although with very great caution, that the similarities stem from the four common beatitudes in their source (B1Mt, B2Mt, B4Mt, B9Mt), and that separate redactional activity by Matthew and Luke best explains the differences (1958: 341–344). While I appreciate Dupont's caution and recognize with Manson that "there is no entirely satisfactory solution of the problem" (49), I prefer, again with Manson, to presume, at least as my working hypothesis, that the four common beatitudes and Luke's four woes were present in Q (see Polag, 1979:84–85). I have two main reasons for this preference.

First, with regard to *form*, I consider that the *fourfold* balance of beatitudes/woes is not only directly visible in Luke but indirectly so in Matthew. Matthew redacted Q's parallelism of four beatitudes and four woes into two sets of four beatitudes. He indicated this balance of 5:3–6 and 5:7–10 both externally, by framing devices, and internally, by keeping the eight beatitudes in the third person. To complete the eight beatitudes he also had to create his B8Mt (5:10) as a doublet from Q's final beatitude which is still visible as B9Mt(5:11–12) = B4Lk (6:22–23). But in Matthew that ninth beatitude is in the second person (*este*) and so it is not so much one

Table 5.11 (cont.)

Luke	Woes
W1Lk(6:24)	Rich
W3Lk(6:25b)	Laughing
W2Lk(6:25a)	Full
W4Lk(6:26)	Praised

more beatitude as a transitional connective to the second person section in 5:13 (*este*) and 5:14 (*este*) which follows (see Dodd, 1955: 405; Guelich: 432). Matthew's structure is indicated in Table 5.12.

Thus Matthew's composition is less a set of nine beatitudes than a substitution of two sets of four beatitudes for one set of four beatitudes and one set of four woes. I emphasize that this is Matthew's *redactional composition* rather than that of his source (but see Michaelis).

Second, with regard to *content*, there are expressions in Matthew's beatitudes that can be interpreted as showing Matthean knowledge of the woes in Luke and therefore in Q (Schürmann, 1966:76–77; Frankemölle: 64). For example, three out of the four woes have similar (Greek) words in Matthew, as follows:

(1) $W_1Lk(6:24)$ "consolation" $= B_2Mt(5:4)$ "comforted"
(2) $W_3Lk(6:25b)$ "mourn" $= B_2Mt(5:4)$ "mourn"
(3) $W_4Lk(6:26)$ "speak" $= B_9Mt(5:11)$ "utter"
     $W_4Lk(6:26)$ "false" $= B_9Mt(5:11)$ "falsely"

It should be noted, however, that the presence of "falsely" in $B_9Mt(5:11)$ is textually doubtful (see Metzger, 1971:12–13).

Those two arguments are neither new nor absolutely compelling, and the presence of Lukan vocabulary in the woes might well weigh hard against them (see Fitzmyer, 1981:636). I therefore include the balance of beatitudes and woes in Q itself, but very tentatively.

Table 5.12

B1Mt (5:3)	Poor	"for theirs is the Kingdom of heaven"
B2Mt (5:4)	Mourning	
B3Mt (5:5)	Meek	
B4Mt (5:6)	Hungry	"righteousness"
B5Mt (5:7)	Merciful	
B6Mt (5:8)	Pure	
B7Mt (5:9)	Peacemakers	
B8Mt (5:10)	Persecuted	"righteousness"
		"for theirs is the Kingdom of heaven"

My present and immediate concern is with the formal cluster of four beatitudes in Q/Luke 6:20–23, which Matt. 5:3–12 expanded into a cluster of nine beatitudes. Their independent versions are given in Table 5.13.

It is quite clear that Aphorism 30 (the fourth beatitude) is quite different in length and content from Aphorisms 27–28–29 (the first three beatitudes). This may well be indicative of earlier stages in the Sermon's development, that is, of a fourth beatitude being added to an earlier unified triad (Strecker, 1972:202; Guelich: 420–421,432; McEleney, 1981:8). If that is correct, the present formal cluster of beatitudes may well have gone through at least three stages: (1) Pre-Q contained *three* beatitudes, as in Luke 6:20b–21; (2) Q contained *four* beatitudes, as in Luke 6:20b–23; (3) Matthew expanded this to *nine* beatitudes, as in 5:3–12.

2. FORMAL CLUSTER OF WOES

This cluster consists of a series of Woes in Aphorisms 76–82 climaxed by the saying on *Wisdom's Envoys* in Aphorism 83 (see Appendix 2). But the Lukan and Matthean versions of this series differ so much in *location*, *sequence*, and even *wording*, at times, that it might seem almost impossible to reconstruct any Q source for such diversified redaction. I agree with Jacobson, however, that "such an attempt at reconstruction may not be so hopeless as is often supposed" (1978:183). I would also note that the nature of the complex as a *series of Woes* tends to make absolute security about the internal sequence less important in any case.

Normally, one presumes that Luke better represents the Q sequence than does Matthew: "Luke has preserved the order of Q and has followed it with great fidelity" (Taylor, 1959:266). One would therefore conclude that the sequence in Luke 11:39b–44,46–52 is that of Q itself (see Polag, 1979:54–57). There are, however, two objections to that solution in this instance. (1) Matthew relocates these Woes into Matt. 23, which is a seried diatribe against the scribes and Pharisees, and it is thus not that clear why his composi-

Table 5.13

APHORISM	MATTHEW/ LUKE	BEATITUDE
27	B1/B1	*Blessed the Poor*
28	B4/B2	*Blessed the Hungry*
29	B2/B3	*Blessed the Weeping*
30	B8-9/B4	*Blessed the Persecuted*

tion there demands such changes of sequence. One would rather have expected the Q sequence to be still visible there despite all additions and insertions, just as the Q sequence of the great sermon in Q/Luke 6:20b–49 is still quite visible, despite all the expansions, in Matt. 5–7 (see Taylor, 1953:29;1959:249–254). (2) On the other hand, and this is much more significant, there are quite clear indications of Luke's redaction within this complex. There is a balanced composition as in Table 5.14. This composition balances three woes against the Pharisees with three against the lawyers (scribes), and it necessitates: (a) twin introductions in 11:37–38 (from Mark 7:1–5?) and 11:45, which have no Matthean parallels; (b) the non–Woe status of 11:39–41 as compared with Matt. 23:25–26; (3) the subordination of 11:49–51 within Luke 11:47–51 rather than as the climactic conclusion to all the Woes, as in Matt. 23:34–36.

In the light of these two objections, I consider that (1) Q contained a series of *seven* Woes against scribes and/or Pharisees, which led to a climactic aphorism on *Wisdom's Envoys* (Matt. 23:34–36; Luke 11:49–51); that (2) Luke redacted this into a quite different sequence, as just outlined; but that (3) Matthew retained the Q sequence in integrating it into his more massive composition in Matt. 23, while still reflecting the seried sevenfold construction of Q's Woes in his own sevenfold Woes at 23:13,15,16,23,25,27,29 (see Lührmann, 1969:43–48; Jacobson, 1978:183–188).

My working hypothesis, therefore, is that the Q sequence was as in Table 5.15 (see Jacobson, 1978:193).

Table 5.13 (cont.)

Q		THOMAS
Matthew	Luke	
5:3	6:20b	54
5:6	6:21a	69b
5:4	6:21b	
5:10		69a
5:11–12	6:22–23	68

Table 5.14

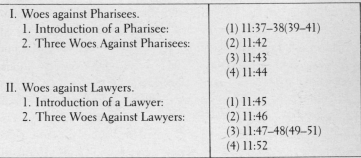

I. Woes against Pharisees.	
1. Introduction of a Pharisee:	(1) 11:37–38(39–41)
2. Three Woes Against Pharisees:	(2) 11:42
	(3) 11:43
	(4) 11:44
II. Woes against Lawyers.	
1. Introduction of a Lawyer:	(1) 11:45
2. Three Woes Against Lawyers:	(2) 11:46
	(3) 11:47–48(49–51)
	(4) 11:52

Table 5.15

Aphorism	Woe	Subject	Matthew	Luke
76	1	*Helping with Burdens*	23:4	11:46
77	2	*Honors and Salutations*	[23:6–7]	11:43
78	3	*On Hindering Others*	23:13	11:52
79	4	*Tithing and Justice*	23:23	11:42
80	5	*Inside and Outside*	23:25–26	11:39–41
81	6	*Like Graves*	23:27–28	11:44
82	7	*The Prophets' Tombs*	23:29–32	11:47–48
83		*Wisdom's Envoys*	23:34–36	11:49–51

This presumes a careful Q composition of seven woes leading up to the Wisdom oracle (see Bultmann: 113–114, as against Manson: 94–96).

Two further questions are, however, much more difficult. First, against whom were the accusations in Aphorisms 76–82 directed?

Second, were they in the form of Woes before Q's usage of them? Three of the aphorisms appear outside Q as follows: (1) Aphorism 77, Woe 2, is in Mark 12:38–40 as a warning against "the scribes"; (2) Aphorism 78, Woe 3, is in *Gos. Thom.* 39a as an accusation against "the Pharisees and the scribes," but possibly also in *Gos. Thom.* 102 as a Woe against "the Pharisees"; (3) Aphorism 80, Woe 5, is in *Gos. Thom.* 89 as an accusation against an unidentified "you."

The expected trajectory of change would have been from (1) scribes to (2) scribes/Pharisees to (3) Pharisees. Morton Smith has explained the "scribes" as "almost certainly a professional class, not a party," like the Pharisees. "They were authorities on the Pentateuch" and "many scribes may have made their living as upperschool teachers, others perhaps gave legal advice, and some were professional drafters and copyists of documents . . . the middle and lower-middle-class schoolteachers, lawyers, and notaries of the Galilean towns, dependent for their status on their limited knowledge of 'the Law,' and therefore devoted to 'the Law,' proud of their knowledge, and pillars of local propriety" (30). He also thinks that "their replacement by Pharisees in the later gospels may perhaps represent a social upgrading of Jesus' milieu as well as the introduction of opponents more important to the later church" (30–31).

With that *general* trajectory in mind, and agreeing that, at least in Galilee, "Jesus' original opponents were the scribes" (Smith: 1978:50), I would conclude that the Q series was (1) a formal cluster of seven Woes and that (2) it already combined both scribes and Pharisees.

Q's formal cluster of seven Woes was greatly expanded by Matthew. In terms of content, the Q sequence can still be discerned behind Matt. 23 (see Table 5.15). In terms of form, the sevenfold structure is also visible, but with different content at times, as the armature for the wider complex: see 23:13,15,16,23,25,27,29. Luke's redaction has developed the complex from a formal cluster into a predominantly structural cluster. This construction in Table 5.14 is very similar to the structural clusters just seen in Mark 4:21–25 and 8:34–9:1.

3. FORMAL CLUSTER OF APOCALYPTIC SAYINGS

There are two different forms to be considered here, and my own terms for them are (1) *apocalyptic sanctions* and (2) *apocalyptic comparisons*.

(1) Apocalyptic Sanctions. This is my term for what Käsemann has called "sentences of holy law." He argued that there is a form throughout the New Testament whose "protasis—sometimes a relative construction, sometimes a conditional, sometimes a participial—echoes the introduction of a statement of legal casuistry, while the apodosis is organized in the style of apodictic divine law" (1969:86). They are "distinguished in content by their combination of a basically apocalyptic outlook with an enthusiasm stemming from prophetic inspiration, in form by the eschatological future of the promise or the curse which follows in the apodosis on the frequently juristic formulations of the conditional sentences" (1969:93). There are sixteen texts involved, but only nine separate aphorisms: (a) four from Paul in Gal. 1:9; 1 Cor. 3:17; 14:38; 16:22; (b) two from both Mark and Q, in (i) Mark 8:38 = Matt. 16:27 = Luke 9:26 and Q/Matt. 10:32–33 = Luke 12:8–9, and in (ii) Mark 4:24 and Q/Matt. 7:1–2 = Luke 6:37–38; (c) one in Mark 11:25 = Matt. 6:14–15; (d) one in Matt. 5:19; and (e) one in Rev. 22:18–19. An example of the form would be that in 1 Cor. 14:38, "If any one does not recognize this, he is not recognized."

Four comments need to be made on Käsemann's analysis.

(a) The *jus talionis* or eye-for-eye principle whereby earthly act begets eschatological reaction is the heart of the form, and this is created primarily by having the same verb in protasis (active) and apodosis (passive). Chiasmus, for example, is only present in 1 Cor. 3:17 (Käsemann, 1969:67) and certainly should not be described as "the principal feature of the form" (Boring, 1976:272).

(b) The more imminently one expects the apocalyptic judgment, the more a present tense can replace the future of the eschatological sanction, as in Paul's four instances.

(c) The agent of the eschatological sanction is usually God, either directly named (1 Cor. 3:17; Mark 11:25 = Matt. 6:14–15; Rev. 22:18–19), or indirectly indicated behind an anathema (Gal. 1:9; 1 Cor. 16:22) or a passive voice (1 Cor. 14:38; Mark 4:24, and Q/Matt. 7:1–2 = Luke 6:37–38; Matt. 5:19). In one case the agent is the passive (Luke 12:9), the "I" of Jesus (Matt. 10:32–33), and the Son of Man (Mark 8:38; Luke 12:8) within versions of the same aphorism from Mark and Q (see Aphorism 89 in Appendix 1).

(d) Käsemann traced this form back to early Christian prophecy, adopting legal forms from the Old Testament in an atmosphere charged with apocalyptic enthusiasm. Others have proposed that "the *form . . .* belongs to the genre of sapiential exhortation in which the sanction corresponds to the action according to a law of immanent justice" (Hill: 271; see Berger, 1970–1971, 1972). That Käsemann's analysis is the more correct will be seen under (3) "Prophetic Correlatives" below.

(2) Apocalyptic Comparisons. This is my term for what Edwards has called "eschatological correlatives." He noted that there were four Son of Man sayings in Q that had a very similar format:

(a) Dialectial Dialogue (*Request for Sign*): Q/Matt. 12:38–40 = Luke 11:29–30.

(b) Aphorism 125 (*As with Lightning*): Q/Matt. 24:27 = Luke 17:24.

(c) Aphorism 126 (*As with Noah*): Q/Matt. 24:37–39a = Luke 17:26–27.

(d) Aphorism 127 (*As with Lot*): Q/Matt. 24:39b = Luke 17:28 –30.

That similar form involves (a) the protasis with "as" (*kathōs, hōsper, hōs*) and a verb in past or present tense, followed by (b) the apodosis with "so" (*houtōs, kata ta auta*) and a "will be" and the "Son of Man." Edwards proposed that this eschatological correlative "was created by the Q community to express its particular theological understanding of the Son of Man who is to come" (1971:54, see also 57,58). Its purpose was to create from biblical or natural experience a content for the imminent expectation of the Son of Man's return and especially of its judgmental aspects.

(3) Prophetic Correlatives. Schmidt has shown very persuasively that both Käsemann's "sentences of holy law" and Edward's "eschatological correlatives" are derived from the same, single Old Testament form, which he terms the "prophetic correlative." It is because of this suggestion that I have renamed the New Testament forms, at least for myself, as *apocalyptic sanctions* and *apocalyptic comparisons*.

For Schmidt (521) the "prophetic correlative" is composed of (a) the protasis with *kathōs* (*hōsper, hōs, hon tropon*) and a verb in past or present tense, followed by (b) the apodosis with *houtōs* and the same or equivalent verb in the future tense. Schmidt cites fourteen examples from Jeremiah(6), Isaiah(4), Ezekiel(3), and Amos(1), as well as two from the Pentateuch, all of which have both a correlative construction (*hōs, hōsper, katha, kathaper*, etc. . . . *houtōs*) and the same verbal root in protasis and apodosis—that is, the Old Testament form has the aspects of both New Testament forms. Apart from these sixteen examples of the combined format in the Old Testament, there are also four instances, from Isaiah(2), Ezekiel(1), and Obadiah(1), that have a correlative structure, but instead of a common verbal stem, they have *estai* in the apodosis, just as in the New Testament *apocalyptic correlatives* studied by Edwards. The two legal examples are especially instructive in showing how both apocalyptic sanctions and comparisons derive from legal/prophetic correlatives. The series of case laws in Lev. 24:17,18 concludes in 24:19–20 with, "When a man causes a disfigurement in his neighbor, *as he has done it shall be done to him*, fracture for fracture, eye for eye, tooth for tooth; *as he has disfigured a man, he shall be disfigured*." So also in Deut. 8:5, "as a man disciplines his son, the Lord your God disciplines you."

Schmidt agrees that both *apocalyptic sanctions* and *apocalyptic comparisons* were forms used by Christian prophets on the model of biblical prophetic language. "The prophetic correlative is usually found in the LXX in the context of *tade legei kyrios* [thus says the Lord]. Christian prophets would be expected to use the same formula. In Acts 21:10–11, Luke tells of a prophet who prefaces his utterance with *tade legei to pneuma to hagion* [thus says the Holy Spirit], and then makes a statement with *houtōs* and a future verb which is correlated to his symbolic act, described with the same verb" (520). Thus *sanctions* and *comparisons* are twin forms of New Testament prophecy based on a single Old Testament (LXX) model but looking now to an imminent apocalyptic judgment.

Schmidt also asks, "Is it correct to consider the 'eschatological correlative' a creation of the Q community? Hardly. Is the 'correlative' fundamentally distinct in origin and locale from the 'sentences'? On the contrary, both appear to be directly developed from the LXX prophetic correlative and both were used by early Christian prophets" (521). It should be noted, however, that the *apocalyptic sanctions* (or "sentences of holy law") appear in very diverse New Testament sources, while the use of *apocalyptic comparisons* (or "eschatological correlatives") is quite specific to Q itself. Thus, even if Q did not create the form, it was Q that used it with a very special emphasis within the New Testament.

(4) Cluster of Apocalyptic Comparisons. Aphorisms 123–131 (see Appendix 1) have such an agreement of *order and content* in Matthew and Luke that there must have been already an integrated apocalyptic discourse in Q (Manson: 141–147; Taylor, 1953:30; 1959:262–263; Polag, 1979:76–79). I consider that (a) Q *must have* contained at least the sequence of Aphorisms 123–124–125–126–127–130, (b) Q *probably* contained Aphorisms 128–130–131 in their Lukan rather than their Matthean positions; (c) Q also *probably* contained Aphorism 129 but *not* in its Lukan position; and (d) Luke 17:25 is the one unit that is *certainly* to be considered a Lukan redactional insertion into Q.

My present concern, however, is only with the formal cluster of *apocalyptic comparisons* composed by these three sayings:

(i)   Aphorism 125 (As with Lightning): Q/Matt. 24:27 = Luke
       17:24

(ii)   Aphorism 126 (As with Noah): Q/Matt. 24:37–39a = Luke
       17:26–27

(iii) Aphorism 127 (As with Lot): Q/Matt. 24:39b = Luke 17:28
       –30

The Q triad is maintained clearly in Luke, but is lost both internally
and externally in Matthew. It is lost internally because the As with
Lot Aphorism in Q/Luke 17:28–30 is reduced to a tiny remnant in
Matt. 24:39b. It is lost externally because of Matt. 24:29–36 (from
Mark 13:24–32), which is now inserted between the immediate Q
sequence of Aphorisms 125 and 126. But Q/Luke 17:24–30 is a
formal cluster of three apocalyptic comparisons.

(5) Cluster of Apocalyptic Sanctions. Aphorism 41: Measure and
Measured was mentioned above under (1) "Apocalyptic Sanctions."
My present concern is how other apocalyptic sanctions have been
composed in formal clusters with Aphorism 41 present as their climactic unit. There is no attempt, however, to make the preceding
apocalyptic sanctions match exactly the form of that climactic Aphorism 41.

(a) Mark 4:24. Aphorism 41 appears as a solitary apocalyptic sanction within Mark's careful composition of 4:1–34. The phrase "and
still more will be given you" (kai prostethēsetai hymin) was probably
added by Mark. It appears in Q as "seek his Kingdom and these
things will be yours as well (kai tauta prostethēsetai hymin) in Q/
Matt. 6:33 = Luke 12:31. It is possible that Mark knew a version of
this Q saying so that "the second part of this clause has been taken
over by Mark" and used to indicate "the abundant eschatological
reward" (Lambrecht, 1974a:290). Be that as it may, Aphorism 41
exists in Mark 4:24 as an isolated apocalyptic sanction.

(b) Q/Matt. 7:1–2 = Luke 6:37–38. The twin versions of Q are
given in Table 5.16.

Table 5.16

Matthew 7:1–2	
Judge not, that you be not judged. For with the judgment you pronounce you will be judged,	
and the measure you give will be the measure you get	

The Q text is actually a flat contradiction of the apocalyptic *jus talionis* or measure for measure, at least with regard to rewards. It is composed of: (i) four *apocalyptic sanctions* in twin negative (judge, condemn) and twin positive (forgive, give) parallelism in Q/Luke 6:37–38a; (ii) the inserted "over-measure" comment in Q/Luke 6:38b, which links and intervenes between preceding and succeeding sections—formally, it has four qualifications to match the proposed sanction, and, materially, it has "measure" to connect with 6:38c and "put" (*dōsousin*) to connect with 6:37–38a ("give," *didote*); and, finally, (iii) Aphorism 34 in Q/Luke 6:38c. Hence the basic complex is a fivefold formal cluster climaxed by Aphorism 34, a fivefold cluster of *apocalyptic sanctions*, but with the final one retaining its formal differentiation from the others.

All of this is much truncated in Matt. 7:1–2. Q's balance of two separate negatives (judge, condemn) and two separate positives (forgive, give) has been reduced to a single negative/positive parallelism (judge not/judge). But, in creating that new 7:2a, Matthew adapted it formally (in Greek) not to the preceding and parallel negative in 7:1 but to the succeeding Aphorism 34 in 7:2b. It is therefore only in Q/Luke 6:37–38 that one can still see Q's formal cluster of five *apocalyptic sanctions*.

Table 5.16 (cont.)

Luke 6:37-38
Judge not, and you will not be judged;
condemn not, and you will not be condemned; forgive, and you will be forgiven; give, and it will be given to you; good measure, pressed down, shaken together running over, will be put into your lap. For the measure you give will be the measure you get back.

(c) 1 *Clem*. 13:2. It was already seen that 1 *Clem*. 13:2 is not dependent on intracanonical sources (see also Stroker: 334–340). The text reads as follows (Lake: 1.30–31; numbers added):

   (i)   Be merciful, that you may obtain mercy.
  (ii)   Forgive, that you may be forgiven.
 (iii)   As ye do, so shall it be done unto you.
 (iv)   As ye give, so shall it be given unto you.
  (v)   As ye judge, so shall ye be judged.
 (vi)   As ye are kind, so shall kindness be shewn you.
(vii)   With what measure ye mete, it shall be measured to you.

Even in English translation, it is clear that (i)–(ii) have the same form (imperative with "that"), that (iii)–(vi) also have a similar form ("as . . . so"), and, once again, that (vii) is the climactic Aphorism 34 which has its own special format, different from (i)–(vi) but the same in 1 *Clement* as in Mark and Q. Hence the formal cluster of five apocalyptic sanctions in Q appears here as a formal cluster of seven. And their thematic unity is underlined by their introduction in 1 *Clem*. 13:1, "remembering the words of the Lord Jesus which he spoke when he was teaching gentleness and longsuffering" (Lake: 1.30–31).

(d) Pol. *Phil.* 2:3a. "Polycarp was the Bishop of Smyrna in the first half of the second century, and was martyred, in all probability, on February 23rd, 155 A.D., at the age of eighty-six" (Lake: 1.280). His "letter to the Philippians is, as we should say, a 'covering letter' for the copies which Polycarp sends of all the Ignatian epistles to which he had access" (1.280).

The text is as follows (Lake: 1.284–285; numbers added):

(i)   Judge not that ye be not judged,
(ii) forgive and it shall be forgiven unto you,
(iii) be merciful that ye may obtain mercy,
(iv) with what measure ye mete, it shall be measured to you again.

That text does not represent independent and extracanonical tradition, but represents an insertion and an alignment of *1 Clem.* 13:2 (*forgive, be merciful*) within Matt. 7:1 (*judge*) and Luke 6:38c (*get back/again, antimetrēthēsetai*) as the canonical wording begins to become more and more official (Koester, 1957a:13 note 1; see also 115–118 and 260). That is, just as Matt. 7:1 reduced Q's fivefold cluster of apocalyptic sanctions to only two, so Pol. *Phil.* 2:3a has reduced the sevenfold cluster in *1 Clem.* 13:2 to a fourfold one. But, once again, there is formal diversity within the preceding triad, yet the final and climactic Aphorism 41 is still in that position and still with its own special format.

In conclusion, then, and abstracting from the distinction between primary and secondary texts, the formal clusters of *apocalyptic sanctions*, although always climaxed by Aphorism 41: *Measure and Measured*, have either two (Matt. 7:1–2), four (Pol. *Phil.* 2:3a), five (Q/Luke 6:37–38), or seven units (1 *Clem.* 13:2).

6

Aphoristic Conclusion

Most smart sayings are derived from metaphor, and also from misleading the hearer beforehand. For it becomes more evident to him that he has learned something, when the conclusion turns out contrary to his expectation, and the mind seems to say, "How true it is! but I missed it."

ARISTOTLE (Freese: 409)

For brevity suits apophthegms and maxims; and it is a mark of superior skill to compress much thought in a little space, just as seeds contain potentially entire trees. Draw out the maxim at full length, and it becomes a lecture or a piece of rhetoric rather than a maxim.

DEMETRIUS (Roberts: 303)

For, as a valuable coin has greatest worth in smallest bulk, so effective speech would seem to indicate much with few words.

PLUTARCH (Perrin: 8.155)

A. APHORISM AS CONCLUSION

Besides being connected to a single aphorism as an *aphoristic compound* or to multiple aphorisms as an *aphoristic cluster*, the isolated aphorism can be connected in conclusion to just about any other linguistic form imaginable. A hint of this was already seen with Aphorism 6 above. The *Let Him Hear* saying was connected (1) to aphorisms, as their beginning in Rev. 13:9, their center in Mark 4:21–25, and their conclusion in Matt. 11:15 and Luke 14:35b; (2) to parables, as their conclusion, in Mark 4:9 = Matt 13:9 = Luke 8:8b (*The Sower*), in Gos. Thom. 8 (*The Wise Fisherman*), 21 (*The Ripened Grain*), 63 (*The Rich Man*), 65 (*The Wicked Tenants*), 96 (*The Leaven*); (3) to dialogues, introducing Jesus's response, in Gos. Thom. 24 and Soph. Jes. Chr. CG III, 105:10–12; BG 8502,107:18–

108:1 (Robinson, 1977:217,221); and (4) to "letters" as their conclusion, in Rev. 2:7,11,17,29; 3:6,13,22. An *aphoristic conclusion* is thus an isolated saying affixed terminally, for example, to miracles, prayers, parables, dialogues, and stories.

B. APHORISM AND MIRACLE

My primary example here is how (1) the *Beelzebul Controversy* that appears in both Mark 3:22–26 and Q/Matt. 12:22–26(9:32–34) = Luke 11:14–18 received, as *aphoristic conclusion*, both (2) Aphorism 69: *Your Sons* and Aphorism 70: *By the Spirit*, an aphoristic compound, in Q/Matt. 12:27–28 = Luke 11:19–20, and (3) Aphorism 5: *Strong Man's House* in Mark 3:27 = Matt. 12:29 = Luke 11:21–22.

1. THE BEELZEBUL CONTROVERSY

The *Beelzebul Controversy* and its aphoristic conclusions are found in both Mark 3:22–27 and Q/Matt. 12:22–30(9:32–34) = Luke 11:14–23. In this case the minor agreements of Matthew and Luke against Mark involve so many phenomena of both *order and content* that they indicate an overlapping of the two traditions (Neirynck, 1974:42 note 136). Indeed, it is almost a classic case of the overlap

Table 6.1

TEXTS ELEMENTS	MARK		
	Mark	Matthew	Luke
SITUATION			
ACCUSATION	3:22	9:34; 12:24	11:15
INTRODUCTION	3:23a		
ANSWER 1	3:23b–26		
ANSWER 2(Aphorism 69)			
ANSWER 3(Aphorism 70)			
ANSWER 4(Aphorism 5)	3:27	12:29	11:21–22
CONCLUSION(Aphorism 71)			

explanation (see Sanders, 1972–1973:460–461). The twin traditions are outlined in Table 6.1.

My present concern is not with the *dialectical story* of the *Beelzebul Controversy* itself. The complex of *Situation, Accusation, Introduction*, and *Answer 1*, in Mark 3:22–26 and Q/Matt. 12:22–26 = Luke 11:14–18, is "the basic section . . . the accusation and the twin images of a divided kingdom and a divided house, an answer in a form typical in Jewish debates. Admittedly it is possible that the saying in Mk. 3:23b–25 (as also the Q parallels) could have existed originally in isolation; yet there are no positive reasons to support this hypothesis, and it seems much more likely that the basic section is a unity" (Bultmann: 13). *Answers 2,3*, and *4*, however, are another question, since "we can clearly track the process of expanding an original apophthegm by the addition of particular sayings right back behind Q and Mark" (Bultmann: 14). My interest is with those sayings used in aphoristic conclusions to the *Beelzebul Controversy*:

2. APHORISMS 69–70 AS APHORISTIC CONCLUSION

(1) This is an *aphoristic compound* whose twin sayings are found only in Q/Matt. 12:27–28 = Luke 11:19–20. (See Table 6.2.)

(2) Aphorism 69 (Q/Matt. 12:27 = Luke 11:19). This saying,

Table 6.1 (cont.)

Q	
Matthew	Luke
(9:32–33)	
12:22–23	11:14
(12:25a)	(11:17a)
12:25b–26	11:17b–18
12:27	11:19
12:28	11:20
12:30	11:23

Table 6.2

Matthew 12:27–28	Luke 11:19–20
If I cast out demons by Beelzebul, by whom do your sons cast them out? If it is by the Spirit of God that I cast out demons, then the Kingdom of God has come upon you.	If I cast out demons by Beelzebul, by whom do your sons cast them out? If it is by the finger of God that I cast out demons, then the Kingdom of God has come upon you.

especially in conjunction with the succeeding one, often causes theological consternation. And this can hardly be solved by simply noting that they had "nothing to do with each other originally" (Bultmann: 162). More to the point is the question of Q's understanding of their present conjunction. Once again we are back, very much back, in the *earlier* Q wisdom theology. "It is certainly true that the juxtaposition of Lk 11:19 and 20 par jeopardizes the eschatological uniqueness of Jesus. But we have seen elsewhere in Q that this was apparently no problem. That is, where Jesus is understood as a messenger of Wisdom, such ideas as this are possible" (Jacobson, 1978:165). Or, again: "That Wisdom sends prophets is not, however, the only way of speaking of the prophets or messengers to Israel. Thus in Lk 11:19f par, we meet the idea that the Kingdom of God comes to expression not only in Jesus but in the Jewish exorcists. Likewise, Lk 11:29–32 par speaks both of the *kerygma* of Jonah and the *sophia* of Solomon. All of these are manifestations of God's reaching out to his people through envoys of various kinds" (1978: 227–228).

(3) Aphorism 70 (Q/Matt. 12:28 = Luke 11:20). This saying "can, in my view, claim the highest degree of authenticity which we can make for any saying of Jesus: it is full of that feeling of eschatological power which must have characterized the activity of Jesus" (Bultmann: 162). And after that, discussions of this aphorism usually emphasized the stratum of the historical Jesus, especially after Dodd connected the unit with realized eschatology (see Berkey). My present

interest is only with its function within an *aphoristic compound* and as an *aphoristic conclusion* to Q's *Beelzebul Controversy*.

The Q conjunction is underlined by three formal correspondences:

Aphorism 69: "if . . . by *(en)* . . . I cast out demons
Aphorism 70: "if . . . by *(en)* . . . I cast out demons

None of this, of course, denies that the two aphorisms were *originally* distinct: the "come upon *you*" is inappropriate for Jesus' opponents (Jacobson, 1978:164). But, for Q, exorcisms both by Jesus and by others are of God: "The Spirit of God is at work in both. What is said here is also found in Lk 12:10 par where it is said that blasphemy against the Son of Man is forgiveable, but not blasphemy against the Spirit" (Jacobson, 1978:165). And that comment raises the question of the saying's content in Q. Was it "Spirit" or "finger" in Q? Has Matt. 12:28 or Luke 11:20 better preserved the Q text?

Manson's answer was that " 'Finger of God' (Lk.) is the true Q text altered by Mt. to 'spirit of God' " (86). But, although this seems obvious and persuasive, it has been repeatedly challenged.

(a) After an analysis of Matthew and Luke's reaction to "Spirit" in Mark or Q, Rodd concluded that "Matthew keeps close to his sources and *never* in the passages examined *adds* references to the Holy Spirit. On the other hand Luke both adds such references, *and deletes them*" (158).

(b) Against the Old Testament background, Hamerton-Kelly concluded that " 'finger of God' is a variation of 'hand of God' which is of no consequence to the idea being communicated" (1964–1965: 168), and considered that Luke has changed Q towards this Old Testament metaphor.

(c) More especially, George points to the phrase "finger of God" in the context of Moses' miracles in Exod. 8:15[19], and concluded that Luke had changed Q towards this biblical prototype. He noted, moreover that just as Luke alone used this metaphor in the New Testament, so he alone used "hand of God" and "arm of God" (1966:462).

The final question is, even granted this penchant for biblicizing, *why* would Luke decide to change the Q text *here*? Among other reasons, that very conjunction of Aphorisms 69 and 70, giving the Spirit alike to Jesus and to other Jewish exorcists, would have "conflicted with his carefully thought-out pneumatology" (Meyer, 1967: 71 note 1). But, if inappropriate for Luke's thought, it is completely appropriate to Q's *earlier* wisdom theology to suggest that Spirit-Wisdom sent *many* messengers, many others besides Jesus himself.

3. Aphorism 5 as Aphoristic Conclusion

This saying is found both in Mark 3:27 = Matt. 12:29 = Luke 11:21–22 and in *Gos. Thom.* 35. That represents, however, a conclusion concerning the aphorism's absence from Q. (See Table 6.3.)

(1) Mark and Q? As Bultmann already noted (14), there was a very strong and early tendency to append *aphoristic conclusions* to the *dialectical story* of the *Beelzebul Controversy*. These appear as

Table 6.3

Matthew 12:29	Mark 3:27	
Or how can one enter a strong man's house	But no one can enter a strong man's house	
and plunder his goods,	and plunder his goods,	
unless he first binds the strong man?	unless he first binds the strong man;	
Then indeed he may plunder his house.	then indeed he may plunder his house.	

Answers 2 and 3 in Q and as *Answer* 4 in Mark. But was *Answer* 4 in Q as well as in Mark, and, if so, is it still to be seen in Luke 11:21–22?

Bultmann (13–14) considered it as part of a continuing Mark and Q overlap: "the same tendency to coalescence had combined it with the original apophthegm also in Q . . . though only after two other originally unattached sayings had been added." So also does Manson, if more cautiously: "We may therefore, though with some hesitation, assign Lk. 11:21f. to Q, and assume that the two replies had got together at a stage in the tradition anterior to Mk. and Q" (85). Finally, Polag considers almost the entire text of Luke 11:21–22 as Q (1977:42; 1979:52–53). None of this of course, is impossible or even unlikely. But (a) Matt. 12:29 follows Mark 3:27 so very closely and (b) Matt. 12:29 and Luke 11:21–22 fail so completely to agree with one another against Mark 3:27 that I prefer to consider that Luke 11:21–22 is not from Q, or even from some independent Lukan source (so Lührmann, 1969:33), but rather that "Q did not contain the parable of the strong man bound" (Jacobson, 1978:163) so that here "Luke has simply expanded on Mark" (Meyer, 1967:71 note 1).

Table 6.3 (cont.)

Luke 11:21–22	*Gospel of Thomas* 35
	It is not possible for anyone to enter the house of a strong man
When a strong man, fully armed, guards his own palace, his goods are in peace; but when	and take it by force
one stronger than he assails him and overcomes him, he takes away his armor in which he trusted,	unless he binds his hands;
and divides his spoil	then he will (be able to) ransack his house.

(2) Mark 3:27. This, then, is the only version of Aphorism 5 in the synoptic tradition. It is kept to fairly minimal format and concerns a general situation: "no one can."

(3) Matt. 12:29. Matthew's content stays extremely close to his Markan source. But, formally, he changed it into a question beginning with "how" (*pōs*). Thus Matthew smoothes his conflation of *Answer* 1 from Q in Matt. 12:26 = Luke 11:18, which is a question beginning with "how" (*pōs*), with this *Answer* 4 from Mark.

(4) *Gos. Thom.* 35. This version is extremely close to Mark 3:27, much more than to Matt. 12:29 (against Schrage: 87). With regard to *form*, (a) the external format is assertion rather than question in Mark and *Thomas*, against Matthew; (b) the internal format has three sections: general negation ("not"/"no one"), specific exception ("unless"), direct result ("then"), in Mark and *Thomas*, but only the last two in Matthew. With regard to *content*, and allowing for the syntactical and translational differences between Greek and Coptic, the main differences are that *Thomas* lacks "his goods" and "first" but contains "his hands," as against Mark. The Coptic text is ambiguous on the object of the intruder's force: "him (*or:* it)" in Guillaumont (1959:23), "it (*or:* him)" in Wilson (Hennecke and Schneemelcher:1.515). But the meaning seems to demand the translation "take it by force," as in Lambdin (122), and this is again close to Mark. In summary, then, the differences between Mark and *Thomas* are performancial variations in content within a remarkably similar format.

(5) Luke 11:21–22. This version is totally different from Mark/ *Thomas* in both form and content (Bartsch, 1959–1960:255–256, as against Quispel, 1958–1959:280–281). The emphasis here has shifted (a) from a general negative ("no one can") to a specific positive ("when one stronger") and, even more importantly, (b) this stronger one's actions are detailed over four steps: (i) "assails," (ii) "overcomes," (iii) "takes away his armor," and (iv) "divides his spoil." As suggested earlier, "Luke has rewritten the (Markan) parable of the strong man" (Jacobson, 1978:158). This is indicated both by the Lukan vocabulary (Jacobson, 1978:196 note 2; Légasse,

1962) and also by the fact that "the resulting parable bears formal resemblances to Lk 11:24–26 (both begin: *hotan . . .* and both are of similar length)" (Jacobson, 1978:158).

(6) Conclusion. The *dialectical story* of the *Beelzebul Controversy* is present in both Mark and Q. In Mark it received Aphorism 5 as *aphoristic conclusion*, but this appears as an isolated saying in *Gos. Thom.* 35. In Q it received the *aphoristic compound* of Aphorisms 69–70 as a first *aphoristic conclusion* and then as a final one, Aphorism 71: *For and Against* in Q/Matt. 12:30 = Luke 11:23. Both Matthew and Luke make the obvious but independent decision to combine the two versions of the *Beelzebul Controversy* so that now it concludes with an *aphoristic cluster* of Aphorisms 69–70–5–71 in their accounts.

C. APHORISM AND PRAYER

1. APHORISM 62 AS APHORISTIC CONCLUSION

(1) My primary example is Aphorism 62: *Father and Son* in Q/Matt. 11:27 = Luke 10:22, which appears there as the *aphoristic conclusion* of Jesus' prayer in Q/Matt. 11:25–26 = Luke 10:21. (See Table 6.4.)

(2) The Q Context. This requires consideration of the following four units (see Appendix 2):

Table 6.4

Matthew 11:25–27	Luke 10:21–22
I thank thee, Father, Lord of heaven and earth, that thou hast hidden these things from the wise and understanding and revealed them to babes; yea, Father, for such was thy gracious will.	I thank thee, Father, Lord of heaven and earth, that thou hast hidden these things from the wise and understanding and revealed them to babes; yea, Father, for such was thy gracious will.
All things have been delivered to me by my Father; and no one knows the Son except the Father, and no one knows the Father except the Son and any one to whom the Son chooses to reveal him.	All things have been delivered to me by my Father; and no one knows who the Son is except the Father, or who the Father is except the Son and any one to whom the Son chooses to reveal him.

(a)	*Revelation to Babes*	Matt. 11:25–26	= Luke 10:21
(b)	*Father and Son*	Matt. 11:27	= Luke 10:22
(c)	*Blessed the Eyes*	Matt. 13:16–17	= Luke 10:23–24
(d)	*Yoke and Burden*	Matt. 11:28–30	

In the light of discussion on these units since the time of Harnack (272–310), I emphasize that my present concern is not with the complex's genuineness as either separate or successive sayings of Jesus (see Hunter, 1961–1962). The more immediate question is whether and where these four units stood in Q. And this question may be rendered with more precision as follows: (a) did Q contain together units 1–2–4, as now in Matt. 11:25–30, while Luke omitted 4 and substituted for it 3, another Q unit but from elsewhere; *or* (b) did Q contain together units 1–2–3–4, so that Matthew relocated 3 while Luke retained it here, and Luke omitted 4 entirely while Matthew retained it here?

On (a). Although Matt 11:25–30 (units 1–2–4) has often been taken as an integrated tristrophic poem, neither the Aramaic (see Manson: 79) nor the scriptural (Cerfaux: 1954–1955) reflections are strong enough to offset the obvious conceptual differences that led Bultmann to assert, "I am convinced that the three 'strophes' of this saying did not originally belong together" (159; see also Suggs, 1970:77–83).

On (b). Manson (78–81) thinks that units 1–2–3 were together in Q, as in Luke 10:21–24, but he insists that Matt. 11:28–30 (unit 4) was not: "it is hardly credible that Lk. would have omitted a saying so entirely after his own heart, if it had stood in his source" (185). This is an impressive objection, but I am even more impressed by the following consideration. Matthew and Luke both have the conjunction of units 1 and 2 from Q, but both Matthew and Luke lack the conjunction of units 3 and 4; that is, *if it was in Q*, they *both* avoided it: Matthew by the relocation of 3, Luke by the omission of 4. I consider it, therefore, quite possible that the conjunction was present in Q, but that both Matthew and Luke considered it inappropriate, presumably because 4 seemed anticlimactic *after* 3.

My working hypothesis is, therefore, that all of units 1–4 stood together in Q, but I would insist that (a) this is certain for 1 and 2; (b) less certain for 3 (but see Taylor, 1953:29–30; Polag, 1979:46–49); and (c) very much less certain for 4. I am primarily persuaded to this position by the comparison of these *four* units with certain "revelation sayings" in other contexts involving gnosticized wisdom as given by Koester (1980b: 244–250). He concludes that "the best hypothesis that would explain this peculiar relationship between Q (Matt. 11:25–30; Luke 10:21–24; perhaps also Matt. 13:35), 1 Corinthians 1–4 and the *Gospel of Thomas* is the assumption that the ultimate source of these sayings was a lost sapiential writing which the Corinthians knew and used in the context of their wisdom theology" (249).

I begin with a consideration of the *prayer* in Q/Matt. 11:25–26 = Luke 10:21 to show its separate identity from the *aphoristic conclusion* in Q/Matt. 11:27 = Luke 10:22.

(3) The Prayer and Q. The mention of "in the Holy Spirit" is presumably a Lukan addition (see Polag, 1979:46–47). More important, however, is the referent of "these things" *in the present Q context* of this saying. When this saying is taken only in terms of *preceding* context "the 'these things' in verse 25 should be understood as referring to eschatological secrets" (Suggs, 1970:89). But, in terms of *succeeding* context, something much more radical is asserted, something that has to do with revelation itself and not only with its apocalyptic consummation. In total Q context this saying is "a reinterpretation of the recalcitrance of Israel. It is now said that it was God's will that Israel did not believe" (Jacobson, 1978:141). This was seen in great detail earlier and needs no further discussion here.

(4) The Prayer and 1 Cor. 1–4. Harnack had already drawn attention to the "coincidence . . . in thought and vocabulary" between Matt. 11:25–26 and 1 Cor. 1:19–21 (301 note 1; see Hunter, 1961–1962:244), and Koester following him, has noted five key words common to the Q saying and 1 Cor. 1–4 (1980b:247):

(1) "hidden	1 Cor. 2:7; 4:5
(2) "wise"	1 Cor. 1:19
(3) "understanding"	1 Cor. 1:19
(4) "revealed"	1 Cor. 2:10; 3:13
(5) "babes"	1 Cor. 3:1

Most significant is the fact, noted by Koester (1980b:247), that the combination *wise and understanding* is "used together only in Matt. 11:25 (Luke 10:21) and in the quotation of Isa. 29:14 in 1 Cor. 1:19–nowhere else in the New Testament." But this is no mere coincidence: "The occurrence of all these terms in 1 Corinthians 1–4 cannot be accidental. Paul confronts wisdom speculations in these chapters and obviously uses the terminology of the Corinthian wisdom teachers. He also seems to allude to some of their standard 'sayings' which must have been closely related to the saying Matt. 11:25. . . ." (1980b:248). That is: (a) the tendency towards a gnosticizing wisdom enthusiasm, which entered Q with this and the succeeding aphorisms, was combatted *initially and internally* inside Q by the addition of such key texts as the inaugurally placed "antienthusiastic polemic in Lk. 4:1–12 par." (Jacobson, 1978:233), and, *ultimately and externally* outside Q by Matthew and Luke combining it with Mark's passion theology; (b) Matthew and Luke, rather than Q itself (but see Robinson, 1962b:86), offer the parallel corrective to such a gnosticizing wisdom as does Paul in 1 Cor. 1–4—namely, the cross, or better, crucified wisdom.

This prayer, therefore, introduces a series of aphorisms that represent a new and different emphasis in Q theology. The problem of Israel's refusal here recedes into the background before enthusiasm over their own divine election and received revelation. This moves Q much closer to primitive stands of Jewish gnosticism, which receive internal correctives in Q's final redaction but which may still be seen operative, without such internal correctives, at Corinth.

(5) The Text of Aphorism 62. The aphorism in Q/Matt. 11:27 = Luke 10:22 follows immediately on Jesus' prayer of thanksgiving in

Q/Matt. 11:25–26 = Luke 10:21. There is, however, a preliminary problem. After an exhaustive review of manuscript and patristic evidence, Winter proposed the following original version of this saying (1956:147):

All things have been committed to me of the Father
And no one knows the Father but the Son
and those to whom the Son [would] reveal him.

That is, the primary change is the claim that the phrase "and no one knows the Son except the Father" is an interpolation. Since this analysis gives much more value to patristic over manuscript evidence, I agree with Suggs's judgment: "I cannot convince myself that the questioned clause should be omitted" (1970:76).

(6) The Saying and Q. The prayer in Q/Matt. 11:25–26 = Luke 10:21 is a completely adequate *thanksgiving* formula all by itself, as can be seen from biblical and extrabiblical parallels (see Robinson, 1964; and Grimm). Hence the immediate conjunction of Aphorism 62 to it means that in Q/Matt. 11:25–27 = Luke 10:21–22 we have "two layers, in that the concluding verse functions as an interpretation of the preceding thanksgiving" (Robinson, 1975:8). But it is an interpretation that considerably radicalizes it and that continues the basic shift in Q theology already noted for the *prayer* itself. There the change involved the Q community and recusant Israel; in Aphorism 62 it involves Jesus and Wisdom. It has been claimed that in Q Jesus is one, even if the primary one, of Wisdom's envoys, and that only in Matthew is Jesus equated with Wisdom itself (Suggs, 1970:127). Thus it was not by Q but only "by Paul at Corinth and by Matthew (in Syria?)" that "the Son is identified with Wisdom" and "this fateful step . . . is a development which was required before the gnosticizing tendencies of their opponents could issue in the developed gnosticism of the second century" (1970:96). I prefer, however, in the light of this present aphorism, to agree with Robinson that "here, *even if at the very latest stage* in the Q tradition, Jesus is not simply cast in the role of one of Sophia's spokesmen, even the culminating one, but rather is described with predications

that are reserved for Sophia itself" (1975:9, my italics). This means that it is necessary to distinguish successive redactional layers of Q theology concerning Jesus and Wisdom: (a) the dominant one has Jesus "as the *primus inter pares*, the most important, of her many spokesmen" (1975:10); (b) a later stage, as in this saying, has "the exclusivity of Sophia . . . attributed to the Son, who is identified with Jesus" (1975:10); (c) a final stage, represented by the Q temptation account, which "marks a shift away from an enthusiastic Christianity into Jewish-Christian scribalism" (Jacobson, 1978:233; see also 44–45, 221–222).

(7) The Saying Outside Q. What appears as a unified aphorism in Q has fragmentary parallels in John and elsewhere. (a) "All things have been delivered to me by my Father" recalls John 3:35, "the Father loves the Son, and has given all things into his hand" (see also 13:3a; 17:2). (b) "And no one knows the Son except the Father, and no one knows the Father except the Son" recalls John 10:15a, "as the Father knows me and I know the Father" (Dodd, 1963:359–361). (c) "And no one knows the Father except the Son and anyone to whom the Son chooses to reveal him" recalls John 14:7, "if you had known me you would have known my Father." Even more interesting, however, is the parallel in the *Dialogue of the Savior* 134:14–15, "and he who does not know the Son, how will he know the [Father]?" (Robinson, 1977:234). In that third comparison it should be noted how the emphasis moves from Son/ Father towards the believer in Q, but from believer towards Son/ Father in John and the *Dialogue*. Koester concludes that "the parallels in the Gospel of John indicate that the transmission of this saying was not restricted to Q; it must have occurred also in older sayings traditions upon which John as well as the *Dialogue of the Savior* depended" (1980b:245). I am more inclined, however, to explain these parallels not as variations on the same aphorism, but as elements and themes that appear elsewhere both separately and differently and that have been combined here in Q's Aphorism 62.

(8) Conclusion. Aphorism 62: *Father and Son*, with its triple mention of "Father," was appended in *aphoristic conclusion* to

Jesus' prayer concerning *Revelation and Babes*, with its double mention of "Father," to form the complex in Q/Matt. 11:25–27 = Luke 10:21–22. In this case, aphorism is appended to prayer.

D. APHORISM AND PARABLE

Aphorisms 132–133 will be considered here in their relationship to the parable of *The Talents/Pounds*, and this will bring up the question of Q's own original conclusion.

Aphorism 132: *Have and Receive*

(1) There are three independent versions: (a) Mark 4:25 = Matt. 13:12 = Luke 8:18b; (b) Q/Matt. 25:29 = Luke 19:26; and (c) *Gos. Thom.* 41. (See Table 6.5.)

(2) Translation. There is one detail worth noting in the translation of the aphorism's first stich. The Greek of both Markan and Q versions reads simply and literally "will be given." It is the English translators (*RSV, JB, NEB, NAB*) who added "more" in all cases. Lambdin's translation has continued this process and indeed expanded it, since there is no "something" and no "more" in the Coptic of *Gos. Thom.* 41. It reads: "to him shall be given" (Guillaumont, 1959:25; Wilson, 1973:515). This will be of significance later on.

(3) Form. This aphorism represents a classic case of that formal difference noted earlier between certain sayings in Mark and Q. In Mark the saying opens with *hos* plus the indicative in both stichs; this is slightly changed by Matt. 13:12 to *hostis* and the indicative; and it is changed more fully by Luke 8:18b to *hos an* with the subjunctive in both stichs. As Best (1976:3) notes, "the rules about the use of the subjunctive and indicative in this kind of clause were not always rigidly observed in Hellenistic Greek." In distinction to this *relatival* format in Mark, the Q version has a *participial* construction for both stichs. These distinctions do not appear in English translation and scarcely change the meaning in any case: "whoever has" in Mark, and "to everyone having" in Q (literally).

Table 6.5

Matthew 13:12	Mark 4:25	Luke 8:18b	
For to him who has	For to him who has	for to him who has	
will more be given, and he will have abundance; but from him who has not, even what he has will be taken away.	will more be given; and from him who has not, even what he has will be taken away.	will more be given, and from him who has not, even what he thinks that he has will be taken away.	

We are dealing, then, with Greek performancial preferences (rather than translational variations) in a double-stich aphorism arranged in positive/negative structure. This diptych or "double-stranded mashal" (Bultmann:81) contains a positive protasis and apodosis followed by a negative protasis and apodosis. This is simple antithetical parallelism.

(4) Mark 4:25. Mark locates this saying as the conclusion of his redactional complex in 4:21–25. It was already formulated in a manner dear to Markan style: a parallelism of "negative-positive" (Neirynck, 1972:89–94). But this parallelism is broken at one point. The negative stich has "even what he has," and this is more patently disruptive and problematic in Greek, which reads literally: "and whoever *has not*, even *what he has* will be taken away."

(5) Matt. 13:12. Apart from Matthew's minor change from *hos* to *hostis*, there is one even more significant change in his use of Mark. He also adds a qualification over and above the Markan text: "and he will have abundance." Thus Matthew has a qualification in both positive and negative stichs.

(6) Luke 8:18b. Apart from the change from indicative to subjunctive already noted, Luke's only significant change over Mark is

Table 6.5 (cont.)

Matthew 25:29	Luke 19:26	*Gospel of Thomas* 41
For to every one who has	I tell you, that to every one who has	Whoever has something in his hand
will more be given, and he will have abundance; but from him who has not, even what he has will be taken away.	will more be given; but from him who has not, even what he has will be taken away.	will receive more, and whoever has nothing will be deprived of even the little he has.

his specification of the negative stich's qualification as "even what *he thinks* that he has."

(7) The Q Context. The aphorism appears at the end of the parable of *The Talents* in Matt. 25:14–30 and of *The Pounds* in Luke 19:11–27 (see Appendix 2).

(a) The former is a single parable, but the latter is a careful and sequential conflation of two separate parables, that of *The Pounds* and of *The Throne Claimant* (Crossan, 1973:100–103).

(b) The differences between *The Talents* and *The Pounds* (apart from that conflation) are precisely such as indicate performancial variation rather than redactional change. Note, especially, the numerical differences: (i) 3 servants, 5/2/1 talents, 5 + 5/2 + 2/1 + 0 returns, in Matthew; but (ii) 10 servants, 1 pound apiece, 1 + 10/ 1 + 5/1 + 0 returns, in Luke. This would indicate independent sources for each version (see Manson: 245–248,312–317).

(c) Yet the inclusion of Aphorism 132 just before the final verse, that is, at exactly the same point for each parable, requires some explanation. The texts can be compared as in Table 6.6.

Table 6.6

Matthew 25:28–30
So take the talent from him, and give it to him who has the ten talents.
Aphorism 132 And cast the worthless servant into the outer darkness; there men will weep and gnash their teeth.

If, then, Matt. 25:14–30 and Luke 19:11–27 represent different versions of *The Talents/Pounds* parable, how do they both have Aphorism 132 located at exactly the same place, that is, not as the last but as the second-to-last verse? In other words, is Aphorism 132 an *aphoristic conclusion* or an integral part of the original parable?

(a) The parable concludes quite adequately with Matt. 25:28 = Luke 19:24. The final verse in Matt. 25:30 is redactionally his own conclusion. And the final verse in Luke 19:27 is that of the conflated parable of *The Throme Claimant* (see also 19:12b,14,15a). This means that Aphorism 132 is appended directly to *The Talents/ Pounds* parable in both Matt. 25:29 and Luke 19:25–26.

(b) It is possible that Matthew's version of the parable lacked the *aphoristic conclusion* and that he took it from the Q/Luke double parable even while refusing that conflated version. But I think it more likely that the parable of *The Talents/Pounds* received Aphorism 132 as its *aphoristic conclusion* at a much earlier stage before it descended either to Matt. 25:14–28 or to become conflated with *The Throne Claimant* in Q/Luke 19:11–27.

(c) Thus Q's concluding verse in 19:27 and Matthew's redactional addition in 25:30 served alike to demote Aphorism 128 from *aphoristic conclusion* to penultimate position.

Table 6.6 (cont.)

Luke 19:24–27
And he said to those who stood by,   "Take the pound from him,   and give it to him who has the ten pounds."   (And they said to him, "Lord, he has ten pounds!")   *Aphorism 132*   But as for these enemies of mine, who did not   want me to reign over them, bring them here   and slay them before me.

(d) I consider Luke 19:25 to be most likely original since, "on balance, both external attestation and transcriptional probabilities favor the retention of the words in the text" (Metzger, 1971:169). It would represent a presumably pre-Q smoothing of the linkage between parable and *aphoristic conclusion*.

(8) *Gos. Thom.* 41. The addition of "in his hand" may be redactional, since *Thomas* seems to have a particular liking for "hand" (17,21c,22b,35,98: see Ménard, 1975:142). The other change is of more significance. The negative stich is again qualified: "even the little he has." It is also possible that *Gos. Thom.* 70 is a much more gnostic version of this saying (Grant and Freedman: 147).

(9) Conclusion. It is clear from Mark and *Thomas* that this was originally a quite isolated saying. I think that the original aphorism (a) was strictly parallel and without any qualifications in either stich; (b) contained twin passives denoting divine action and eschatological challenge; and (c) offered a startling paradox to its transmission. The stages of internal hermeneutical development would be: (a) the qualification of the negative stich by "even what he has" in the earliest period; (b) the secondary specifications of this initial qualification, not by Mark 4:25 but by both Luke 8:18b ("thinks") and *Gos. Thom.* 41 ("little"); (c) the qualification of the positive stich by Matt. 13:12 = 25:29 ("and he will have abundance"); and, finally, (d) the further qualifications added to the positive stich by modern

English translators who added "more" to the synoptic tradition or "something" and "more" to the Thomistic version. It is, in other words, the challenge of the double paradox with its apparent double impossibility of the haver receiving and the non-haver losing, which forced the transmission along an internal trajectory of qualification and specification.

I used Aphorism 132 here, however, primarily for its external bonding with the parable of *The Talents/Pounds*. It is *possible* that the saying became an *aphoristic conclusion* only in Q/Luke 19:26, and thence into Matt. 25:29. But I think it is *more probable* that the linkage took place before Q and even before the performancial variations of Matt. 25:14–28 and pre-Q/Luke 19:12a,13,15b–24.

Aphorism 132: *On Twelve Thrones*

(1) There is only one version to be considered, in Q/Matt. 19:28 = Luke 22:28–30. (See Table 6.7.)

(2) The Q Context. I am presuming the following stages and contents for the general Q context of this aphorism.

(a) Pre-Q involved the appending of Aphorism 132: *Have and Receive* to the parable of *The Talents/Pounds*.

(b) Q created the double and conflated parable of *The Pounds/Throne Claimant*, but with Aphorism 132 still in its original place

Table 6.7

Matthew 19:28	Luke 22:28–30
Truly, I say to you, in the new world, when the Son of man shall sit on his glorious throne, you who have followed me	You are those who have continued with me in my trials; and I assign to you, as my Father assigned to me, a kingdom, that you may eat and drink at my table in my kingdom,
will also sit on twelve thrones, judging the twelve tribes of Israel.	and sit on thrones judging the twelve tribes of Israel.

at the end of the *Pounds* section. This double parable was created by Q either from two originally independent parables or else, more simply, by a creative expansion of the one original parable of *The Pounds* to include the motifs of *The Throne Claimant*.

(c) Luke 19:11–27 retained the complex as he found it in Q.

(d) Matthew found the conflated or expanded version radically unsuitable to precede his climactic 25:31–46, so he chose instead another version of the original parable from his own special sources. This version, however, also concluded with Aphorism 132, because, as just noted, that *aphoristic conclusion* had been added at a much earlier stage of the transmission. Under the influence of Q/Luke 19:27's punitive conclusion (actually from *The Throne Claimant* sequence), Matthew added on his own 25:30 so that the punishment of the failed servant is more lethally obvious there than in the original parable, which ended as Matt. 25:28 = Luke 19:24.

As a Q composition, the double parable of *The Pounds/Throne Claimant*, with its double emphasis on servants and citizens, served to give the Q community's history of salvation. It contained both a warning to those within (servants) and a judgment on those without (citizens).

I consider, therefore, that the following sequence represented the conclusion of Q as an integrated document:

(i)   Aphorisms 123–128, 130–131 (see Appendix 2).
(ii) Double Parable with Aphorism 132 included (Q/Luke 19: 22–27).
(iii) Aphorism 133: *On Twelve Thrones* (Q/Matt. 19:28 = Luke 22:28–30).

My main argument for this proposal is that Aphorism 133 (as in Q/Luke 22:28–30 rather than Matt. 19:28) links verbally and thematically, directly and immediately, to the conclusion of the conflated parable in Q/Luke 19:12–27:

(a)   Q/Luke 19:12,15,27: "Kingdom . . . Kingdom . . . rule"
(b)   Q/Luke 22:29,30:   "Kingdom . . . Kingdom"

The Kingdom Jesus received in the double parable is that in which the disciples share in the concluding aphorism.

(3) Q/Matt. 19:28 = Luke 22:28–30. The original verb of the Q opening is lost behind the "you who have followed me" (*hymeis hoi akolouthēsantes moi*) and "you who have continued with me" (*hymeis . . . hoi diamemenēkotes met' emou*) of Matt. 19:28 and Luke 22:28 (Bultmann: 158). But the present format of Luke 22:28, and especially its mention of "trials," is redactionally Lukan (Dupont, 1974:362). Matthew's opening is an even more redactional version of Q. I consider that the quite unusual formulation of Q/ Luke 22:29 is due to the connection in Q between this aphorism and the immediately preceding double parable in Q/Luke 19:11–27 (see 19:12,15). But Matthew, having replaced Q's double parable with an independent version lacking any such conflation in 25:14–29, replaced the theme of the "Kingdom" in Q/Luke 22:29–30a with "in the new world, when the Son of man shall sit on his glorious throne" (see 25:31; Vielhauer, 1957:67–68; Dupont, 1964: 364–368). Thus Matthew also removed any mention of Q's "that you may eat and drink at my table in my Kingdom," although this idea is known in general in Aphorisms 109 and 110 from Q/Matt. 8:11–12 = Luke 13:28–29. But Matthew and Luke agree on Q's statement concerning the judgment thrones. Matthew may better represent Q here with "twelve thrones" since Luke, having just told of Judas' betrayal in 22:21–23, would have preferred the vaguer "thrones" (Dupont, 1964:369–370; see Polag, 1979:78–89).

(4) Conclusion. I have suggested that Aphorism 132: *Have and Receive* was added in *aphoristic conclusion* to the parable of *The Talents/Pounds* at a very early and pre-Q stage. But Aphorism 133: *On Twelve Thrones* was used by Q not only as the *aphoristic conclusion* of the new double parable of *The Pounds/Throne Claimant*, but also as the climactic promise that ended the entire document. Q itself ended with Aphorism 133 (see Bammel, 1970), but as in Luke 22:(28)29–30 rather than in Matt. 19:28. It linked with and derived its unusual "Kingdom" formulation from Q's immediately preceding double parable in Q/Luke 19:11–27 (but see Manson: 216–217, 337–339; Vassiliadis: 70; Polag, 1979:78–89).

E. APHORISM AND DIALOGUE

I distinguish between *dialogue* and *story* even though the latter may easily contain the former. What is significant, however, is that the former *need not* contain the latter. And this becomes especially important for the gnostic transmission of the Jesus tradition. Compare, for example, how the *dialectical dialogue* of *Gos. Thom.* 104 appears as a *dialectical story* in Mark 2:18–20 and is heightened there by the presence of Mark 2:18, which is omitted in Matt. 9:14 = Luke 5:33. My example here concerns a *dialectical dialogue*.

Aphorism 118: *Against Divorce*

(1) There are three independent versions to be considered: (a) 1 Cor. 7:10–11; (b) Mark 10:11–12 = Matt. 19:9; and (c) Q/Matt. 5:32 = Luke 16:18. (See Table 6.8.)

(2) 1 Cor. 7:10–11. Paul is replying (7:1) with general principles (7:2–7) applied to three specific groups within the Corinthian community: (a) "to the unmarried and the widows" in 7:8–9; (b) "to the married" in 7:10–11; and (c) "to the rest," that is, to those in mixed Christian-pagan marriages, in 7:12–16. The middle case is specifically cited as "to the married I give charge, not I but the Lord, that . . ." (7:10a).

(a) The Verbs. Different verbs are used for the act of the wife ("separate," *chōristhēnai*) and of the husband ("divorce," *aphienai*); and, while the latter verb is active, the former could be read either as middle ("separate herself from") or passive ("be separated from"). The context in 7:1–16 clearly favors a reading that equates each verb ("separate" = "divorce") and therefore gives "separate" a middle-voice interpretation. Thus the verb used for the husband's action in 7:11b is used for the actions of *both* husband and wife in 7:12–13, while the verb used for the wife's action in 7:10b is used for both cases in 7:15. Within the Pauline context, then, 7:10b + 11b indicate a Greco-Roman legal setting where either party could initiate divorce proceedings. It does not seem necessary to postulate a prepauline reading against the background of Jewish law wherein either

Table 6.8

Mark 10:11–12	Matthew 19:9	Matthew 5:32	
Whoever divorces his wife and marries another, commits adultery against her; and if she divorces her husband and marries another, she commits adultery.	And I say to you: whoever divorces his wife, except for unchastity, and marries another commits adultery.	It was also said, "Whoever divorces his wife, let him give her a certificate of divorce." But I say to you that every one who divorces his wife, except on the ground of unchastity, makes her an adulteress; and whoever marries a divorced woman commits adultery.	

(i) the husband is forbidden to *divorce* and the wife to *separate* (Vawter: 536), or (ii) the husband is forbidden to divorce and (tautologously?) the wife to be divorced (Fitzmyer, 1976:199). If divorce is possible for both, it is forbidden equally to both by 1 Cor. 7:10–11.

(b) The Sequence. The sequence in 7:10b + 11b is wife (10b) and then husband (11b). Throughout all of 7:1–16 Paul fluctuates his sequence as follows:

male/female//female/male	(7:2)
male/female//female/male	(7:3)
female/male//male/female	(7:4)
female/male//male/female	(7:10–11)
male/female//female/male	(7:12–13)

Table 6.8 (cont.)

Luke 16:18	1 Corinthians 7:10–11
Every one who divorces his wife	
and marries another commits adultery,	
and he who marries a woman divorced from her husband commits adultery.	that the wife should not separate from her husband (but if she does, let her remain single or else be reconciled to her husband)— and that the husband should not divorce his wife.

    male/female//female/male   (7:14)
    female/male//male/female   (7:16)

Thus the sequence in 7:10–11 is simply part of Paul's constant evenhandedness in his treatment of the sexes throughout this entire matter of celibacy, marriage, and divorce.

(c) The "Exception." But it is precisely that consistent parallelism and evenhandedness concerning sexual rights and duties throughout 7:1–16 that calls special attention to the one-sided clause in 7:11a: "(but if she does, let her remain single or else be reconciled to her husband)." The problem is quite precise: Against the background of his careful and evenhanded parallelism of male and female throughout 7:1–16, why does Paul have a specification to the wife's case in 7:10b–11a, but none to the husband's case in 7:11b? I deem it most unlikely that the specification represents the reflection of a dominical "saying prohibiting the remarriage of a divorced woman" (see Catchpole: 107) as part of the overall double-stich prohibition of divorce. Fitzmyer's suggestion is much more plausible: "One wonders, however, whether this is really a Pauline 'permission' or a mere concession to a factual situation, perhaps reported to him from the Corinthian community" (1976:200). Only the wife is mentioned here, because Paul is dealing with a specific case from Corinth involving a wife who divorced her husband. This may also, of course, have persuaded him to place the prohibition in the sequence wife/husband in 7:10–11. But, apart from such emphases, the specification applies just as much to both, since 7:10b–11b is quite absolute.

(3) Mark and Matthew. It will be necessary to look both at the *dialectical dialogue* in Mark 10:2–9 = Matt. 19:3–8 and at the *aphoristic conclusion* in Mark 10:11–12 = Matt. 19:9.

(a) Mark 10:2–12 = Matt. 19:3–12. Matthew's text is a careful external restructuring and internal rephrasing of Mark's, but with appended materials of his own as well (Crossan, 1968:7–9). *Externally:* (i) Matthew accepts Mark's distinction between *nondisciples* in 10:2–9 (on the problematic "Pharisees" of 10:2, see Metzger, 1971: 103–104), and *disciples* in 10:10–12; but he gives all of Mark 10:2–11 to his *nondisciples* (Pharisees) in 19:3–9 while adding a more appropriately specific unit for the *disciples* in 19:10–12 from his own special materials (see Moloney); (ii) Mark's structure of (*a*) question in 10:2, (*a'*) counter-question in 10:3, (*b*) answer in 10:4, (*b'*) counter-answer in 10:5–9, has become in Matthew a rhythm of (*a*) question in 19:3, (*b*) answer in 19:4–6, (*a'*) counter-question in 19:7, (*b'*) counter-answer in 19:8–9 (note Bultmann: 41, despite 27). *Internally:* (i) Matt. 19:3 *may* have added "Pharisees" instead of "crowds" (implicit) in Mark 10:2a (see Metzger, 1971:103; Crossan, 1968: notes 3 and 5); (ii) Matt. 19:3 adds "for any cause" to Mark 10:2; (iii) Matt. 19:9 adds "except for unchastity" (*porneia*) to Mark 10:11; and (iv) Matt. 19:9 accepts only that part of Mark 10:11–12 that is consistent with "divorce itself being placidly assumed to be an exclusively male prerogative" (Vawter: 532).

(b) Mark 10:2–9 = Matt. 19:3–8. On the one hand, then, Matthew has redacted Mark's *disciples* unit (10:10–12) inside his version of the dialogue to allow for his own special disciples unit in 19:10–12. This external restructuring scarcely affects the meaning of the unit. On the other hand, the internal changes are much more significant. In Mark there is an absolute prohibition of divorce addressed (possibly) to the crowds rather than the Pharisees. But in Matthew the debate is now recast "in terms of the Hillel-Shammai dispute" (Fitzmyer, 1976:206) over adequate reasons for divorce, and, more importantly, there is now one exception where divorce is permitted (demanded?)—that is, in the case of *porneia*. This refers to the specific situation of the Matthean community, but against the general problem of *porneia* in Acts 15:20,29 (see Crossan, 1968:16–26). Fitzmyer concludes that "another aspect of the exceptive phrases [in Matt. 5:32; 19:9] was undoubtedly to handle the situation of Gentiles who were coming into it [Matthew's mixed Jewish-Gentile community] and already found themselves in the marital condition proscribed for Jews by Lv 18:6–18. Just as the letter of James enjoined certain matters on the Gentile Christians of the local churches of Antioch, Syria, and Cilicia, so Matthew's exceptive phrases solve a problem for Gentile Christians living in the same community with Jewish Christians, who were still observing Mosaic regulations" (1976:211, and see especially 221). But in all of this we are seeing intensive external and internal Matthean redaction of his Markan source (Crossan, 1968:7–9; Catchpole: 93–110; Fitzmyer, 1976:205–207), and it is not necessary, even if of course possible, to postulate independent Matthean tradition for the dialogue (Vawter: 532). Neither can the argument that the question of Mark 10:2 would be meaningless in Jesus' contemporary Palestine disprove this hypothesis of Markan over Matthean priority for the dialogue. If Jesus could be asked whether he accepted the Roman law on tribute in 12:13–17, he could also be asked whether he accepted the Jewish law on divorce in 10:2–9. The question is at least *possible*, whether one accepts (Fitzmyer, 1976:213–222) or rejects (Vawter: 532–534) the possible evidence that the Qumran Essenes rejected divorce.

(c) Mark 10:11–12 = Matt. 19:9. Mark joined together the originally separate *dialectical dialogue* in 10:2–9 with the *aphoristic saying* in 10:11–12 by his redactional device of *nondisciples* outside and *disciples* inside (see Mark 4:10 and 7:17). But his internal redactions are even more important.

The Markan aphorism opens in 10:11 within a formulation appropriate to, but of course contradicting, Jewish law: "whoever divorces his wife and marries another commits adultery." And Matt. 19:9 is content to follow Mark this far *but no farther*. Mark, however, first continues with (i) "against her" in 10:11, and this "is almost certainly a Marcan addition made in the light of what is to be said in v. 12. It is an explicative addition, which makes Jesus' words express the fact that adultery against a woman is something now to be considered" (Fitzmyer, 1976:204–205); and then (ii) "v. 12 is a further Marcan extension of the first logion, introduced to suit the contingencies of Gentile Christian communities in areas where Roman and Greek law prevailed and where a woman was permitted to divorce her husband" (1976:205).

Mark, then, is Matthew's only source for his 19:3–9, but Mark's own aphorism in 10:11–12 is a double-stich version which, as with Paul's 1 Cor. 7:10–11, has the wife's stich (*ean autē apolysasa*) phrased rather differently than the husband's (*hos an apolysē*). But once again, as with Paul, has Mark expanded an original single-stich prohibition (10:11) or rephrased an original double-stich one (10:11–12)?

(4) Q/Matt. 5:32 = Luke 16:18. That Matt. 5:32 and Luke 16:18 represent the Q version of this aphorism (Bultmann: 26) rather than two independent versions (Q and M; so Manson: 136,157) is confirmed by a consideration of the openings involved. This is another of these instances seen earlier where a relatival format appears in

Mark but a participial one is preferred in Q. In the present aphorism the twin stichs of Mark 10:11–12 have the relatival "whoever" (*hos an*) and the conditional "if" (*ean*), but of these Matt. 19:9 accepts only the former (*hos an*). And the twin stichs of Luke 16:18 (Q) have two participial constructions (*pas ho . . . ho*) while Matt. 5:32a accepts the former (*pas ho*) but reverts to relatival form (*hos ean*), as in 19:9, for the latter.

In Q/Luke 16:18 the aphorism's position seems dictated primarily by the Lukan redaction of Luke 16, and in Q/Matt. 5:32 it is also relocated and reset to form one of the antitheses of his Sermon on the Mount (Taylor, 1953:30; 1959:249–250; Polag, 1979:74–75).

The basic problem of the synoptic texts is the content of Q's double-stich version, since it is clear that "the direction of the Q saying has been radically changed by someone, either by Matthew or by Luke" (Vawter: 530). The exceptive clause in Matt. 5:32 ("except on the ground of unchastity") is akin to Matthew's qualification already seen for 19:9 ("except for unchastity") and is part of the Matthean redaction, not the Q tradition. But, leaving this aside, what was Q's original double-stich version?

In terms of *form* Luke 16:8 is closer to Q, since it has a double participial format (*ho . . . ho*) while Matt. 5:32 has a split participial (*ho*) and relatival (*hos ean*) construction. This latter change is an intrusion from Mark 10:11–12 (*hos an . . . ean*) through Matt. 19:9 (*hos an*) into Matt. 5:32b (*hos ean*).

In terms of *content* the problem is much more difficult, and it does not reside in the second stich (Matt. 5:32b = Luke 16:18b), which contains exactly the same change. It resides in the first stich of Matt. 5:32a where "a man who repudiates his wife is said to make her an adulteress . . . he puts her in jeopardy of adultery by declaring her free of a bond which he has no right to dissolve," as compared with that of Luke 16:18a where "the husband himself becomes an adulterer by marrying another woman after repudiating his wife" (Vawter: 530). In other words, Matt. 5:32 indicates the exclusively male viewpoint of Jewish divorce law in *both* stichs, while Luke 16:18 has split the viewpoint between the mutuality of Greco-Ro-

man law (18a) and the masculinity of Jewish law (18b). I conclude,
therefore, that despite the Matthean redactional setting of 5:31
(from Matt. 19:7) and the Matthean redactional exception in 5:32a,
the version in 5:32 is closer to Q than is Luke 16:18 (with Crossan,
1968:10–11 and Vawter: 530–531 against Fitzmyer, 1976:200–203).

There is, however, one obvious objection to that conclusion.
Since Matt. 19:9 had rephrased Mark 10:11–12 from a Greco–Roman to a Jewish formulation, might not Matt. 5:32 have done the
same to a Greco–Roman form in Q? This would be a very serious
objection if Luke 16:18 had been *consistently* formulated within
Greco–Roman divorce law, for example, if it had read: "every one
who divorces his wife and marries another commits adultery, *and
she who divorces her husband and marries another commits adultery.*" But since the second stich of Q (Matt. 5:32b = Luke 16:18b)
was formulated in terms of Jewish law, I conclude that so also was
the first, as still visible in Matt. 5:32a but not in Luke 16:18a.

(5) Conclusion. The earliest recoverable version of Aphorism
118 is in Q, as still visible in the text of Matt. 5:32, once its redactional setting and exceptive clause are removed. It was a double-
stich aphorism formulated within the exclusively male orientation
of Jewish divorce law and it stated that, since husband could not
divorce his wife, any such attempt rendered wife and new husband
adulterous just as if no such attempt had ever been made. In effect:
Whoever can divorce (i.e. the husband), cannot do so! This aphorism then moved along two somewhat contradictory internal trajectories. One internal trajectory used the opportunity granted by the
double-stich format (first husband/second husband) to reformulate
the stichs (husband/wife) in terms of Greco-Roman mutuality in
divorce proceedings. This process is indicated in the first stich of
Luke 16:18, but is clearly visible in 1 Cor. 7:10–11 and Mark 10:11–
12. In effect: Whoever can divorce (i.e., husband or wife), cannot
do so! But the second internal trajectory makes exceptions to this
absolute prohibition, whether formulated for Jewish (Matt. 5:32a =
19:9a) or Greco–Roman law (1 Cor. 7:12–16; see Crossan, 1968:26–
29). The external trajectory has the aphorism remain in isolated

conjunction in Q/Luke 16:18 (despite Bammel, 1958), but it is re-dacted by Matt. 5:31–32 within his antitheses for the Sermon on the Mount (5:31–32 = 19:7,9) and by Paul within the context of 1 Cor. 7:1–16.

It was Mark, however, who appended the saying as an *aphoristic conclusion* in 10:11–12 to the *dialectical dialogue* of Mark 10:2–9. The conjunction was facilitated internally because of the common prohibition of divorce in dialogue and aphorism and externally by the typical redactional device of 10:10. Later Matt. 19:3–9 tightened the Markan construction for his own complex in 19:3–12.

F. APHORISM AND STORY

The use of an *aphoristic conclusion* at the end of a story is quite common in Mark. Two examples of this were seen already but in other contexts. Aphorism 3: *Patches and Wineskins* (Mark 2:21–22 = Matt. 9:16–17; Luke 5:36–38) is appended to the *dialectical story* in Mark 2:18–20 = Matt. 9:14–15 = Luke 5:33–35. But there is no such conjunction in the parallels for that aphorism in *Gos. Thom.* 47b or the *dialectical dialogue* in *Gos. Thom.* 104. Aphorism 4: *Man and Sabbath* (Mark 2:27–28 = Matt. 12:8 = Luke 6:5) is terminally affixed to another *dialectical story* in Mark 2:23–26 = Matt. 12:1–7 = Luke 6:1–4. Later, there will be another instance with Aphorism 19: *Kingdom and Children* (Mark 10:15 = Luke 18:17) appended to the *aphoristic/dialectical story* in Mark 10:13–14,16. Three other examples will be considered here.

Aphorism 2: *Came for Sinners*

(1) There are four independent versions to be considered: (a) Mark 2:17b = Matt. 9:13b = Luke 5:32; (b) *Barn.* 5:9; (c) 1 Tim. 1:15; and (d) Luke 19:10. (See Table 6.9.)

(2) The Markan Context. The general Markan context of 2:1–3:6 was discussed earlier. It is now a question of the more immediate context in 2:13–17. I consider this to be composed of five separable units: (a) *By the Sea* in 2:13; (b) *Call of Levi* in 2:14; (c) *Eating with*

Table 6.9

Matthew 9:13b	Mark 2:17b	Luke 5:32
For I came not to call the righteous, but sinners.	I came not to call the righteous, but sinners.	I have come not to call the righteous, but sinners to repentance.

Levi in 2:15; (d) the dialectical story on *Eating with Sinners* in 2:16–17a; and (e) Aphorism 2: *Came for Sinners* in 2:17b. The major analytical issue is whether Mark 2:17a and 2:17b were originally two separate and independent aphorisms out of which was developed the *aphoristic story* of 2:16–17, or whether, as I shall argue, 2:17b is an *aphoristic conclusion* appended by Mark to the *dialectical story* in 2:16–17a.

(3) Mark 2:13–15. The *call* in 2:13–14 is told in close parallel to the earlier ones in 1:16–20: (a) "passing . . . by (*para*) the sea" and "beside (*para*) the sea . . . passing"; (b) "saw" disciples-to-be at work; (c) "said . . . 'Follow me' "; and (d) new disciples abandon older work and "followed him." The *sea/call* conjunction in 2:13–14 leads to *meal* in 2:15. This phrase is Mark's own redactional link between 2:13–14 and the pre-Markan unit in 2:16–17a. It simply locates the event of 2:16–17a at Levi's house by using most of the vocabulary of 2:16 to create 2:15. But this also establishes a triad of *sea/call/meal* in 1:16a, 16b–20,31, in 2:13,14,15, and later in 3:7, 13–19,20. That is, each of these three complexes follows a set conjunction that underlines the importance of *sea/call/meal* in Markan theology (see Kelber, 1974:45–65).

(4) Mark 2:16–17. I am in complete agreement with Hultgren that this unit does not repeat "a specific event in the life of Jesus"

Table 6.9 (cont.)

Epistle of Barnabas 5:9	1 Timothy 1:15	Luke 19:10
	The saying is sure and worthy of full acceptance,	
that "he	that Christ Jesus	For the Son of man
came	came	came
	into the world	to seek and
not to call the	to save	to save
righteous, but		
sinners"	sinners.	the lost.

(1971:208; 1979:109). But I would debate his suggestion that "from a formal point of view the story appears to have been constructed from two sayings attributed to Jesus (2:17a and 17b) and a setting, which is artificial. The two sayings consist of a proverb . . . and an I saying" (1979:109). He suggests, in other words, that (a) 2:17a and 17b were originally isolated sayings; that (b) they were formed into an aphoristic compound; and that (c) this then became the basis for creating an aphoristic story, as in 2:16–17. That is not at all impossible, but I propose instead that (a) a *dialectical story* in 2:16–17a received (b) an *aphoristic conclusion* from the originally independent 2:17b. And the debate is of some importance for transmissional history in general. The primary reason for my counter-suggestion is Oxy P 1224.

(5) Mark 2:16–17a. Oxy P 1224 was already seen in considering Aphorism 71. An independent version of that saying appeared within an aphoristic cluster on the *recto* of the second fragment. On the *verso* of that same fragment there is a version of Mark 2:16–17a. The texts are given in Table 6.10. I consider that Oxy P 1224 is independent of the intracanonical versions of this unit. In general the transmission's tendency is to transfer attacks on Jesus to attacks on his disciples: "It is further characteristic that Mk 2:15f.; Matt 17:24, raises a question about the conduct of Jesus, though the

Table 6.10

Mark 2:16–17a	Oxyrhynchus Papyrus 1224
And the scribes of the Pharisees when they saw that he was eating with sinners and tax collectors,	And the scribes and [Pharisees] and pries when they sa[w] him, were angry [that with sin]ners in the midst he [reclined] at table.
said to his disciples, "Why does he eat with tax collectors and sinners?" And when Jesus heard it, he said to them, "Those who are well have no need of a physician, but those who are sick."	But Jesus heard [it and said:] The h[ealthy need not the physician.]

question is not put direct to him, but to the disciples" (Bultmann: 49). But in Oxy P 1224 there are no disciples present and the accusation is made against Jesus himself. Then in Mark 2:16 the objection is made against Jesus but to the disciples. Finally, in Luke 5:30 the objection is made against and to the disciples themselves.

There is, however, a more serious difficulty concerning the precise ending of the unit in Oxy P 1224. In the transcription cited above (Hennecke and Schneemelcher: 1.114) the fragment breaks off with "the he[althy. . . ." The document's original editors noted that "both fragments are from the top of leaves" and that "it is likely that the column was of no great height, and it may be estimated at about twenty lines at most" (Grenfell and Hunt, 1914:1,2). So the column certainly contained other lines after that final break. There is, apparently, one single letter still visible in the center of the next line, but it is so uncertain and the rest of that line is so completely gone that the original editors made no attempt to identify it (1914: 5,8). But whatever may have followed in Oxy P 1224 there is *at least no evidence* that it contained any parallel to Mark 2:17b or even to the phrase "but those who are sick" of 2:17a.

In the light of Oxy P 1224, therefore, I consider it better to take the story in Mark 2:16–17a as a separate unit to which 2:17b has been added later as an *aphoristic conclusion*.

(6) Aphorism or Dialectic. But, even if 2:17b be left aside, should 2:16–17a be considered as an *aphoristic story* composed out

of the originally independent aphorism in 2:17a, or is it a unified *dialectical story* in 2:16–17a?

The problem is already evident in Bultmann. On the one hand, he says that "the point of the story, expressed in Jesus' words in v. 17, has no very close connection with the situation described. The saying was thus originally unattached, and v. 15 is simply a story designed for it" (18). And again: "This individual analysis of the Synoptic controversy dialogues has further shown that we must always raise the question whether we are dealing with an unitary composition, or whether the scene is a secondary construction for a saying originally in independent circulation. If the saying is comprehensible only in terms of its contextual situation, then it clearly has been conceived together with it. But that is commonly not the case either in the controversy or scholastic dialogues. Instances such as Mk. 2:15–17 . . . where the artificiality of the composition is clear as day . . . show that the arguments were in many cases already there before the narratives themselves" (46–47). But then, on the other hand, he admits that "it is even more precarious to try to indicate which of the logia Jesus could have taken from secular wisdom and made his own. In itself it is obviously by no means impossible that he should have taken the widespread figure of the doctor who tends the sick and not the healthy (Mk. 2:17), and used it to defend his own way of going to work. . . . It is necessary to see that the tradition has taken many logia from popular wisdom and piety into itself, and to reckon with the fact that it has done so now and then because Jesus has made use of or coined such a saying" (104–105).

I cannot imagine that the piece of proverbial obviousness (see Taylor, 1966:207) in 2:17a, whether stemming from Jesus or the tradition, could ever have been transmitted as an aphorism in search of a setting, as an *aphoristic saying* on its way to becoming an *aphoristic story*. Were it ever so transmitted at all, it would surely have been along with the present setting, that is, as a *dialectical story*. Or, and this seems even more likely, certain situations—that is, certain *typical* problematic incidents—may well have been transmitted, and thereafter situation begets saying, or uses an available proverbial saying, rather than the reverse phenomenon. This will be discussed more fully below, but it is already and clearly necessary to distinguish between *aphoristic stories*, where the saying begets the setting, and *dialectical stories*, where both are created together or where, sometimes, the setting may beget the saying. It is not enough to cite Bultmann's general dictum that "the sayings have commonly generated the situation, not vice-versa" (47).

(7) Mark 2:17b. I consider this to be an independent saying affixed as *aphoristic conclusion* to Mark 2:16–17a, and with that conjunction facilitated, in content, by the parallelism of *well/sick* and *righteous/sinners*, and in form, by the negative/positive (*ouk/alla*) construction of both 2:17a and 2:17b.

After his own insertion of Matt. 9:13a, Matthew follows Mark 2:17b in 9:13b. But Luke adds "to repentance" in 5:32b.

(8) *Barn.* 5:9. The document called *Epistle of Barnabas* is anonymous and "is either a general treatise or was intended for some community in which Alexandrian ideas prevailed, though it is not possible to define either its destination, or the locality from which it was written, with any greater accuracy" (Lake: 1.337). The comment in *Barn.* 16:14 "points to the heathen rebuilding of the temple of Jupiter on the temple site in Jerusalem, on the eve of the Bar-Cochba War of A.D. 132–135; this would date the *Letter* about A.D. 130–131, when Hadrian ordered the building of the new city" (Goodspeed and Grant:20). Koester has argued that the method of Old Testament allegorical exegesis used in *Barnabas* rendered any need for the canonical gospels superfluous, even if they were available at the time and place of its composition (1957a:157,260).

The text of *Barn.* 5:8–9 is as follows: "Furthermore, while teaching Israel and doing such great signs and wonders he preached to them and loved them greatly; but when he chose out his own Apostles who were to preach his Gospel, he chose those who were iniquitous above all sin to show that 'he came not to call the righteous but sinners,'—then he manifested himself as God's Son" (Lake:1.356–357). There are three points to be noted. (a) The form is again negative/positive (*ouk/alla*). (b) The saying is given in third ("he came") rather than first person ("I came"). (c) The saying de-velops the theme of the Sinner-Apostle, as in 1 Cor. 15:9–11. It is not just a question of Jesus' calling sinners in general, but of the Sinner-Apostle in particular. This version is quite independent of any intracanonical texts (so Koester, 1957a:138–145,157,260).

(9) 1 Tim. 1:15. The full text of 1 Tim. 1:12–17 is quite clearly a "Pauline" commentary on 1 Cor. 15:8–11. It thus continues the theme of Sinner-Apostle from there, but it also associates the apho-rism with Paul himself. It is an independent version, both from intracanonical and extracanonical versions (see Koester, 1957a:144). The saying is introduced with a standard formula, "the saying is sure" (see 1 Tim. 3:1; 4:9; 2 Tim. 2:11; Titus 3:8). It is in third-person construction, but with only the positive rather than the negative/positive formulation. And the positive verb is now "save" rather than "call."

This means that a basic *Came for Sinners* saying is being trans-mitted in two different versions. One is negative/positive: "*came* not to call the righteous, but *sinners*," as in Mark 2:17b and *Barn.* 5:9. Another is positive only: "*came* to save *sinners*" in 1 Tim. 1:15.

(10) Luke 19:10. This is an *aphoristic conclusion* to the anecdote in Luke 19:1–9. "For the Son of Man came to seek and save the lost." It is another version of the positive-only trajectory just seen in 1 Tim. 1:15. The agent is now "Son of Man" rather than "I" (Mark 2:17b) or "Christ Jesus" (1 Tim. 1:15); the verb is again "save" as in 1 Tim. 1:15, but "the lost" appears instead of "sinners." I presume the *aphoristic conclusion* is pre-Lukan (despite Bultmann: 34).

(11) Luke 9:55 ms. Certain lesser manuscripts of Luke 9:55 read as follows (see critical apparatus): "But he turned and rebuked them, and he said, 'You do not know what manner of spirit you are of; for the Son of man came not to destroy men's lives but to save them.' " This brings together the two versions of the aphorism. It is in nega-tive/positive format, as in Mark 2:17b or *Barn.* 5:9, but it has the verbs "save" and "destroy" (*apolesai*) just as in Luke 19:10, "to save the lost" (*apolōlos*). I consider it a later and dependent conjunction of the twin streams of Aphorism 2.

(12) 2 *Clem.* 2:4,7. This pseudo-letter of pseudo-Clement of

Rome, dating "probably from the half century between 120 and 170 A.D." (Lake: 1.127), contains the following in 2:4–7: "And another Scripture also says, 'I came not to call righteous, but sinners'; He means that those who are perishing must be saved, for it is great and wonderful to give strength, not to the things which are standing, but to those which are falling. So Christ also willed to save the perishing, and he saved many, coming and calling us who were already perishing" (Lake: 1.130–131). Once again there is a conjunction of the twin streams of Aphorism 2. In 2 *Clem.* 2:4 there is an explicit citation of the negative/positive version, as in Mark 2:17b or *Barn.* 5:9. This is secondary to the intracanonical texts (see Koester, 1957a:64–66,71,109,260). But later, as the text concludes in 2 *Clem.* 2:7, the positive-only version appears, "Christ . . . coming and calling," and the double "save(d)/perishing" (*apollymena*). It is more difficult to decide whether 2 *Clem.* 2:7 is dependent on Luke 19:10, or simply represents another version of that positive-only variant (see Koester, 1957a:108–109).

(13) *Conclusion.* Aphorism 2 is an independent saying used in *aphoristic conclusion* to the dialectical story in Mark 2:16–17a. The saying has been transmitted along two lines: (a) Positive/Negative ("call") in Mark 2:17b ("I") and *Barn.* 5:9 ("he"). (b) Positive ("save") in 1 Tim. 1:15 ("Christ Jesus") and Luke 19:10 ("Son of man"). These twin lines come together later in (c) Luke 9:55 ms and (d) 2 *Clem.* 2:4–7. The basic aphorism (*Jesus came for sinners*) is applied to the Apostle-Sinner in 1 Tim. 1:15 (Paul), *Barn.* 5:9 (Apostles), Mark 2:17b (Levi), and to the non-apostle-sinner, Zacchaeus, in Luke 19:1–10. But Mark 2:16–17 has also widened the reference to others besides apostles, and this movement is continued in later and dependent texts (Luke 9:55 ms; 2 *Clem.* 2:4–7).

Aphorism 20: *Camel and Needle*

(1) There is only one independent version to be considered: Mark 10:25 = Matt. 19:24 = Luke 18:25. (See Table 6.11.)

(2) Matt. 19:24 and Luke 18:25. The versions in Matthew and

Table 6.11

Matthew 19:24	Mark 10:25	Luke 18:25
It is easier for a camel to go through the eye of a needle than for a rich man to enter the kingdom of God	It is easier for a camel to go through the eye of a needle than for a rich man to enter the kingdom of God.	For it is easier for a camel to go through the eye of a needle than for a rich man to enter the kingdom of God.

Luke have some small changes over Mark that appear in Greek but not in English translation. There are three minor agreements against Mark (Neirynck, 1974:137). For example, they both (note critical apparatus) avoid Mark's predilection for a "compound verb followed by the same proposition" (Neirynck, 1972:75), or preceded by it as in 10:24b and 25. Otherwise they remain wisely close to this formidable aphorism in Mark.

(3) Mark 10:25. Walter has analyzed Mark 10:17–31 as (a) story in 10:17–24a to which Mark has appended (b) 10:24b–27 and (c) 10:28–31. But Bultmann's analysis is much better: (a) a "genuine apothegm" or aphoristic story in 10:17–22; (b) a "saying (or two) about riches with a subsequent discussion with the disciples" in 10:23–27; (c) "a saying about rewards in the Kingdom of God, which comes in answer to a question by Peter" in 10:28–30; (d) "and finally, v. 31, the saying about the first and the last" (21–22). Thus the immediate context of the aphorism about *Camel and Needle* is in 10:23–27. I consider this to be a completely redactional Markan creation (against Légasse, 1962) intended to frame centrally and interpret carefully the startling saying of Jesus in 10:25 (see also Pryke: 166). In terms of *form* Mark has composed his unit in a mildly chiastic manner:

(a) "Jesus looked . . . said . . . " (10:23)
(b) "and the (*hoi de*) disciples . . . amazed . . . " (10:24a)
(c) Aphorism (*with muting introduction*) (10:24b–25)
(b') "And they (*hoi de*) . . . exceedingly astonished . . . " (10:26)
(a') "Jesus looked . . . said . . . " (10:27)

But more importantly, in terms of *content*, he has two statements before the aphorism in 10:23b and 24b and another two after it in 10:26b and 10:27b that together render the impossibility stated in 10:25 less hopeless by first describing it as "very difficult" (10:23b = 24b) and then as impossible for men but possible for God (10:26b,27b). Thus the total effect of Mark's framing dialogue in 10:23–27 is to mute the apodictic impossibility of 10:25. This muting process, begun in the Markan contextual framing, is continued within the manuscript transmission of this aphorism throughout all three synoptic versions. It is as if the startling combination of comedy in literal content and tragedy in metaphorical meaning was almost too much for those who had to copy this saying. Thus several manuscript witnesses substituted *kamilon*, a rope or ship's hawser, for *kamēlon*, a camel. "The change was facilitated by the circumstance that *i* and *ē* came to be pronounced alike in later Greek (both words were pronounced kah'mee-lon)" (Metzger, 1971:169, see also 50 and 106).

(4) *Gos. Naz.* 16. There is also a version of this aphorism in the *Gospel of the Nazaraeans* (Hennecke and Schneemelcher: 1.149). Should this be considered as primary or secondary, as independent or dependent on the intracanonical version? This will involve some preliminary discussion on that extracanonical gospel itself.

(a) Jewish-Christian Gospels. There is, first of all, the general problem of the Jewish-Christian gospels (JG) and their identity. "The Church fathers hand down the title of only one JG, that of the Gospel of the Hebrews. . . . On the basis of their accounts it is possible to see in this Gospel of the Hebrews either with Jerome the Gospel of the Nazaraeans or with Epiphanius that of the Ebionites or with Eusebius an independent entity and so to distinguish it from each of these. . . . Thus the number of the JG—whether there be one, two or three such gospels—is uncertain, the identification of the several fragments is also uncertain, and finally the character and the relationship to one another of the several JG is uncertain" (Hennecke and Schneemelcher: 1.118). Vielhauer, just cited, concludes that there are three Jewish-Christian gospels: (i) *The Gospel of the Nazaraeans*, (ii) *The Gospel of the Ebionites*, and (iii) *The Gospel of the Hebrews*, and he describes that first text as "a Gospel read in a Semitic speech (Aramaic or Syriac), which is attested by Hegesippus and Eusebius, Epiphanius and Jerome, which according to the latter was in use among the Nazaraeans, the Syrian Jewish Christians, and which showed a close relationship to the canonical Matthew" (Hennecke and Schneemelcher: 1.139).

(b) *Gospel of the Nazaraeans* and Matthew. There is, next, the specific problem of that "close relationship" between Matthew and the *Gospel of the Nazaraeans*. What exactly is the connection? Vielhauer himself holds that "its literary character shows the GN secondary as compared with the canonical Mt.; again, from the point of view of Form Criticism and the history of tradition, as well as from that of language, it presents no proto-Matthew but a development of the Greek Gospel of Matthew" (Hennecke and Schneemelcher: 1.146).

(c) *Gos. Naz.* 16 and Matt. 19:16–24. The conjunction between the *dialectical story* of *The Rich Man* and Aphorism 20: *Camel and Needle* is outlined in Table 6.12. That figure makes it clear how Matthew and Luke both delete the deliberate redactional redundancy of Mark 10:23–24 ("to his disciples") by retaining only Matt. 19:23 ("to his disciples") and Luke 18:24 ("to the rich man"). But the more important point is whether *Gos. Naz.* 16 is to be con-

Table 6.12

	Mark	Matthew	Luke	Gospel of the Nazaraeans
Dialectical Story of *The Rich Man*	10:17–22	19:16–22	18:18–23	16a
Connection ("Jesus said")	10:23a	19:23a	18:24a	16b
Mark: Framing Generalization(1)	10:23b	19:23b	18:24b	
Mark: Amazement of Disciples	10:24a			
Mark: Framing Generalization(2)	10:24b			
Aphorism 20: *Camel and Needle*	10:25	19:24	18:25	16c

sidered a primary or independent version or simply a secondary and indeed tertiary version—that is, dependent on Matt. 19:16–24, which is itself dependent on Mark 10:17–25?

Vielhauer considers *Gos. Naz.* 16 to be secondary to Matt. 19: 16–24. It is his first example after asserting that "alike in its narratives and in its discourse material it proves itself for the most part secondary in comparison with Mt." (Hennecke and Schneemelcher:1.144). Apart from points of "fictional development . . . Jesus and Peter are seated; the rich man who has been spoken to scratches his head," there is this more significant theological development that "whilst in Mt. vs. 21 the giving away of one's goods to the poor expresses how extremely serious a thing it is to follow Christ, in the GN it is motivated by charity; the transformation of eschatological into ethical ideas, so characteristic of the development of the tradition, is evident" (1.144).

Jeremias, on the other hand, notes that *Gos. Naz.* 16 "is remarkably compact and consistent and possesses a clearer unity than the Matthean version, which bears visible traces of being a revision of the Markan form. That excludes the assumption that what we have here is a re-working of the Matthean version" (1964:46). He con-

Table 6.13

Matthew 19:16–17a	Mark 10:17b–18
one came up	a man ran up and
	knelt before him,
to him, saying,	and asked him,
"Teacher, what	"Good Teacher, what
good deed must I do,	must I do
to have eternal life?"	to inherit eternal life?"
And he said to him	And Jesus said to him,
"Why do you ask me	"Why do you call me
about what is good?	good?
One there is who is good.	No one is good but God alone.
If you would enter life,	You know
keep the commandments."	the commandments"

cludes that in *Gos. Naz.* 16 "we have here an independent version of the story of the Rich Young Man" (47).

This dispute has ramifications beyond the present instance because it is an example of classically bad methodology. In comparing an intracanonical and extracanonical text it is all too simple to argue for or against dependence, especially if one mistakenly presumes that secondary features in extracanonical texts must necessarily be *secondary to intracanonical versions.* Proper method requires the initial differentiation of traditional and redactional elements in the intracanonical text, the bracketing of all traditional materials as ambiguous, and separate focus on whether redactional elements from the intracanonical are found in the extracanonical version. If such are present, dependence is proved.

The present case is fortunately, an almost perfect instance for such methodology. The opening lines of the complex are given in Table 6.13.

Luke is willing to accept the Markan Jesus' refusal of the title "good." But Matthew is not so inclined: Note the conclusion to Matt. 20:15, "do you begrudge my generosity," which reads, literally, "is your eye evil because I am good." Matthew shifts the adjec-

Table 6.13 (cont.)

Luke 18:18–19	*Gospel of the Nazaraeans* 16
a ruler	The other of the two rich men
asked him,	said to him:
"Good Teacher, what	Master, what
shall I do	good thing must I do
to inherit eternal life?"	that I may live?
And Jesus said to him,	He said to him:
"Why do you call me good?	
No one is good but God alone.	
You know	Man, fulfill the law
the commandments."	and the prophets.

tive "good" from "teacher" to "deed," and then rephrases Jesus' counter-question (see Wenham, 1982). I consider Matt. 19:16–17 as clear a redactional rephrasing of Mark 10:17–18 as one could imagine. Yet *Gos. Naz.* 16 is but a further and better solution along the same track. It keeps the question as in Matt. 19:16 and omits completely the now rather vacuous counter-question in Matt. 19:17. There is, clearly, no independent version of *The Rich Man* or Aphorism 20 in *Gos. Naz.* 16. What is there is an excellent rewriting of the Matthean text by a very creative author.

(5) Conclusion. The saying on *Camel and Needle* was appended as *aphoristic conclusion* in Mark 10:25 to the dialectical story of *The Rich Man* in Mark 10:17–22. It was there imbedded in the quite emphatic Markan redundancy of 10:23–24. Later versions retained this combination of story and aphorism, but steadily removed the Markan redactional elements, so in the secondary versions of Matt. 19:16–24 = Luke 18:18–25 and the tertiary version of *Gos. Naz.* 16. But nobody succeeded in changing very much the implacable perfection of the aphorism itself.

7
Aphoristic Dialogue

To create things on which time may try its teeth in vain; to be concerned both in the form and the substance of my writing, about a certain degree of immortality—never have I been modest enough to demand less of myself. The aphorism, the sentence, in both of which I, as the first among Germans, am a master, are the forms of "eternity"; it is my ambition to say in ten sentences what everyone else says in a whole book,—what everyone else does *not* say in a whole book.

FRIEDRICH NIETZSCHE (Levy: 16.111)

People find difficulty with the aphoristic form: this arises from the fact that today this form is *not taken seriously enough*. An aphorism, properly stamped and molded, has not been "deciphered" when it has simply been read; rather, one has then to begin its *exegesis*, for which is required an art of exegesis.

FRIEDRICH NIETZSCHE (Kaufmann: 22–23)

An aphorism is a link from a chain of thoughts; it demands that the reader re-establish this chain from his own resources; this is to demand very much. An aphorism is a presumption.

FRIEDRICH NIETZSCHE (Mautner, 1933:54)

A. PROBLEMS AND TERMS

"Are you moved by the many who are dying now?"
"I weep for the survivors, and there are more of those."

That citation of Karl Kraus (Zohn: 88) on the First World War contains implicitly the problem of this chapter. The aphorism is in question and answer format and, while the answer is not meaningless in itself, the saying's force depends on the dialectic of question and answer and not just on the answer alone. In my terms, it compresses both the *aphoristic* and *dialectical traditions* into a single aphorism. And Kraus's dialectical aphorism can also serve as intro-

duction to a problem continuing from classical into contemporary
analysis.

1. CLASSICAL ANALYSIS

In Greco-Roman education "the *Progymnasmata* were a group of
elementary exercises for teaching composition, for writing and
speaking. They led by a graded series of exercises from the less
difficult to the more difficult, and culminated in speech-making.
For this reason, the later stages were handled by the rhetor" (Spencer, 1976:102–103). The student's first progression was, for example, through (1) *Fable*, (2) *Story*, (3) *Chreia*, and (4) *Gnome*. It is in
the relationship between those third and fourth units of speech and
stages in education that a problem begins—for us.

We know about those literary genres and pedagogical steps from
the written exercise books of grammarians such as Aelius Theon of
Alexandria in the early second century A.D., Hermogenes of Tarsus
in the later second century, and Aphthonius of Antioch in the late
fourth or early fifth century. These teachers agree very closely on
the definition and division of the *chreia*, as may be seen in the texts
given and translated by Taylor and Nicklin (Taylor, 1946:75–90).
First, "such sayings are called *chreiai* (from *hē chreia*—'need') probably because they were maxims which were taught to school children to impress their memories with views, ideas, and statements
which would be serviceable for the various 'needs' they would
experience in later walks of life" (Spencer, 1976:90). But it is also
likely that they were "useful" in philosophical propaganda before
being used in pedagogical instruction (Spencer, 1976:158–160).
Second, for definition, there is a third century A.D. Oxyrhynchus
papyrus fragment (Anonymous: 157–158) in the translation of Nicklin (Taylor, 1946:82):

> What is the Chreia? It is an Apomnemoneuma (i.e. memorandum)
> which is succinct, with reference to some person, told to his credit.
>
> Why is the Chreia an Apomnemoneuma? Because it is kept in mind in
> order that it may be quoted.

Why is it 'succinct'? Because, in many cases, if told at length it becomes either a narrative or something else.

Why is it 'told of some person'? Because, in many cases, without a personal reference, a succinct Apomnemoneuma becomes either a Gnomē or something else.

Why is it called a Chreia? Because of its serviceability.

Third, the standard division of the *Chreia* depends on whether the response is (1) a saying, (2) an action, or (3) both saying and action (Taylor, 1946:83; Spencer, 1976:109–113). The problem surfaces clearly in these distinctions and in the examples given for that first category, the purly verbal *Chreia* (Spencer, 1976:110): "Diogenes the philosopher, having been asked by someone how he might become of high regard, answered, 'By giving least thought to how he might become esteemed" (Theon), or "Plato said that the Muses dwell in the souls of the fit" (Hermogenes), or "Plato's saying that seedlings of virtue burst forth through sweat and toil" (Aphthonius).

The term *Chreia* covers aphorisms, dialogues, actions, or stories *as long as the climactic saying is attributed to some historical personage*. For example, the essential difference between *Chreia* and *Gnome* is that the former is so attributed, but the latter is not. Put crudely but accurately: "A stitch in time saves nine" is a *Gnome*, but "Jesus said: a stitch in time saves nine" is a *Chreia*. This is a very important point. It is not at all that the Greco-Roman grammarians were confused in their categories and divisions. It is that their essential distinction was between (1) attribution to a known and named historical person or (2) "attribution" to an anonymous source in ancient wisdom. "The attitude of the times was the reverse of ours. We view a maxim as if it had an existence and authority of its own, apart from its author. If we approve of it, we may be interested to find who was its author, and willing to value him for its sake. But, to them, the maxim, however impressive, had to come from an accredited person to carry the greatest weight. In short, the maxim was required to be a dictum" (Taylor, 1946:79–80). Or again: "the Chreia was, to the Hellenic mind, a fundamental form.

We have to recollect, however, that it was not merely a literary form, but essentially a historical statement—So-and-So, who was a known, historical figure, actually said or did this" (87). This concern with historical (or, for us, pseudohistorical) attribution shows up not only in how the Greco-Roman grammarians distinguished between *Chreia* and *Gnome*, but also in the first and last of the eight headings under which the poor student had to treat the given *Chreia*. The first step was a eulogy of the historical person involved and the final step reverted to that worthy in conclusion (Spencer, 1976:104–105).

The position of Marcus Fabius Quintilianus (c. A.D. 35–100), Spain's gift to Roman rhetoric, is more complicated than that of the grammarians. It is especially important to consider *together* the two sections in his *Institutio Oratoria* where the subject appears—that is, in 1.9:3–5 and 8.5:1–35 (Butler: 1.156–159 and 3.280–301). Note, however, how the Greek *chreia* appears latinized as *chria*.

The *Institutio Oratorio* 1.9:3–5 distinguishes quite clearly between three types of pedagogical exercises "in certain rudiments of oratory for the benefit of those who are not yet ripe for the schools of rhetoric," and these are the writing of "*aphorisms* [*sententiae*], *moral essays* (*chriae*), and *delineations of character* (*ethologiae*). . . . In all of these exercises the general idea is the same, but the form differs: *aphorisms* are general propositions, while *ethologiae* are concerned with persons [*quia sententia universalis est vox, ethologia personis continetur*]" (Butler: 1.156–159). Colson finds it curious that Quintilian should not have said "concerned with persons" of the *chria* as well as of the *ethologia* or *aetiology*, and he suggests that the text be amended accordingly (151 note 2). But I think this may presume a misunderstanding of Quintilian's meaning here. I do not think that his distinction between the "*vox universalis*" and the "*personis continetur*" refers to attribution and source but to application and use. Quintilian presumes that both *sententia* and *chria* stem from known and named persons, but that they are distinguished in that the former applies to a wide variety of situations while the latter applies to some particular, individual, or personal situation. Having made that basic distinction between his first and third type (1.9:3), he proceeds immediately to focus on the second type, the *chria*, in detail (1.9:4–5). This is somewhat in between the "*vox universalis*" and the "*personis continetur*" distinction; but, once again, the distinction is in use not source, in application not attribution. It is quite clear that all the formal openings by which Quintilian distinguishes the *chria*, such as "he said" or "in answer to this he replied," presume in the concrete a named personage. Thus he can state that, "of *moral essays* [*Chriarum*] there are various forms: some are akin to *aphorisms* [*sententiae*] and commence with a simple statement 'he said' or 'he used to say'" (1.9:4). I consider that this interpretation is confirmed by the way the phrase "*vox universalis*" is used again in the later discussion of 8.5:4 (Butler: 3.282–283).

In the *Institutio Oratoria* 8.5:1–35 the terminology, but not the theory, shifts a little. Now the overarching term is *sententia*, and it is used for "striking reflexions such as are more especially introduced at the close of our periods, a practice rare in earlier days, but carried even to excess in our own" (8.5:2). Quintilian breaks the sententia into two major species, an older and a more modern one. (1) "Although all the different forms are included under the same name, the oldest type of *sententia*, and that in which the term is most correctly applied, is the aphorism, called *gnōmē* by the Greeks. Both the Greek and the Latin names are derived from the fact that such utterances resemble the decrees or resolutions of public bodies. The term, however, is of wide application [*est autem haec vox universalis*] (indeed, such reflexions may be deserving of praise even when they have no reference to any special context), and is used in various ways" (8.5:3). Quintilian's "*vox universalis*" is here the universality of application and not the anonymity of attribution. This is also clear in the examples that follow. Sometimes Quintilian cites the author by name but, even when he does not do so explicitly, the examples are not proverbs but quotations and, once again, a named author is presumed behind them (see 8.5:4–7; note footnotes in Butler: 3.282,284). But it is especially evident in his concluding comment: "Such reflexions are best suited to those speakers whose authority is such that their character itself will lend weight to their words. For who would tolerate a boy, or a youth, or even a man of low birth who presumed to speak with all the authority of a judge and to thrust his precepts down our throats" (8.5:8). The other major type of *sententia* is declared to be "more modern," and the examples cited are cases of the *chria*; but there is no specific title used for them. Once again we are dealing primarily with known and named persons (8.5:15–25).

I conclude that, for Quintilian, the *sententia*, whether distinguished from the *chria* as species from species (1.9:3) or genus from species (8.5), is always presumed to have behind it a known, named, and preferably authoritative source, just as does the *chria* itself. In this he agrees substantially with the later grammarians. But while they clearly distinguish the *gnome* as being an anonymous saying, of universal application (a proverb), Quintilian considers it as an authored saying, of universal application (an aphorism).

What we are seeing here, for grammarians and rhetoricians alike, is the "renewed interest in exemplary figures in Hellenistic philosophy since the first century B.C." (Georgi: 534). Thus attribution (even, for us, pseudo-attribution) or anonymity was a crucial distinction, apparently overriding here such distinctions as aphorism, dialogue, action, or story. But this also bequeathes us with a problem, since it does not distinguish where we may want to do so—that is, its fundamental categories may not coincide with our own needed ones. And, worse still, we might not even notice that fact.

2. CONTEMPORARY ANALYSIS

The problem has resurfaced, however, in contemporary discussion. Since classical times the genre in question has been termed both *apophthegma* and *chreia* and, although "apophthegms do not have the breadth of applicability which makes the chreiai useful for so many situations in life" (Spencer, 1976:163), they may be taken for here and now as synonymous. The problem returns in Bultmann's magisterial work on the Synoptic tradition. His first two major sections were entitled "The Tradition of the Sayings of Jesus" (11–205) and "The Tradition of the Narrative Material" (209–317), that is, *sayings* and *stories*. He commented on that division (11):

> It also seems to me a secondary matter whether one begins with say-
> ings or stories. I start with sayings. But I should reckon as part of the
> tradition of the sayings a species of traditional material which might well
> be reckoned as stories—viz. such units as consist of sayings of Jesus set in
> a brief context. I use a term to describe them which comes from Greek
> literature, and is least question-begging—'apophthegms.' The subsequent
> course of this present inquiry will justify my taking the apophthegms
> before the sayings of Jesus that are not placed in a particular framework.
> The chief reason is that many apophthegms can be reduced to bare
> dominical sayings by determining the secondary character of their frame,
> and can thus be compared, in the following part of the book, with other
> sayings of Jesus.

There is an ambiguity hidden in that phrase "secondary character of their frame." A frame may be *historically secondary*, in that it came later than the saying it holds. In that case the saying existed separately and independently of the frame. Or: A frame may be *hermeneutically secondary*, in that it is less important than the saying it holds. But in that case the saying never existed separately or independently of the frame.

Bultmann then divided his "Sayings" section into "Apoph-thegms" (11–69) and "Dominical Sayings" (69–205). The former category includes (1) *conflict*, (2) *scholastic*, and (3) *biographical* apophthegms, and that initial ambiguity remains present throughout the analysis. On the one hand, he proposes a clear distinction between "unitary" and "non-unitary" apophthegms: "we must always raise the question whether we are dealing with an unitary composition, or whether the scene is a secondary construction for a saying originally in independent circulation. If the saying is comprehensible only in terms of its contextual situation, then it clearly has been conceived together with it" (47). On the one hand, he repeatedly asserts: "in general the sayings have produced a situation, not the reverse" (21) or "the sayings have commonly generated the situation, not vice-versa" (47), or "the situation has frequently been composed out of the dominical saying" (61). But surely the unitary apophthegms would have situation and saying quite simultaneous, so that dialectic rather than sequence is here the heart of the composition. And Bultmann's ambiguity has been continued and sometimes even increased in later works.

In his 1971 dissertation and 1979 publication, Hultgren divides the Synoptic conflict stories into "unitary" and "non-unitary" (1971:132–178,179–274; 1979:67–99,100–148), but many of his "non-unitary" ones involve what are actually *aphoristic conclusions* —that is, situations where an isolated saying is appended to a "unitary" story, for example, *Plucking Grain on the Sabbath* in Mark 2:23–28 (1971:217–224, 1975:111–115). Yet such aphoristic additions or conclusions are a quite separate question from the basic distinction of unitary and non-unitary apophthegms, as Bultmann already reminded us: "we must of course keep this question of the unity of the conception quite distinct from that of a secondary expansion by the addition of other sayings" (47 note 1).

It seems to me that the ambiguity inherited from Bultmann's initial analysis is still present in some very recent and very sophisticated studies rightly seeking a more adequate typology of apophthegms or pronouncement stories. There are three such functional typologies to be considered: (1) by Aune (1978:64–67) on the wisdom stories in the "Dinner of the Seven Wise Men" from *Plutarch's Moralia* (Babbitt:2.348–449); (2) by Tannehill (1981:1–13,101–119) on the pronouncement stories of the Jesus tradition; and (3) by Robbins (1981b:29–52), who combines those twin typologies into a more developed third possibility, and tests it on *Plutarch's Lives* (Perrin, 1914–1926). Since Robbins has thus connected Aune and Tannehill, the three analyses may be compared as in Table 7.1, with no great difference to be made between the terms wisdom stories and pronouncement stories, for the moment. I would also insist that each author's categories are to be compared and not just equated with similar ones in another.

My present concern is not with the basic validity of those excellent analyses, but with one single problem that is not really dis-

Table 7.1

	Aune	Robbins			Tannehill
Wisdom Saying					
Wisdom Story	Gnomic	Aphoristic	Description		Description
			Inquiry		Inquiry/Test
	Agonistic	Antagonistic	Correction	Self	
				Direct	Correction
				Indirect	
			Dissent	Objection	Objection
				Rebuff	
		Affirmative	Commendation	Self	
				Direct	Commendation
				Indirect	
			Laudation		
	Paradigmatic				

cussed in either Tannehill or Robbins. I emphasize this point because Robbins's term "aphoristic stories" is *not* the same as my own "aphoristic dialogues" or "aphoristic stories." For Robbins "aphoristic stories" are one of the three sub-types of "pronouncement stories," one where the "interaction . . . is friendly or natural, because confrontation with ideas rather than people governs the dynamics. The primary character's interaction with the idea addressed in the final utterance takes precedence over his interaction with people either within the setting or outside of it" (Robbins: 1981b:32). Neither, by the way, is there an equation between Kee's older term "aphoristic narratives" (1977:144), which is simply another term for "pronouncement stories," and my own expressions "aphoristic dialogues" and "aphoristic stories." None of those terms concerns itself with the specific situation of an aphoristic saying being later developed into an aphoristic dialogue or story. But in Robbins's analysis the problem is latent in his combination of "interaction" and "aphoristic."

Aune, however, has specifically surfaced the problem in "The Dinner of the Seven Wise Men" by noting that "Plutarch has ap-

parently elaborated the single structural element in the wisdom saying into the two-part structure characteristic of wisdom stories"
(1978:64). Among his examples (96–97) is a series of wisdom sayings
(my aphoristic sayings) from Thales in Diogenes Laertius' *Lives of
Eminent Philosophers* I.35 (Hicks: 1.36–37), which Plutarch converts into wisdom stories (my aphoristic dialogues). There are six
sayings, of which Plutarch uses five in his set of nine dialogues. He
also changes the sequence, and in Table 7.2 I have taken the liberty
of adapting Diogenes Laertius' order to that of Plutarch to facilitate
comparison. In Aune's terms: Wisdom sayings have become wisdom stories. In my terms: Aphoristic sayings have become aphoristic dialogues.

I propose, therefore, two essential distinctions. The first is between (1) the aphoristic tradition and (2) the dialectical tradition.
The *aphoristic tradition* includes everything in this present book,
and especially where aphoristic sayings are latterly developed into
aphoristic dialogues or stories. These are usually "set-up" phenomena so that there will be no interaction, dynamics, or dialectic be-

Table 7.2

Thales in Diogenes Laertius	Thales in Plutarch
Of all things that are, the most ancient is God, for he is uncreated	What is the oldest thing? God, said Thales, for God is some-thing that has no beginning
The greatest is space, for it holds all things.	What is greatest? Space; for while the universe contains within it all else, this contains the universe.
The most beautiful is the universe, for it is God's workmanship.	What is most beautiful? The Universe; for everything that is ordered as it should be is a part of it.
The wisest, time, for it brings everything to light.	What is wisest? Time, for it has discovered some things already, and shall discover all the rest.
The strongest, necessity, for it masters all.	What is strongest? Necessity; for that alone is insuperable.

tween situation and/or address and the climactic saying. It will destroy the validity of any typology based on "interaction" to include such units among the data. The *dialectical tradition* includes all those cases where dialectic exists between, on the one hand, the *situation and/or the address*, and, on the other, the *action and/or the response*. In this tradition, even if the second part has meaning by itself, it takes on its full import only in interaction or dialectic with the first part. And in many cases the second part is vacuous or meaningless when taken by itself or as an independent aphorism. I would insist on the importance of this distinction for those working on the Jesus tradition or for any analysis that includes it. How important it is elsewhere is another question but, at least, Aune has shown it operative in one essay of Plutarch.

The second essential distinction is between (1) *dialogue* and (2) *story*. I am quite aware that either can develop into the other and that dialogue often points outside itself to story just as story often contains dialogue within it. But granted all that, I think the distinction is again important, at least for the Jesus tradition and especially for understanding the gnostic and catholic developments within it. Think, for example, of the absolutely artificial way in which the letter *Eugnostos the Blessed* (CG III,3, and V,1) is turned into the dialogue *The Sophia of Jesus Christ* (CG III,4, and BG 8502,3) by inserted questions from Matthew, Philip, *Thomas*, Mariamne, Bartholomew, or the disciples in general (Robinson, 1977:206–228; Robinson and Koester: 84,90; Koester, 1979:536–537). Accordingly, my terms will be *aphoristic dialogues*, studied in the present chapter, then *aphoristic stories*, to be considered in the next chapter. But *dialectical dialogues* and *stories* fall outside the scope of the present book. We shall see, however, those points within the aphoristic tradition where developments towards or linkages with the dialectical tradition could be established.

3. THE TWO TRADITIONS

(1) Before continuing with *aphoristic dialogues*, I shall consider one complex in illustration of the preceding discussion. It has three units:

   (a) *Foxes Have Holes:*   Matt. 8:19–20 =   Luke 9:57–58 and
                                                                      Gos. Thom. 86
   (b) *Let the Dead:*   Matt. 8:21–22 =   Luke 9:59–60
   (c) *On Looking Back:*   Luke 9:61–62

(2) The Q Context. There are three units in Luke and two in Matthew. What was Q's text and context?

With regard to *external* context, this unit followed immediately upon Q/Matt. 11:2–19 = Luke 7:18–35, and this is still visible in the word-linkage between Son of Man in Q/Matt. 11:19 = Luke 7:34 and Q/Matt. 8:20 = Luke 9:58 (see Taylor, 1953:29; 1959:265–266; Polag, 1979:42–43; and Appendix 2).

With regard to *internal* context, the main problem is whether the Q complex contained two units as in Matthew or three as in Luke. Manson suggests that Luke 9:61–62 is not Q but from Luke's own special sources (73), but Lührmann dismisses it as a secondary expansion (1969:58 note 5), presumably from Luke himself. Although the question is delicate, I consider that Q had the aphoristic triptych, for two reasons. First, it is possible at least to suggest a reason why Matthew would have omitted it and also changed completely the sequence of the second aphorism in Q/Matt. 8:21–22 = Luke 9:59–60 from a triple-stich to a double-stich dialogue. Kingsbury (1975: 115) has said that "the most striking feature about Matthew's use of the Son of Man is that it assumes a totally 'public'—as opposed to 'confessional'—character. In addition, except for the 'righteous' in the scene of the Last Judgment, it marks the people in view of whom it is used as being unbelievers or opponents of Jesus." He finds this Matthean process set forth "in sharp relief" in the antithetical scenes of 8:18–22 as foliows:

  unbelieving: scribe/Teacher/Son of Man
  believing: disciple/Lord/Me

Thus there is at least a quite plausible reason why Matthew himself would have eliminated the third unit and then brought the first two into sharper and more balanced contrast. Second, Luke 9:60b, "but as for you, go and proclaim the Kingdom of God," is most likely a Lukan addition to make the startling comment of 9:60a somewhat more positive. It is absent from Matt. 8:21–22 where, were it present, it would make better sense in any case since there, unlike Q/Luke, we are dealing with a "disciple." But if Luke added 9:60b to Q for the second unit, it could well indicate that the third unit, which also contains the phrase "Kingdom of God," was present in Q and that Luke borrowed it thence.

I consider, therefore, that the three units were in Q, and that this is confirmed by a consideration of their content and their form. In *content*, they all deal with "following" Jesus and the first and last ones have the phrase "I will follow you" in Q/Luke 9:57 = 61. It may also be significant that they are framed by mentions of Son of Man and Kingdom of God in Q/Luke 9:58 = 62, just as the Beatitudes were framed by Kingdom of God and Son of Man in Q/Luke 6:20b = 22. But it is in *form* that the careful construction is most obvious. All three are *dialogues* in *comment/response* rather than *question/answer* format. But the stich structure is as follows: (a) man/Jesus, (b) Jesus/man/Jesus, (c) man/Jesus. That is, twin double-stich dialogues ("I will follow you") frame a central triple-stich dialogue ("Follow me").

(3) Aphorism 53: *Foxes Have Holes*. There are two independent versions to be considered: (a) Q/Matt. 8:19–20 = Luke 9:57–58; and (b) *Gos. Thom.* 86. (See Table 7.3.)

(a) Q. The "scribe/Teacher" in Matt. 8:19 is redactional as is, most likely, the Lukan expression, "as they were going along the road." Luke has just started, in 9:51–19:28, Jesus' long final journey to Jerusalem (see George, 1967:109–112). But after those items, the unit is remarkably the same.

Jacobson has drawn attention to a certain discrepancy between *comment* and *response* in Q. The comment says, "I will follow you *wherever you go*." The response seems to warn that Jesus is a homeless wanderer. Yet, surely, the man has just offered to become exactly that. Jacobson therefore proposes "that behind Lk 9:58 par

Table 7.3

Matthew 8:19–20	Luke 9:57–58	*Gospel of Thomas* 86
And a scribe came up and said to him, "Teacher, I will follow you wherever you go." And Jesus said to him, "Foxes have holes, and birds of the air have nests; but the Son of man has nowhere to lay his head."	As they were going along the road, a man said to him, "I will follow you wherever you go." And Jesus said to him, "Foxes have holes, and birds of the air have nests; but the Son of man has nowhere to lay his head."	Jesus said, "[The foxes have their and the birds have [the nests, but the Son of m no place to lay his hea and rest."

stands the idea of Wisdom which can find no resting place" (1978: 132). Suggs has noted that, "Both Sirach and 1 Enoch speak of Wisdom's search for a resting place among men. In Sirach, the search has a happy ending; Wisdom 'pitched her tent in Jacob' (24:8) and found 'a resting place in the beloved city' (24:11). But the fragment embedded in 1 Enoch 42 reports sadly that Wisdom was forced to return to heaven because she could find no dwelling-place among men" (1970:44). That latter text says that, "Wisdom found no place where she could dwell, and her dwelling was in heaven. Wisdom went out in order to dwell among the sons of men, but did not find a dwelling; Wisdom returned to her place and took her seat in the midst of the angels. And iniquity came out from her chambers; those whom she did not seek she found, and dwelt among them, like rain in the desert, and like dew on a parched ground" (Knibb: 2.42; see also 1 Enoch 94:5). Hence, the Q meaning of this aphorism is not just that Jesus is a homeless wanderer but that he has been rejected and cast out. And, quite obviously, Jesus as Son of Man is brought into very, very close conjunction with or even indirect equation with Wisdom herself. I consider, therefore, that Jacobson is quite correct in taking this aphorism "More as a statement about Jesus than as a statement about discipleship" (1978:133). And when one recalls that Q's first section ended with

John and Jesus (as Son of Man) rejected precisely as Wisdom's children in Q/Matt. 11:18–19 = Luke 7:33–35, the appropriateness of Q's starting this second section with Jesus (as Son of Man) rejected and homeless like Wisdom herself is quite obvious (Jacobson, 1978: 132).

(b) *Gos. Thom.* 86. The manuscript of Coptic *Thomas* is slightly but, from start to finish, increasingly damaged at the top and bottom outside corners of its pages. This aphorism begins at the bottom of one page and continues onto the next and is, therefore, doubly damaged. Hence the large amount of reconstructed text within square brackets in its first half.

There is, first of all, the immediate formal difference in that, while Q was an *aphoristic dialogue*, this is an *aphoristic saying*. And, since this eliminates any discrepancy between comment and response, that is between voluntary wandering and involuntary rejection, the meaning of *Gos. Thom.* 86 is not and was not necessarily that of Q. Therefore what Bultmann said long before *Thomas* was discovered must now be recalled: "it is plain that the dominical saying could have circulated without any framework. That must indeed have been the case if *ho huios tou anthrōpou* has been incorrectly substituted for 'man.' And 'man' must have been in fact the original meaning; man, homeless in this world, is contrasted with the wild beasts" (28). Koester, citing Bultmann, notes that *Thomas* never "uses the title 'Son of man' for Jesus or any other figure," so that "the decisive question is whether *Thomas* presupposes a stage of the synoptic tradition in which a titular usage of the term *Son of man* had not yet developed" (Robinson and Koester: 170,171 note 34). As with the saying in *Gos. Thom.* 42, "Become passers-by,"so also does this saying bespeak a homelessness for humanity within this world. And, although this has been denied (Strobel: 223), the addition of "and rest" after "to lay his head" points the aphorism towards a gnostic interpretation (Gärtner: 60–61). This is true not so much of the text itself, even with that addition, but of its contextual association with the theme of Rest or Repose in *Gos. Thom.* 2(Oxy

P 654.2),50,51,60, and 90 (Vielhauer, 1964:292–299). Indeed, there are "two terms, the Place and the Rest (or Repose)" brought together in *Gos. Thom.* 86, and even though "both are found in the New Testament, though usually in a general and non-technical sense," they are used in Thomas in a more specific and gnostic understanding (Turner and Montefiore: 110). In other words, *Gos. Thom.* 86 is much more contextually than textually gnostic (Robinson and Koester: 140–141).

In terms of my present concern, therefore, Aphorism 53, as *aphoristic saying*, has become *aphoristic dialogue* in Q. It belongs, however, to the aphoristic tradition.

(4) *Let the Dead.* There is only one independent version of this dialectical dialogue to be considered: Q/Matt. 8:21–22 = Luke 9: 59–60. (See Table 7.4.)

It is Matthew who changed Q's triple-stich *aphoristic dialogue* (Jesus, man, Jesus) to a double-stich one for the purpose of antithetical parallelism with the preceding saying. But in so doing he left two hanging threads. In Q/Luke 9:57–62 it is "a man" (*tis*), "another," and "another" in 9:57,59,61. But Matt. 8:19 begins with "a scribe" and then moves to "another of the disciples" in 8:21. Also, he retains the "first" in 8:21 but now it "comes very awkwardly in Mt.'s account. Of the two, Lk.'s account is to be preferred" (Manson: 73).

Table 7.4

Matthew 8:21–22	Luke 9:59–60
Another of his disciples	To another he said, "Follow me."
said to him,	But he said,
"Lord, let me first go and bury my father." But Jesus said to him, "Follow me,	"Lord, let me first go and bury my father." But he said to him,
And leave the dead to bury their own dead."	"Leave the dead to bury their own dead; but as for you, go and proclaim the Kingdom of God."

Is this unit aphoristic or dialectical tradition? For Bultmann it is "improbable" that the saying itself "could ever have been an independent saying" (29). In my terms, therefore, he would be considering it a dialectical dialogue. I agree with this since, despite the alternative possibility that an aphoristic dialogue has been built up from an aphoristic saying with the structural help of 1 Kings 19:19–20, it is much more likely that both "situation" and "saying" were in dialectic from the unit's inception.

(5) Aphorism 54: *On Looking Back*. There is only one version, as in Luke 9:61–62,

> Another said, "I will follow you, Lord; but let me first say farewell to those at my home." Jesus said to him, "No one who puts his hand to the plow and looks back is fit for the Kingdom of God."

In 1 Kings 19 Elijah casts his mantle on Elisha while he was plowing (19). Elisha responded: "Let me kiss my father and my mother, and then I will follow you" (20). He then proceeded to make sacrifice of the oxen using their yokes for fire (21). Thus, while the would-be disciple's response is quite similar in Q/Luke 9:61 = 1 Kings 19:20, the mention of the plow in Q/Luke 9:62 and 1 Kings 19:19,21 is totally different. I would suggest that the *aphoristic saying* in Q/Luke 9:62 has been developed into an *aphoristic dialogue* by bringing in the comment of Elisha. The development was, of course, facilitated by the common theme of *plowing* in both cases.

(6) Conclusion. The threefold complex in Q/Luke 9:57–62 frames a dialectical dialogue with two aphoristic ones. It is not my purpose with this terminology to propose a scholarly guessing game on what *might be* aphoristic and what *might be* dialectical. What is important is not just a debate over product but an understanding of process. There are certain sayings whose only force or whose total force occurs in dialectic with their preceding situation and/or address, be it question, comment, or request. That is the dialectical tradition. And there are other sayings, certainly in the Jesus tradition at least, which appear quite separately as aphoristic sayings and

also elsewhere as aphoristic dialogues and stories. As such they are best interpreted within the aphoristic tradition.

B. APHORISM AND DIALOGUE

There are three situations to be considered. First, there are those cases where, within independent or primary versions, one is aphoristic saying while the other is aphoristic dialogue. Examples would be Aphorisms 8,45,53,64,104,124 in Table 7.5. Second, there are instances, within dependent versions, where the primary one is aphorism while the secondary one is dialogue. Examples would be Aphorisms 20,21,24,54,56 and 86, 121 in Table 7.5. These latter instances confirm the general presumption that aphoristic dialogue

Table 7.5

Aphorism	Aphoristic Saying
8	*Gos. Thom.* 14c; Mark 7:15; Matt 15:11
45	Q/Matt. 7:17–18(12:33a) = Luke 6:43
53	*Gos. Thom.* 86
64	Q/Matt. 11:28–30; *Gos. Thom.* 90
104	Q/Luke 12:54–56
124	*Gos. Thom.* 3 Mark 13:21 = Matt. 24:23 Q/Matt. 24:26 = Luke 17:23
20	(Pre-Mark)
21	(Pre-Mark)
24	Mark 12:35–37a = Luke 20:41–44
54	(Pre-Q)
56 86	Q/Matt. 10:16a = Luke 10:3 ⎱ Q/Matt. 10:28 = Luke 12:4–5 ⎰
121	Q/Luke 17:4
106	Q/Matt. 7:13–14
131	Q/Matt. 24:28

is itself a later development of aphoristic saying. Third, however, are those cases of reversed development, cases where a primary version has dialogue, but à dependent version has only the saying. Examples are Aphorisms 106 and 131 in Table 7.5. This is a reminder that formal tendencies, or laws, however dominant, are always reversible in individual cases.

The next step for this chapter is to consider various ways in which aphorisms become dialogues.

C. SIMPLE APHORISTIC DIALOGUE

In the simple aphoristic dialogue, or *saying-as-response*, the address to Jesus, be it question, request, or comment, is minimal and usu-

Table 7.5 (cont.)

Aphoristic Dialogue
Mark 7:17, 18b, 20; Matt. 15:15, 17, 18
Gos. Thom. 43c
Q/Matt. 8:19–20 = Luke 9:57–58
Dial. Sav. 141:3–6
Q/Matt. 16:1–3; *Gos. Thom.* 91
Gos. Thom. 51 and 113 Luke 17:20–21
Mark 10:25 = Matt. 19:24 = Luke 18:25
Mark 10:29–30 = Matt. 19:29–Luke 18:29b–30
Matt. 22:41–46
Q/Luke 9:61–62
2 Clem. 5:2–4
Q/Matt. 18:21–22
Q/Luke 13:23–24
Q/Luke 17:37

ally derived verbally from the saying's own content. The address is a "set-up" for the saying itself. I do not mean that the address adds nothing at all to the saying in such cases. In one sense, of course, it does not. But, in another, the very dialogue form asserts implicitly that questions can and should be asked and that answers can and will be given. And when one considers what happens as dialogue develops, especially among the gnostic traditions, it would be very unwise to consider that these first and very simple steps from aphorism to dialogue were not fateful indeed (see Robinson and Koester: 74–84; Koester, 1979,1980b).

Aphorism 104: *Knowing the Times*

(1) There are two independent versions to be considered: (1) Q/ Matt. 16:1–3 = Luke 12:54–56; and (b) *Gos. Thom.* 91. (See Table 7.6.)

Table 7.6

Matthew 16:1–3	Luke 12:54–56	
And the Pharisees and Sadducees came, and to test him they asked him to show them a sign from heaven.		
He answered them, "When it is evening, you say 'It will be fair weather; for the sky is red.'	He also said to the multitudes, "When you see a cloud rising in the west, you say at once, 'A shower is coming'; and so it happens.	
And in the morning, 'It will be stormy today, for the sky is red and threatening.'	And when you see the south wind blowing, you say, 'There will be scorching heat'; and it happens.	
You know how to interpret the appearance of the sky, but	You hypocrites! You know how to interpret the appearance of the earth and sky; but why do	
you cannot interpret the signs of the times."	you not know how to interpret the present time?"	

(2) The Q Text. There is a special problem concerning Matt. 16:2–3 that has resulted in its being placed within brackets in the third edition of *The Greek New Testament* and the twenty-sixth edition of the Nestle-Aland *Novum Testamentum*. "The external evidence for the absence of these words is impressive. . . . The question is how one ought to interpret this evidence. Most scholars regard the passage as a later insertion from a source similar to Lk 12.54–56, or from the Lukan passage itself, with an adjustment concerning the particular signs of the weather. On the other hand, it can be argued (as Scrivener and Lagrange do) that the words were omitted by copyists in climates (e.g. Egypt) where red sky in the morning does not announce rain" (Metzger, 1971:41). The manuscript evidence is indeed impressive, but I am still more inclined to consider it original in Matt. 16:2–3 and to explain its omission as suggested above. It is quite understandable and even usual for

Table 7.6 (cont.)

Gospel of Thomas 91
They said to Him, "Tell us who you are so that we may believe in you."
He said to them,
"You read the face of the sky and of the earth, but you have not recognized the one who (or: that which) is before you, and you do not know how to read this moment."

scribes to harmonize synoptic texts as they copy them. But this scribe would have had to effect an almost classic performancial variation on Luke 12:54–56 and then locate it in a completely different but verbally quite appropriate context in Matthew. What has been effected, in other words, is disharmony rather than harmony. This would only be plausible if one insists that the scribe knew the Matthean version quite independently of Luke 12:54–56 and considered that it had to be added to Matthew's text. This would indicate, at a minimum, that Matt. 16:2–3 represents an independent performancial variation on Luke 12:54–56 prior to any scribal inclusion of it in Matthew's text. Finally, there is the problem of a possible word-linkage between

(a) Aphorism 104 (Q?/Matt. 16:2–3 = Luke 12:54–56): "interpret" (*diakrinein*).
(b) Aphorism 105 (Q?/Matt. 5:25–26 = Luke 12:57–59): "judge" (*krinete*).

The verb *diakrinein* is only in Matt. 16:3, and the verb *krinete* is only in Luke 12:57. Unless this is pure coincidence, it could indicate that those sayings were word-linked successively in Q.

At minimum, then, Matt. 16:2–3 would have to be considered an independent performancial variation inserted scribally into Matt. 16:2–3. And, at maximum, it would represent a pre-Matthean or Matthean performancial variation on the Q/Luke 12:54–56 text. I am not convinced it is simple scribal interpolation (but see Bultmann: 116; Manson: 121).

Matthew and Luke give different indications for

good weather: evening red sky (good) and western cloud (rain)
bad weather : morning red sky (storm) and southern wind (heat)

in that order. But in Matthew it is twice a case of the "appearance of the sky" (16:3), while in Luke 12:56 it is a case of the "appearance of earth and sky," that is, the wind is evident on earth while the cloud is evident in the sky.

In terms of my present concern, Q/Luke 12:54–56 is an aphoristic saying but Matt. 16:1–3 has made it an aphoristic dialogue. This was effected, however, not just by creating a preliminary address but by inserting the aphorism within the dialectical dialogue *Request for Sign*, which is present both in Mark 8:11–12 and also Q/Matt. 12:38–40(16:4) = Luke 11:(16)29–30. This process was also facilitated by the word-linkage between (a) "sign/heaven (*ouranos*)" in Matt. 16:1 = Mark 8:11 = Luke 11:16 and (b) "sky (*ouranos*)/ signs" in Matt. 16:2–3 (see Polag, 1979:66–67).

(3) *Gos. Thom*. 91. In terms of form the *Thomas* text is an aphoristic dialogue, as in Matt. 16:1–3, rather than an aphoristic saying, as in Q/Luke 12:54–56.

There are six *dialectical* (13,18,52,79,104,114) and thirteen *aphoristic dialogues* (3,6,12,21,22b,24,37,43,51,53,61b,91,113) in the *Gospel of Thomas*, and this means that *dialogue* is its next most frequent form after that of the single, isolated *aphorism* itself. Even the parable of *The Mustard Seed* appears as dialogue in *Gos. Thom*. 20. Of those twenty dialogues twelve are single interchanges between the Disciples and Jesus, in that order: 6,12,18,20,22b,24,37, 43,51,52,53,113. Another six have as addressees either named disciples such as Mary (21), Salome (61b), Simon Peter (114), or, more generally, "a woman" (79), or simple "they" (91,104). These six cases, like the other twelve, are all single interchanges with Jesus always as respondent. A possible exception is 61b where, despite manuscript difficulties, there seems to have been a double interchange between Salome and Jesus. The final two instances, however, are quite special. In *Gos. Thom*. 3 there is an implicit aphoristic and even dialectical dialogue which will be discussed more fully later. Finally and most unusually, in *Gos. Thom*. 13 Jesus speaks to the disciples and is answered by Simon Peter, Matthew, and Thomas. Then Jesus speaks only to Thomas, giving him preferential treatment above the others. It then concludes with the only case in the *Gospel of Thomas* where an interchange takes place *without* Jesus: the disciples ask Thomas a question and he responds to them.

Gos. Thom. 91 fits, then, into the more usual single-exchange dialogue with Jesus as respondent, but it is also one of the two dialogues initiated by an unnamed "they."

In terms of content, there are two important differences between

Gos. Thom. 91 and Q/Luke 12:54–56. *Thomas* gives no concrete examples of weather indications, yet he does mention "the face of the sky and of the earth," and this fits with the types of indications mentioned in Luke: cloud and wind. But the more significant change is that, corresponding to the opening question—"They said to Him, 'Tell us who You are so that we may believe in You' "— the *aphoristic dialogue* contains "but you have not recognized the one who (or: that which) is before you." This is best seen as "a gnosticized reworking of the saying we have known from Luke 12: 56" (Sieber: 220). It is to be read along with *Gos. Thom.* 5 and 52 and "suggests the description of the epiphany of a heavenly thing, a veritable theophany" (Turner and Montefiore: 88; Gärtner: 139–140).

(4) Conclusion. In content, the emphasis in Q/Luke 12:54–56 was on the *kairos* and this is still the emphasis in the performancial variation of this saying created by Matthew and inserted at 16:2–3. But *Gos. Thom.* 91 has changed this in both form and content so that the preliminary concrete weather indications are completely omitted and it is Jesus as Revealer who receives primary emphasis. In form, however, the main difference is that the implicit dialogue in Q/Luke had become an explicit aphoristic dialogue in both Matthew and *Thomas*. And in these cases aphoristic is already heading towards dialectical dialogue as "correction" intrudes from Jesus in *Thomas* and "testing inquiry" from the addresses in Matthew (see Tannehill, 1981:103; Perkins, 1981:123).

Aphorism 8: *From the Mouth*

(1) There are three independent versions to be considered: (a) Mark 7:15; (b) Matt. 15:11; and (c) *Gos. Thom.* 14c. (See Table 7.7.)

(2) Mark 7:1–23. Bultmann (17) had already suggested that Mark 7:15 was not the original aphoristic climax of the polemical apophthegm in 7:1–8 or 7:1–13 because (a) it deals with unclean food not unwashed hands; (b) "it is like Mark to enlarge apophthegms by such additions," for example, in 2:27–28; and (c) 7:14 is his redac-

Table 7.7

Matthew 15:11	Mark 7:15	*Gospel of Thomas* 14c
Not what goes into the mouth defiles a man, but what comes out of the mouth this defiles a man.	There is nothing outside a man which by going into him can defile him; but the things which come out of a man are what defile him.	For what goes into your mouth will not defile you, but that which issues from your mouth— it is that which will defile you.

tional connective, using the same distinction of *parabolic teaching to the crowds outside* and *explanation for the incomprehending and rebuked disciples inside*, as in 4:1 = 7:14 and 4:10 + 13 = 7:17–18a (so also Pryke: 50–52,156,161). Although this position has been debated (see Lambrecht, 1977:28–39), the debate itself, as well as the appearance of the isolated aphorism in *Gos. Thom.* 14c, make it necessary to study Mark 7:15, among the aphorisms, as aphoristic dialogue, rather than leaving it with the apophthegms, as dialectical dialogue.

(3) Mark 7 and Q. There are two *separable* problems both arising from the differentiation of *food* into pure and impure: (a) washing vessels and hands before eating (see Lambrecht, 1977:48 note 76); and (b) eating itself. These must be considered separately.

(a) *Washing.* Q has preserved in Aphorism 80: *Inside and Outside* (Matt. 23:25–26 = Luke 11:39–41) a saying concerning washing. Here the metaphorical challenge moves along the axes of outside/inside and utensils (explicit)/persons (implicit). But the point of the original aphorism can be seen much more clearly in *Gos. Thom.* 89. It is a radical attack on the very validity of the outer/inner *distinction* itself. In Q the point has already moved from utensils to persons: see Q/Matt. 23–25b = Luke 11:39b, and note Matthew's "they are full" against Luke's "you are full." Luke 11:41 consummates this personalization process.

(b) *Eating.* This is the problem behind the saying in Mark 7:15, Matt. 15:11, Acts 11:8, and *Gos. Thom.* 14c. Here the axes are going in/coming out and food/words and it is explicitly connected with persons not vessels.

(c) *Washing and Eating.* But in Mark 7 these two separable problems are quite legitimately unified into a single discourse that attacks their common root in food purity and impurity. Thus the *washing* problem appears in 7:1–13 and the *eating* problem in 7:14–23. What is most significant, however, is that the outside/inside dichotomy from the former debate has now infiltrated into the latter. (See Table 7.8.)

Two points should be underlined. Outside/Inside is always in that sequence and always uses *exōthen/esōthen*—except for Matt. 23:26 (*entos/ektos*).

This means, therefore, that in studying the aphorism *From the Mouth* we must watch for interference from that other aphorism on *Inside and Outside.*

(4) Luke. Luke has omitted the entire discussion on food purity/impurity from Mark 7 presumably because of his section more appropriately placed in Acts 10–11. When the Lord commands Peter to eat indiscriminately, "Peter said, 'No, Lord; for I have never eaten anything that is common or unclean' " in 10:14. But in retelling his vision in Jerusalem Peter says, "I said, 'No Lord; for nothing common or unclean has ever entered my mouth' " (11:8). That final phrase, "entered my mouth" (*eisēlthen eis to stoma mou*), must be remembered for future discussion.

(5) Matt. 15:11. It is commonly accepted that Matt. 15:1–20 has rather drastically rearranged and rephrased Mark 7:1–23 (Morgenthaler: 173) for both stylistic and theological reasons. But there is something more important than this. In comparing his version of the aphorism in 15:11 with that in Mark 7:15, and his repetition of

Table 7.8

	Matthew 15:11	Mark 7:15	Luke
Outside		7:15, 18	
Inside		7:21, 23	

it in 15:17,18 with those in Mark 7:18b,20, two items stand out forcibly. (i) Matthew has nothing about the *Outside/Inside* dichotomy of Mark 7:15,18,21,23. (ii) Matthew mentions "the mouth" (*stoma*) in 15:11a,11b,17,18 and Mark never does so. Indeed the differentiation is quite pointed. (See Table 7.9.)

These considerations persuade me to accept "the possibility . . . that Matthew here replaced Mark 7:15 with another version of the saying from his special material" (Sieber: 192). It is clear from Acts 11:8 that Luke also knows an aphorism about pure and impure food *going into the mouth*, and this confirms its existence. One might even conjecture that it could have been in Q, whence into Matt. 15:11 and Acts 11:8. But, in any case, Matthew has substituted the *into/out of the mouth* version for Mark's *outside/inside* one.

(6) Mark 7:15. Pryke (50) has said that "the whole passage vv. 14–23 . . . is a Markan construction including dominical sayings to which are appended lists of sins, similar in kind to passages in the Pauline epistles." Mark has built the complex (a) by taking the double-stich negative/positive saying in 7:15ab; (b) repeating 7:15a in 7:18b and then adding the commentary of 7:19; and (c) repeating 7:15b in 7:20 and then adding the commentary of 7:21–23. Thus the aphorism has been redactionally repeated in 7:15 and 7:18b,20.

As already argued, the *outside/inside* dichotomy in Mark 7:15 (18b,20) is a combination with and intrusion for that same distinction in Q/Matt. 23:25–26 = Luke 11:39–41. But the *going into/ coming out of* dichotomy is original to this aphorism. This is indicated by its presence in Matt. 15:11; Acts 11:8; *Gos. Thom.* 14c, and despite the fact that those verbs are favorite redactional ones for Mark (Lambrecht, 1977:58–60).

(7) *Gos. Thom.* 14c. The Thomistic version is obviously closer to

Table 7.8 (cont.)

Gospel of Thomas 14c	Matthew 23:25–26	Luke 11:39–40
	23:25a, 26b	11:39a, 40a
	23:25b, 26a	11:39b, 40b

Table 7.9

Mark 7	Matthew 15
"outside" (15)	"into the mouth" (15:11a)
"outside" (18)	"out of the mouth" (15:11b)
"inside" (21)	"into the mouth" (15:17)
"inside" (23)	"out of the mouth" (15:18)

the Matthean-Lukan than to the Markan since it has the *going into the mouth/coming out of the mouth* dichotomy rather than the *outside/inside* distinction. It has been argued that this proves that "the Gospel of Thomas here follows Matthew" and is dependent on him (McArthur, 1960:286; see Schrage: 55; Ménard, 1975:101). But this does not explain why the Synoptic texts are in the third person while the Thomistic version is in the second person (Sieber: 193).

The accusation concerning *washing* is made against Jesus in Q (= Luke 11:38) and he replies, naturally, in the second person in Q/Luke 11:39–40 = Matt. 23:25–26, but this has become an accusation against Jesus' disciples in Mark 7:1–2,5 to which the aphorism in 7:15 speaks in the third person. The general tendency of the tradition is to change an attack on Jesus into an attack on his disciples (Bultmann: 48). This development appears concerning *washing* as Q(= Luke 11:38) reappears in Mark 7:1–2,5, and also concerning *eating* as Gos. Thom. 14c reappears in Matt. 15:11(17,18). "It seems more likely, therefore, that the second person, a defence of Jesus himself, is the original" (Sieber: 193).

One final point. In the *second* half of the aphorism in Mark 7:20 (but not in 7:15b), in Matt 15:11b = 18, and in Gos. Thom. 14c, there is a *casus pendens* followed by a resumptive demonstrative pronoun, presumably for emphasis. This will have to be retained in the recoverable original while remembering that this usage "is normal in Greek, but unattested in Hebrew or Aramaic" contemporary with the New Testament (Maloney: 126).

(8) Conclusion. In terms of content, the original aphorism had no outside/inside dichotomy, but contrasted what goes into the

mouth (innocent foods) with what comes out of the mouth (guilty words). In so doing it deliberately played along the borders of physical and spiritual, literal and metaphorical. And it denied quite radically and absolutely the value of spirituality connected with pure and impure categories of food. In terms of form the saying is a simple aphorism in *Gos. Thom.* 14c. But in Mark it has become part of a carefully constructed complex involving (a) a dialectic in 7:1–13 with the authorities; (b) the aphorism addressed to the crowds in 7:14–15; and (c) the aphorism broken down into 7:18b and 20 and then commented on in 7:19 and 21–23, but now addressed to the rebuked (7:18a) and incomprehending disciples. Although Matt. 15:11 seems an independent version, he has followed Mark's combination of it into this complex. He has developed the dialogue with the disciples in two stages, however: first the disciples in general in Matt. 15:12–14 (not in Mark), and then Peter in particular in 15:15, but with the disciples's question from Mark 7:17.

D. SPLIT APHORISTIC DIALOGUE

In the split aphoristic dialogue, or *saying-as-address-and-response*, the aphorism is divided between address and response so that the latter is no longer comprehensible by itself. It could be termed a pseudo-dialectical dialogue.

Aune, as seen earlier, has already noted how Plutarch split traditional sayings into dialogues by giving half the saying as address and the other half as response. Koester has proposed the same phenomenon within the *Dialogue of the Savior* from Nag Hammadi (III,5): "The main source used by the author was a dialogue between Jesus and several of the disciples. This dialogue is based on a traditional collection of sayings comparable to 'Q' or the *Gospel of Thomas* (II,2); in fact, many of the sayings used or alluded to in the dialogue have parallels in the *Gospel of Thomas*. The individual sayings of Jesus are quoted, expanded, and interpreted, and thus a dialogue is formed" (in Robinson, 1977:229; see also Pagels and Koester: 67–68). He suggests, for example, that *Dial. Sav.* 142:5–9, "Judas said,

'Tell me, Lord, what is the beginning of the way?' He said, 'Love and goodness. For if there had been one of these dwelling with the archons, wickedness would never have come to be" (Robinson, 1977:236), "was constructed probably" from the saying, "The beginning of the way is love and goodness" (Koester, 1980b:252; see also 1979:545).

One could hardly find a more perfect example of this process than the way in which a Homeric couplet appears as a dialogue between Alexander and Diogenes among examples of the *chreia* cited in Aelius Theon of Alexandria. The saying to Atreus is from *The Iliad* 2:24–25 (see Murray: 1.52–53), the dialogue is from Spengel (2.98) in the translation by Spencer (112–113, see also 470). Since the Greek is verbatim the same, I translate Homer to agree with Spencer, as in Table 7.10.

Another interesting example, but not, of course in genetic relationship, is the way in which *The Golden Rule* is attributed to Jesus as a saying in Q/Matt. 7:12 = Luke 6:31, "and as you wish that men would do to you, do so to them," but is attributed to Aristotle as a split aphoristic dialogue. Diogenes Laertius' *Lives of Eminent Philosophers* V.21 reports that, "To the question how we should behave to friends, he answered, 'As we should wish them to behave to us'" (Hicks: 1.464–465). One can easily imagine this version of *The Silver Rule* (only for friends?) as a saying: We should behave to

Table 7.10

Homer's Saying	Theon's Dialogue
	Alexander, the king of the Macedonians, standing above Diogenes as he slept said,
It is not proper for a man who counsels to sleep all night,	"It is not proper for a man who counsels to sleep all night," and Diogenes answered,
(one) to whom the people have been entrusted and on whom so much rests.	"(one) to whom the people have been entrusted and on whom so much rests."

friends as we should wish them to behave to us. The twin versions, apart from the wider demands of the Jesus one, are but performancial transpositions of the twin halves of the same idea.

Aphorism 64: *Yoke and Burden*

(1) There are possibly four independent versions to be considered: (a) Q/Matt. 11:28–30; (b) *Gos. Thom.* 90; (c) *Pist. Soph.* 95; and (d) *Dial. Sav.* 141:3–6. (See Table 7.11.)

(2) Q and Matt. 11:28–30. Despite the obvious uncertainties, I am presuming that this aphorism stood in Q immediately after Aphorisms 62–63 (see Koester, 1980b:244 note 19). It continues this rhapsodic interpolation of later Q wisdom theology. And yet the central verse, Matt. 11:29, seems to mute somewhat the staggering claim of the (for Matthew) immediately preceding Q/11:27. I propose that Q contained *only* Matt. 11:28,30 and that Matthew himself inserted 11:29 within the Q saying. In Q/Matt. 11:28 + 30, Jesus is again Wisdom itself since *he* now promises what *it* supplied in Sir. 51:26 (yoke) and 51:27 (rest). My reasons for that proposal are not so much internal considerations, although the clearest Matthean redactional element, the use of "gentle," is in 11:29. This is elsewhere only in Matt. 5:5, 21:5, and 1 Pet. 3:4 in the New Testament. The following external evidence prompts the suggestion.

(3) *Gos. Thom.* 90. *Thomas's* version is not dependent on that of Matthew (Sieber:139; as against Schrage, 1964:173). Instead, "both go back to wisdom traditions which have been subjected to gnosticizing transformations" (Betz, 1967:20). Koester has suggested that "except for 'lordship' instead of 'burden' (Matt. 11:30) this shorter version could be more original than Matthew's" (1980b:246). Bauer would agree and even consider that "lordship" could be more original (1961:105). I prefer to follow Koester rather than Bauer primarily because "burden" reappears in *Pist. Soph.* 95 and *Dial. Sav.* 141:3–6. Indeed, the force of the aphorism seems intensified if there is some comparison made between heavy or difficult burdens (from elsewhere) and light or easy burdens (from Jesus). I propose, therefore, that, while *Thomas's* version is more original than that of

Table 7.11

Matthew 11:28–30	*Gospel of Thomas* 90	
Come to me, all who labor and are heavy-laden,	Come unto Me,	
and I will give you rest. Take my yoke upon you, and learn from me; for I am gentle and lowly in heart, and you will find rest for your souls.		
For my yoke is easy, and my burden is light.	for My yoke is easy and My lordship is mild, and you will find repose for yourselves.	

Matt. 11:28–30, it is not more original than Q/Matt. 11:28 + 30 since *Thomas* lacks any equivalent to Q's "all who labor and are heavy laden (burdened)."

(4) *Pist. Soph.* 95. The English collector Dr. A. Askew bought a Coptic parchment codex from a London bookseller in 1773, and this Codex Askewianus was purchased by the British Museum at his death in 1785. In the meanwhile it had been introduced to the scholarly world as *Pistis Sophia*, a title inserted for Book II by a later hand. There are, however, two separate works included under this traditional title, and both are translations from Greek originals. Books I–III "correspond to the three books of one and the same work, probably composed between 250 and 300"; but Book IV "is in reality a distinct work, composed in the *first* half of the 3rd century and thus older than those which precede it" (Hennecke and Schneemelcher: 1.250–51).

There is a version of Aphorism 64 in Book II, Chapter 95: "Because of this now I said to you once: 'Everyone who is weary and heavy-laden (lit. oppressed with care and troubled by their burden)

Table 7.11 (cont.)

Pistis Sophia 95	Dialogue of the Saviour 141:3–6
Everyone who is weary and heavy-laden, come to me and I will give you rest.	Matthew said, "Why do we not put ourselves to rest at once?"
For my burden is light and my yoke is compassionate.	The Lord said, "(You will) when you lay down these burdens."

come to me and I will give you rest. *For* my burden is light and my yoke is compassionate" (Schmidt and MacDermot: 219–220 or 438–441; Greek word italicized). In context, the "heavy burden" is explained as: the whole world and all the matter or material cares within it; and the *light burden* of those who have "renounced" the material world is: the mystery of the Ineffable, the Godhead. One must "renounce" the former for the latter. This could, of course, be simply an abbreviated and slightly changed quotation from Matthew 11:28–30. But Betz has noted that "the Matthean vs. 29 is missing, and we cannot explain the omission on the grounds of gnostic theology," and I would therefore agree with his conclusion that "we are dealing with wisdom sayings, originally independent, which were gnosticized and then were taken up in different variants into the Gospel of Matthew, the Gospel of Thomas, and the Pistis Sophia" (1967:20). Matthew would thus be an expanded, and *Thomas* a contracted version of a saying whose more original form is still visible in *Pistis Sophia*.

(5) *Dial. Sav.* 141:3–6. This document, which was mentioned

earlier in this chapter, "contains some forty-seven questions and answers" (Perkins, 1980:108). The core of the composition is described by Pagels and Koester as: "*Dialogue* between 'the Lord,' Judas, Miriam, and Matthew. This original dialogue is the other's *primary source*. It is woven throughout the whole of the present *Dialogue of the Savior*; is based on a traditional collection of the sayings of Jesus, analogous to the synoptic *Sayings Source*. Parallels with *Matthew* occur more frequently (10 times) than those with *Mark, Luke,* or *John*: yet parallels to the *Gospel of Thomas* occur 16 times" (73).

Both "rest" and "burden" appear within the aphoristic saying itself in Q/Matt. 11:28–30 and *Pist. Soph*. 95. But they are split in *Dial. Sav*. 141:3–6 so that "rest" appears in Matthew's question and "burdens" appears in Jesus' answer. Koester has argued that the aphoristic dialogue in *Dial. Sav*. 141:3–6 is independent of Matthew (1980b:246). In this document the "burdens" are interpreted by the next interchange between Matthew and Jesus where the latter comments (141:10–13): "When you leave behind you the things that will not be able to follow you, than you will put yourselves to rest" (Robinson, 1977:236). Obviously, however, this version is extremely constricted and indeed but barely still visible.

(6) Conclusion. In terms of content, the "burden" is the "Pharisaic law" for Matthew (Betz, 1967:22; see also Maher). For Q, "Jesus has taken the place of the hypostasized Wisdom" (22), and thence "a tendency towards Gnosticism" (22) becomes more fully developed and evident in *Pist. Soph*. 95, *Dial. Sav*. 141:3–6, 10–13, and *Gos. Thom*. 90 (see Vielhauer, 1964). In terms of form, the aphoristic saying as in *Pist. Soph*. 95 is expanded by the addition of 11:29 into Matt. 11:28–30 and contracted into *Gos. Thom*. 90. But only in *Dial. Sav*. 141:3–6 does it appear as a split aphoristic dialogue.

Aphorism 24: *Son of David*

(1) There are two independent versions to be considered: (a) Mark 12:35–37a = Matt. 22:41–45 = Luke 20:41–44; and (b) *Barn*. 12:10b,11b. (See Table 7.12.)

(2) *Barn.* 12:10–11. It was already seen that *Barnabas* is independent of the synoptic tradition. And there is no internal evidence for a dependence of *Barn.* 12:10–11 on Mark 12:35–37, to which, despite its "footstool" as in Luke 20:43, it is closest among the three synoptics (Koester, 1957a:145–146).

Barn. 12:10–11 (Lake:1.386–387) opens with, "See again Jesus, not as son of man, but as Son of God, but manifested in a type in the flesh" (10a). Then follows the argument from Ps. 101:1 (10b) and another from Isa. 45:1 (11a). The unit closes with another framing, "See how David calls him Lord and does not say Son" (11b). The two biblical proofs are word-linked by "right hand," that of God in Ps. 110:1 (10b), that of Jesus in Isa. 45:1 (11a). But the present emphasis of the text is on the use of Ps. 110:1 to prove that Jesus is David's Lord and not David's Son.

(3) Luke 20:41–44. Luke's makes only minor changes over Mark. He omits the situational opening in Mark 12:35a, addresses the question to "the scribes" in Luke 20:39 = 41, and then omits the specific pointing of the question *against* the scribes as in Mark 12:35b. He also quotes from Ps. 110:1 using "stool for thy feet'" just as in Acts 2:35. He thus avoids the conflation of Ps. 110:1b and 8:6b present in Mark.

(4) Matt. 22:41–46. Matthew's changes over Mark are primarily of a *formal* nature. As Bultmann (51) noted this "is a passage that does not appear in Mark in the form of a debate, but in Matt. 22:41–46, it becomes a controversy dialogue, in which, on this occasion, Jesus himself launches the attack." This last point is important because, in the process of changing the aphoristic saying in Mark into an aphoristic dialogue or polemical apophthegm, Matthew gave a clear indication of the secondary nature of his creation. "It is characteristic of the primitive apophthegm that it makes the occasion of a dominical saying something that happens to Jesus. . . . It is a sign of a secondary formation if Jesus himself provides the initiative" (Bultmann: 66). Thus, in rephrasing Mark's text, Matthew introduces the Pharisees in 22:41 but has Jesus open with a question in 22:42a, then gives their reply in 22:42b, and concludes with Jesus' counter-question in 22:43–45.

Table 7.12

Matthew 22:41–45	Mark 12:35–37a
Now while the Pharisees were gathered together, Jesus asked them a question, saying, "What do you think of the	And as Jesus taught in the temple, he said, "How can the scribes say that
Christ? Whose son is he?" They said to him "The son of David." He said to them, "How is it then that David, inspired by the Spirit, calls him Lord, saying, 'The Lord said to my Lord, Sit at my right hand, till I put thy enemies under thy feet'? If David then calls him Lord, how is he his son?"	the Christ is the son of David? David himself, inspired by the Holy Spirit declared, 'The Lord said to my Lord, Sit at my right hand, till I put thy enemies under thy feet'? David himself calls him Lord; so how is he his son?"

(5) Mark 12:35–37a. I consider 12:35–37a to be a redactional creation by Mark himself. The arguments for this position are minor ones pertaining to form and major ones pertaining to content.

(a) Form. The form is chiastically arranged around the central citation from Ps. 110:1:

(a)	" . . . is the son of David?"	(12:35b)
(b)	"David himself . . . (declared) . . . Lord . . .	(12:36a)
(c)	Ps. 110:1	(12:36b)
(b')	"David himself (calls) . . . Lord . . .	(12:37a)
(a')	" . . . is he his son?"	(12:37b)

The outer frames are given interrogatively (12:35b = 37b) and such a "double question" is quite characteristic of Markan style (see Nei-

Table 7.12 (cont.)

Luke 20:41–44	*Epistle of Barnabas* 12:10b, 11b
But he said to them, "How can they say that the Christ is	Since therefore they are going to say that the Christ is
David's son?	David's son,
For David himself says in the Book of Psalms,	David himself prohesies, fearing and understanding the error of the sinners,
'The Lord said to my Lord, Sit at my right hand, till I make thy enemies a stool for thy feet.' David thus calls him Lord; so how is he his son?"	"The Lord said to my Lord sit thou on my right hand until I make thy enemies thy footstool." .... See how David calls him Lord, and does not say Son.

rynck, 1972:125), as is the "inclusion" in which they are arranged (132).

(b) Content. Mark's redactional creativity is to be understood against the following pre-Markan tradition.

(i) The use of Ps. 110:1 with regard to Jesus as the exalted Lord is both pre-Markan and extremely primitive. In discussing the combination of Ps. 110:1 in Acts 2:34–35 with Ps. 16:8–11 in Acts 2:25–28, Lindars (1961:45) has said that Ps. 110:1 "was probably in use in the Church at a very much earlier date, and that it was perhaps the most important of the scriptures used with the argument from literal fulfilment." This very early usage of Ps. 110:1 is also indicated by the fact that "the Exaltation of which it speaks was originally an alternative way of talking about the Resurrection, though it slips into denoting a separate, successive act" (1961:45).

(ii) The name of David is specifically associated with this Ps. 110:1 in Acts 2:34–35 just as it was with Ps. 16:8–11 in Acts 2:25, 29. The purpose of this specific mention is to prevent or refute the obvious Jewish answer that these psalm texts referred to David and not to Jesus. In other words, the argument in Acts 2 was that David could not be the subject of Ps. 110:1 and that, therefore, Jesus as the Christ was the subject about which David spoke.

(iii) But *Barn.* 12:10–11 had not only gone beyond this, it had actually gone against it. Acts 2:30–31 was content to say, "Being therefore a prophet, and knowing that God had sworn with an oath to him that he would set *one of his descendants* upon his throne, he foresaw and spoke of the resurrection of *the Christ.*" In *Barnabas*, however, the argument is that Jesus is David's Lord, not David's Son at all. It should be underlined, also that in *Barnabas*, none of this is placed on the lips of Jesus: it is an assertion by *Barnabas* himself (Koester, 1957a:146).

(iv) Mark concludes his citation of Ps. 110:1 with "under thy feet" (*hypokatō tōn podōn sou*). This change is also pre-Markan since, as Lindars (1961:50) has shown, "a notable feature of these references is that consideration of Ps. 110.1b often involves conflation with Ps. 8.7." Thus Mark cites Ps. 110:1 (Ps. 109:1 in LXX) already conflated with Ps. 8:6 (Ps. 8:7 LXX), as shown in Table 7.13.

The conflation was facilitated, of course, by the similarity between the Greek of 110:1b and 6b, but "the special value of this psalm [Ps. 8] is that it enabled Christian thinkers to express the concept of the risen Lord as the 'inclusive representative' [Dodd] of

Table 7.13

Psalm 110:1	Psalm 8:6
Sit at my right hand,	Thou has given him dominion over the works of thy hands;
till I make your enemies your footstool (*hypopodion tōn podōn*)	thou has put all things under his feet (*hypokatō tōn podōn*)

redeemed humanity. It is a psalm of praise for man's redemption in and through the person of Jesus, crucified and risen" (Lindars, 1961:168–169). The conflation of Ps. 110:1b and 8:6b is therefore also pre-Markan.

With regard to *content*, Mark's major redactional change is that he has placed the argument on the lips of Jesus himself. What was an assertion by *Barnabas*—"See how David calls him Lord and does not say Son"—is now a rhetorical question by Jesus: "David himself calls him Lord; so how is he his son?" in Mark 12:37. This must be understood within Markan theology. Kelber (1974:92–97) has shown that Mark (i) mentions Son of David only as Jesus approaches Jerusalem and its opposition to him; (ii) uses it there three times, with blind Bartimeus in 10:46–52, at the formal entrance in 11:1–10, and finally in the temple in 12:35–37; (iii) locates it among the teaching of the "scribes"; and, thereby, I would add, (iv) leaves it open whether Jesus speaks against Jewish or Jewish-Christian scribal authorities (see also Mark 3:22a and 7:1b). But, above all, Kelber suggests "a progressive exposure of the inadequacy of the title as Jesus approaches the seat of Davidic hopes: the confession of the blind Bartimaeus at Jericho, the wrong acclamation at the outskirts, and Jesus' personal rejection in the temple" (96). Thus, for example, it is critically important that Mark gives no citation from Zech. 9:9 (see Matt. 21:4–5) while describing the acclamation of the Jerusalem crowds in 11:9–10. The scriptures do not support the Son of David title for Mark.

(6) Conclusion. This is an almost classic case of a progression from (a) a non-saying of Jesus in *Barn.* 12:10b,11b to (b) a saying of Jesus in Mark 12:35–37, and to (c) a dialogue in Matt. 22:41–45. But even in Mark or *Barnabas* the unit stands on the border between aphoristic and dialectial traditions. Aphorisms that debate with oneself or with absent others ("they say") can easily become full dialectical dialogues. This is the point of closest contact between aphorism and dialectic. Since *Barnabas* and Mark had a "they," it was quite simple for Matthew to create not only a split aphoristic dialogue by placing "the son of David" on the lips of the

now explicit opponents, but also a dialectical dialogue. Aphorism 24 is, therefore, an example both of *split* (Matthew) and implicit (*Barnabas*, Mark) aphoristic dialogue, and as this latter it stands on the very border or interface of the aphoristic and dialectical traditions.

E. TRANSPOSED APHORISTIC DIALOGUE

Koester has said that Jesus' "sayings can also be used in order to formulate a question of the disciples. Thus, in a dialogue, questions may in fact represent traditional sayings and are not necessarily editorial products" (1980b:252). I term this a transposed aphoristic dialogue, or *saying-as-question*, because the saying of Jesus is transposed as address onto the lips of the disciples, and a new saying or an explanation of the original saying is then given by Jesus himself.

In some cases this transposition is direct and obvious since the disciple *explicitly* quotes a saying as being from Jesus in posing the question and asking for the explanation. For example, there is the *Epistula Apostolorum*, "a remarkable document from the time of the battle between Christianity and Gnosticism" (Hennecke and Schneemelcher: 1.190) or, more accurately, between catholic and gnostic Christianity. In terms of its date, "the opposition against a Gnosticism that still exercises a strong influence puts the writing in the 2nd century. The free and easy way with which the author uses and treats the New Testament writings could point to the first half of that century. The questions concerning the end of the world and the Lord's return still have very immediate significance. That also points to an early period" (Hennecke and Schneemelcher: 1.190–191). In terms of form, it "represents an orthodox attempt to use the same weapons as the Gnostics. There, orthodox convictions about the life and death of Jesus and his bodily resurrection are related in a dialogue between the Risen Lord and the twelve" (Perkins, 1980: 202). Most of this anti-gnostic revelation dialogue is composed of questions and answers, about fifty in all (*Ep. Apost.* 13–50). The questions are not posed by individual disciples but by a general or choral "we said to him." In the following example, from *Ep. Apost.* 41 (Coptic), the disciples explicitly cite a saying of Jesus in asking him their question (Hennecke and Schneemelcher: 1.220):

> We said to him, "O Lord, it is you who said, 'Do not call (anyone) father upon earth, for one is your father who is in heaven and your master.' Why do you now say to us, 'You will be father of many children and servants and masters'?" But he answered and said to us, "As you have said. For truly I say to you, whoever will hear you and believe in me, he [will receive from] you the light of the seal through [me] and baptism through me; you will [become] fathers and servants and masters."

This form of transposed aphoristic dialogue in which the saying of Jesus is explicitly cited as such in the disciples's question reaches a certain structural consummation in the *Pistis Sophia*. The writing contained in Books I–III of that codex has many instances where a disciple explicitly cites a saying of Jesus and then gives an interpretation of it. In the dialogue all that Jesus does is approve the explanation. For example, in *Pist. Soph.* 52, "Mariam sprang up again, she said: 'Yes, O Lord. This is what thou didst say to us once: "The last will become first and first will become last." Now the first, which were created before us, are the *invisible ones*, *since* they existed before mankind, they and the gods and the archons; and the men who will receive *mysteries* will precede them in the Kingdom of Heaven.' Jesus said to her: '*Excellent*, Mariam.'" (Schmidt and MacDermot: 98 or 196–197; Greek words italicized). The dialogue here is almost that of the comprehensive examination. Mary Magdalene cites and interprets Aphorism 111: *First and Last*, and Jesus responds with approval. Or, again, in the second book at *Pist. Soph.* 87, she cites and interprets Aphorisms 111 and 6, and Jesus' answer simply commends her: "Maria Magdalene sprang up and said . . . 'My Lord, thou has once said to us: "The first will be last and the last will be first." That is, the last are the whole *race* of mankind who will be first within the Kingdom of the Light before those of all the *places* of the height, which are themselves first. Because of this *now*, my Lord, thou hast said to us: "He who has ears to hear, let him hear": that is, thou didst wish to know whether we have *grasped* every word which thou has said. This *now* is the word, my Lord.' Now it happened when she finished speaking these words, the *Saviour* marvelled greatly at the *answers* to the words which she gave, because she had completely become *pure Spirit*. Jesus answered and said to her: '*Excellent*, thou *pure spiritual* one, Maria. This is the interpretation of the discourse' " (Schmidt and MacDermot: 199–200 or 398–401; Greek words italicized).

These few examples indicate the intensive development *from saying to dialogue to discourse* that took place especially within gnostic Christianity but also within those strands of catholic Christianity, such as the gospel of John or the *Epistola Apostolorum*, which were formally closest to it (see Gärtner: 17–27; Robinson and Koester: 71–85).

In this section, however, I am primarily interested in cases where the *transposed aphoristic dialogue* does not have any explicit citation of the content of the disciple's question as being a saying of Jesus. In such cases one is only sure it is a transposed dialogue if the question is known from elsewhere as an independent saying. This is the situation in the following examples.

Aphorism 56: *Lambs Among Wolves*
Aphorism 86: *Whom to Fear*

(1) There are two quite separate aphorisms, Aphorism 56 in Q/Matt. 10:16a = Luke 10:3 and Aphorism 86 in Q/Matt. 10:28 = Luke 12:4–5, which are secondarily integrated into a transposed aphoristic dialogue in 2 *Clem.* 5:2–4. (See Table 7.14.)

(2) Aphorism 56 in Q/Matt. 10:16a = Luke 10:3. This opened the "mission discourse" in Q (Taylor, 1953:29; 1959:254; Polag, 1979:44–45). Opening and metaphor will be discussed separately.

(a) Opening. The saying opens with the solemn statement: "Behold, I send you out" (*idou apostellō hymas*). This phrase, as *idou (ego) apostellō*, appears in two other very important Q texts. First, it is found in the Mal. 3:1/Exod. 23:20 texts applied by Jesus to John in

Table 7.14

Matthew 10:16a + 10:28	Luke 10:3 + 12:4–5	2 Clement 5:2–4
		For the Lord said,
	Go your way;	
Behold, I send you out	behold, I send you out	"Ye shall be
as sheep in the midst	as lambs in the midst	as lambs in the midst
of wolves.	of wolves.	of wolves,"
		and Peter answered
		and said to him,
		"If then the wolves
		tear the lambs?"
		Jesus said to Peter, "Let
		the lambs have no fear of
		the wolves after their death;
	I tell you, my friends,	
And do not fear	do not fear	and do ye have no fear of
those who kill the body	those who kill the body, and	those that slay you, and
but cannot kill the soul;	after that have no more that	can do nothing more to you,
rather	they can do. But I will warn	but
fear him	you whom to fear: fear him	fear him
who can destroy	who, after he has killed,	who after your death
both body and	has power to cast into hell;	hath power over body and
soul		soul, to cast them into
in hell.		the flames of hell."
	yes, I tell you, fear him!	

Q/Matt. 11:10 = Luke 7:27. Second, and much more important, is its use in the oracle of doom uttered by divine Wisdom at the dawn of creation in Q/Luke 11:49 but changed in Matt. 23:34 (Aphorism 83). When the present saying is placed against the background of that latter text and especially against the general background of the rejection of Wisdom and Wisdom's envoys by Israel, Jesus' use of the solemn opening becomes extremely significant. It is another slight, indirect, and ambiguous indication (see Q/Matt. 8:19–20 = Luke 9:57–58) that, even in Q itself and despite flat contradictions at times (see Q/Matt. 12:32 = Luke 12:10), there was an increasing equation of Jesus with Wisdom itself. Thus, for example, Robinson has suggested with regard to Q/Matt. 11:27 = Luke 10:22 (Aphorism 62) that, "even if at the very latest stage in the Q tradition, Jesus is not simply cast in the role of one of Sophia's spokesmen, even the culminating one, but rather is described with predications that are reserved for Sophia herself" (1975:9). It is not then only with Matthew's use of Q that this equation of Jesus and Sophia takes place. Thus, although Suggs is quite correct in insisting that Matthew makes this equation much more clearly and fully (Jesus as Sophia-Torah), the equation was indirectly if ambiguously present in Q itself (see Suggs, 1970:96, 127).

(b) Metaphor. With the opening so understood, the terrible negativity of the saying's metaphor becomes inevitable. Whether the preceding aphorism, the *Harvest is Great*, is taken positively for the salvific ingathering of the elect or negatively for the punitive threshing of the doomed, one presumes that the laborers will prevail. But here in this aphorism it is a case of a mission without hope. This is so in Q/Luke 10:3, although Matthew's change of "lambs" to "sheep" as well as his addition in Matt. 10:16b render it somewhat more hopeful. In Q we are *not* dealing with wandering charismatics whose homelessness symbolizes eschatological urgency (see Theissen: 33), but rather does this "mission discourse" place on Jesus' lip an autobiography of the Q community's past history within Israel. It is foretold as a hopeless mission because it has been experienced precisely as such. "In fact, the 'Mission Charge' should not be understood as a 'mission' at all but as an *errand of judgment*. For what is related is a remarkable process which, apparently counting on few positive results, has 'laborers' sent out for the central purpose of distinguishing, merely by their reception, between the elect and the damned" (Jacobson, 1978:134). It is, in other words, less a program for the future than a description of the past. And what one notices here is how from one end of Q to the other there is a steadily increasing virulence of the polemic against Israel (see Appendix 2).

(3) Aphorism 86 in Q/Matt. 10:28 = Luke 12:4–5. This appears as a quite separate saying in the fourth, final, and apocalyptic section of Q (see Appendix 2). The concluding phrase, "Yes, I tell you," is

characteristic of Q (Manson: 107): see, for example, Q/Matt. 11:9b = Luke 7:26 or Q/Matt. 23:36 = Luke 11:51 (see Jacobson, 1978: 192).

(4) 2 *Clem.* 5:2–4. This pseudo-letter of pseudo-Clement of Rome, dating "probably from the half century between 120 and 170 A.D." (Lake 1.127), contains Aphorisms 56 and 86 within a dialogue. The dialogue has three strophes: Jesus (Aphorism 56), Peter (Aphorism 56 transposed), and Jesus (Aphorism 86). Is this complex independent of intracanonical tradition?

Schneemelcher judges that, "in spite of reminiscences of Mt. 10:16 and 10:28 and parallels . . . a special tradition can be traced here," but "the fact that the saying 2 Clem. 12,2 also has the form of a dialogue cannot however be brought forward in support of the view that 5,2–4 is also derived from the Gospel of the Egyptians" (Hennecke and Schneemelcher: 1.172, see 168–169; so also Ropes: 146–147). Jeremias, on the other hand, rightly unimpressed by the creative and persuasive value of "Let not the lambs fear the wolves *after they are dead*" (i.e. the lambs), concludes that dialogue "is a not strikingly successful combination of two separate sayings by means of an artificial connecting link" (1964: 38–39). Koester has shown that the citations in 2 *Clement* stem from a harmonized sayings collection based on Matthew and Luke, from independent noncanonical tradition, and from redactional creativity by the work's author (1957a:109–111). The *content* of 2 *Clem.* 5:2–4 is dependent on intracanonical data, although this is possibly indirect (that is, through the use of an already harmonized version of Matthean-Lukan sayings) (1957a:94–99). The *form*, which probably derived from 2 *Clement* itself, is not only a dialogue, but one in which a saying of Jesus is transposed onto the lips of a questioning disciple. And this is very far from the usual mode of questioning found, for example, within the synoptic tradition itself (see Koester, 1957a:98).

(5) Conclusion. Although the content of "II Clement's version represents a secondary development of the synoptic material, not an independent tradition" (Stroker: 302), the form is a fascinating ex-

ample of a *transposed aphoristic dialogue* in the process of composition. Jesus first gives Aphorism 56 and then Peter quotes it in posing his question. Finally Jesus reuses Aphorism 56 as an introduction to Aphorism 86.

Aphorism 120: *Reproving and Forgiving*
Aphorism 121: *Unlimited Forgiveness*

(1) There is only one independent version to be considered for Aphorism 120: Q/Matt 18:15 = Luke 17:3 and also for Aphorism 121: Q/Matt. 18:21–22 = Luke 17:4, but there is a very interesting secondary version in *Gos. Naz.* 15a. (See Table 7.15.)

(2) The Q Context. The two units that are combined together in Luke 17:3 and 4 appear in Matt. 18:15 (16–17) and 21–22 as two very different and textually separated sayings. It is quite possible, therefore, to consider that Luke and Matthew "come through different lines of tradition" for these pericopes (see Manson: 209; also

Table 7.15

Matthew 18:15, 21–22	Luke 17:3–4	Gospel of the Nazarea■
	Take heed to yourselves;	
If your brother sins against you, go and tell him his fault, between you and him alone.	if your brother sins, rebuke him,	
If he listens to you, you have gained your brother.	and if he repents, forgive him;	
. . . .		
Then Peter came up and said to him, "Lord, how often shall my brother sin against me, and I forgive him? As many as seven times?		He [*namely Jesus*] said:
	and if he sins against you seven times in the day, and turns to you seven times, and says, "I repent," you must forgive him.	If thy brother has sinne■ with a word and has m■ thee reparation, receiv■ seven times in a day.
		Simon his disciple said■ him: Seven times in a ■ The Lord answered an■ to him: Yea, I say unto■ until seventy times seven times.
Jesus said to him, "I do not say to you seven times, but seventy times seven."		

139). Taylor makes the same judgment: "The verbal agreements are slight, and from these it is impossible to maintain that the two versions are derived from one common source" (1959:260). But he also notes that "there is agreement in the succession of themes (offences and forgiveness)" (260), so that there is a common *sequence*, now, of:

(a) Aphorism 119: Matt. 18:7   = Luke 17:1
(b) Aphorism 120: Matt. 18:15   = Luke 17:3
(c) Aphorism 121: Matt. 18:21–22 = Luke 17:4

It must therefore be considered at least as "possible that the Q form was available to Matthew" (so Bultmann: 141–142 note 2). I conclude, then, but from *sequence* rather than *wording*, that Q/Luke 17:3–4 was available to Matthew for his overall redactional composition of Matt. 18. A much more difficult question is whether Matthean redaction alone or special Matthean tradition is necessary to explain the present changed state of Q/Luke 17:3–4 in Matt. 18: 15(16–17) and 21–22. "To what degree all this was already united with the 'Rule for the Congregation' in a special tradition which Matthew took over, or to what degree this was done by Matthew himself, remains a question. However, we should not suppose that the Evangelist gave any of the sayings their first editorial shape; they received their form beforehand" (Bornkamm, 1970:39). It is certainly true that the legal and communal nature of the composition in Matt. 18 severely limits the possibilities of redactional creativity. But I would still leave open the question of whether Matthew himself redacted Q/Luke 17:3–4 into Matt. 18:15(16–17) and 18:21–22. I would also leave open the wider question of Q context. The original Q sequence may well have been (see Appendix 2):

(a) Aphorism 117: Matt. 5:18   = Luke 16:17
(b) Aphorism 118: Matt. 5:32   = Luke 16:18
(c) Aphorism 119: Matt. 18:7   = Luke 17:1
(d) Aphorism 120: Matt. 18:15   = Luke 17:3
(e) Aphorism 121: Matt. 18:21–22 = Luke 17:4

If that was so (see Polag, 1979:74–75), there may have been a connection between (a) legal fidelity, (b) scandal (as legal infidelity?), and (c) forgiveness (for legal infidelity?), already present in Q.

(3) Aphorism 120. The Q/Luke 17:3 form is rather basic and obvious: sins/rebuke//repents/forgive. Matt. 18:15–17 is quite different: "the disciplinary instructions in verses 15–17 clearly constitute a unity . . . in all probability, developed from the Q-logion which is preserved in Luke 17:3" (Bornkamm, 1970:39). Q/Luke 17:3 had two conditional stichs with *ean*, and there is a general presumption of a positive outcome. This is also true of the twin *if* (*ean*) stichs of Matt. 18:15. This is simply Q/Luke 17:3 rephrased to prepare it as a lead-in to 18:16–17. But the tone changes drastically in the three appended *if* stichs of that 18:16–17. Here "the general drift of the sayings group undoubtedly moves toward the most extreme disciplinary possibility: the exclusion of the impenitent sinner by the assembled congregation" (Bornkamm, 1970:40). Hence while Q/Matt. 18:15 = Luke 17:3 has two positive *if* stichs, Matt. 18:16–17 has three negative *if* stichs: "if he does not/if he refuses/if he refuses. . . ." There is, in other words, no need to postulate an independent Matthean tradition for Matt. 18:15, and the way it carefully rephrases Q/Luke 17:3 in preparation for and connection with the succeeding Matt. 18:16–17 makes it much more likely that Matt. 18:15–17 is a deliberate Matthean expansion of Q/Matt. 18:15 = Luke 17:3.

(4) Aphorism 121. Although the case of Aphorism 121 is more difficult than that of Aphorism 120, I would suggest that here also Matt. 18:21–22 is a redactional restatement of Q/Luke 17:4. But, from a formal and subgeneric point of view, this is a quite fascinating change.

(a) Form in Aphorism 121. In my preceding example, 2 *Clem*. 5:2–4 had Peter repeat Jesus' Aphorism 56 as a question, so that we could see the *transposed aphoristic dialogue* in the process of formation. Here there is a similar phenomenon. Peter repeats Jesus' Aphorism 121 as a question, but we only know it was first a saying of

Jesus because of Q/Luke 17:4. It is gone as a saying of Jesus from Matthew 18:21–22. It should also be noted that 21–22 is not just a neutral but a corrective dialogue (see also Bornkamm, 1970:41).

(b) Content in Aphorism 121. The opposition of "seventy times seven" to "seven times" (recall Gen. 4:24) seems to make Matthew's forgiveness much more generous than Q/Luke's. But Q/Luke had "seven times *in the day*," so that both versions actually speak of *unlimited forgiveness*, stated, however, with different numerical symbolism. The advantage of Matthew's version is that he has created a contrast with the unlimited *un*forgiveness of Lamech in Gen. 4:24, not that he has improved on the mercy of Q/Luke.

(5) *Gospel of the Nazaraeans*. The question of the relationship between Matt 18:21–22 and *Gos. Naz.* 15a is difficult and controversial. Apart from the general assessment discussed before, Vielhauer has commented specifically on *Gos. Naz.* 15a: "As regards the discourse material of the GN there are occasions when a late stage of the tradition history can clearly be recognized in it. . . . In the saying on forgiveness (No. 15) the sin of the brother is, as compared with Mt. 18:21f., limited to sins of the tongue, to insulting language" (Hennecke and Schneemelcher: 1.145). But there is a specific problem with deriving *Gos. Naz.* 15a secondarily from Matt. 18:21–22. Jeremias has already noted this (Hennecke and Schneemelcher: 1.87) and has said that, "The case for the originality and independence of the new version of the logion is clearly borderline. . . . On the other hand it is uncertain whether it is a secondary modification of Matt. 18.21f or an independent version thereof. It is difficult to be quite sure" (1964:95). I think, however, that it is possible and necessary to go beyond that position.

Gos. Naz. 15a cannot be based on Matt 18:21–22 alone. In terms of *form*, the saying-as-question of Peter in Matt 18:21 appears here as a saying of Jesus. This, however, could be argued as a modification of Matt. 18:21–22, although the purpose for the change is not immediately evident: It would seem better to let Jesus contradict Peter than himself. But it is the *content* that is the real problem.

Gos. Naz. 15a has three elements in the first saying of Jesus that do not derive from Matt. 18:21 but are present in Q/Luke 17:4: (a) the conditional ("if") opening, (b) the mention of repentance, and (c) the specification "in a (the) day" (see also Jeremias, 1964:94). Hence one would have to consider *Gos. Naz.* 15a as at least "a conflation of the Lukan and Matthean passages" (Stroker: 287).

I consider it best, therefore, to take *Gos. Naz.* 15a as a conflation of Q/Luke 17:4 and Matt. 18:21–22 (see Koester, 1957b:231). But what is of present interest is the form, and especially its precise similarity to the preceding case of 2 *Clem.* 5:2–4. In *Gos. Naz.* 15a Jesus gives an aphoristic saying, then Peter repeats it as a question, and finally Jesus gives a second aphorism. But while 2 *Clem.* 5:2–4 used the device to link two separate aphorisms together (56 and 86), *Gos. Naz.* 15a uses it to link two different versions of the same aphorism (121) together.

(6) Conclusion. Matt. 18:21–22 is a classic example of a transposed aphoristic dialogue effected on the saying in Q/Luke 17:4. But the secondary and conflated version in *Gos. Naz.* 15a actually gives a glimpse of the transposition *as it were* in process. This conflation still has Jesus give the aphorism, then Peter repeat it as a question, before Jesus finally gives the alternative version of it.

8

Aphoristic Story

To think aphoristically is the attempt to avoid the imperfection of per
fection in thought.

HANS KASPER (Margolius: 81)

A. PROBLEMS AND TERMS

This section presumes and continues what was said in the parallel
portion of the preceding chapter. I presume, in other words, the
distinction proposed there between *aphorism* and *dialectic*, on the
one hand, and between *dialogue* and *story*, on the other.

There are three points to be made concerning the distinctions
proposed by Greco-Roman grammar and rhetoric concerning the
linguistic form called *chreia* (*chria*), that is, "a concise and pointed
account of something said or done, attributed to some particular
person" (Theon, in Taylor: 76); or "a concise exposition of some
memorable saying or deed, generally for good counsel" (Hermogenes, in Baldwin: 26); or "a brief bit of advice bearing appropriately
on some person" (Aphthonius, in Nadeau: 266).

The first point is the importance of the distinction between
named and unnamed authorship which was seen already and needs
no further comment. The second point is the distinction made between three general types of climactic *response*: (1) by word alone,
(2) by deed alone, (3) by word plus deed. "All three grammarians
[Theon, Hermogenes, Aphthonius] say that the chreiai have three
types: 'verbal' (*logikai*), 'active' (*praktikai*), and 'mixed' (*miktai*)," in
the summation of Spencer (109). The third point underlines that
triple distinction as being based only on the modes of *response* and
not at all on the modes of the *stimulus* where, of course, a similar

triad is equally possible. One could imagine a full typology of the basic *chreia* as follows:

(1) *stimulus:* address and/or situation,
(2) *response:* saying and/or deed.

There is already a faint hint of this in the great rhetorician Quintilian, whose *Institutio Oratoria* (1.9:4) divided the *chreia* (*chria*) into four, not three, types: "Of *moral essays* [*chriarum*] there are various forms: (1) some are akin to *aphorisms* [simile sententiae] and commence with a simple statement 'he said' or 'he used to say': (2) others give the answer to a question and begin 'on being asked' or 'in answer to this he replied,' (3) while a third and not dissimilar type begins, 'when someone has said or done something.' (4) Some hold that a *moral essay* [*chriam*] may take some action as its text" (Butler: 1.158–159; numbers added). You will notice a gesture towards the distinction between a dialogue and a story in the separation suggested between his second and third types. It is, however, only a gesture.

Therefore I distinguish first between the aphoristic and dialectical tradition—that is, between units where the setting is simply a frame for the climactic saying and units where setting and saying are in interactive relationship so that the saying is hermeneutically banal or even grammatically incomplete without the setting. And I distinguish second within the aphoristic tradition between aphoristic dialogues—that is, units composed of *address* (question, remark, request) and *response*, and aphoristic stories—that is, units composed of *situation*, with or without *address*, and *response*. I insist on this distinction, once again, at least for the Jesus tradition, and out of respect for the fateful trajectories chosen differently by the gnostic and catholic destinies.

B. APHORISM AND STORY

One point must be emphasized immediately. All four of the intracanonical gospels are narratives, and the narrative framework permeates those particular writings from beginning to end. They are not simply discourses with an initial narrative setting as, for example, those gnostic revelation dialogues where "the setting is usually a small part of the whole" (Perkins, 1980:37). And they are even farther removed linguistically from a genre such as the *logoi sophōn* or "sayings of the sages" identified by Robinson (Robinson and Koester: 71–113). There are, for example, four dialectical stories (60,72,99,100) and one aphoristic story (22) in the *Gospel of Thomas*, but the overarching genre is that of a sayings collection. So also with "the treatise called 'Pirkē Aloth', or 'Sayings of the Fathers' . . . a collection of maxims, mostly ethical and religious, uttered by Jewish teachers within a period extending from the third century B.C. to the third century A.D." (Charles: 2.686). This is the second-to-last tractate of the fourth division (*Nezikin*, or "Damages") of *The Mishnah* (see Danby: 446–461), the "code of the oral Torah, promulgated by Judah the Patriarch in *ca*. 200 A.D." (Neusner, 1979:xxi). But among, and almost lost among all those sayings, are two aphoristic stories, one towards the start and another in the appended last chapter.

In *m. 'Abot* 2:7 the following story is recorded of Hillel (*ca*. 20 B.C.), "Moreover he saw a skull floating on the face of the water and he said unto it, Because thou drownedst they drowned thee and at the last they that drowned thee shall be drowned" (Danby: 448). The *saying* itself is "an epigram of retribution" and "the original is in Aramaic," although the introductory *setting* is in Hebrew (Charles: 2.696). In my terms this is a classic example of an aphoristic story, because "a 'historical' narrative setting is invented for the saying" so that "a separate logion . . . is given a narrative setting" (Neusner, 1979:20).

The chapter *m. 'Abot* 6 "is a very late gloss to the five chapters of Aboth. It was probably added because of the common liturgical use of Aboth since the eleventh century as a reading on the six Sabbath afternoons between Passover and Pentecost, when a sixth section was called for" (Danby: 458–459 note 12). In *m. 'Abot* 6:9 the following story is told by R. Jose ben Kisma, one of the third gen-

eration of Tannaim, or "repeaters" of the Oral Law (c. A.D. 120–
140): "I was once walking by the way and a man met me and
greeted me and I returned his greeting. He said to me, 'Rabbi, from
what place are thou?' I answered, 'I come from a great city of Sages
and scribes.' He said to me, 'If thou wilt dwell with us in our place
I will give thee a thousand thousand golden *denars* and precious
stones and pearls.' I answered, 'If thou gavest me all the silver and
gold and precious stones and pearls in the world I would not dwell
save in a place of the Law" (Danby: 460–461; this is *m*. 'A*bot* 6:10
in Charles: 2.713). This aphoristic dialogue with two exchanges
appears as an aphoristic story, but barely, because of the initial
situation, "walking by the way and. . . ." But the dialogue and its
narrative setting has been created to frame and build up to the
climactic saying of the rabbi.

In the *Gospel of Thomas* or in the tractate 'A*bot*, then, the stories
stand out among the dominant surrounding sayings; but in the intracanonical gospels the reverse is true. There sayings, no matter
how isolated, are always held within the overarching frames of the
basic gospel story. I am presently concerned, however, with the
smaller narrative units created to frame individual sayings. For this
purpose I do not consider the overall narrative mode as turning all
sayings into stories automatically.

There is one striking feature of the aphoristic stories to be studied in this chapter. There are several dialectical stories in the
Gospel of Thomas (for example, in *Gos. Thom.* 60, 72,99,100), and
there are several dialectical stories in Q (for example, Q/Matt. 12:
22–26 = Luke 11:14–18 or Q/Matt. 11:2–6 = Luke 7:18–23 or
Q/Matt. 12:38–40 = Luke 11:(16)29–30 or Q/Matt. 8:21–22 = Luke
9:59–60). But, except for *Gos. Thom.* 22a, there are no aphoristic
stories in either Q or the *Gospel of Thomas*. That is one side of the
feature. The other is the number of aphoristic stories created by
Mark himself—created, it would seem, as one of the major tech-
niques in maintaining the narrative modality of his writing. The
five cases in this present chapter are spread over Mark 6,9,10,11,
13,14,15.

Aphorism 7: *Prophet and Physician*

(1) There are four independent versions: (a) Mark 6:4 = Matt. 13:57; (b) Luke 4:24; (c) John 4:44; and (d) *Gos. Thom.* 31. (See Table 8.1.)

(2) John 4:44. At first glance "Jn 4:44 echoes the Mt-Mk tradition" (Fitzmyer, 1974:402), and one almost leaves it at that. Like Mark 6:4a it begins with *hoti* (" 'this *hoti* when introducing direct speech is equivalent to our colon (:); it is very common in Mark and John perhaps owing to the influence of Aramaic,' " (thus Pryke: 74, note 2, citing Zerwick), and mentions the three key Markan words (*prophet, honor, country*) although in a different order and format. But Brown (1966:188) has noted that the succeeding verse in John 4:45 has "welcomed" and that this "verb *dechesthai* occurs only here in the Johannine works" (1966:186) but appears in another form as "acceptable" (*dektos*) in Luke 4:24. And it may be even more important that the same word, *dektos*, appears in the Greek source of *Gos. Thom.* 31. Thus it must be considered possible "that Mark, Luke and John all drew the saying from variant strains of tradition"

Table 8.1

Matthew 13:57	Mark 6:4	Luke 4:24	John 4:44	*Gospel of Thomas* 31
A prophet is not without honor except in his own country and in his own house.	A prophet is not without honor, except in his own country, and among his own kin, and in his own house.	Truly, I say to you, no prophet is acceptable in his own country.	a prophet has no honor in his own country.	No prophet is accepted in his own village; no physician heals those who know him.

(Dodd, 1963:239). Hence "honor" appears in Mark (Matthew) and John while "acceptable" occurs in Luke and Thomas (and John?).

(3) Matt. 13:57. Matthew follows Mark closely, save for the total excision of "and among his own kin."

(4) Mark 6:4. The absence of "and among his own kin" everywhere else, as well as the negative attitude of Mark towards Jesus' relatives, makes it most likely that this phrase has been redactionally inserted by Mark to point the opposition more precisely as coming from Jesus' family (Crossan, 1973b:102–104; Lambrecht, 1974b: 252–253). The double-negative format is also probably Markan (Neirynck, 1972:88).

(5) Luke 4:24. Apart even from some minor changes in common with Matthew (Neirynck, 1974:106,214), Luke has major differences from Mark. (a) He opens with: "Truly, I say to you . . . ." (b) He has a different format: "No prophet is" instead of "A prophet is not." (c) He uses "acceptable" (*dektos*) instead of "without honor" (*atimos*). But (d) he concludes, as does Mark, with "in his own country." The opening phrase, "Truly, I say to you" (*amēn legō hymin*) appears only six times in Luke but over twice as much again in Mark and still twice as often again in Matthew (Schlier: 337). Luke usually omits, shortens, or modifies it, and its presence always indicates Lukan sources: three times from Mark (Mark 10:15 = Luke 18:17; Mark 10:29 = Luke 18:29; Mark 13:30 = Luke 21:32) and three times from his special sources (Luke 4:24; 12:37; 23:43). This alone, and apart from other Lukan changes, raises the possibility that Luke has another version besides Mark 6:4 for this aphorism (see Schramm: 37).

(6) *Gos. Thom.* 31. This saying is found both in the Coptic version of *Thomas* from Nag Hammadi and among its Greek texts from Oxyrhynchus. I have already discussed the Oxyrhynchus Papyri in general and Oxy P 655 and Oxy P 654 in particular. *Gos. Thom.* 31 is contained in Oxy P 1, the last of the triad to be seen in detail. Oxy P 1 is part of a codex page, written on both sides, measuring 15 × 9.7 cm., "but its height was originally somewhat greater, as it is unfortunately broken at the bottom" (Grenfell and Hunt, 1897:6; see 1898:1–3). In the case of the present aphorism, however, the

Greek text is very well preserved. The English translation reads as in Table 8.2.

In attempting to compare these versions either with one another or with the synoptics, one must acknowledge immediately the syntactical difficulties in comparing Greek and Coptic. One can, however, discipline the comparison somewhat by noting how the translators handled the parallel synoptic texts in transforming the Greek New Testament into Coptic (Horner).

In comparing the twin versions of *Gos. Thom.* 31 with one another, three points may be noted. (a) "No prophet is" and "a prophet is not" in Greek can be translated by the same impersonal negative verb preceding the word "prophet" in Coptic—that is, by (*m*)*m*e*n*, "there is no . . . ." Both Mark 6:4 ("a prophet is not") and Luke 4:24 ("no prophet is") are so translated in the Coptic New Testament. (b) Similarly, there is probably no difference between "village" and "homeland," since the Greek word *patris* (homeland) is translated as *time* (village) in the Coptic versions of Mark 6:4, Matt. 13:54,57, Luke 4:24, and John 4:44. In effect, *at least originally*, whatever term was used, it was "village" that was intended. (c) Finally, there is the difference between "heals" and "works cures." But, once again, the difference is inconsequential since the Coptic has the Greek loan-word *therapeuein* ("to cure, heal") in Coptic format as *eptherapeue* while the Greek version has *poiei therapeias* ("work cures"). In other words the two versions are probably as identical as texts in totally different languages can be.

When one compares the different versions of the *prophet* saying in John, Mark, Luke, and *Thomas*, it seems evident that we are dealing with performancial variations that do not allow or need any

Table 8.2

Coptic Version (*Gospel of Thomas* 31)	Greek Version (Oxyrhynchus Papyrus 1)
Jesus said, "No prophet is accepted in his own village; no physician heals those who know him."	Jesus says, "A prophet is not acceptable in his own homeland, nor does a physician work cures on those who know him."

further decision concerning the oral original. Thus, for example, the use of "honor" in Mark and Luke and of "acceptable" in Luke and *Thomas* are free performancial variations that allow of no further direct choice between them. I tend, however, to prefer the Luke-*Thomas* term because of a major indirect consideration. This has to do with the far more interesting question of whether we are dealing with a single-stich aphorism about a prophet or a double-stich aphorism concerning a *prophet/physician* parallelism. If one accepts the double-stich saying as the more original, one tends also to prefer its wording as well.

But, in everything seen so far, the main difference is the prophet/physician parallelism, which appears only in *Thomas*. Even before the 1945 discovery of the Coptic *Gospel of Thomas*, Bultmann had followed Emil Wendling's 1908 thesis that the aphorism in Oxy P 1 was more original than that in Mark 6:4 (Bultmann: 31; see also Robinson and Koester: 129–131). His argument was that "it is hardly likely that the double proverb has grown out of Mk 6:1–6, the reverse is on the other hand probable: the second half of the twin proverb is transposed in the story, and the *ginōskontes auton* becomes the *syggeneis* of Mk 6:4" (31). This *is* more probable than Jeremias's suggestion that *Gos. Thom.* 31a "is expanded by the addition of the parallel saying" in 31b (1964:36; see also Ménard: 127). The reason for the greater probability was already noted by Bultmann, and it can be strengthened since the discovery of the Coptic version. Both Mark 6:5 (*etherapeusen*) and Luke 4:23 (*therapeuson*) mention "curing" in either the succeeding or preceding verse to their prophet aphorism. And Luke cites another proverb in 4:23 that invites a counter-proverb such as that in *Gos. Thom.* 31b. In other words both the Markan and Lukan tradition, and here independently of each other, (a) kept the prophet saying, (b) removed the physician saying, but (c) let its earlier presence be seen residually in Mark 6:5 and Luke 4:23. It could even be suggested, against Bultmann but following his basic intuition, that the *ginōskontes auton* of Thomas reappears in Mark's "in his house" (*en tē oikia autou*).

(7) Conclusion. It was already seen that *contraction* and *expan-*

sion can often take place within the aphoristic core itself so that it is impossible to decide between single- and double-stich versions of an aphorism. In the present case, however, it seems most likely that the best recoverable text is in *Thomas*, either Greek or Coptic (see Sieber: 21, as against Schrage: 75). The tradition was more interested in Jesus as a literal prophet than as a metaphorical (or literal) physician, so it was almost inevitable that the second stich of the saying fell away. It is still somewhat visible, however, in Mark, much more in Luke, but not at all in John.

In terms of this present chapter's emphasis (that is, the development from aphoristic saying to aphoristic story) one begins again with *Gos. Thom.* 31. There the unit appears as a straight aphoristic saying. And it is really the same in John 4:44, although the aphorism is placed in the somewhat uneasy context of Jesus' relations with Jerusalem in 4:43–44. It is not yet, however, an aphoristic story, save for the general overarching narrativity of the gospel as a whole. In Mark 6:1–6a = Matt. 13:56–58 it is developed into a fullblown aphoristic story redolent with Markan polemical and theological interests. And in Luke 4:16–30 the saying in 4:24 is taken up into an even larger narrative framework, which serves for Luke as a graphic summary of all that is to come thereafter.

Aphorism 14: *Leader as Servant*

(1) There are two independent versions to be considered: (a) Mark 10:42–45 = Matt. 20:25–28 and so into Mark 9:35 = Matt. 23:11 = Luke 9:48c; and (b) Luke 22:25–27. (See Table 8.3.)

(2) Introduction. This complex will be separated into two sections for easier discussion: (a) the first part is in Mark 9:35 = Matt. 23:11 = Luke 9:48c, which I will propose is developed from Mark 10:42–44 = Matt. 20:25–27, and also in Luke 22:25–26; (b) the second part is in Mark 10:45 = Matt. 20:28, and also in Luke 22:27.

(3) Mark 9:35. This aphorism is part of the word-linked cluster of 9:33–50. In wider context it is the central one of three sections of "corrective teaching" immediately following upon "misunderstand-

Table 8.3

Matthew 23:11	Luke 9:48c	Mark 9:35	
He who is greatest among you shall be your servant.	for he who is least among you all is the one who is great.	If any one would be first, he must be last of all and servant of all.	

ing by disciples." The three units have word-linked openings (Neirynck, 1966:64):

(a) "if any one would" (8:34)   "whoever would" (8:35)
(b) "if any one would" (9:35)
(c)   "whoever would" (10:43,44)

This linkage involves both the conditional and relatival openings and the use of "would" (*thelō*), which is redactionally Markan in this auxiliary usage (see Turner, 1926–1927:356–357).

Table 8.3 (cont.)

Mark 10:42–45	Matthew 20:25–28	Luke 22:25–27
You know that those who are supposed to rule over the Gentiles lord it over them, and their great men exercise authority over them. But it shall not be so among you; but whoever would be great among you must	You know that the rulers of the Gentiles lord it over them, and their great men exercise authority over them. It shall not be so among you; but whoever would be great among you must	The kings of the Gentiles exercise lordship over them and those in authority over them are called benefactors. But not so with you; rather let the greatest among you become as the youngest,
be your servant, and whoever would be first among you must be slave of all.	be your servant, and whoever would be first among you must be your slave;	and the leader as one who serves.
For the Son of man also came not to be served but to serve, and to give his life as a ransom for many.	even as the Son of man came not to be served but to serve, and to give his life as a ransom for many.	For which is the greater, one who sits at table, or one who serves? Is if not the one who serves? But I am among you as one who serves.

Mark 9:35b (a) opens in conditional format, (b) continues in positive/negative sequence, (c) contains a stich-and-a-half: first (*prōtos*)-last(*eschatos*)/servant (*diakonos*), and (d) remains in the third person although it is actually addressed to the disciples.

(4) Matt. 23:11. Neither Matt. 18:1–5 nor Luke 9:46–48 accepted the loose combination of Mark 9:33–35 and 36–37 (Neirynck, 1966:68,73). Each rewrote the twin units into tighter combination. Matthew rewrote Mark 9:33–34 from a personal dispute into an abstract question and then completely rephrased and relocated

Mark 9:35 into Matt. 18:4. As a postscript to this redaction Matthew placed a single-stich version of Mark 9:35 at his own Matt. 23:11: "greatest" (*meizōn*) from Mark 9:34 = Matt. 18:1,4, and "servant" (*diakonos*) from Mark 9:35. There is, therefore, no independent tradition in Matt. 23:11.

(5) Luke 9:48c. Luke restructures Mark into: (a) Luke 9:46 = Mark 9:33–34; (b) Luke 9:47–48ab = Mark 9:36–37; and (c) Luke 9:48c = Mark 9:35. But Luke 9:48c is also a quite total rephrasing of Mark 9:35: (i) participial format ("he who," *ho* . . .); (ii) single-stich structure; (iii) negative/positive sequence: "least (*mikroteros*)/ great (*megas*); (iv) addressed directly to the disciples ("among you all"); and (v) with the word "great" (*megas*) as in Mark 10:43b later. In the light of all that, and especially in view of the verb used ("is," with *hyparchōn*), Luke 9:48c is most likely a redactional restatement by Luke of Mark 9:35b.

(6) Mark 10:42–44 and Luke 22:25–26. There is an obvious parallelism in position and content between Jesus' rebuke of the disputes among the disciples in Mark 9:33–35 and 10:35–44. Luke omitted completely the incident in Mark 10:35–40. But he has a version of Mark 10:42–44 in Luke 22:25–26. Although the opening in Luke 22:24 may have been influenced by the opening of the parallel dispute in Mark 9:34 = Luke 9:46, both the context and text of Luke 22:25–26 indicate that it is "independent of Mk. and derived from Lk's special source" (Manson: 337).

Despite minor variations, however, the structure of Mark 10:42–44 and Luke 22:25–26 are exactly similar, as in Table 8.4.

Table 8.4

Mark 10:42–44		Luke 22:25–26	
(a) Gentiles	{ rule/lord / great men/authority	(a) Gentiles	{ kings/lordship / authority/benefactors
(b) "But it shall not be so among you"		(b) "But not so with you"	
(a') Disciples	{ great/servent / first/slave	(a') Disciples	{ greatest/youngest / leader/serves

The structure is similar because it is very, very tightly composed and this taut *a* (double stich), *b* (single stich), *a'* (double stich) held firm even as the expressions for superiors and inferiors changed as performancial variations.

(7) Matt. 20:25–27. This is verbatim from Mark 10:42–44, for all practical purposes.

(8) Mark 9:35 and Mark 10:42–44. I would propose that Mark redactionally doubled his 10:42–44 into 9:35 as part of his overall structuring of 8:27–10:45. This explains the stich-and-a-half format of 9:35 and the fact that two of its three terms (first, last, servant) reappear in 10:42–44 (servant, first). Thus the saying in 9:35 derives from 10:42–44, just as the apostolic dispute in 9:33–34 derives from that in 10:35–41 (Fleddermann: 58–61).

(9) Mark 10:45 and Luke 22:27. This is the second part of Aphorism 14 to be considered. In themselves Mark 10:45 (= Matt 20:28) and Luke 22:27 might not even be considered as variations of the same saying. It is only when the common sequence of Mark 10:42–45 and Luke 22:24–27 is examined that this arises as a question. (See Table 8.5.)

What is common between Mark 10:45 and Luke 22:27 is their thematic conjunction and word-linkage ("serv-") with the preceding units; what is different between them is that the servant is "I" (Jesus) in Luke but "the Son of Man" in Mark, and also that the opening in Luke 22:27a (sits/serves/sits) and the conclusion in Mark 10:45b (life as ransom) are quite particular to each.

(10) Luke 22:27. Luke 22:24–26 and 27 are not two juxtaposed

Table 8.5

Mark	Luke
[10:35–41 (James and John vs. the others)]	22:24 (dispute over greatness)
10:42 (rule/lord//great/authority)	22:25 (king/lordship//authority/benefactor)
10:43 (not so with you)	22:26a (not so with you)
10:44 (great/servant//first/slave)	22:26b (greatest/youngest//leader/serves)
	22:27a (metaphorical question and answer)
10:45a ("Son of Man" as servant)	22:27b ("I" as servant)
10:45b (life as ransom)	

aphorisms but rather a logically, verbally, and formally integrated complex. *Logically*, the world's way (25) is to be reversed by the disciples (26) just as its procedure (27a) is contradicted by Jesus himself (27b). *Verbally*, the connections are as follows:

22:24.	the greatest(*meizōn*)	
22:26.	the greatest(*meizōn*) . . .	as one who serves (*diakonōn*)
22:27a.	the greater(*meizōn*) . . .	one who serves (*diakonōn*)
22:27b.		as one who serves (*diakonōn*)

Formally, it was noted before that there are many instances of sayings with a relatival opening in Mark that are found elsewhere (Q, John) with a participial format. This is true also of Mark 10:43–44 (*hos an* twice) and of Luke 22:26b (participial *ho* twice). But this participial usage continues into Luke 22:27 (four times) so that it is not a question of "servant" (*diakonos*) but of "serving" (*diakonōn*). Hence Luke 22:24–27 is a well-integrated unit.

The Lukan complex, and what may be a completely recast dramatization of its tradition in John 13:4–17, are located at the Last Supper. This is quite appropriate for Luke because "in the New Testament *diakoneō* to serve primarily and originally means 'to wait at table' " (Tödt: 210). But apart from this general appropriateness between aphorism and *table* situation, the connection with the Last Supper seems redactional, even if quite possibly pre-Lukan.

(11) Mark 10:45. There are three separate questions to be studied and, even though they are all connected, they should not be confused.

(a) Son of Man and 10:45a. Their contexts make it clear that Mark 10:45a and Luke 22:27b are variants of the same aphorism, but it is equally clear that Luke has "*I* am among you as one who serves" while Mark has "*the Son of man* came not to be served but to serve." The question this raises must be carefully phrased and circumscribed: it is *not* whether Mark 10:45 or Luke 22:27 is more original, and not even whether Mark 10:45a or Luke 22:27b is more original, but whether "I" or "Son of Man" is more original.

Perrin, for example, says: "Lohse has argued convincingly that both Mark 10:45 and . . . Luke 22:27 have independent histories in the tradition of the church, the former in a more Semitic and the latter in a more Hellenistic area. . . . So the balance of probability is that the Son of Man is the more original and that the I-saying was formed from it" (1971:185; but see 1970:211). On the other hand, Jeremias showed that most Son of Man sayings have versions or parallels *without* that phrase, that these former instances are secondary, and that Mark 10:45a/Luke 22:27b is such a situation (1967b:161,166). One cannot, therefore, use any overall conclusions on Mark 10:45/Luke 22:27 originality to decide on Son of Man/I originality therein. As Colpe cautiously concludes: "The *egō* in Lk. might well be original . . . Mk. might well have substituted the title Son of Man for the first person *egō*" (448; so also Tödt: 208).

(b) Son of Man and 10:45b. The saying in 10:45 has been declared emphatically to belong "to the oldest Palestinian tradition of dominical sayings" (Colpe: 455), but this has also been just as flatly denied, since "the assumption that the logion arose in Palestine cannot be proved; the Semitic coloring can be explained from the influence of the OT or of the linguistic usage in Hellenistic-Jewish Christianity and, in light of the history of the saying, this latter is more probable" (Strecker, 1968:432 note 30a). Leaving aside, then this problem of origins, what of the conjunction between the Son of Man and this saying in 10:45b?

My proposal is that Mark himself linked the term "Son of Man" with 10:45b as part of his general creation of the suffering Son of Man theme. This thesis *in no way* presumes that Mark created either the apologetical or soteriological traditions concerning Jesus' suffering and passion, but it does propose that Mark was the first who inserted the title Son of Man into such traditions. I have two arguments for this proposal in connection with 10:45.

(i) Jeremias. This is a general argument based on Jeremias' proposal that the "oldest layer" of Son of Man sayings is composed of those twelve units that have no parallels *without* the term Son of Man: Matt. 8:20; 10:23; 24:27; 24:37(39b); 25:31; Mark 13:26; 14: 62; Luke 17:22,30; 18:8; 21:36; John 1:51 (1967:172). Leaving aside for now any criticism of that list, I intend only to underline the fact that there are no suffering Son of Man sayings included on it.

(ii) Perrin. This is a far more important argument and it is based on, although differing with, the conclusions of Perrin's own analysis. Perrin distinguished "two distinct traditions using (*para*)*didonai* of the passion in the New Testament: (1) an apologetic (*para*)*didonai* tradition using the verb in the passive . . . and (2) a soteriological (*para*)*didonai* tradition using the verb in the active with a relexive object. . . ." (1970:207). In that former tradition only Mark and those texts directly (see Mark 9:31 = Matt. 17:22 = Luke 9:44; Mark 10:33 = Matt. 20:18 = Luke 18:31; Mark 14:41 = Matt. 26:45) or indirectly (see Matt. 26:2 and Luke 24:7) dependent on him have the title Son of Man. The others have Jesus/Lord (see 1 Cor. 11:23; Rom. 4:25; Perrin, 1970:205). Turning to the latter tradition, one finds exactly the same pattern as in the former. Perrin cites eight texts where: (a) an agent of salvation, (b) gives himself (*didonai* or *pardidonai heauton*), (c) on behalf of (*hyper*), (d) others. The agent is either "the man Christ Jesus" (1 Tim. 2:5–6), "Jesus Christ" (Tit. 2:13–14), "Lord Jesus Christ" (Gal. 1:3–4), "Son of God" (Gal. 2:20), and "Christ" (Eph. 5:2,25). Against these diverse titles, it is only in Mark 10:45 that the agent is the Son of Man. The case can be sharpened by contrasting Mark 10:45 with 1 Tim. 2:5–6, which is closest to it (see Table 8.6):

It seems to me that this second (*para*)*didonai* tradition cries out

Table 8.6

Mark 10:45	1 Timothy 2:5–6
the Son of man . . . to give his life (*dounai tēn psychēn autou*) as a ransom (*lytron*) for many (*anti pollōn*)	the man Christ Jesus, who gave himself (*dous heauton*) as a ransom (*antilytron*) for all (*hyper pantōn*)

for the same conclusion as did the first one: It is Mark who first inserted the title Son of Man into the traditions concerning the suffering and passion of Jesus.

(c) The Unity of 10:45. Presuming, then, that it was Mark who inserted the title Son of Man into this verse, there is one final question to ask. Was the unit already composed of 10:45a and 10:45b before Mark, or did he first combine it into its present unity? I propose that Mark added 10:45b at the same time as he inserted Son of Man into 10:45a and thereby created the present unit. This is supported by the absence of any equivalent to Mark 10:45b in Luke 22:27. Mark's redactional creation, unique among all the Son of Man sayings (Tödt: 208–209), thus served as an appropriate climax to the themes of suffering and humility that interweave throughout all of 8:31–10:45. Indeed, by this combination of the paradoxical authority of the *earthly* Son of Man (10:45a) with the salvific passion of the *suffering* Son of Man (10:45b), Mark has created a first and most appropriate climax to all he has said heretofore concerning those twin aspects of the Son of Man, in 2:10,28 (as earthly) and 8:31; 9:12,31; and 10:33 (as suffering).

Barrett has denied that it is the specific Suffering Servant of Isa. 52:13–53:12 which lies behind this verse, but rather the far more general Old Testament motif of expiatory death for God's people, from Moses (Exod. 32:30) to the Maccabean martyrs (2 Mac. 7:37–38). He concludes that this latter "background . . . is such that a creative mind working upon it could produce a saying such as that recorded in Mark" (1959:15; see also 1972). I conclude that this "creative mind" belonged to Mark himself.

(12) Conclusion. In terms of the aphorism itself, there are independent variants in Mark 10:42–45 = Matt. 20:25–28, and in Luke 22:25–27. Mark 9:35 = Matt. 23:11 = Luke 9:48c is a Markan redactional and abbreviated doublet of that Mark 10:42–45. In terms of aphoristic stories, the introduction in Luke 22:24 (from Mark 9:34 = Luke 9:46) turns his 22:25–27 into something of a story or at least a dialogue. But it is especially Mark who developed the aphorism into

two separate stories, each quite critical of the disciples. The first
story is in 9:33–35, "And they came to Capernaum; and when he
was in the house he asked them, 'What were you discussing on the
way?' But they were silent; for on the way they had discussed with
one another who was the greatest. And he sat down and called the
twelve; and he said to them, 'If any one would be first, he must be
last of all and servant of all.'" The second story is in 10:35–45. The
dreadfully inappropriate request of James and John in the *dialectical
story* of 10:35–40 leads into the statement in 10:41—"And when the
ten heard it, they began to be indignant at James and John." This

Table 8.7

Mark 11:22–23	Matthew 21:21	Matthew 18:19	
Have faith in God. Truly, I say to you,	Truly, I say to you, if you have faith	Again I say to you, if two of you agree on earth about anything they ask,	
	and never doubt, you will not only do what has been done to the fig tree but even		
whoever says to this mountain, "Be taken up and cast into the sea," and does not doubt in his heart, but believes that what he says will come to pass, it will be done for him.	if you say to this mountain "Be taken up and cast into the sea," it will be done.	it will be done for them by my Father in heaven.	

then introduces the unit in 10:42–45, so that in the context of 10:41–45 we are dealing with an *aphoristic story*. So this time Mark got two *aphoristic stories* out of a single saying.

Aphorism 23: *Moving a Mountain*

(1) There are four independent versions to be considered: (a) Mark 11:23 = Matt. 21:21; (b) Matt. 18:19; (c) *Didasc.* XV; and (4) *Gos. Thom.* 48 and 106. There is also a reference to the aphorism in 1 Cor. 13:2 and a possible one in Ign. *Eph.* 5:2. (see Table 8.7.)

Table 8.7 (cont.)

Didascalia XV	Gospel of Thomas 48	Gospel of Thomas 106
	If two make peace with each other in this one house,	When you make the two one, you will become the sons of man,
If two shall agree together		
and shall say to this mountain: Take and cast yourself in the sea,	they will say to the mountain "Move away,"	and when you say, "Mountain, move away,"
it will happen.	and it will move away.	it will move away.

(2) Mark 11:12–21. For Mark the cursing (11:12–14) and withering (11:20–21) of the fig tree frame the incident in the Temple
(11:15–19). In Mark the central episode is not a *cleansing* but a
symbolic destruction of the Temple in its perfectly legitimate fiscal,
sacrificial, and cultic activities: "Jesus not only puts an end to the
temple's business operation, but he also suspends the practice of
cult and ritual. At this point the temple no longer operates. It is
shut down in all its functions" (Kelber, 1974:101). So also with the
fig tree incident: "In the context of Mark's framing design the fig
tree stands for the temple, and the disaster which befell the tree
illustrates what occurred to the temple . . . Mark's compositional
arrangement, dooming of fig tree—temple incident—withering of
fig tree, is meant to highlight an eschatological temple crisis" (Kelber, 1974:102). All of this, of course, is handled very differently in
the cleansing-healing-acclaiming trilogy of Matt. 21:12–16.

(3) Mark 11:22–25. As already seen, this is a redactional cluster
of four aphorisms, with Mark having created Mark 11:22 as the
cluster's programmatic preamble. Its presence emphasizes faith as
well as prayer for the whole complex. Leaving aside Mark 11:22 for
the moment, the interest here is on how Mark 11:23 is developed by
the Markan composition from aphorism into dialogue.

(4) Mark 11:23. Also, as already seen, most of 11:23b is redactionally Markan ("and does not doubt . . . come to pass"). That
means that the pre-Markan 11:23 is now incomplete and must be
restored from other independent versions of this aphorism. But before and apart from Mark's redaction, the aphorism's emphasis was
on the power of prayer and indeed of combined prayer, on the
prayer of *two* persons, rather than on the power of faith as such.

In terms of my present concern, Mark merged Aphorism 23 into
his redactional complex by turning it into dialogue: "And Peter
remembered [the previous day's cursing] and said to him, 'Master,
look! The fig tree which you cursed has withered.' And Jesus answered them . . . " (11:21). Aphorism 23 is now Jesus' response to
Peter's comment.

(5) Matt. 21:21. Matthew redacted Mark's text to smooth and

tighten its compositional unity and to destroy in that process Mark's careful framing combination of "evacuated" Temple and withered fig tree. In Matt. 21:19 cursing and withering are immediate and simultaneous. But he retains Mark's dialogue connection: "When the disciples saw it they marveled, saying, 'How did the fig tree wither at once?'" (21:20). This picks up his preceding "withered at once" from 21:19b. Thus Aphorism 23 still appears as aphoristic dialogue in Matt. 21:20–21. Two other changes may also be noted in Matthew. (a) *Externally*, he has united Mark 11:20–21 (fig tree) more closely with 11:22–23 (mountain) by having the fig tree infiltrate into the aphorism ("not only . . . but even . . ."), possibly helped by the "tree" in Q/Luke 17:6. (b) *Internally*, he reformulated Mark 11:22–23 to (i) a single and initial mention of faith, (ii) an immediate mention of "never doubt," (iii) then the "mountain," and (iv) directly, "it will be done (*genēsetai*)."

(6) Matt. 18:19. This is a separate aphorism from its presently succeeding one in Matt. 18:20, on which see *Gos. Thom.* 30 (and Attridge, 1979). It asserts the power of combined (double) prayer but it has no mention of moving mountains. Matthew has also established verbal links between 18:19 and 21:21, for example, "it will be done" (*genēsetai*).

(7) *Thomas*. Turner has suggested that the "spirituality implied in the Gospel of Thomas is a type of unitive mysticism. The theme of unity runs through the document as a whole. In two sayings it replaces the synoptic 'faith' as the force which removes mountains (Sayings 48 and 106). The second saying has a more distinctively gnostic ring than the first" (Turner and Montefiore: 105). Quispel has even said that 106 has "targumized" 48 by "hinting at the reunion of the opposites, male and female, above and below, inner and outer" (1958–1959:288). But it is probably also true that *Thomas* now reads 48 in the light of 106 (Ménard, 1975:150), since there is already a thematic complex in 46–49 on this subject (see Turner and Montefiore: 80).

Both *Gos. Thom.* 48 and 106 retain the apodosis concerning moving the mountain, but each has changed the protasis in different ways. My hypothesis is that the original protasis was about combined (double) prayer but (a) in 48 it now concerns peaceful coexistence and (b) in 106 it now concerns primordial undifferentiation, both of which are hermeneutical variations on that original theme. Neither text has any mention of the mountain being cast into the sea, which was also omitted from Matthew's conflation of Aphorism 122 (Q/Matt. 17:20b = Luke 17:5–6) and Aphorism 23 (Mark 11:23 = Matt. 21:21) in Matt. 17:20. I do not see any direct contact between Matt. 17:20 and Gos. Thom. 48 or 106, but simply a common tendency to mute just a little the startling hyperbole of the aphorism's promise.

(8) Didasc. XV. In none of those versions seen so far was there a clear combination of (a) double prayer and (b) moved mountain. The former unit was clear in Matt. 18:19, only residually visible in Gos. Thom. 48 or 106, and gone completely from Mark 11:23. The latter element was gone from Matt. 18:19, quite clear in shortened form in Gos. Thom. 48 and 106 (no sea), but clear and full in Mark 11:23. In the Didasc. XV, however, both units appear together and are full and clear.

"Written in Greek, the Didascalia has reached us in a complete form only in an early Syriac translation. But in addition to this we have extensive fragments of an ancient Latin version, which cover about two-fifths of the whole text and include both the beginning and the end. And further, though no manuscript of the original Greek has yet been found, considerable portions of the Greek text are recoverable (if, too often, only in an approximate form) from the fourth-century Apostolic Constitutions, the compiler of which made the Didascalia the basis of his first six books" (Connolly: xi). In terms of function "the book has naturally been classed with that family of documents which we know as the church orders, among which it forms a third in point of time to the Didache and the Apostolic Tradition of Hippolytus" (Connolly: xxvi–xxvii). Questions concerning place and time of origin are more problematic: "As to the region from which the Didascalia comes and the date at which it was written there is now a large measure of agreement within certain limits: Syria or Palestine, and the third century, is the general verdict of scholars" (Connolly: lxxxvii).

The context of *Didasc*. XV concerns discipline in the order of widows, and warns against widows who "will not sit beneath the roof of their houses and pray and entreat the Lord, but are impatient to be running after gain" (Connolly:134–135). Against such squabbling, it cites what "is written in the Gospel," but with an interesting difference between the Syriac and Latin versions of the lost Greek original (Connolly:134–135), as in Table 8.8. What is a single-stich aphorism in the Latin is a double one in the Syriac. It should also be noted that the parallel section to *Didasc*. XV in the *Apostolic Constitutions* III.7:2 omits totally any reference to this citation (Funk: 1.192–193). This latter work, written around A.D. 375–400, has its "first six books . . . based on the *Didascalia*, the seventh begins with a version of the *Didache*, and the chief known source of the eighth is the *Apostolic Tradition* of Hippolytus" (Connolly: xx).

It is possible, of course, to consider these citations as a redacted conflation of the *double prayer* from Matt. 18:19 with the *mountain/sea* from Matt. 21:21 (so Achelis and Flemming: 345). This conflation would have been more originally obvious in the Syriac, but less so in the abbreviated version of the Latin. But this does not explain *Gos. Thom*. 48 and 106.

I propose, therefore, that *Didasc*. XV is an independent version and not a Matthean conflation. Its earliest and best recoverable form is in the single-stich Latin version: "Duo si convenerint in unum et dixerint monti huic: Tolle et mitte te in mari, fiet" (Con-

Table 8.8

Didascalia XV (Syriac)	Didascalia XV (Latin)
If two shall agree together and shall ask concerning anything whatsoever, it shall be given them. And if they shall say to a mountain that it be removed and fall into the sea, it shall be done.	If two shall agree together and shall say to this mountain: Take and cast yourself in the sea, it will happen.

nolly: 135; see also Hennecke and Schneemelcher: 1.302). This metaphoric and hyperbolic aphorism was expanded into the double-stich saying in the Syriac version so that the abstracted generalization of the first stich interpreted the metaphoric exaggeration of the second stich. The version in Matt. 18:19 is a further "improvement" on the saying, in that it has now omitted completely the second half. And *Apost. Con.* III.7:2 has solved it even more radically by omitting it totally. *Gos. Thom.* 48 and 106, however, still continue the tradition of the original single-stich Latin version from *Didasc.* XV.

The possibility of canonically independent versions in the *Didascalia*, and especially of contacts between such versions and *Thomas*, has been suggested before. In a doctoral dissertation at Harvard University in 1973, Cox studies seven units in the *Didascalia* and concluded that, "Although one cannot speak with certainty until the evidence is equally analyzed, I doubt seriously that the Greek Didascalist cited *immediately* from any of the canonical gospels. My doubt is based on (i) the fact that the Didascalist, while he not infrequently, when citing from the *Tanak*, indicates specifically the title of the source from which he cites, never, when citing from the 'Gospel,' indicates specifically the title of the source from which he draws, other than that it is the 'Gospel,' and (ii) the fact that all of the '*logoi*' analyzed in these 'studies' probably derive *immediately* from collections of *logoi Jesu* . . . much like Q and the *Gospel of Thomas*, collections gathered together for various theological, paraenetic, and apologetic motives. And this should not surprise us since Syria, the home of the *Didascalia*, was the home of just such collections ('gospels') from the earliest period" (576–577).

(9) Ign. *Eph.* 5:2. The fact of Ignatius' independence from the intracanonical gospels has been discussed before. In his letter to the Ephesians Ignatius says: "if the prayer of one or two has such might, how much more has that of the bishop and of the whole Church" (Lake: 1.178–179). It is quite doubtful whether Ignatius is here referring to our present aphorism at all (see Koester, 1957a:38–39) and I simply mention it as a possibility. If he has it in mind, he has

changed its protasis to "one or two" lest the bishop, as "one," be undermined by "two" non-episcopal prayers. Ignatius would prefer the bishop to move the mountain.

(10) 1 Cor. 13:2. What of Paul's comment in 1 Cor. 13:2, "if I have all faith, so as to remove mountains, but have not love, I am nothing"? Does this prove a knowledge, and criticism, of an aphorism combining faith and mountain, a conjunction claimed above to be redactionally Markan?

It is possible, of course, that Paul has simply created the expression in 1 Cor. 13:2 for his context since " 'uprooting mountains' as an idiom for doing the impossible" is a Jewish hyperbole, "but the association of this power with faith is not attested" (Robinson and Koester: 41 note 29). In that case the relationship between the present aphorism and 1 Cor. 13:2 is strictly coincidental. There are two points, however, which render coincidence unlikely. First, we have already seen contacts between the prayer in Q/Matt. 11:25–26 = Luke 10:21, which precedes the Q/Aphorisms 62–68 and 1 Cor. 1–4. That is, the problem of gnostic enthusiasm is already known as a Corinthian phenomenon opposed at least in its effects by Paul. Second, any gnosticizing edition of Aphorism 23 would have to avoid the emphasis on double or combined prayer either as in *Gos. Thom.* 48 and 106 or, more simply, by replacing double prayer by personal and individual faith. I am inclined, therefore, to consider that the Corinthian gnostics are using the present aphorism, but with personal faith replacing common (double) prayer. "In that case Paul's allusion to the saying would be remarkable, in that the word of the Lord is not used as final authority settling the issue. Rather, Paul criticizes it; or, more exactly, he criticizes the use made of it, much as in the case of speaking in tongues, where Paul recognizes a religious experience as a divine gift and still criticizes its misuse. First Cor. 13:2 might then tend indirectly to suggest that the Corinthians were misusing sayings of the Lord" (Robinson and Koester: 41).

(11) Conclusion. The original aphorism is best seen in *Didasc.* XV with both protasis (double prayer) and apodosis (mountain to sea) intact. The first part or protasis remains in Matt. 18:19, is

reflected in *Gos. Thom.* 48 and 106, but is gone completely from Mark 11:23. The second part or apodosis remains fully in Mark 11:23 (mountain/sea) and partially in *Gos. Thom.* 48 and 106 (mountain), but is gone completely from Matt. 18:19. The original emphasis was on the power not just of faith or of prayer but of *double or common prayer*.

In terms of form, and the concerns of the present chapter, the *aphoristic saying* remains as such in all versions outside of Markan influence. But Mark has created an *aphoristic dialogue* leading from the address in 11:21, through the introductory saying created as 11:22, into the response of Jesus in 11:23. And he has then developed this into an *aphoristic story* by linking the dialogue into the narrative of the cursed and withered fig tree, which pointedly frames the . Temple's symbolic destruction. Matt. 21:20–21, despite all other changes over his Markan source, follows him in the development from saying to dialogue and on into story.

Aphorism 25: *The Temple's Destruction*

(1) There is only one independent version to be considered: Mark 13:2 = Matt. 24:2 = Luke 21:6. (See Table 8.9.)

(2) Mark 13. The discourse of Jesus in Mark 13 is strikingly different from all of Jesus' other discourses in Mark. In some chapters, such as Mark 2 or 10 or 12, there are clear delineations and separations by theme and subject, time and place, speakers and hearers. And even in those chapters where the theme seems more unified (for example, in 4:1–34; 7:1–23; 9:30–50) there are explicit breaks in place and audience (4:10; 7:17) or at least in speaker (9:33,38). But above all there are those implicit breaks through such phrases as "and he said (to them)." Such implicit breaks appear in 4:11,21,24,26,30 and in 7:9,14,18,20. But in Mark 13 there is but a single break separating 13:1–2 and 3–37. Thus 13:3–37 is the single sustained discourse of Jesus in Mark that lacks even the minimal implicit break of "and he said (to them)."

Bultmann claimed that Mark 13:5–27 "is a Jewish Apocalypse

Table 8.9

Matthew 24:1–2	Mark 13:1–2	Luke 21:5–6
Jesus left the temple and was going away, when his disciples came to point out to him the

buildings of the temple. But he answered them, "You see all these, do you not? Truly, I say to you, there will not be left here one stone upon another, that will not be thrown down." | And as he came out of the temple, one of his disciples said to him, "Look, Teacher, what wonderful stones and what wonderful buildings!" And Jesus said to him, "Do you see these great buildings?

There will not be left here one stone upon another, that will not be thrown down." | And as some spoke of the temple, how it was adorned

with noble stones and offerings, he said, "As for these things which you see, the days will come when there shall not be left here one stone upon another that will not be thrown down." |

with a Christian editing" (125). This claim, made with no documentary evidence, presumably arises from two considerations: (a) Mark is a collector and an editor rather than a composer and an author; but (b) Mark 13:5–27 is clearly a compositional unity and not just a collection of units and pericopes. Bultmann's judgment has had its own following but, as his first point or presupposition has become increasingly challenged by redactional criticism on Mark, it must at least be considered possible that the present *unity* not only of 13:5–27 but indeed of all 13:1–37 is a Markan creation. This conclusion depends on the intensely Markan development of this section in terms of both structure and theology.

In terms of *structure* Lambrecht (1965, 1967) has proposed a very persuasive chiastic format of: A(5–23) with a(5–6), b(7–8), c(9–13), b'(14–20), a'(21–23); B(24–27); A'(28–37) with a(28–29), b(30), c(31), b'(32), a'(33–36), and the climactic and concluding 37. Even though Lambrecht believes that Mark 13 took five units from a redaction of the Q source, he insists that such sources in no way constituted a compositional unity such as the present Mark 13. This latter is a strictly Markan composition (1966:360). His proposed structure has been corroborated more recently by the analysis of Rousseau (1975; see also Robbins, 1981a:111).

In terms of *theology* this chapter gives evidence of characteristically Markan eschatology (see Kelber, 1974:109–128). Thus (a) the destruction of the Temple in 13:5–23 is clearly differentiated from and succeeded by (b) the coming of the Son of Man "after that tribulation" in 13:24–27; and (c) although the destruction will take place within this generation (13:30), just as will the coming (9:1), the two events are distinct and consecutive even if closely connected, just as are the slow greening of the fig tree and the sudden coming of summer, in 13:28–37.

I would conclude that the lack of internal breaks in 13:5–37, as well as the specifically Markan structure and theology, bespeak intense authorial creativity and compositional control by Mark over this most crucial chapter. None of this precludes the possibility that Mark 13 contains individual units taken from either Jewish or Christian sources, but it negates any sustained pre-Markan source for this chapter, whether a pre-Markan Jewish apocalyptic "flyer" (Walter; Pesch; Flückiger) or even a Markan midrash on Dan. 7 (Hartmann).

(3) Mark 13:1–2. That preceding section serves, however, to draw attention to 13:1–2 and 13:3–4, since the only breaks occur between 13:1–2 and 13:3–4 and between 13:3–4 and 13:5–37. The break between 13:1–2 and 3–4 has Jesus deliver his speech "while enthroned upon the eschatological counter mountain and looking upon the temple whose downfall he has in mind" (Kelber, 1974: 112). Even more importantly, the break separates Jesus' comment on the Temple's destruction in 13:2 from the *mistaken* question of the disciples in 13:4. It is their presumption that the destruction of the Temple is *coincident and synonymous* (13:4a = 4b) with the advent of the Son of Man and the end of the world that is refuted by Jesus' careful delineation and separation of these two successive events in 13:5–37.

(4) Matt 24:2 = Luke 21:6. The minor agreements against Mark indicate synoptic preference for the future tense against the Markan

aorist as well as dislike for his doubled emphatic negative (see Nei-rynck, 1974:161,239). Otherwise Matt. 24:2 stays close to Mark 13:2. The introductory clause in Luke 21:6, "the days will come when" (*eleusontai hēmerai en hais*) indicates his connection of this proph-ecy to the preceding one in 19:43, "the days shall come" (*hēxousin hēmerai*), and the succeeding one in 23:29, "the days are coming when" (*erchontai hēmerai en hais*).

In the Greco-Roman tradition of the *chreia* and apophthegm the address (question, comment, or request) is often given with indirect discourse and with participial constructions, especially such devices as the genitive absolute, as here in Luke 21:5. This moves the dia-logue or story swiftly and smoothly towards its climax in the hero or sage's saying. And in that tradition, and for the same reason, the "he said" or "he answered" is often inserted within the saying itself, *as if* Luke 21:5–6 read: "as for these things which you see," he said, "there shall not be left here one stone upon another that will not be thrown down." In the Jesus tradition, however, double direct dis-course, with the verb of address and response placed initially before each unit, is by far the more normal construction.

(5) Luke 19:41–44. The full text of 19:41–44 reads, "And when he drew near and saw the city he wept over it, saying, 'Would that even today you knew the things that make for peace! But now they are hid from your eyes. For the days shall come upon you, when your enemies will cast up a bank about you and surround you, and hem you in on every side, and dash you to the ground, you and your children within you, and they will not leave one stone upon another in you; because you did not know the time of your visita-tion.' "

Dupont has argued that Luke 19:44b is independent of Mark 13:2 so that the phrase "they will not leave one stone upon another" in 19:44b is a separate witness to that text (1971:312–319). I am not convinced that this analysis is correct, especially when it is con-sidered against the background of certain other texts in Luke.

There are four Lukan texts to be considered before any decision can be made on 19:44b: (a) *Jerusalem Indicted* in Q/Matt. 23:37–39

= Luke 13:34–35; (b) *Jerusalem Destroyed* here in Luke 19:42–44; (c) *Jerusalem Abandoned* in the heavily redacted version of Mark 13:14–20 in Luke 21:20–24 (note how Mark 13:15–16 = Matt. 24: 17–18 is relocated into Luke 17:31–32); and (d) *Jerusalem Mourned* in Luke 23:27–31.

I am persuaded by the arguments of Boring (1982:171–173,224–225) and Neyrey that Luke has taken (a) from Q and then developed the sequence of (b)–(c)–(d) as its extension so that Jesus makes a judgment on Jerusalem's fate three more times: as he enters the city in 19:42–44, within the city in 21:20–24, and as he leaves the city in 23:27–31. In other words, both Luke 19:42–44 and 23:27–31 are his own creations but with close regard for the form and content of the given text in Q/Matt. 23:37–39 = Luke 13:34–35. In such a situation the presence of the "stone upon stone" unit in Luke 19:44b is best seen as a usage of Mark 13:2 = Matt. 24:2 = Luke 21:6 once again in Luke 19:44b. There is, therefore, no independent version of Aphorism 25 in Luke 19:44b.

(6) Conclusion. Aphorism 25 is of special interest because it has

Table 8.10

Mark 14:58	Matthew 26:61	Mark 15:29
We heard him say,	This fellow said,	Aha! you who
"I will destroy this temple that is made with hands, and in three days I will build another, not made with hands."	"I am able to destroy the temple of God, and to build it in three days."	would destroy the temple and build it in three days, save yourself…

been argued in both directions. If one accepts the analysis of Dupont (1971) and rephrases it in my terms, than an *aphoristic saying* found independently in Luke 19:44b has been converted into an *aphoristic story* in Mark 13:2. But I am more convinced that the movement has been in the other direction. The tradition began with an *aphoristic story* in Mark 13:2 and was thereafter converted by Luke himself into an *aphoristic saying*, or at least part of one, in Luke 19:42–44. This is a salutary reminder that the movement is not always in the one direction, not always from saying to story, but sometimes in the opposite direction as well.

Aphorism 26: *Jesus and Temple*

(1) There are three independent sources to be considered: (a) Mark 14:58 = Matt. 26:61; Mark 15:29 = Matt. 27:40; (b) *Gos. Thom.* 71; and (c) John 2:19. (See Table 8.10.)

(2) *Gos. Thom.* 71. The original manuscript is more damaged than indicated in Lambdin. Wilson (Hennecke and Schneemelcher: 1.518) gives the text as, "Jesus said: I will des[troy this] house,

Table 8.10 (cont.)

Matthew 27:40	Gospel of Thomas 71	John 2:19	Acts 6:14
You who would destroy the temple	I shall destroy [this] house,	Destroy this temple,	we have heard him say that this Jesus of Nazareth will destroy this place . . .
and build it in three days, save yourself . . .	and no one will be able to rebuild it.	and in three days I will raise it up.	

and none shall be able to build it [again]." Nevertheless, it is clear that we have here "a form of the charge brought against Jesus" in Mark 14:58 (Wilson, 1960a:114). If one considers *Thomas* to be dependent on the canonical gospels, this text intends to contradict the gospel promise of the resurrection (Ménard, 1975:172), or possibly indicates "a period after the final destruction of the Temple in Jerusalem, when no hope remained of its rebuilding" (Wilson, 1960a:115). But, if *Thomas* is independent of the gospels, this text may well indicate an even more primitive version than our present gospel ones.

Gos. Thom. 71 could be read as announcing the destruction of the body-house or world-house, but there is nothing to render this reading inevitable. In other words, the aphorism makes just as much sense as a statement about the Second Temple rebuilt after the destruction of the First Temple. It may also be noted that when the Coptic New Testament came to translate the Greek verbs for "destroy" (*katalyō*) and "build" (*oikodomeō*) in Mark 14:58 = Matt. 26:61, it used the same two verbs, *šoršr* and *kot*, as in the Coptic text of *Gos. Thom.* 71.

(3) Mark 13:1–2. This is Mark's own Aphorism 25: *The Temple's Destruction*. But Mark has also conflated some elements from the pre-Markan Aphorism 26: *Jesus and Temple* into that earlier one. Mark 13:1–2 is part of the "redactional text of Mark" (Pyrke: 170), wherein Mark: (a) combined these two traditions by taking two elements from Aphorism 25, "be left" (*aphethę̄*) and "stone upon another" (*lithos epi lithon*), and two from Aphorism 26, "be thrown down" or "destroyed (*katalythę̄*) and "built," contained indirectly as "buildings" (*oikodomai*); (b) combined them chiastically with "stones/buildings//buildings/stone"; and (c) combined them with a characteristically Markan "double negative" (*ou mē . . . hos ou mē*) in 13:2b, and "synonymous expression" in 13:1–2 (Neirynck, 1972: 88,105). It must be underlined, however, that this combination does not have Jesus say that he himself will destroy the Temple. This will be significant for the later understanding of Mark 14:58 and 15:29.

Why did Mark 13:1–2 allow the pre-Markan Aphorism 26 to infiltrate into his own newly created Aphorism 25? On the one hand, Mark teaches that Jesus himself *symbolically destroyed* the Temple in 11:12–21: "in the context of Mark's framing design the fig tree stands for the temple, and the disaster which befell the tree illustrates what occurred to the temple" (Kelber, 1974:102). And God himself concurred in this *symbolic destruction* in 15:38. On the other hand, Mark 13 wishes emphatically to separate both chronologically and theologically the *physical destruction* of the Temple and the advent of the Son of Man (13:14–23/24–27). In such a context Jesus cannot announce that he himself will physically destroy the Temple, since such a prophecy *means for Mark* that destruction and advent are synonymous and concomitant events. Thus in 13:1–2 Jesus may announce the Temple's physical destruction by God, but not by himself.

(4) Mark 14:58. In his doctoral dissertation Donahue (103–138) argued that *the Greek text* of Mark 14:58 (a) is a carefully composed chiasm of A(destroy), B(with hands), C(three days), B'(without hands), A'(build); wherein (b) "Mark has created a single saying by joining two traditions, one which affirms opposition to the temple, the other which points to the community as the substitute for the destroyed temple" (109), so that (c) 14:58 "for Mark, is a true statement on the lips of Jesus" (135). He continues to maintain that position, although others have not found it very persuasive (compare Kelber, 1976:66–71 with 121–129 and 168–172).

I would argue, on the other hand, that (a) 14:58 is precisely what Mark says it is: a false accusation (14:47). The quotation in 14:58 is not what Jesus said since, *as far as Mark is concerned, what Jesus truly said is* 13:2. In other words, Mark once again distinguishes between the destruction of the Temple in 14:57–58 and the advent of the Son of Man in 14:62. Jesus did not say "I will destroy the Temple, etc.," that is, Jesus did not equate the destruction of the Temple and the return of the Son of Man in glory. Therefore (b) I interpret "another, not made with hands," not as the ecclesiastical community after the resurrection but the eschatological community after the parousia. Hence (c) the "in three days" at the chiastic core of 14:58 is not the "after three days" of 8:31; 9:31; 10:34. The phrase denotes "immediately" for Mark and does not seem to have taken on the sacred constancy of "on the third day." Its use again denies that Jesus would destroy the Temple and *immediately* constitute the eschatological dwelling place. I would emphasize that this is Mark's understanding of the situation and not necessarily anyone else's view of the prophecy. Finally, (d) leaving aside for the moment the question of the chiastic form of 14:58, it seems most likely that its *content* represents a teaching of the false prophets opposed in 13:6, 21–22 rather than a Markan creation from previously independent traditions (see also Nickelsburg, 1980:176–182; as against Juel: 204–209). And John 2:19 may well be an independent witness to that pre-Markan prophecy.

(5) Matt. 26:61. Matthew rather drastically changes his Markan source: "I am able to destroy the temple of God, and to build it in three days." So stated, Matthew probably considers the accusation as also quite false, as a boast about miraculous physical power: "I am able" (see 26:59). Luke omits it completely.

(6) Mark 15:29. This is simply a condensed repetition of 14:58, but once again the false accusation is placed on the lip of Jesus' opposition. Mark's obvious unconcern with the chiastic structure of 14:58, or even with the accurate repetition of its content (no "another" here), may tend to confirm that he neither created 14:58 himself nor believes in its truth.

(7) Matt. 27:40. This is close to Mark 15:29, but even closer to the earlier chiastic structure of Mark 14:58 = Matt. 26:61. Once again, Luke omits it completely.

(8) Acts 6:14. This makes it clear why Luke omitted Mark 14:58 and 15:29. The "false" accusation (6:13) is now brought against Stephen: "for we have heard him say that this Jesus of Nazareth will destroy this place." I see no proof of independent Lukan tradition in this citation since (a) the "false witnesses" of 6:13 reflects the "bore false witness" of Mark 14:57, and (b) the "we have heard" of 6:14 reflects the "we heard" of Mark 14:58. The context of Acts 6:14 precludes any mention of "building."

(9) John 2:19. Brown has concluded that "the material in John ii 13–22 is not taken from the Synoptic Gospels, but represents an independent tradition running parallel to the Synoptic tradition" (Brown: 1.120). Since I was not able to consider Mark 14:58 as a Markan creation, it is certainly possible that John 2:19 represents a reflection of the prophecy independently contained in Mark 14:58. In this case, however, it is also clear that John 2:19–22 represents a distinctively Johannine interpretation of the prophecy. John 2:19 has Jesus challenge the Jews: "Destroy (*lysate*) this temple, and in three days I will raise (*egerō*) it up." Thus (a) the Jews, *not Jesus*, will destroy the temple, which is now interpreted as Jesus' body at the crucifixion: 19a = 21; (b) Jesus will raise it up at the resurrection: 19b = 22; and the Markan verbs (*katalyō* and *oikodomeō*) must now be changed to *lyō* and *egeirō*. This *crucifixion/resurrection* is, of course, quite different from Mark's *catastrophe/parousia*, but, facilitated by the "in three days," it enables John to keep the prophecy on Jesus' lip without declaring it false. In other words, whether independent of Mark or not, it has been heavily redacted and brilliantly reinterpreted in its present Johannine setting. That means that, even if John 2:19 is independent of Mark 14:58 and 15:29, it does not tell us anything new about this strand of tradition.

(10) Conclusion. For *Gos. Thom.* 71 the saying is given in *direct* discourse as an aphorism of Jesus (no rebuilding possible!). It is rephrased from a threat to a challenge in John 2:19, developed then into a dialogue in 2:18–20, explained for the reader in 2:21–22, and the entire *aphoristic dialogue* is attached to the symbolic destruction of the Temple in John 2:14–17, "The Jews then said to him, 'What sign have you to show us for doing this?' Jesus answered them, 'Destroy this temple, and in three days I will raise it up.' The Jews then said, 'It has taken forty-six years to build this temple, and will you raise it up in three days?' But he spoke of the temple of his body." The *aphoristic saying* has become part of an *aphoristic story*.

But it is Mark who has effected the move from aphorism to story most brilliantly. The aphorism was used apparently as an assertion of the coincidence of Jesus' parousia and the Temple's fall by those whom Mark opposes in Mark 13. So understood he considers it a false assertion and assigns it, in indirect discourse, to false witnesses and mocking onlookers. What Jesus said was not Aphorism 26 but Aphorism 25, for Mark. In the process Mark created an aphoristic story concerning the *false* witnesses at the trial in 14:55–59 and the mocking passersby at the cross in 15:29. An aphoristic saying has, in other words, generated two separate aphoristic stories in this case. Finally, Acts 6:14, drawing an obvious parallel between the fate of Jesus and of Stephen, copies the Markan aphoristic story from 14:55 –59 into its own Acts 6:8–15. Saying becomes story becomes type.

9

Aphoristic Model

Aphorism is exaggeration, extravagant language; the road of excess which leads to the palace of wisdom.

Aphorism is recklessness; it goes too far. Intellect is courage; the courage to risk its own life; to play with madness.

Aphorism, the form of the mad truth, the Dionysian form.

Aphoristic form is suicide, or self-sacrifice; for truth must die. Intellect is sacrifice of intellect, or fire; which burns up as it gives light.

Broken flesh, broken mind, broken speech. Truth, a broken body: fragments, or aphorisms; as opposed to systematic form or methods.

Systematic form attempts to evade the necessity of death in the life of the mind as of the body; it has immortal longings on it, and so it remains dead. The rigor is *rigor mortis*; systems are wooden crosses, Procrustean beds on which the living mind is pinned.

Aphorism is the form of death and resurrection: "the form of eternity."

NORMAN O. BROWN (187–188)

A. APHORISTIC POWER

In the first chapter I gave several citations from Francis Bacon on the generative power of the aphorism. "Aphorisms, representing a knowledge broken, do invite men to enquire farther," and "aphorisms . . . did invite men, both to ponder that which was invented, and to add and supply further," and again, "aphorisms doth leave the wit of man more free to turn and toss, and to make use of that which is so delivered to more several purposes and applications."

Two distinctions are now in order. Bacon is talking of what I would term hermeneutic power rather than mimetic power. This latter is the aphorism's power of provoking others to create aphorisms for themselves. This phenomenon is exemplified by earlier prophets and later evangelists creating aphorisms for Jesus just as he himself had once done for them. This was not considered here because it would have required a more complete analysis of the entire aphoristic Jesus tradition. A full and complete analysis of the aphoristic tradition would have to consider not only the hermeneutically controlled generativity of Jesus' aphorisms, but also their mimetically controlled generativity.

A second distinction might be proposed between internal and external hermeneutic in the aphoristic tradition. Bacon is talking of internal hermeneutic, of the textual and contextual power of aphorism to provoke thought and discussion, application and interpretation. This internal generative power was seen both textually and contextually for every single aphorism in this book.

In this concluding chapter, however, I consider the phenomenon of external hermeneutic, or of what I would term *modal hermeneutic*. This is aphorism's generative power in creating all those phenomena that served as chapter headings throughout the book. This *modal hermeneutic* is especially important as aphoristic sayings generate either aphoristic dialogues and aphoristic stories and Jesus is thereby tied to human discourse and human history.

This external hermeneutic's generative power is organized as a generative model in Figure 9.1. The axes of the model depend on whether the aphorism is (1) kept as a separate and single aphorism in *isolation*, or combined with one or several other aphorisms in *combination*; and also whether the aphorism is (2) expanded into a story as *narrative*, or expanded into a dialogue as *discourse*. As noted before, that last distinction between narrative and discourse trajectories is a fateful one for the catholic and gnostic traditions within early Christianity. I also presume that further work on the aphoristic tradition will serve either to change that model and/or to fill out more options along its proposed axes. (See Figure 9.1.)

B. APHORISTIC PARADIGM

(1) I have retained as conclusion the aphorism that best exemplifies the diverse possibilities of the aphoristic model. This is Aphorism

Figure 9.1 Generative Model for the Aphoristic Tradition

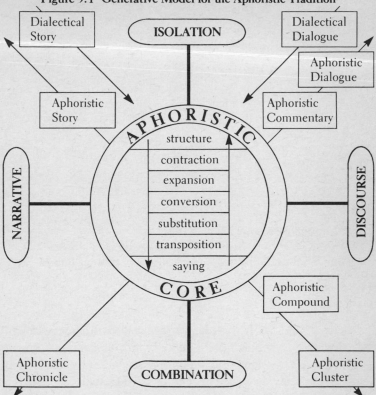

19: *Kingdom and Children*. There are four independent versions to be considered: (a) Matt. 18:3; (b) Mark 10:15 = Luke 18:17; (c) John 3:3,5; and (d) *Gos. Thom.* 22. (See Table 9.1.)

That figure gives only the parallel texts of the *aphoristic saying* itself. Its fuller context will have to be studied, however, in each case.

(2) Mark 10:13–16.

And they were bringing children to him, that he might touch them; and the disciples rebuked them. But when Jesus saw it he was indignant, and said to them, "Let the children come to me, do not hinder them; for to

Table 9.1

Matthew 18:3	Mark 10:15	Luke 18:17	
Truly, I say to you, unless you turn and become like children, you will never enter the kingdom of heaven.	Truly, I say to you, whoever does not receive the kingdom of God like a child shall not enter it.	Truly, I say to you, whoever does not receive the kingdom of God like a child shall not enter it.	

such belongs the kingdom of God. Truly, I say to you, whoever does not receive the kingdom of God like a child shall not enter it." And he took them in his arms and blessed them, laying his hands upon them.

The text will be discussed in terms of both general context and immediate context.

(a) General Context. It was already seen that there is very careful redactional construction linking all of Mark 8:27–10:45 together into three major sections. But within that second or middle section itself there was also evidence of very deliberate parallelism between the episodes in Mark 9:36–39 and 10:13–16, as seen earlier in Table 3.10.

From Table 3.10, however, it becomes quite evident whence the theme of "receiving" the Kingdom was derived in 10:15. It is not in any way pre-Markan, but it represents Mark's rephrasing of his pre-Markan 10:15 in order to underline the verbal and thematic parallel with 9:37 (B/B'). Hence any consideration of Mark 10:15 must imagine a pre-Markan version that contained nothing about "receiving" the Kingdom as a child.

(b) Immediate Content. Bultmann had already suggested "treating v. 15 as an originally independent dominical saying, inserted into

Table 9.1 (cont.)

John 3:3	John 3:5	*Gospel of Thomas* 22
Truly, truly, I say to you, unless one is born anew,	Truly, truly, I say to you, unless one is born of water and the Spirit,	
he cannot see the kingdom of God.	he cannot enter the kingdom of God.	These infants being suckled are like those who enter the Kingdom.

the situation of vv. 13–16" (32). But he also held that "the point of v. 14 is quite different from that of v. 15: v. 14 simply states that children have a share in the Kingdom of God" (32). I accept the first point, but do not agree at all with the second.

(i) Mark 10:15. I agree that this is an independent *aphoristic saying*. This will be confirmed by later considerations of both Matt. 18:3 and John 3:3,5. In these three independent texts there is an aphorism with similar construction: (a) solemn opening, "Truly, I say to you," with the usual doubling of the "Truly" in John; (b) protasis formulated negatively; (c) apodosis, also formulated negatively; and (d) the same verb, "enter," in Mark 10:15; Matt. 18:3; and John 3:5.

(ii) Mark 10:13,14,16. Bultmann said that "vv. 13–16 are a complete apophthegm without v. 15" (32) and he located Mark 10:13, 14,16 among the biographical apophthegms (see also Spencer: 351–356). Tannehill locates 10:13–16 among those "hybrid pronouncement stories which combine . . . correction and commendation" (103). In my terminology Mark 10:13,14,16 is a *dialectical story*. The saying of Jesus is: "Let the children come to me, do not hinder them; for to such belongs the kingdom of God." This saying *could* make sense by itself, as its frequent citation within the Christian tradition has proved. But the emphatic and double opening with its positive ("let") and negative ("do not") imperative bespeaks at least an implicit dialectic with some previous position. It is not, therefore, an *aphoristic story* but rather a *dialectical story*.

It is possible, but not much more, to argue that there was a pre-Markan *aphoristic story* present in 10:13a + 14b and that Mark, by introducing the conflict between the disciples and Jesus in 13b + 14a, has himself turned this into a *dialectical story*. One might even point to the "Jesus saw" in Mark 10:14 (not accepted by either Matt. 19:14 or Luke 18:16) and the "Jesus saw" in *Gos. Thom.* 22a as evidence for such a pre-Markan *aphoristic story* in 10:13a + 14b.

I think, however, that a more radical solution is called for. It was Mark himself who created the entire *dialectical story* in 10:13,14,16 and imbedded the pre-Markan but redactionally rephrased 10:15 within it. This suggestion is supported by three considerations. (a) Structures. I have already drawn attention to how Mark built 10:13–16 in verbal parallel with the two incidents in Mark 9:36–37 and 9:38–39 (see Table 3.10). (b) Expressions. The Markan penchant for dualism and especially for a positive followed by a negative appears in 10:14 (Neirynck, 1972:84,92, see also 99,115,122). (c) Words. Pryke places all of 10:13 and 16 in "the redactional text of Mark" (165, see also 18,24,105,107,108,109, and, on *gar*, see 128, despite 126,133,134).

(3) Matt. 18:1–4.

At that time the disciples came to Jesus, saying, "Who is the greatest in the kingdom of heaven?" And calling to him a child, he put him in the midst of them, and said, "Truly, I say to you, unless you turn and become like children, you will never enter the kingdom of heaven. Whoever humbles himself like this child, he is the greatest in the kingdom of heaven."

This unit will also be discussed in terms of both context and content.

(a) Matt. 18:1–5. The parallels between Matt. 18:1–5 and Mark are as follows:

Matt. 18:1   =   Mark 9:33–34
Matt. 23:11 =   Mark 9:35
Matt. 18:2   =   Mark 9:36
Matt. 18:3   =   Mark 10:15
Matt. 18:4   —
Matt. 18:5   =   Mark 9:37a

This means that Matthew removed Mark 10:15 from its sequence in Mark 10:13–16 = Matt. 19:13–15 = Luke 18:15–17 and inserted it into his own smoother reformulation of Mark 9:33–37. He has thus united the two child aphorisms of Mark 9:36–37; 10:15, that is, he has noted but rewritten Table 3.10 above.

(b) Matt. 18:3. That preceding description raises the question whether Matt. 18:3 is just his version of Mark 10:15 or might be an independent version. On the one hand, Bultmann states emphatically that "Matt. 18:3 . . . is clearly not an independent tradition, but is the Matthean form of Mk. 10:15 in another context" (32). On the other, Lindars has argued persuasively that, "even on the assumption of Markan priority, the version of the saying in Mt. 18.3 must be regarded as equally likely to represent the original as the version in Mk. 10.15" (1980–1981:288). He cites four reasons for his conclusion: (i) the better balance of verb and adverbial clause in both protasis and apodosis of Matt. 18:3 over Mark 10:15; (ii) the verb "enter" of Matt. 18:3 is less redactionally and contextually derivative than the "receive" of Mark 10:15 (ex Mark 9:37); (iii) Matt. 18:3 uses the plural "like children" despite the fact that Mark 10:15 has a singular and that such a singular fits far better than a plural with the other singulars in Matt. 18:2,4,5; the plural is thus presumably pre-Matthean; (iv) Jeremias noted that "in the Septuagint we have a whole series of double expressions which paraphrase 'again' and are analogous in structure to the *straphēte kai genēsthe hos ta paidia*" (1971:155), that is, "turn and become" means "become again." This Semitism is a final and most important indication that Matt. 18:3 is independent of and even more original than the version in Mark 10:15.

Matt. 18:3 is thus another version of the *aphoristic saying* found in another context in Mark 10:15.

(c) Matt. 18:4. In the table of parallels between Mark 18:1–5 and Mark that was given above, there was no Markan parallel to Matt. 18:4. It is clear that 18:1 and 18:4 serve as frames for the materials in between, since they both conclude with "the greatest in the kingdom of heaven." But Matt. 18:4 does much more than close the complex in 18:1–4. In and by itself it almost reads like an independent aphorism. It is what I term an *aphoristic commentary*, that is, a unit that looks like an aphorism but which is appended to a preceding independent aphorism in order to comment on it. It deserves the title *aphoristic commentary* because it is formally modeled on the aphorism itself. This distinguishes it from the more obvious *commentary on an aphorism*. But it also makes it much more difficult to distinguish it from *aphoristic compounds* (two aphorisms together) or even *aphoristic clusters* (more than two aphorisms together).

By the appendage of Matt. 18:4 to 18:3 Matthew tells us how he interprets the *Kingdom and Children* saying: To become like a child is to become humble like a child.

(4) John 3:1–10.

Now there was a man of the Pharisees, named Nicodemus, a ruler of the Jews. This man came to Jesus by night and said to him, "Rabbi, we know that you are a teacher come from God; for no one can do these signs that you do, unless God is with him." Jesus answered him, "TRULY, TRULY, I SAY TO YOU, UNLESS ONE IS BORN ANEW, HE CANNOT SEE THE KINGDOM OF GOD." Nicodemus said to him, "How can a man be born when he is old? Can he enter a second time into his mother's womb and be born?" Jesus answered, "TRULY, TRULY, I SAY TO YOU, UNLESS ONE IS BORN OF WATER AND THE SPIRIT, HE CANNOT ENTER THE KINGDOM OF GOD. That which is born of the flesh is flesh, and that which is born of the Spirit is spirit. Do not marvel that I said to you, 'YOU MUST BE BORN ANEW.' The wind blows where it wills, and you hear the sound of it, but you do not know whence it comes or whither it goes; so it is with every one who is born of the Spirit." Nicodemus said to him,

"How can this be?" Jesus answered him, "Are you a teacher of Israel, and yet you do not understand this?"

My working hypothesis concerning Johannine and Synoptic relationships involves *both* (a) the presence of Synoptically independent traditions concerning Jesus' words and deeds in John, *and also* (b) the influence of the Synoptics on the final construction of the Johannine Gospel itself (see Smith, 1979–1980:443).

(a) John 3:3,5. The independence proposed for Matt. 18:3 is confirmed by a consideration of John 3:3,5 which, despite Johannine reformulation and baptismal adaptation, is another witness to the independent version underlying Matt. 18:3 (Dodd: 358–359; Brown: 1.143–144).

With regard to content, Lindars (1980–1981) has proposed that (i) John 3:5a ("of water and the Spirit") is his own reformulation of 3:3a ("anew"), and 3:3b ("see") is his own reformulation of 3:3b ("enter"): hence, "anew" (*anōthen*) and "enter" are prejohannine; that (ii) "John's *anōthen* can bear the meaning 'again,' and so represents a more idiomatic translation of the Aramaic phrase which appears in Matthew's version as *straphēte kai* ["turn and"]" (290); that (iii) John's term "born" (*gennethē*) is linguistically close to Matt. 18:3's "become" (*genēsthe*) although, of course, they are not the same root; and that (iv) in adapting his source and dropping any mention of children, "John intended the meaning 'from above' in verse 3, contrary to the required meaning [anew, again] of the underlying source" (292).

(b) John 3:1–10. What John has done with the aphorism is quite fascinating. (i) John 3:2b–10 is a dialogue between Nicodemus and Jesus in three exchanges: 2b/3, 4/5–8, and 9/10. (ii) It is structured so that Nicodemus gets one assertion (2b) and two questions (4,9), while Jesus gets two assertions (3, 5–8) and one question (10). And (iii) the unit is framed by the ironic contrast between the "teacher" in 3:3 and 3:10.

But the most interesting feature is the way that the *aphoristic saying* has been tripled to form the armature of the dialogue in 3:3,5,7. In this case *aphoristic saying* has been developed into *aphoristic dialogue* with three exchanges. But each time the aphorism is cited it is varied a little. In 3:3 the apodosis has the Johannine term "see" rather than the traditional "enter" (see Brown: 1.501–503). In 3:5 the protasis has the new expression, which is of paramount importance for 3:5–8, "of water and the Spirit." And in 3:7 there is only an abbreviated version of the protasis as in 3:3.

After the twin citations of the aphorism in 3:5 and 7 John adds, as had Matt. 18:4 after 18:3, what I term *aphoristic commentary*. Thus, in 3:6 and 8, appear sentences that read like aphorisms, sentences that could be imagined as independent sayings in their own right but which are given, however, in a format that copies that of the basic aphorism which they interpret.

Finally, one could say that the aphorism concerning *Kingdom and Children*, having become a triple dialogue in 3:2b–10, is located as an aphoristic story within the overall narrative of John's gospel by 3:1–2a.

This is a small but significant confirmation of the first working hypothesis proposed by Koester concerning the development of Johannine dialogues and monologues from traditional sayings of Jesus (1979:553). And what comes next, from *Gos. Thom.* 22, seems an equal confirmation of his second proposed working hypothesis. This postulates the necessity of establishing not only material, but especially formal trajectories for the transmission of canonically independent Jesus sayings from, for example, (i) Papyrus Egerton 2 (Bell and Skeat; see Mayeda); (ii) through such Nag Hammadi texts as the *Gospel of Thomas*, the *Dialogue of the Savior* (see Pagels and Koester), and the *Apocryphon of James*, on into (iii) the dialogues and monologues of John's gospel (Koester, 1979:553–554; also 1980a:119–126; 1980b:250–256).

(5) *Gos. Thom.* 22.

Jesus saw infants being suckled. He said to His disciples, "These infants being suckled are like those who enter the Kingdom." They said to Him,

"Shall we then, as children, enter the Kingdom." Jesus said to them, "When you make the two one, and when you make the inside like the outside, and the outside like the inside, and the above like the below, and when you make the male and the female one and the same, so that the male not be male nor the female female; and when you fashion eyes in place of an eye, and a hand in place of a hand, and a foot in place of a foot and a likeness in place of a likeness; then will you enter [the Kingdom]."

(a) *Gos. Thom.* 22b. Robinson has shown most persuasively how the original *Kingdom and Children* aphorism has moved along two hermeneutical trajectories. One is the "orthodox" baptismal interpretation represented by John 3:1–10 and developed in later patristic texts (1962a:106–107). The other is the "unorthodox" and gnostic interpretation represented here by *Gos. Thom.* 22b: "When one considers that repudiation of sex was a condition to admission to some Gnostic groups, somewhat as baptism was a condition of admission into the church at large, it is not too difficult to see how a logion whose original *Sitz im Leben* was baptism could be taken over and remolded in the analogous *Sitz im Leben* of admission to the sect" (1962a:108). Thus Jesus' reply in *Gos. Thom.* 22b involves a fourfold "when you make," each of which contains the obliteration of bodily differences, and each of which is known by itself or in various combinations from other gnostic sources (save the fourth). Thus "when you make the two one" reappears in *Gos. Thom.* 106, and combined as "when the two become one and the male with the female (is) neither male nor female" in the *Gospel of the Egyptians* (Hennecke and Schneemelcher: 1.168). These, and Robinson's more detailed examples (1962a:108,281–284), show that the setting and saying in *Gos. Thom.* 22a have been redactionally expanded in typically gnostic terms by the dialogue of 22b. "The result is a logion all but transformed beyond recognition, were it not that the hint provided by the basic structure is confirmed by the introduction, in which it becomes clear that the logion grew out of the saying about the children" (Robinson, 1962a:109).

The only factor not adequately explained in all this is the meaning of the fourth and final "when you make" concerning eye-hand-foot. "It is tempting to propose an emendation of the text" (Kee: 312) so that it would recommend eye to replace eyes, hand hands, and foot feet. But that, as Kee admits, is but a plausible guess, and Robinson can only note Mark 9:43,45,47 and add a question mark. But however one explains that final "when you make (fashion)," it is clear that "a collection of various traditions" (Robinson, 1962a:283 note 46) has been appended to the *Kingdom and Children* aphorism. This means that one cannot dismiss the possibility of independent tradition in *Gos. Thom.* 22a simply because of the gnostic interpretation(s) now attached to it in 22b (against Kee: 314). Any decision on 22a must be made apart from its present much longer dialogic conclusion in 22b.

(b) *Gos. Thom.* 22a. This will be considered in terms of both form and content.

(i) Form. Here is a classic example of an *aphoristic story*, that is, of an *aphoristic saying* developed into narrative. A setting or situation is given with "Jesus saw infants being suckled." But this situation is already verbally contained within the aphorism itself: "He said to His disciples, 'These infants being suckled are like those who enter the Kingdom.'" On the one hand, this adds little to the aphorism itself, but, on the other, it significantly chooses the narrative mode (situation) over the discourse mode (address) to develop the aphorism. Notice also that the incident begins with Jesus, with something *from Jesus* rather than something *to Jesus*. It begins when "Jesus saw." This recalls Bultmann's observation that, "It is characteristic of the primitive apophthegm that it makes the occasion of a dominical saying something that happens to Jesus (with the exception of the stories of the call of the disciples). It is a sign of a secondary formation if Jesus himself provides the initiative" (66).

(ii) Content. The aphoristic saying in Mark 10:15; Matt. 18:3; John 3:3,5 appears as a double negative ("unless . . . not"), but the *dialectical story* in Mark 10:14 and the *aphoristic story* in *Gos.*

Thom. 22a are positive. The shift from saying to story has involved the shift from negative to positive as well.

(c) *Gos. Thom*. 22. The whole unit of 22 involves three steps. First, the *aphoristic saying* is developed into an *aphoristic story* in 22a. Second, this is hermeneutically expanded by means of *aphoristic dialogue*. A single exchange is created between disciples and Jesus. Their question simply picks up the language of Jesus' original saying in 22a. Three, the reply of Jesus almost overpowers the original saying in length, but it is an *aphoristic commentary* in form. If one leaves aside 22a and the opening question of 22b, the rest of 22b could be taken as an originally independent saying. It is, however, an *aphoristic commentary*, that is, a unit that looks like an independent aphorism but is appended as interpretative commentary to a preceding aphorism.

(6) *Gos. Thom*. 46.

> Jesus said, "Among those born of women, from Adam until John the Baptist, there is no one superior to John the Baptist that his eyes should not be lowered (before him). Yet I have said, whichever one of you comes to be a child will be acquainted with the Kingdom and will become superior to John."

This is another version of the saying found in Q/Matt. 11:11 = Luke 7:28, where the "least" in the Kingdom is "greater" than John. Baker has drawn attention to other versions of this aphorism in "the homilies that pass under the name of Macarius" and which "continue to perplex scholars as to their true author, place of origin and sources" although "recent work has brought strong arguments for Asia Minor and perhaps Syria as the place and the last quarter of the fourth century as the time of composition" (215). Pseudo-Macarius' versions speak first of the "least one" (*mikroteros*) as being greater than John, then equate such with the "apostles," and conclude that such a "little one" (*mikros*) is greater than John (Migne: 713CD). That final text is the same as the one found in *Gos. Thom*. 46b, since the Coptic word *kwi* can be translated either as "a child" or "a little one." *Gos. Thom*. 46b therefore translates either "whichever one of you comes to be a child" (Lambdin; see also Guillaumont *et al.*) or "he who shall be among you as a little one" (Wilson, 1973:515). This change from "least one" to "little one" is significant, "for the New Testament wishes to say that all in the Kingdom are greater than John, therefore, even the least—*mikroteros*. Whereas the Gospel of Thomas and Macarius mean that only those who are small—*mikros*—are greater than John" (Baker: 218). Quispel (1964) has explained the relationship between *Thomas* and Macarius by proposing "that Macarius most probably knew the *Gospel of Thomas* and alluded to it in his writings" (227), and he concludes by asserting that he is "not in the least astonished that Macarius used the *Gospel of Thomas,* because so many Syrian writers before him had done the same" (234).

I consider, therefore, that there has been an infiltration from *Gos. Thom.* 22 into 46b, which (a) mitigates the denigration of John and (b) substitutes "shall know (be acquainted with) the Kingdom" for "shall enter the Kingdom." Gärtner has summarized the situation as follows: "The categorical statement in Matt. 11.11 has been reshaped so as to state the condition for admittance into the Kingdom, 'the one among you who becomes like a little one (a child) shall know the kingdom.' The resemblance to Logion 22a is striking. Indeed, behind the alteration we may discern a gnosticizing tendency which has as its object to emphasize the important term 'little,' referring to the Gnostic. This tendency is supported by another alteration, the phrase 'know the kingdom.' The New Testament uses such expressions as 'to enter the kingdom of God,' or 'to receive the kingdom of God,' but never 'to know the kingdom of God'" (224).

(7) Conclusion. In terms of the aphoristic model, this saying is something of a paradigmatic case.

(a) The *aphoristic saying* is still quite visible in Matt. 18:3 and Mark 10:15, but in that latter case it is appended to and in the former case integrated into an aphoristic story.

(b) The saying appears as an *aphoristic story* in *Gos. Thom.* 22a.

(c) But the Markan redaction in 10:13,14,16 turns this aphorism into a dialectical story. The unit is now directed pointedly and critically against the recalcitrant disciples. Mark 10:13,14,16 thus represents a classic interface between aphoristic and dialectial traditions.

(d) The saying is developed along the discourse rather than the narrative trajectory in *Gos. Thom.* 22b and John 3:1–10. In the former case a single interchange takes place between disciples and Jesus and in that process the original aphorism of 22a is completely reinterpreted into 22b. In that latter case an exquisitely subtle movement of three interchanges between Nicodemus and Jesus serves, once again, to rephrase and reinterpret the original aphorism from 3:3 through 3:5–8.

(e) Finally, there is a phenomenon noted on the aphoristic model as *aphoristic commentary*—that is, sayings that look and sound like independent aphorisms so that we could well be reading an aphoristic compound or even cluster. But they are actually creative commentaries whose contents bow in form to the units they interpret. This process is only noted here because its study belongs to future work. Aphoristic commentary and the wider trajectories of internal aphoristic expansion are so important that they demand much fuller analysis than is possible in this book.

Epilogue

What is missing of course is his voice. That was available only for a short time, and for those few to whom he gave so generously of his unique spirit. *His voice.* Those seated beside him at the same table . . .

The words go on; they flow through his silence. That silence which was his last considered choice. For wasn't it enough for them to know that he had been there; could they not have pooled their memories of his presence? But this was not to be. The hand of one of those closest to him sifted among his belongings; fingers tightened on sheets covered with black ink.

We have read those words — read and recited over and over again — and understood nothing. The experts still express astonishment that he could speak of the Garden as if he had been there in person. Some of them even revel in the opaque, counting the tiny prisms made with the points of their pens.

They can not grasp what goes deeper than their lives. Not a choice for darkness, but for the earliest light: before the forest awakens, before the intruder arrives.

LAWRENCE FIXEL, "The Master," in *The Scale of Silence* (Santa Cruz, CA: Kayak Books, 1970), p. 39

Appendix 1:
Corpus of Aphorisms
Presumed in This Book

APH.	MARK			Q	
	Matthew	Mark	Luke	Matthew	Luke
1	4:17b	1:15			
2	9:13b	2:17b	5:32		
3	9:16–17	2:21–22			
4	12:8	2:27–28	6:5		
5	12:29	3:27	11:21–22		
6	13:9 13:43b	4:9 4:23	8:8b		
7	13:57	6:4			
8		7:15			
9	16:6	8:15	12:1b		
10	16:21 17:9b 17:12b 17:22b–23 20:18–19 26:2 26:24 26:45b	8:31 9:9b 9:12b 9:31 10:33–34 14:21 14:41	9:22 9:44b 17:25 18:31–33 22:22 24:7		

MATTHEW	LUKE	JOHN	*THOMAS*	OTHER
	19:10			*Barn.* 5:9 1 Tim. 1:15
	5:36–38		47b(2–3)	
			35	
11:15	14:35b		8 21 24 63 65 96	Rev. 2:7 Rev. 2:11 Rev. 2:17 Rev. 2:29 Rev. 3:6 Rev. 3:13 Rev. 3:22 Rev. 13:9 *Soph. Jes. Chr.* CG III, 97:21–23; 　98:22–23; 　105:10–12; BG 8502,107:18–108:1
	4:24	4:44	31	
15:11			14c	(Acts 11:8)

APH.	MARK			Q	
	Matthew	Mark	Luke	Matthew	Luke
11	16:26a	8:36	9:25		
12	16:26b	8:37			
13	16:28	9:1	9:27		
14	23:11 20:25–28	9:35 10:42–45	9:48c		
15	10:42	9:41			
16	18:6	9:42	17:2		
17	18:8–9 5:29–30	9:43–48			
18		9:49			
19		10:15	18:17		
20	19:24	10:25	18:25		
21	19:29	10:29–30	18:29b–30		
22	21:21a	11:22			
23	21:21b 17:20b	11:23			
24	22:41–45	12:35–37a	20:41–44		
25	24:2	13:2	21:6 (19:44b)		
26	26:61 27:40	14:58 15:29			
27				5:3	6:20b
28				5:6	6:21a
29				5:4	6:21b
30				5:10 5:11–12	6:22–23
31					6:24
32					6:25a
33					6:25b
34					6:26
35				5:43–44	6:27–28

MATTHEW	LUKE	JOHN	THOMAS	OTHER
	22:25–27	(13:4–17)		
				1 Clem. 46:8b
18:3		3:3	22a	
		3:5		
18:19			48	*Didasc.* XV
			106	1 Cor. 13:2
				Ign. *Eph.* 5:2
				Barn. 12:10–11
		2:19	71	Acts 6:14
			54	
			69b	
			68	
			69a	

APH.	MARK			Q	
	Matthew	Mark	Luke	Matthew	Luke
36				5:39b–41	6:29
37				5:42	6:30
38				7:12a	6:31
39				5:45–47	6:32–35
40				5:48	6:36
41		4:24		7:1–2	6:37–38
42				15:14	6:39
43				10:24–25a	6:40
44				7:3–5	6:41–42
45				7:17–18 12:33a	6:43
46				7:16a = 20 12:33b	6:44a
47				7:16b	6:44b
48				12:34b, 35	6:45a
49				12:34c	6:45b
50				7:21	6:46
51				11:7–11	7:24–28
52				11:12–13	16:16
53				8:19–20	9:57–58
54					9:61–62
55				9:37–38	10:2
56				10:16a	10:3
57	10:9–10	6:8–9	9:3		10:4
58	10:10b–13	6:10	9:4	10:10b–13	10:5–7
59	10:7–8, 14	6:11	9:5	10:7–8, 14	10:8–11
60				11:21–24	10:13–15
61	18:5	9:37	9:48ab	10:40	10:16

MATTHEW	LUKE	JOHN	*THOMAS*	OTHER
			95	
			6b	*Did*. 1:2b
				1 *Clem*. 13:2
		13:16 15:20		
			26	
			43b	
				Ign. *Eph*. 14:2
			45a	
			45bc	
			45d	
				P. Egerton 2
			78 46	
			86	
		4:35	73	
				1 Tim. 5:18
			14b	1 Cor. 10:27
		5:23 12:44–45 13:20		Ign. *Eph*. 6:1

APH.	MARK			Q	
	Matthew	Mark	Luke	Matthew	Luke
62				11:27	10:22
63				13:16–17	10:23–24
64				11:28–30	
65	6:14–15	11:25		6:12	11:4a
66				7:6	
67	21:22	11:24		7:7–8	11:9–10
68				7:9–11	11:11–13
69				12:27	11:19
70				12:28	11:20
71		9:40	9:50b	12:30	11:23
72				12:41–42	11:31–32
73				12:43–45	11:24–26
74		4:21	8:16	5:15	11:33
75				6:22–23	11:34–36
76				23:4	11:46
77	23:6–7a	12:38b–40	20:46–47		11:43
78				23:13	11:52
79				23:23	11:42
80				23:25–26	11:39–41
81				23:27–28	11:44
82				23:29–32	11:47–48
83				23:34–36	11:49–51
84		4:22	8:17	10:26	12:2
85				10:27	12:3

MATTHEW	LUKE	JOHN	THOMAS	OTHER
			90	*Dial. Sav.* 141:3–6 *Pist. Soph.* 95
5:23–24				*Did.* 14:2 *Did.* 8:2
			93	*Did.* 9:5
		14:13–14 15:7 15:16 16:23–24 16:26	2 92 94	
				Oxy P 1224
			33b	
				Dial. Sav. 125:18–126:1
			39a 102	
			89	
				2 Esdr. 1:32
			5b 6b	
			33a	

APH.	MARK			Q	
	Matthew	Mark	Luke	Matthew	Luke
86				10:28	12:4–5
87				10:29	12:6
88				10:30	12:7a
89	16:27	8:38	9:26	10:32–33	12:8–9
90	12:31	3:28–29		12:32	12:10
91	10:19–20	13:11			12:11–12
92				10:23	
93				6:25–26, 28b–30	12:22–24, 27–38 (32)
94				6:27	12:25
95				6:31–33	12:29–31
96					12:32
97				6:19–20	12:33b
98				6:21	12:34
99				24:43	12:39
100	24:42	13:32 13:33 13:35		24:44 24:50	12:40 12:46
101					12:48b
102					12:49–50
103				10:34–36	12:51–53
104				16:1–3	12:54–56
105				5:25–26	12:57–59
106				7:13–14	13:23–24
107				25:10–12	13:25
108				7:22–23	13:26–27
109				8:11b–12	13:28
110				8:11a	13:29

MATTHEW	LUKE	JOHN	*THOMAS*	OTHER
				Rev. 3:5 2 Tim. 2:12b
			44	
			36 Oxy P 655	
			Oxy P 655	
			76b	
			21c 103	1 Thess. 5:2 2 Pet. 3:10 Rev. 3:2–3 Rev. 16:15
25:13				Rev. 3:2–3 *Did*. 16:1
			10	
			16	
			91	
				2 Esdr. 1:30b, 39–40
				2 Esdr. 1:38

APH.	MARK			Q	
	Matthew	Mark	Luke	Matthew	Luke
111	19:30	10:31		20:16	13:30
112				23:37–39	13:34–35
113				10:37	14:26
114	16:24	8:34b	9:23	10:38	14:27
115		9:50a		5:13	14:34–35a
116				6:24	16:13
117				5:18	16:17
118	19:9	10:11–12		5:32	16:18
119	26:24	14:21	22:22	18:7	17:1
120				18:15	17:3
121				18:21–22	17:4
122				17:20b	17:5–6
123					17:22
124	24:23	13:21		24:26	17:23
125				24:27	17:24
126				24:37–39a	17:26–27
127				24:39b	17:28–30
128	24:17–18	13:15–16	17:31		
129	16:25	8:35	9:24	10:39	17:33
130				24:40–41	17:34–35
131				24:28	17:37
132	13:12	4:25	8:18b	25:29	19:26
133				19:28	22:28–30

MATTHEW	LUKE	JOHN	*THOMAS*	OTHER
			4b	
				2 Esdr. 1:30a, 32, 33
			55a 101a	
			55b 101a	
			47a	
				1 Cor. 7:10–11
				1 *Clem.* 46:8a
	17:20–21		3a (22b) (46b) 51 113	2 *Clem.* 13:2 *Gos. Eg.* (f)
		12:25		
			61a	
			41	

Appendix 2: Sequence of Q Presumed in This Book

Part 1: Jesus and John

Aphorism	Content	Matthew	Luke
	Coming of John	3:1,5b	3:2b,3a
	Citation of Isa. 40:3	3:3	3:4
	John's Sermon	3:7 – 12	3:7 – 9,16 – 17
	[Jesus' Baptism?]	[3:13 – 16]	[3:21 – 22a]
	Jesus' Temptations	4:1 – 4,5 – 7,8 – 11	4:1 – 4,9 – 13,5 – 8
27	Blessed the Poor	5:3	6:20b
28	Blessed the Hungry	5:6	6:21a
29	Blessed the Sad	5:4	6:21b
30	Blessed the Persecuted	5:10,11 – 12	6:22 – 23
31	Woes Against Riches		6:24
32	Woe Against Satiety		6:25a
33	Woe Against Laughter		6:25b
34	Woe Against Praise		6:26
35	Love Your Enemies	5:43 – 44	6:27 – 28
36	The Other Cheek	5:39b – 41	6:29
37	Give Your Goods	5:42	6:30
38	The Golden Rule	7:12a	6:31
39	Better Than Sinners	7:46 – 47	6:32 – 35
40	As Your Father	5:48	6:36
41	Measure and Measured	7:1 – 2	6:37 – 38
42	The Blind Guide	15:14	6:39
43	Disciple and Servant	10:24 – 25a	6:40
44	Speck and Log	7:3 – 5	6:41 – 42
45	Tree and Fruit	7:17 – 18;12:33a	6:43
46	By Its Fruit	7:16a 20;12:33b	6:44a
47	Grapes and Thorns	7:16b	6:44b
48	From One's Treasure	12:34b,35	6:45a

Part 1: Jesus and John (cont.)

Aphorism	Content	Matthew	Luke
49	Heart and Mouth	12:34c	6:45b
50	Hear or Obey	7:21	6:46
	Two Builders	7:24 – 27	6:47 – 49
	The Centurion's Servant	8:5 – 13	7:1 – 2[3 – 6a]6b – 10
	The Baptist's Question	11:2 – 6	7:18 – 19 [20] 21 – 23
51	Jesus on John	11:7 – 9,11a	7:24 – 26,28a
	Wisdom's Children	11:16 – 19	7:31 – 35

Part 2: Jesus and Disciples

Aphorism	Content	Matthew	Luke
53	Foxes Have Holes	8:19 – 20	9:57 – 58
	Let the Dead	8:21 – 22	9:59 – 60a
54	On Looking Back		9:61 – 62
55	Harvest is Great	9:37 – 38	10:2
56	Lambs Among Wolves	10:16a	10:3
57	On the Road	10:9 – 10a	10:4
58	In the House	10:10b,12 – 13	10:5 – 7
59	At the Town	10:7 – 8,14	10:8 – 11
60	Cities of Woe	10:15;11:20 – 24	10:12 – 15
61	Receiving the Sender	10:40	10:16
	Revelation to Babes	11:25 – 26	10:21
62	Father and Son	11:27	10:22
63	Blessed the Eyes	13:16 – 17	10:23 – 24
64	Yoke and Burden	11:28 – 30	
	The Lord's Prayer	6:9 – 13	11:2 – 4
66	Pearls Before Swine	7:6	
67	Ask, Seek, Knock	7:7 – 8	11:9 – 10
68	Good Gifts	7:9 – 11	11:11 – 13

Part 3: Jesus and Opponents

Aphorism	Content	Matthew	Luke
	Beelzebul Controversy	12:22 – 26	11:14 – 18
69	Your Sons	12:27	11:19
70	By the Spirit	12:28	11:20

Part 3: Jesus and Opponents (cont.)

Aphorism Content	Matthew	Luke
71	For and Against	12:30	11:23
	Request for Sign	16:4;12:38 – 40	11:16,29 – 30
72	Solomon and Jonah	12:41 – 42	11:31-32
73	The Returning Demon	12:43 – 45	11:24 – 26
	Blessed the Hearers		11:27 – 28
74	Lamp and Bushel	5:15	11:33(8:16)
75	Eye as Lamp	6:22 – 23	11:34 – 36
76	Helping with Burdens	23:4	11:46
77	Honors and Salutations	23:6 – 7	11:43
78	On Hindering Others	23:13	11:52
79	Tithing and Justice	23:23	11:42
80	Inside and Outside	23:25 – 26	11:39 – 41
81	Like Graves	23:27 – 28	11:44
82	The Prophets' Tombs	23:29 – 32	11:47 – 48
83	Wisdom's Envoys	23:34 – 36	11:49-51

Part 4: Jesus and Apocalypse

Aphorism Content	Matthew	Luke
84	Hidden Made Manifest	10:26	12:2
85	Open Proclamation	10:27	12:3
86	Whom to Fear	10:28	12:4 – 5
87	God and Sparrows	10:29	12:6
88	Numbered Hairs	10:30	12:7a
89	Before the Angels	10:32 – 33	12:8 – 9
90	All Sins Forgiven	12:32	12:10
91	Spirit Under Trial	(10:19 – 20)	12:11 – 12
92	Cities of Israel	10:23	
93	Food and Clothing	6:25 – 30	12:22 – 28
94	Added Span	6:27	12:25
95	Seek the Kingdom	6:31 – 33	12:29 – 31
96	Little Flock		12:32
97	Treasure in Heaven	6:19 – 20	12:33b
98	Heart and Treasure	6:21	12:34
	The Waiting Servants		12:35 – 38
99	Knowing the Danger	24:43	12:39
100	The Unknown Time	24:44	12:40
	Steward and Servants	24:45 – 51	12:41 – 46
	Servants and Beatings		12:47 – 48a

Part 4: Jesus and Apocalypse (cont.)

Aphorism	Content	Matthew	Luke
101	Much and More		12:48b
102	Fire on Earth		12:49 – 50
103	Peace or Sword	10:34 – 36	12:51 – 53
104	Knowing the Times	[16:2 – 3]	12:54 – 56
105	Before the Judgment	5:25 – 26	12:57 – 59
	The Mustard Seed	13:31 – 32	13:18 – 19
	The Leaven	13:33	13:20 – 21
106	The Narrow Door	7:13 – 14	13:23 – 24
107	The Closed Door	25:10 – 12	13:25
108	Depart From Me	7:22 – 23	13:26 – 27
109	Patriarchs and Kingdom	8:11b – 12	13:28
110	Gentiles and Kingdom	8:11a	13:29
111	First and Last	20:16	13:30
112	Jerusalem Indicted	23:37 – 39	13:34 – 35
	The Great Supper	22:2 – 10	14:16 – 24
113	Hating One's Family	10:37	14:26
114	Carrying One's Cross	10:38	14:27
115	Salting the Salt	5:13	14:34 – 35a
	The Lost Sheep	18:12 – 14	15:4 – 7
	The Lost Coin		15:8 – 10
116	Serving Two Masters	6:24	16:13
52	Kingdom and Violence	11:12 – 13	16:16
117	One Dot	5:18	16:17
118	Against Divorce	5:32	16:18
119	Woe for Scandal	18:7	17:1
120	Reproving and Forgiving	18:15	17:3
121	Unlimited Forgiveness	18:21 – 22	17:4
122	Faith's Power	17:20	17:5 – 6
123	Days Are Coming		17:22
124	When and Where	24:26	17:23
125	As with Lightning	24:27	17:24
126	As with Noah	24:37 – 39a	17:26 – 27
127	As with Lot	24:39b	17:28 – 30
129	Saving One's Life	10:39	17:33
130	Taken or Left	24:40 – 41	17:34 – 35
131	Corpse and Vultures	24:28	17:37
	Citizens and Servants		19:11 – 27
132	Have and Receive	25:29	19:26
133	On Twelve Thrones	19:28	22:28 – 30

Bibliography

Achelis, H., and J. Flemming
    1904   *Die Syrische Didaskalia.* TU(NF) 10.2. Leipzig: Hinrichs.

Adams, Francis
    1939   *The Genuine Works of Hippocrates.* Baltimore, MD: Williams & Wilkins.

Anonymous
    1912   *Papiri Greci e Latini.* Vol I: Nos. 1–112. Pubblicazioni della Società Italiana per la ricerca dei Papiri greci e latini in Egitto. Florence: Ariani. (No. 85 [pp. 157–158] edited by Teresa Lodi.)

Asemissen, H. U.
    1949   "Notizen über den Aphorismus." Pp. 159–176 in *Der Aphorismus* (Neumann, 1976b) = *Trivium* 7:144–161.

Attridge, Harold W.
    1979   "The Original Text of Gos. Thom., Saying 30." *BASP* 16: 153–157.

Auden, W. H., and L. Kronenberger, eds.
    1981   *The Viking Book of Aphorisms.* 1962. Reprint. New York: Viking.

Aune, David E.
    1978   "Septem Sapientium Convivium (Moralia 146B–164D)." Pp. 51–105 in *Plutarch's Ethical Writings and Early Christian Literature.* Edited by H. D. Betz. Studia ad Corpus Hellenisticum Novi Testamenti 4. Leiden: Brill.

Babbitt, Frank C., *et al.*
    1927–   *Plutarch's Moralia.* LCL. 16 vols. Cambridge, MA: Harvard University Press.

Bacon, Francis
    1857–1874   *The Works of Francis Bacon.* Edited by J. Spedding, R. L.

---

*In general, the abbreviations for texts and documents, journals, and serials used in this book are those suggested by the *Journal of Biblical Literature* 95 (1976):331–346 and the *Catholic Biblical Quarterly* 38 (1976):437–454.

Ellis, and D. D. Heath. 14 vols. London: Longman. (Facsimile reproduction, Stuttgart/Bad Cannstatt: Friedrich Frommann Verlag Günther Holzboog, 1963.)

Baker, A.
1964   "Pseudo-Macarius and the Gospel of Thomas." VC 18:215 –225.

Baldwin, Charles S.
1928   Medieval Rhetoric and Poetic. New York: Macmillan.

Bammel, E.
1958   "Is Luke 16,16–18 of Baptist's Provenience?" HTR 51:101–106.
1969   "Rest and Rule." VC 23:88–90.

Barrett, C. K.
1959   "The Background of Mark 10:45." Pp. 1–18 in New Testament Essays: Studies in Memory of Thomas Walter Manson 1893–1958. Edited by A. J. B. Higgins. Manchester: Manchester University Press.
1972   "Mark 10.45: A Ransom for Many." Pp. 20–26 in his own New Testament Essays. London: SPCK.

Bartsch, H. W.
1959–1960   "Das Thomas-Evangelium und die synoptischen Evangelien. Zu G. Quispels Bemerkungen zum Thomas-Evangelium." NTS 6:249–261.

Bauer, J. B.
1961   "Das milde Joch und die Ruhe, Matth. 11,28–30." TZ 17:99–106.

Beare, F. W.
1960   "The Sabbath Was Made for Man?" JBL 79:130–136.

Bell, J. Idriss, and T. C. Skeat
1935a   Fragments of an Unknown Gospel and Other Early Christian Papyri. London: Oxford University Press.
1935b   The New Gospel Fragments. London: Oxford University Press.

Berger, K.
1970–1971   "Zu den sogenannten Sätzen heiligen Rechts." NTS 17:10 –40.
1972   "Die sog. 'Sätze heiligen Rechts' im N.T. Ihre Funktion und Ihr Sitz im Leben." TZ 28:305–330.

Berkey, R. F.
1963   "EGGIZEIN, PHTHANEIN, and Realized Eschatology." JBL 82: 117–187.

Best, E.
1970   "Discipleship in Mark: Mark 8.22–10.52." *SJT* 23:323–337.
1974   "Mark's Preservation of the Tradition." Pp. 21–34 in *L'É-vangile selon Marc* (Sabbe, 1974.)
1976   "An Early Sayings Collection." *NovT* 18:1–16.
Betz, H. D.
1967   "The Logion of the Easy Yoke and of Rest (Matt 11:28–30)." *JBL* 86:10–24.
Birdsall, J. N.
1962   "Luke XII.16ff. and the Gospel of Thomas." *JTS* 13:332–36.
Black, M.
1978   "Jesus and the Son of Man." *JSNT* 1:4–18.
Borgen, P.
1979–1980   "The Use of Tradition in John 12.44–50." *NTS* 26:18–35.
Boring, M. E.
1976   "The unforgivable Sin Logion Mark III 28–29/Matt XII 31–32/Luke XII 10: Formal Analysis and History of the Tradition." *NovT* 18:258–279.
1982   *Sayings of the Risen Jesus: Christian Prophecy in the Synoptic Tradition.* SNTSMS 46. New York: Cambridge University Press.
Bornkamm, G.
1970   "The Authority to 'Bind' and 'Loose' in the Church in Matthew's Gospel: The Problem of Sources in Matthew's Gospel." *Perspective* 11:37–50.
Bradley, F. H.
1930   *Aphorisms.* Oxford: Clarendon.
Brown, N. O.
1966   *Love's Body.* New York: Vintage.
Brown, Raymond E.
1962–1963   "The Gospel of Thomas and St. John's Gospel." *NTS* 9:155–177.
1966–1970   *The Gospel according to John I–XII and XIII–XXI.* AB 29–29A. 2 vols. Garden City, NY: Doubleday.
1979   *The Community of the Beloved Disciple.* New York: Paulist.
Bultmann, R.
1963   *The History of the Synoptic Tradition.* Translated by John Marsh. New York: Harper & Row.

Burney, Charles Fox
1925   *The Poetry of Our Lord.* Oxford: Clarendon.
Butler, B. C.
1960   "The Literary Relations of Didache, Ch. XVI." *JTS* 11:
            265–283.
Butler, Harold Edgeworth (tr.)
1920–1922   *The Institutio Oratoria of Quintilian.* LCL. 4 vols. Cam-
            bridge, MA: Harvard University Press.
Carlston, C. E.
1980   "Proverbs, Maxims, and the Historical Jesus." *JBL* 99:87–
            105.
Catchpole, D. R.
1974   "The Synoptic Divorce Material As a Traditio-Historical
            Problem." *BJRL* 57:92–127.
Cerfaux, L.
1954–1955   "Les Sources Scripturaires de Mt., XI, 25–30." *ETL* 30:
            740–746, 31:331–342.
Charles, R. H.
1913   *The Apocrypha and Pseudepigrapha of the Old Testament.*
            2 vols. Oxford: Clarendon.
Clark, D. J.
1975   "Criteria for Identifying Chiasm." *LingBib* 35:63–72.
Collins, John J.
1979   "The Jewish Apocalypses." *Semeia* 14:21–59.
1980   "Proverbial Wisdom and the Yahwist Vision." *Semeia* 17:
            1–17.
Colpe, Carsten
1972   *"ho huios tou anthrōpou."* Pp. 400–477 in *Theological Dic-
            tionary of the New Testament.* Edited by Gerhard Frie-
            drich. Translated by Geoffrey W. Bromiley. Vol. 8. Grand
            Rapids, MI: Eerdmans.
Colson, F. H.
1921   "Quintilian 1.9 and the 'Chria' in Ancient Education."
            The Classical Review 35:150–154.
Connolly, R. Hugh
1929   *Didascalia Apostolorum.* The Syriac Version translated
            and accompanied by the Verona Latin Fragments. Oxford:
            Clarendon.
Cox, James John Charles
1973   *Studies in the Determination and Evaluation of the
            Dominical Logoi as Cited in the Original Text of the Greek*

'*Didascalia Apostolorum.*' Harvard University, Ph.D. dissertation (microfilm).

Crossan, John Dominic
1968   "Divorce and Remarriage in the New Testament." Pp. 1–40 in *The Bond of Marriage.* Edited by W. W. Bassett. Notre Dame, IN: University of Notre Dame Press.
1973a   *In Parables.* New York: Harper & Row.
1973b   "Mark and the Relatives of Jesus." *NovT* 15:81–113.

Crum, W. E.
1939   A *Coptic Dictionary.* Oxford: Clarendon.

Danby, H.
1967   *The Mishnah.* London: Oxford University Press.

Dehandschutter, B.
1973   "L'Évangile selon Thomas: témoin d'une tradition prélucanienne?" Pp. 287–297 in *L'Évangile de Luc* [Neirynck, 1973].

de la Potterie, I. (ed.)
1967   *De Jésus aux Évangiles. Tradition et Rédaction dans les Évangiles synoptiques.* BETL 25. Gembloux: Duculot & Paris: Lethielleux.

Dewey, Joanna
1973   "The Literary Structure of the Controversy Stories in Mark 2:1–3:6." *JBL* 92:394–401.
1980   *Markan Public Debate: Literary Technique, Concentric Structure, and Theology in Mark 2:1–3:6.* SBLDS 48. Chico, CA: Scholars Press.

Dihle, A.
1962   *Die goldene Regel. Eine Einführung in die Geschichte der antiken und frühchristlichen Vulgärethik.* Studienhefte zur Altertumswissenschaft 7. Göttingen: Vandenhoeck & Ruprecht.

Dodd, Charles Harold
1955   "The Beatitudes: A Form-Critical Study." Pp. 404–410 in *Mélanges bibliques rédigés en l'honneur de André Robert.* Travaux de l'institut catholique de Paris 4. Paris: Bloud & Gay. (= Pp. 1–10 in Dodd, *More New Testament Studies.* Grand Rapids, MI: Eerdmans, 1968.)
1963   *Historical Tradition in the Fourth Gospel.* London: Cambridge University Press.

Donahue, John R.
1973   *Are You the Christ? The Trial Narrative in the Gospel of Mark.* SBLDS 10. Cambridge, MA: SBL.

Dupont, Jacques
1958   *Les Béatitudes. La problème littéraire. Les deux versions du Sermon sur la montagne et des Béatitudes.* Nouvelle édition entièrement refondue. Bruges: Abbaye de Saint André & Louvain: Nauwelaerts.

1964   "Le logion des douze trônes (Mt 19,28; Lc 22,28–30)." *Bib* 45:355–392.

1969   *Les Béatitudes, Tome II: La bonne nouvelle.* EBib. Rev. Ed. Paris: Gabalda.

1971   "Il n'en serra pas laissé pierre sur pierre (Marc 13,2; Luc 19,44)." *Bib* 52:301–320.

1973   *Les Béatitudes, Tome III: Les Évangélistes.* EBib. Rev. Ed. Paris: Gabalda.

1975   (ed.) *Jésus aux origines de la christologie.* BETL 40. Gembloux: Duculot & Louvain: Leuven University Press.

Edwards, Richard A.
1971   *The Sign of Jonah in the Theology of the Evangelists and Q.* SBT 2/18. Naperville, IL: Allenson.

Eichner, Hans
1970   *Friedrich Schlegel.* Twayne's World Authors Series. New York: Twayne.

Fadiman, Clifton
1967   "Lec and the Art of the Aphorism." Pp. 5–23 in Stanislaw J. Lec, *Unkempt Thoughts.* Translated by Jacek Galazka. New York: Minerva.

Firchow, Peter (tr.)
1971   *Friedrich Schlegel's* Lucinde *and the Fragments.* Minneapolis, MN: University of Minnesota Press.

Fitzmyer, Joseph A.
1968   Review of M. Black, *An Aramaic Approach to the Gospels and Acts* (3rd ed. Oxford: Clarendon, 1967) in *CBQ* 30: 417–428.

1973–1974   "The Contribution of Qumran Aramaic to the Study of the New Testament." *NTS* 20:382–407 = Pp. 85–113 in Fitzmyer, *A Wandering Aramean* (1979b).

1974   "The Oxyrhynchus Logoi of Jesus and the Coptic Gospel according to Thomas." Pp. 355–433 in Fitzmyer, *Essays on the Semitic Background of the New Testament.* London: Chapman, 1971 = SBLSBS 5. Missoula, MT: Scholars Press, 1974 (updated revision of *TS* 20 (1959) 505–560).

1975   "Methodology in the Study of the Aramaic Substratum of Jesus' Sayings in the New Testament." Pp. 73–102 in *Jésus*

(Dupont, 1975) = (slightly revised) Pp. 1–27 in Fitzmyer, *A Wandering Aramean* (1979b).

1976   "The Matthean Divorce Texts and Some New Palestinian Evidence." *TS* 37:197–226.

1979a   "Another View of the 'Son of Man' Debate." *JSNT* 4:58–68.

1979b   "The New Testament Title 'Son of Man' Philologically Considered." Pp. 143–160 in Fitzmyer, *A Wandering Aramean: Collected Aramaic Essays*. SBLMS 25. Missoula, MT: Scholars Press.

1980   "The Aramaic Language and the Study of the New Testament." *JBL* 99:5–21.

1981   *The Gospel according to Luke I–IX*. AB 28. Garden City, NY: Doubleday.

Fixel, Lawrence

1970   *The Scale of Silence*. Santa Cruz, CA: Kayak.

Fleddermann, H.

1981   "The Discipleship Discourse (Mark 9:33–50)." *CBQ* 43:57–75.

Fletcher, D. R.

1964   "Condemned to Die. The Logion on Cross-Bearing: What Does It Mean?" *Int* 18:156–164.

Flückiger, F.

1970   "Die Redaktion der Zukunftsrede in Mark. 13." *TZ* 26:395–409.

Forster, L.

1968   "Friedrich Schlegel's Literary Manifesto." *Acta Germanica* 3:99–109.

Frankemölle, H.

1971   "Die Makarismen (Mt 5,1–12; Lk 6,20–23). Motive und Umfang der redaktionellen Komposition." *BZ* 15:52–75.

Freese, John Henry (tr.)

1926   *Aristotle: The Art of Rhetoric*. LCL. Cambridge, MA: Harvard University Press.

Funk, Francis Xavier

1905   *Didascalia et Constitutiones Apostolorum*. 2 vols. Paderborn: Schoeningh.

Garitte, G.

1957   "Le premier volume de l'édition photographique des manuscrits gnostiques coptes et l' 'Évangile de Thomas.' " *Muséon* 70:59–73.

1960a   "Les 'Logoi' d'Oxyrhynque et l'apocryphe copte dit 'Évang-
             ile de Thomas.' " *Muséon* 73:151–172.
1960b   "Les 'Logoi' d'Oxyrhynque sont traduits du copte." *Musé-
             on* 73:335–349.

Gärtner, B.
1961   *The Theology of the Gospel According to Thomas*. Trans-
             lated by E. J. Sharpe. New York: Harper.

George, A.
1966   "Note sur quelques traits lucaniens de l'expression 'Par le
             doigt de Dieu' (Luc XI,20)." *SciEccl* 18:461–466.
1967   "Tradition et rédaction chez Luc. La construction du
             troisième Évangile." Pp. 100–129 in *De Jésus aux Évang-
             iles* [de la Potterie].

Georgi, Dieter
1972   "The Records of Jesus in the Light of Ancient Accounts of
             Revered Men." Pp. 527–542 in *SBL 1972 Proceedings*. 2
             vols. (continual pagination). Edited by Lane McGaughy.

Gils, F.
1962   " 'Le sabbat a été fait pour l'homme et non l'homme pour
             le sabbat' (Mc, II,27). Réflexions à propos de Mc, II,27–28."
             RB 69:506–523.

Glover, R.
1958–1959   "The *Didache's* Quotations and the Synoptic Gospels."
             NTS 5:12–29.

Goodspeed, E. J., and R. M. Grant
1966   *A History of Early Christian Literature*. Revised and en-
             larged edition. Chicago: University of Chicago Press.

Grant, R. M., and D. N. Freedman
1960   *The Secret Sayings of Jesus*. Garden City, NY: Doubleday.

Grenfell, B. P., and A. S. Hunt
1897   *LOGIA IĒSOU: Sayings of Our Lord from an Early Greek
             Papyrus*. London: Frowde.
1898   *The Oxyrhynchus Papyri: Part I*. London: Oxford Univer-
             sity Press.
1904a   *The Oxyrhynchus Papyri: Part IV*. London: Oxford Uni-
             versity Press.
1904b   *New Sayings of Jesus and Fragment of a Lost Gospel from
             Oxyrhynchus*. London: Frowde.
1914   *The Oxyrhynchus Papyri: Part X*. London: Oxford Univer-
             sity Press.

Griffiths, J. G.
1969–1970   "The Disciple's Cross." *NTS* 16:358–364.

Grimm, W.
1973   "Der Dank für die empfangene Offenbarung bei Jesus und
             Josephus. Parallelen zu Mt 11,25–27." *BZ* 17:249–256.

Guelich, R. A.
1976   "The Matthean Beatitudes: 'Entrance-Requirements' or
             Eschatological Blessings?" *JBL* 95:415–434.

Guillaumont, A., *et al.*
1959   *The Gospel according to Thomas.* Leiden: Brill, New York:
             Harper & Row.
1960   "Les *Logia* d'Oxyrhynchos sont-ils traduits du copte?"
             Muséon 73:325–333.

Haenchen, E.
1963   "Die Komposition von Mk viii 27–ix 1 und Par." *NovT*
             6:81–109.

Hahn, F.
1971   "Die Bildworte vom neuen Flicken und vom jungen Wein
             (Mk. 2,21 f parr)." *EvT* 31:357–375.

Hamerton-Kelly, R. G.
1964–1965   "A Note on Matthew xii.28 par. Luke xi.20." *NTS* 11:167
             –169.

Harmon, A. M., *et al.*
1913–1967   *Lucian.* LCL. 8 vols. Cambridge, MA: Harvard University
             Press.

Harnack, Adolf
1908   *The Sayings of Jesus.* The Second Source of St. Matthew
             and St. Luke. Translated by J. R. Wilkinson. New York:
             Putnam's.

Hartmann, L.
1966   *Prophecy Interpreted. The Formation of Some Jewish
             Apocalyptic Texts and of the Eschatological Discourse Mark
             13 par.* Translated by N. Tomkinson and J. Gray.
             ConB:NT 1. Lund: Gleerup.

Hay, L. S.
1970   "The Son of Man in Mark 2:10 and 2:28." *JBL* 89:69–75.

Hennecke, Edgar, and Wilhelm Schneemelcher
1963–1965   *New Testament Apocrypha.* Edited by R. McL. Wilson. 2
             vols. Philadelphia: Westminster.

Hicks, R. D. (tr.)
1925   *Diogenes Laertius: Lives of Eminent Philosophers.* LCL. 2
             vols. Cambridge, MA: Harvard University Press.

Hill, D.
1973–1974   "On the Evidence for the Creative Rôle of Christian Prophets." *NTS* 20:262–274.

Hoffmann, P.
1967   *"Pantes ergatai adikias.* Redaktion und Tradition in Lc 13:22–30." *ZNW* 58:188–214.

Hofius, O.
1960   "Das koptische Thomasevangelium und die Oxyrhynchus-Papyri Nr. 1, 654 und 655." *EvT* 20:21–42,182–192.

Holman, C. Hugh
1972   A *Handbook to Literature.* 3rd ed. New York: Bobbs-Merrill.

Hommel, H.
1966   "Herrenworte im Lichte sokratischer Überlieferung." *ZNW* 57:1–23.

Horner, G. (Ed.)
1898–1905   *The Coptic Version of the New Testament in the Northern Dialect, otherwise called Memphitic and Bohairic.* 4 vols. Oxford: Clarendon.
1911–1924   *The Coptic Version of the New Testament in the Southern Dialect, otherwise called Sahidic and Thebaic.* 7 vols. Oxford: Clarendon.

Hultgren, Arland John
1971   *Jesus and His Adversaries: A Study of the Form and Function of the Conflict Stories in the Synoptic Tradition.* Union Theological Seminary, Th.D. dissertation. Ann Arbor, MI: University Microfilms International.
1972   "The Formation of the Sabbath Pericope in Mark 2:23–28." *JBL* 91:38–43.
1979   *Jesus and His Adversaries.* Minneapolis, MN: Augsburg.

Hunt, A. S.
1911   *The Oxyrhynchus Papyri: Part VIII.* London: Oxford University Press.

Hunter, A. M.
1961–1962   "Crux Criticum — Matt. xi.25–30 — A Re-appraisal." *NTS* 8:241–249.

Jacobson, Arland Dean
1978   *Wisdom Christology in Q.* Claremont Graduate School, Ph.D. dissertation. Ann Arbor, MI: University Microfilms International.
1982   "The Literary Unity of Q." *JBL* 101:365–389.

Jeremias, Joachim

1963   *The Parables of Jesus*. Rev. ed. New York: Scribner's.

1964   *Unknown Sayings of Jesus*. Translated by R. H. Fuller. 2nd ed. New York: Macmillan.

1967a   *The Prayers of Jesus*. SBT 2/6. Naperville, IL: Allenson.

1967b   "Die älteste Schicht der Menschensohn-Logien." ZNW 58: 159–172.

1971   *New Testament Theology*. New York: Scribner's.

Juel, D.

1977   *Messiah and Temple. The Trial of Jesus in the Gospel of Mark*. SBLDS 31. Missoula, MT: Scholars Press.

Käsemann, Ernst

1969   "Sentences of Holy Law in the New Testament." Pp. 66–81 in his *New Testament Questions of Today*. Philadelphia: Fortress. (= "Sätze heiligen Rechtes im Neuen Testament." *NTS* 1 [1954–1955] 248–260 = Pp. 69–82 in his *Exegetische Versuche und Besinnungen II*. Göttingen: Vandenhoeck and Ruprecht, 1960).

Kaufmann, W. (ed.)

1967   *On the Genealogy of Morals* and *Ecce Homo*. New York: Random House (Vintage).

Kee, A.

1969   "The Question About Fasting." *NovT* 11:161–173.

Kee, Howard C.

1963   " 'Becoming a Child' in the Gospel of Thomas." *JBL* 82: 307–314.

1978   *Jesus in History*. New York: Harcourt Brace Jovanovich.

Kelber, Werner H.

1974   *The Kingdom in Mark*. Philadelphia: Fortress.

1976   (ed.) *The Passion in Mark*. Philadelphia: Fortress.

1983   *The Oral and Written Gospel*. Philadelphia: Fortress.

Keynes, Geoffrey (ed.)

1966   *The Complete Writings of William Blake*. New York: Oxford University Press.

Kingsbury, Jack Dean

1975   *Matthew: Structure, Christology, Kingdom*. Philadelphia: Fortress.

Klijn, A. F. J.

1962   "The 'Single One' in the Gospel of Thomas." *JBL* 81:271–278.

Knibb, M. A., with E. Ullendorff

1978   *The Ethiopic Book of Enoch*. 2 vols. Oxford: Clarendon.

Koester, Helmut
1957a   *Synoptische Überlieferung bei den Apostolischen Vätern.*
         TU 65. Berlin: Akademie.
1957b   "Die ausserkanonischen Herrenworte als Produkte der
         christlichen Gemeinde." ZNW 48:220–237.
1978   "Mark 9:43–47 and Quintilian 8.3.75." HTR 71:151–153.
1979   "Dialog und Spruchüberlieferung in den gnostischen Text-
         en von Nag Hammadi." EvT 39:532–556.
1980a   "Apocryphal and Canonical Gospels." HTR 73:105–130.
1980b   "Gnostic Writings as Witnesses for the Development of the
         Sayings Tradition." Pp. 238–256 (with discussion on pp.
         256–261) in *The Rediscovery of Gnosticism. Vol I: The
         School of Valentinus.* Studies in the History of Religions:
         Supplements to *Numen* 41/1. Leiden: Brill.

Kraft, R. A.
1961   "Oxyrhynchus Papyrus 655 Reconsidered." HTR 54:253–
         262.

Kugel, James L.
1981   *The Idea of Biblical Poetry: Parallelism and Its History.*
         New Haven, CT: Yale University Press.

Kuhn, H.-W.
1971   *Ältere Sammlungen im Markusevangelium.* SUNT 8. Göt-
         tingen: Vandenhoeck & Ruprecht.

Kuhn, K. H.
1960   "Some Observations on the Coptic Gospel according to
         Thomas." Muséon 73:317–323.

Lafontaine, R., and P. Mourlon Beernaert
1969   "Essai sur la structure de Marc, 8,27–9,13." RechSR 57:
         543–561.

Lake, Kirsopp (tr.)
1930   *The Apostolic Fathers.* LCL. 2 vols. Cambridge, MA:
         Harvard University Press.

Lambdin, Thomas O.
1977   "The Gospel of Thomas." Pp. 118–130 in *The Nag Ham-
         madi Library in English* (Robinson, 1977).

Lambrecht, J.
1965   "Redactio Sermonis Eschatologici." VD 43:278–287.
1966   "Die Logia-Quellen von Markus 13." Bib 47:321–360.
1967   *Die Redaktion der Markus-Apokalypse.* AnBib 28. Rome:
         Biblical Institute.

1974a   "Redaction and Theology in Mk., IV." Pp. 269–307 in *L'Évangile selon Marc* (Sabbe).

1974b   "The Relatives of Jesus in Mark." *NovT* 16:241–258.

1977   "Jesus and the Law. An Investigation of Mk 7,1–23." *ETL* 53:24–82.

Layton, Bentley

1968   "The Sources, Date and Transmission of *Didache* 1.3b–2.1." *HTR* 61:343–383.

Légasse, S.

1962   " 'L'homme fort' de Luc XI 21–22." *NovT* 5:5–9.

1963–1964   "Jésus a-t-il annoncé la Conversion Finale d'Israël? (A propos de Marc X.23–27)." *NTS* 10:480–487.

Levy, Oscar (ed.)

1964   *The Complete Works of Friedrich Nietzsche.* 1909–1911. 18 vols. New York: Russell & Russell.

Lewis, A. Smith

1910   *The Old Syriac Gospels or Evangelion Da-Mepharreshê.* London: Gilbert & Rivington/Clowes & Sons.

Lindars, Barnabas

1961   *New Testament Apologetic.* London: SCM.

1980–1981   "John and the Synoptic Gospels: A Test Case." *NTS* 27:287–294.

Lohse, E.

1960   "Jesu Worte über den Sabbat." Pp. 79–89 in *Judentum, Urchristentum, Kirche: Festschrift für Joachim Jeremias.* Edited by Walther Eltester. BZNW 26. Berlin: Töpelmann.

Lord, A. B.

1971   *The Singer of Tales.* New York: Atheneum.

Lührmann, Dieter

1969   *Die Redaktion der Logienquelle.* WMANT 33. Neukirchen-Vluyn: Neukirchener Verlag.

1972   "Liebet eure Feinde (Lk 6,27–36/Mt 5,39–48)." *ZTK* 69:412–438.

Magill, C. P.

1973   "Two Types of German Prose Miniature." Pp. 79–89 in *Deutung und Bedeutung: Studies in German and Comparative Literature presented to Karl-Werner Maurer.* Edited by B. Schludermann *et al.* The Hague: Mouton.

Maher, M.

1975–1976   " 'Take my yoke upon you' (Matt. xi.29)." *NTS* 22:97–103.

Maloney, Elliott Charles
1979   A *Study of Semitic Interference in Marcan Syntax*. Ford-
            ham University, Ph.D. dissertation. Ann Arbor, MI: Uni-
            versity Microfilms International.

Manson, T. W.
1979   *The Sayings of Jesus*. Grand Rapids, MI: Eerdmans, 1979.
            (= Part II of *The Mission and Message of Jesus*. London:
            SCM, 1937. Reissued as separate volume in 1949).

Marcovich, M.
1969   "Textual Criticism on the *Gospel of Thomas*." *JTS* 20:53–
            74.

Margolius, Hans
1963–1964   "On the Uses of Aphorisms in Ethics." *Educational
            Forum* 28:79–85.

Marxsen, W.
1969   *Mark the Evangelist*. Translated by J. Boyce *et al*. Nash-
            ville, TN: Abingdon.

Mautner, F. H.
1933   "Der Aphorismus als literarische Gattung." Pp. 19–74 (with
            1973 postschrift on pp. 73–74) in *Der Aphorismus* (Neu-
            mann, 1976b) = *Zeitschrift für Aesthetik und Allgemeine
            Kunstwissenschaft* 27(1933) 132–175.

1959   "Introduction." Pp. 1–40 in *The Lichtenberg Reader: Se-
            lected Writings of Georg Christoph Lichtenberg*. Edited by
            F. H. Mautner and H. Hatfield. Boston: Beacon.

1966   "Maxim(e)s, Sentences, Fragmente, Aphorismen." Pp.
            399–412 (with 1973 postscript on pp. 411–412) in *Der
            Aphorismus* [Neumann, 1976b] = Pp. 812–819 in *Actes
            du IVe Congrès de l'Association Internationale de Littéra-
            ture Comparée. Freiburg i.U. 1964*. The Hague: Mouton.

Mayeda, Goro
1946   *Das Leben-Jesu-Fragment Papyrus Egerton 2 und seine
            Stellung in der urchristlichen Literaturgeschichte*. Bern:
            Haupt.

McArthur, H. K.
1960   "The Dependence of the Gospel of Thomas on the Synop-
            tics." *ExpTim* 71:286–287.

McEleney, N. J.
1981   "The Beatitudes of the Sermon on the Mount/Plain."
            CBQ 43:1–13.

Mees, M.
1971   "Schema und Dispositio in ihrer Bedeutung für die For-

mung der Herrenworte aus dem *1. Clemensbrief*, Kap. 13,2." *VetChr* 8:257–272.

1972   "Das Herrenwort aus dem Ersten Clemensbrief, Kap 46,8 und seine Bedeutung für die Überlieferung der Jesusworte." *Augustinianum* 12:233–256.

Meeus, X. de
1961   "Composition de Lc. XIV, et genre symposiaque." *ETL* 37: 847–870.

Ménard, J.–E.
1975   *L'Évangile selon Thomas*. NHS 5. Leiden: Brill.

Metzger, Bruce M.
1971   *A Textual Commentary on the Greek New Testament*. New York: United Bible Societies.

Meyer, P. D.
1967   *The Community of Q*. University of Iowa, Ph.D. dissertation. Ann Arbor, MI: University Microfilms International.

Michaelis, C.
1968   "Der Pi-Alliteration der Subjektsworte der ersten 4 Seligpreisungen in Mt. V 3–6 und ihre Bedeutung für den Aufbau der Seligpreisungen bei Mt., Lk. und in Q." *NovT* 10:148–161.

Migne, J.–P.
1903   *Patrologiae Cursus Completus: Series Graeca 34*. Paris: Garnier.

Mill, John Stuart
1973   "Aphorisms: A Fragment." Vol I, Pp. 206–210 in his *Dissertations and Discussions, Political, Philosophical, and Historical*. 2 vols. New York: Haskell House.

Moloney, F. J.
1979   "Matthew 19,3–12 and Celibacy. A Redactional and Form Critical Study." *JSNT* 2:42–60.

Moravcsik, G.
1964   " 'Hund in der Krippe'. Zur Geschichte eines griechischen Sprichwortes." *Acta Antiqua* 12:77–86.

Morgenthaler, R.
1971   *Statistische Synopse*. Zurich-Stuttgart: Gotthelf.

Morley, John
1910   "Aphorisms." Pp. 54–102 in his *Studies in Literature*. London: Macmillan.

Mourlon Beernaert, P.
1973   "Jésus controversé. Structure et théologie de Marc 2,1–3,6." *NRT* 95:129–149.

Muddiman, J. B.
1975   "Jesus and Fasting (Marc 2,18–22)." Pp. 271–281 in *Jésus*
            (Dupont, 1975).

Murray, A. T.
1924–1925   *Homer: The Iliad*. LCL. 2 vols. Cambridge, MA: Harvard
            University Press.

Myers, Jacob M.
1974   *I and II Esdras*. AB 42. Garden City, NY: Doubleday.

Nadeau, Ray
1952   "The Progymnasmata of Aphthonius in Translation."
            Speech Monographs 19:264–285.

Nagel, W.
1960   "Neuer Wein in alten Schläuchen (Mt 9,17)." VC 14:1–8.

Neirynck, Frans
1966   "The Tradition of the Sayings of Jesus: Mark 9,33–50."
            Pp. 62–74 in *The Dynamism of Biblical Tradition*. Con-
            cilium. Theology in the Age of Renewal 20: Scripture.
            New York: Paulist.

1972   *Duality in Mark*. BETL 31. Louvain: Leuven University
            Press. (= *ETL* 47 [1971] 144–198, 394–463; 48 [1972]
            150–209).

1973   (ed.) *L'Évangile de Luc. Problèmes littéraires et théolo-
            giques*: Mémorial Lucien Cerfaux. BETL 32. Gembloux:
            Duculot.

1974   *The Minor Agreements of Matthew and Luke against Mark
            with a Cumulative List*. BETL 37. Gembloux: Duculot.

1975   "Jesus and the Sabbath. Some Observations on Mk II,27."
            Pp. 227–270 in *Jésus* (Dupont, 1975).

Neumann, Gerhard
1976a   *Ideenparadiese: Untersuchungen zur Aphoristik von Lich-
            tenberg, Novalis, Friedrich Schlegel und Goethe*. Munich:
            Fink.

1976b   *Der Aphorismus: zur Geschichte, zu den Formen und Mö-
            glichkeiten einer literarischen Gattung*. Wege der Forsch-
            ung 356. Darmstadt: Wissenschaftliche Buchgesellschaft.

Neusner, Jacob
1979   *From Politics to Piety: The Emergence of Pharisaic Juda-
            ism*. 2nd ed. New York: KTAV.

Neyrey, J. H.
1983   "Jesus' Address to the Women of Jerusalem (Lk. 23.27–31)
            —A Prophetic Judgment Oracle." NTS 29:74–86.

Nickelsburg, G. W. E.
    1980   "The Genre and Function of the Markan Passion Narra-
                    tive." *HTR* 73:153–184.

    1981   *Jewish Literature between the Bible and the Mishnah.*
                    Philadelphia: Fortress.

Ong, Walter J.
    1977   *Interfaces of the Word.* Ithaca, NY: Cornell University
                    Press.

Pagels, Elaine, and Helmut Koester
    1978   "Report on the *Dialogue of the Savior.*" Pp. 66–74 in *Nag
                    Hammadi and Gnosis.* Edited by R. McL. Wilson. NHS
                    14. Leiden: Brill.

Perelman, C., and L. Olbrechts-Tyteca
    1969   *The New Rhetoric: A Treatise on Argumentation.* Trans-
                    lated by J. Wilkinson and P. Weaver. Notre Dame, IN:
                    University of Notre Dame Press.

Perkins, Pheme
    1981   "Pronouncement Stories in the Gospel of Thomas."
                    Semeia 20:121–132.

Perrin, Bernadette
    1914–1926   *Plutarch's Lives.* LCL. 11 vols. Cambridge, MA: Harvard
                    University Press.

Perrin, Norman
    1968   "The Creative Use of the Son of Man Traditions by
                    Mark." *USQR* 23:357–365.

    1970   "The Use of (*para*)*didonai* in Connection with the Passion
                    of Jesus in the New Testament." Pp. 204–212 in *Der Ruf
                    Jesu und die Antwort der Gemeinde.* Festschrift für Joa-
                    chim Jeremias. Edited by E. Lohse, with C. Burchard and
                    B. Schaller. Göttingen: Vandenhoeck & Ruprecht.

    1971   "The Christology of Mark: A Study in Methodology." *JR*
                    51: 173–187.

Perrin, Norman, and Dennis C. Duling
    1982   *The New Testament: An Introduction.* 2nd ed. New York:
                    Harcourt Brace Jovanovich.

Perry, Ben Edwin
    1952   *Aesopica: 1. Greek and Latin Texts.* Urbana, IL: Univer-
                    sity of Illinois.

    1965   *Babrius and Phaedrus.* LCL. Cambridge, MA: Harvard
                    University Press.

Pesch, R.
1968   *Naherwartungen. Tradition und Redaktion in Mk 13.*
            Düsseldorf: Patmos.

Petersen, N. R.
1980   "The Composition of Mark 4:1–8:26." *HTR* 73:185–217.

Polag, Athanasius
1977   *Die Christologie der Logienquelle.* WMANT 45. Neukirc-
            hen-Vluyn: Neukirchener Verlag.
1979   *Fragmenta Q: Textheft zur Logienquelle.* Neukirchen-
            Vluyn: Neukirchener Verlag.

Pryke, E. J.
1978   *Redactional Style in the Marcan Gospel.* SNTSMS 33.
            London: Cambridge University Press.

Quecke, H.
1963   " 'Sein Haus seines Königreiches'. Zum Thomasevangeli-
            um 85.9f." *Muséon* 76:47–53.

Quispel, G.
1957   "The Gospel of Thomas and the New Testament." *VC* 11:
            189–207.
1958–1959   "Some Remarks on the Gospel of Thomas." *NTS* 5:276–
            290.
1964   "The Syrian Thomas and the Syrian Macarius." *VC* 18:
            226–235.

Robbins, Vernon K.
1981a   "Summons and Outline in Mark: The Three-Step Progres-
            sion." *NovT* 23:97–114.
1981b   "Classifying Pronouncement Stories in Plutarch's *Parallel
            Lives.*" *Semeia* 20:29–52.

Roberts, W. Rhys
1932   *Demetrius: On Style.* Pp. 255–487 in *Aristotle: The Poet-
            ics; "Longinus": On the Sublime; Demetrius: On Style.*
            LCL. Cambridge, MA: Harvard University Press.

Robinson, James M.
1962a   "The Formal Structure of Jesus' Message." Pp. 91–110 in
            Current Issues in New Testament Interpretation. Essays in
            Honor of Otto A. Piper. Edited by W. Klassen and G. F.
            Snyder. New York: Harper & Bros.
1962b   "Basic Shifts in German Theology." *Int* 16:76–97.
1964   "Die Hodajot-Formel in Gebet und Hymnus des Früh-
            christentums." Pp. 194–235 in *Apophoreta: Festschrift für
            Ernst Haenchen zu seinem siebzigsten Geburtstag am 10.*

Dezember 1964. Edited by W. Eltester and F. M. Kettler. BZNW 30. Berlin: Töpelmann.

1975   "Jesus as Sophos and Sophia: Wisdom Tradition in the Gospels." Pp. 1–16 in *Aspects of Wisdom in Judaism and Early Christianity*. Edited by R. L. Wilken. Notre Dame, IN: University of Notre Dame.

1977   (Director) *The Nag Hammadi Library in English*. Edited by Marvin M. Myer. New York: Harper & Row.

Robinson, James M., and Helmut Koester

1971   *Trajectories through Early Christianity*. Philadelphia: Fortress.

Rodd, C. S.

1961   "Spirit or Finger." *ExpTim* 72:157–158.

Ropes, James Hardy

1896   *Die Sprüche Jesu die in den kanonischen Evangelien nicht überliefert sind*. Eine kritische Bearbeitung des von D. Alfred Resch gesammelten Materials. TU 14.2. Leipzig: Hinrichs.

Rousseau, F.

1975   "La structure de Marc 13." *Bib* 56:157–172.

Sabbe, M. (ed.)

1974   "L'Évangile selon Marc. Tradition et rédaction. BETL 34. Gembloux: Duculot.

Sanders, E. P.

1972–1973   "The Overlaps of Mark and Q and the Synoptic Problem." *NTS* 19:453–465.

Satake, A.

1976   "Das Leiden der Jünger 'um meinetwillen.'" ZNW 67:4–19.

Schlier, H.

1964   "amēn." Pp. 335–338 in *Theological Dictionary of the New Testament*. Edited by Gerhard Friedrich. Translated by Geoffrey W. Bromiley. Vol. 1. Grand Rapids, MI: Eerdmans.

Schmidt, C., and V. MacDermot

1978   *Pistis Sophia*. The Coptic Gnostic Library. NHS 9. Edited by R. McL. Wilson. Leiden: Brill.

Schmidt, Daryl

1977   "The LXX *Gattung* Prophetic Correlative." *JBL* 96:517–522.

Schneider, G.
1970   "Das Bildwort von der Lampe. Zur Traditionsgeschichte
            eines Jesus-Wortes." ZNW 61:183–209.

Schrage, W.
1964   Das Verhältnis des Thomas-Evangeliums zur synoptischen
            Tradition und zu den koptischen Evangelienübersetzungen.
            BZNW 29. Berlin: Töpelmann.

Schramm, T.
1971   Der Markus-Stoff bei Lukas. SNTSMS 15. New York:
            Cambridge University Press.

Schürmann, H.
1963   "Das Thomasevangelium und das lukanische Sondergut."
            BZ 7:236–260.
1966   "Die Warnung des Lukas vor der Falschlehre in der 'Pre-
            digt am Berge' Lk 6,20–49." BZ 10:57–81.

Sieber, J. H.
1966   A Redactional Analysis of the Synoptic Gospels with Re-
            gard to the Question of the Sources of the Gospel According
            to Thomas. Claremont Graduate School, Ph.D. disserta-
            tion. Ann Arbor, MI: University Microfilms International.

Smith, D. M.
1979–1980   "John and the Synoptics: Some Dimensions of the Prob-
            lem." NTS 26:425–444.

Smith, Logan Pearsall
1928   "Introduction." Pp. 1–50 in his A Treasury of English Aph-
            orisms. London: Constable.

Smith, Morton
1978   Jesus the Magician. New York: Harper & Row.

Snyder, G. F.
1976–1977   "The Tobspruch in the New Testament." NTS 23:117–
            120.

Spencer, Richard Albert
1976   A Study of Form and Function of the Biographical Apoph-
            thegms in the Synoptic Tradition in the Light of their Hel-
            lenistic Background. Emory University, Ph.D. dissertation.
            Ann Arbor, MI: University Microfilms International.

Spengel, Leonhard von
1853–1856   Rhetores Graeci. Leipzig: Teubner (= Frankfurt: Miner-
            va, 1966).

Stanton, G. N.
1977   "5 Ezra and Matthean Christianity in the Second Cen-
            tury." *JTS* 28:67–83.

Stephens, James
1975   *Francis Bacon and the Style of Science*. Chicago: Univer-
            sity of Chicago Press.

Stephenson, R. H.
1980   "On the Widespread Use of an Inappropriate and Restric-
            tive Model of the Literary Aphorism." *Modern Language
            Review* 75:1–17.

Stern, J. P.
1959   *Lichtenberg: A Doctrine of Scattered Occasions*. Blooming-
            ton, IN: Indiana University Press.

Strack, H. L., and Paul Billerbeck
1922–1928   *Kommentar zum Neuen Testament aus Talmud und Mi-
            drasch*. 4 vols. Munich: Beck.

Strecker, G.
1968   "The Passion- and Resurrection Predictions in Mark's Gos-
            pel (Mark 8:31; 9:31; 10:32–34)." *Int* 22:421–442 (= ZTK
            64 (1967) 16–39).
1972   "Les macarismes du discours sur la montagne." Pp. 185–
            208 in *L'Évangile selon Matthie. Rédaction et théologie*.
            Edited by M. Didier. BETL 29. Gembloux: Duculot (=
            NTS 17 (1970–1971) 255–275).

Strobel, A.
1963   "Textgeschichtliches zum Thomas-Logion 86 (Mt 8,20/
            Luk 9,58)." VC 17:211–224.

Stroker, William Dettwiller
1970   *The Formation of Secondary Sayings of Jesus*. Yale Univer-
            sity, Ph.D. dissertation. Ann Arbor, MI: University Mi-
            crofilms International.

Suggs, M. J.
1970   *Wisdom, Christology, and Law in Matthew's Gospel*.
            Cambridge, MA: Harvard University Press.

Tannehill, Robert C.
1981   "Introduction: The Pronouncement Story and Its Types"
            and "Varieties of Synoptic Pronouncement Stories."
            Semeia 20:1–13 and 101–119.

Taylor, R. O. P.
1946   *The Groundwork of the Gospels*. Oxford: Blackwell.

Taylor, Vincent
    1953   "The Order of Q." *JTS* 4:27–31.
    1959   "The Original Order of Q." Pp. 246–269 in *New Testament Essays: Studies in Memory of Thomas Walter Manson 1893–1958*. Edited by A. J. B. Higgins. Manchester: Manchester University Press (= pp. 90–94 and 95–118, respectively, in Taylor, *New Testament Essays*. Grand Rapids, MI: Eerdmans).
    1966   *The Gospel according to St. Mark*. 2nd ed. New York: St. Martin's Press.

Theissen, G.
    1978   *Sociology of Early Christianity*. Translated by J. Bowden. Philadelphia: Fortress.

Till, W. C.
    1959   "New Sayings of Jesus in the Recently Discovered Coptic 'Gospel of Thomas.'" *BJRL* 41:446–458.

Tödt, H. E.
    1965   *The Son of Man in the Synoptic Tradition*. Translated by D. M. Barton. The New Testament Library. Philadelphia: Fortress.

Topliss, Patricia
    1966   *The Rhetoric of Pascal*. Leicester University Press.

Turner, C. H.
    1926–1927 "Marcan Usage: Notes, Critical and Exegetical, on the Second Gospel: VIII." *JTS* 28:349–362.

Turner, H. E. W., and H. Montefiore
    1962   *Thomas and the Evangelists*. SBT 1/35. Naperville, IL: Allenson.

Ungar, Frederick (ed.)
    1977   *No Compromise: Selected Writings of Karl Kraus*. New York: Frederick Ungar Publishing Company.

Vassiliadis, P.
    1978   "The Nature and Extent of the Q-document." *NovT* 20:49–73.

Vawter, Bruce
    1977   "Divorce and the New Testament." *CBQ* 39:528–542.

Vermes, Geza
    1967   "The Use of *br nš / br nš'* in Jewish Aramaic." Pp. 310–328 in M. Black, *An Aramaic Approach to the Gospels and Acts*. 3rd ed. Oxford: Clarendon.

1973   *Jesus the Jew*. New York: Macmillan.

1978a   "The Present State of the 'Son of Man' Debate." *JJS* 29: 123–134 (extended version of 1978b).

1978b   "The 'Son of Man' Debate." *JSNT* 1:19–32.

Vickers, Brian

1968   *Francis Bacon and Renaissance Prose*. Cambridge: Cambridge University Press.

Vielhauer, P.

1957   "Gottesreich und Menschensohn in der Verkündigung Jesus." Pp. 51–79 in *Festschrift für Günther Dehn*. Neukirchen: Verlag der Buchhandlung der Erziehungsvereins Neukirchen.

1964   "ANAPAUSIS: Zum gnostischen Hintergrund des Thomasevangeliums." Pp. 281–299 in *Apophoreta* (see Robinson, 1964).

Walter, N.

1962   "Zur Analyse von Mc 10:17–31." ZNW 53:206–218.

1966   "Tempelzerstörung und synoptische Apokalypse." ZNW 57: 38–49.

Wenham, J. W.

1982   "Why Do You Ask Me about the Good? A Study of the Relation between Text and Source Criticism." *NTS* 28:116–125.

Williams, J. G.

1981   *Those Who Ponder Proverbs: Aphoristic Thinking and Biblical Literature*. Sheffield, England: Almond Press.

Wilson, R. McL.

1960a   *Studies in the Gospel of Thomas*. London: Mowbray.

1960b   " 'Thomas' and the Growth of the Gospels." *HTR* 53:231–250.

1963   (tr.) "The Gospel of Thomas." Vol 1, Pp. 511–522 in Hennecke and Schneemelcher.

Winter, P.

1956   "Matthew XI 27 and Luke X 22 from the First to the Fifth Century." *NovT* 1:112–148.

Zohn, Harry (ed.)

1976   *Half-Truths and One-and-a-Half Truths. Karl Kraus: Selected Writings*. Montreal: Engendra Press.

Index of Aphorisms

The first number in an entry is the aphorism number.

Index of Authors

Index of Citations

Intracanonical citations are in biblical order; extracanonical citations are in alphabetical order.